ENVIRONMENTAL SECURITY
CONCEPTS, CHALLENGES, AND CASE STUDIES
JOHN M. LANICCI, ELISABETH HOPE MURRAY, AND JAMES D. RAMSAY

AMERICAN METEOROLOGICAL SOCIETY

Authors are listed on the cover and title pages in alphabetical order.

Paperback ISBN: 978-1-944970-41-3
eISBN: 978-1-944970-42-0

Published by the American Meteorological Society
45 Beacon Street, Boston, Massachusetts 02108

For more AMS Books, see http://bookstore.ametsoc.org.

The mission of the American Meteorological Society is to advance the atmospheric and related sciences, technologies, applications, and services for the benefit of society. Founded in 1919, the AMS has a membership of more than 13,000 and represents the premier scientific and professional society serving the atmospheric and related sciences. Additional information regarding society activities and membership can be found at www.ametsoc.org.

Library of Congress Cataloging-in-Publication Data

Names: Lanicci, John M., editor.
Title: Environmental security : concepts, challenges, and case studies /
  [edited by] John Lanicci, Elisabeth Hope Murray, James Ramsay.
Other titles: Environmental security (American Meteorological Society)
Description: First [edition]. | Boston, MA : American Meteorological Society,
  2019. | Includes bibliographical references and index.
Identifiers: LCCN 2018049831 (print) | LCCN 2018055211 (ebook) | ISBN
  9781944970420 (ebook) | ISBN 9781944970413 (pbk. : alk. paper)
Subjects: LCSH: Environmental management. | Environmental risk assessment. |
  Environmental protection. | Global environmental change.
Classification: LCC GE300 (ebook) | LCC GE300 .E626 2019 (print) | DDC
  658.4/083—dc23
LC record available at https://lccn.loc.gov/2018049831

CONTENTS

Foreword   vii
Preface   ix
Acknowledgments   xi

1   Introduction   1

1.1   What Are the Environment and Security, and How Should the Concept of Environmental Security Be Defined? *Jarrod Hayes, Elisabeth Hope Murray, John M. Lanicci, and James D. Ramsay,*   3

  1.1.1   Creating Working Definitions for Environment and Security   4

  1.1.2   A Brief History of the Environmental Security Discipline   6

  1.1.3   Defining Environmental Security   8

  1.1.4   Disaggregating Environmental Security   9

  1.1.5   Fitting Environmental Security into a Larger Security Strategy in the United States   10

  1.1.6   The Missing Link: Human Security   10

1.2   Defining Climate Change: Causes, Impacts, and Institutions. *Elisabeth Hope Murray*   15

  1.2.1   Introduction to Climate Change   15

  1.2.2   First Assessment Report—1990 (and Supplemental Reports—1992)   17

  1.2.3   Second Assessment Report—1995   17

  1.2.4   Third Assessment Report—2001   17

  1.2.5   Fourth Assessment Report—2007   17

  1.2.6   Fifth Assessment Report—2013, 2014   18

2   Natural Resources: Their Access and Relationship to Security   21

2.1   Food Scarcity and Conflict in an Era of Climate Change. *Linda Kiltz and James D. Ramsay*   25

  2.1.1   Introduction   25

  2.1.2   Impact of Climate Change on Agriculture   26

  2.1.3   Environmental Change and Scarcity-based Conflict   29

  2.1.4   Pathways to Conflict   30

    2.1.4.1   The Resource Scarcity Pathway   30

    2.1.4.2   The "Weak State" Pathway   32

    2.1.4.3   The Migration Pathway   34

  2.1.5   Conclusion   35

2.2   Energy Security. *Terrence M. O'Sullivan*   41

  2.2.1   Introduction   41

  2.2.2   The Energy Pyramid and the Law of Tolerance   43

  2.2.3   Defining and (Re-)Framing Energy Security   44

2.2.4 Sources of Energy Used in the U.S. (and Global) Economy 45

2.2.5 Slouching toward the Renewables Future 46

2.2.6 Sustainable/Renewable Energy as Security: the Methods 47

    2.2.6.1 Wind Power 47

    2.2.6.2 Solar Power 48

    2.2.6.3 Solar Thermal Power on Utility Scale 48

    2.2.6.4 Solar PV Power on Utility Scale 48

    2.2.6.5 Distributed Solar Capacity 48

2.2.7 The Economics of Energy Security: The Calculus of Energy Return on Investment 49

2.2.8 A Tidy Linkage between Energy and Food Security 49

2.2.9 Climate, Energy and Food Economics 50

2.2.10 Energy, Food and Water Resource Instability, and War 50

2.2.11 U.S. Energy Policy: Two Steps Forward, One Step Back? 50

    2.2.11.1 Current Energy Policy 51

2.2.12 Conclusion 52

2.3 Water Security: Challenges and Adaptations. *Terrence M. O'Sullivan, Elisabeth Hope Murray, John M. Lanicci, and James D. Ramsay* 55

2.3.1 Introduction 55

2.3.2 Biogeochemical Cycling and the Role of Water 57

    2.3.2.1 Water Use 59

2.3.3 What Is Water Security? 59

2.3.4 The Water-Population-Food-Energy Nexus 62

2.3.5 Issues Related to Water Security 63

2.3.6 The Growing Confluence of Climate Change, Environmental Stresses, and Food and Water Insecurity 64

2.3.7 Water: Access and Security 65

2.3.8 Conclusion 65

2.4 Case Study: ISIS Oil Looting and Environmental Security in Iraq and Syria. *Melinda Negrón-Gonzales* 69

2.4.1 Oil as Essential 69

2.4.2 ISIS Oil Looting and Smuggling 70

2.4.3 Impact on Environmental and Human Security 71

2.4.4 International Efforts to Stop ISIS's Oil Looting and Smuggling 73

2.4.5 Conclusion 76

2.4.6 Discussion Questions 76

2.5 Case Study: Water and Power—International and Substate Water Allocation Conflicts. *Christiane J. Fröhlich* 79

2.5.1 Introduction 79

2.5.2 The Falkenmark Water Stress Index 79

2.5.3 The Myth of the "Water War" 80

2.5.4 The Jordan Basin: Water as an Instrument of Power 81

2.5.5 Conclusion: What Must Be Done 83

2.5.6 What You Should Know from Here 84

2.5.7 Discussion Questions 84

2.6 Case Study: Limits to Growth and Insecurity. *Damien Short* 87

2.6.1 Introduction 87

2.6.2 Extreme Energy 89

2.6.3 The Role of Neoliberal Capitalism 90

2.6.4 The Athabasca Tar Sands Example 91

2.6.5 Concluding Thoughts 93

3 Natural Disasters and Environmental Security 99

3.1 Natural Hazards Overview. *John M. Lanicci* 103

3.1.1 Introduction 103

3.1.2 Tropical Cyclones 104

3.1.3 Floods 107

3.1.4 Droughts 109

3.2 Vulnerability, Natural Disaster, and Disaster Management. *John M. Lanicci* 113

3.2.1 Introduction 113

3.2.2 A Simplified Model of Natural Hazards Vulnerability 113

3.2.3 The Pressure and Release Disaster Onset Model 116

3.2.4 Disaster: When Hazard Meets Vulnerability 118

3.2.5 Disaster Management 119

    3.2.5.1 Mitigation 120

    3.2.5.2 Preparedness 120

    3.2.5.3 Response 121

    3.2.5.4 Recovery 121

3.2.6 The Case Studies for This Unit 121

3.3 Natural Hazards Vulnerability along the U.S. Gulf Coast: The Case of Hurricane Katrina. *John M. Lanicci* 123

   3.3.1 Introduction 123

   3.3.2 Natural Hazards in the Gulf Coast Region 123

      3.3.2.1 Physical Geography 123

      3.3.3.2 Natural Hazards Climatology 124

   3.3.3 A Basic Vulnerability Analysis 126

      3.3.3.1 Economics 127

      3.3.3.2 Infrastructure 127

      3.3.3.3 Demographics 127

      3.3.3.4 Vulnerability Analysis Results 127

   3.3.4 Disaster Preparedness in the Gulf Coast Region 131

   3.3.5 What Went Wrong with Katrina? 132

3.4 Media Impacts on Natural Disaster and Policy. *John R. Fisher and John M. Lanicci* 137

   3.4.1 Introduction 137

   3.4.2 Traditional Media Coverage of Hurricane Katrina and Changes to U.S. Disaster Management Policy in Its Aftermath 138

   3.4.3 The Evolving Role of Social Media in the Wake of Recent Natural Disasters 139

   3.4.4 Conclusions 141

3.5 War and Weak Institutions as Contributors to Natural Disasters. *Edin Mujkic, Lauren Bacon Brengarth, and John M. Lanicci* 145

   3.5.1 Introduction 145

   3.5.2 The Balkan Wars of the 1990s 146

   3.5.3 Problems with Postwar Disaster Management in Bosnia and Serbia 147

   3.5.4 The Balkan Floods of May 2014 148

   3.5.5 Discussion 151

4 Conflict and Environmental Security 155

4.1 Environmental Security and Conflict. *Elisabeth Hope Murray* 159

   4.1.1 Introduction 159

   4.1.2 Links, Correlation, and Causality 159

   4.1.3 Conflict between MDCs and LDCs 160

   4.1.4 Conflict between and within MDCs 164

   4.1.5 Conflict between and within LDCs 166

   4.1.6 Conclusions 169

4.2 An Environment of Insecurity: The Relationship between Environmental Change and Violent Conflict in Northwest Kenya. *Jan-Peter Schilling* 177

   4.2.1 Overview 177

   4.2.2 Introduction 177

   4.2.3 Northwest Kenya 179

   4.2.4 Environmental Change and Violent Conflict in the Region 180

   4.2.5 Violent Conflict and Human Security 181

      4.2.5.1 Loss of Human Life 182

      4.2.5.2 Loss of Livestock 182

      4.2.5.3 Loss of Resources and Homes 182

   4.2.6 Environments of Insecurity 182

   4.2.7 Local Conflicts and National and Global Processes 184

   4.2.8 Conclusions 185

   4.2.9 Acknowledgments 185

   4.2.10 Discussion Questions 185

4.3 U.S. Military Strategy and Arctic Climate Change. *Tobias T. Gibson* 189

   4.3.1 Overview 189

   4.3.2 Introduction 189

   4.3.3 Recent Ice Melt in the Arctic 190

   4.3.4 Economic Impacts of the Opening of the Arctic 190

   4.3.5 The Arctic and U.S. Security 191

   4.3.6 The Arctic and UNCLOS 193

   4.3.7 Conclusions 194

   4.3.8 Discussion Questions 195

5 Concluding Points: Integrating Environmental Security into National Security Planning. *James D. Ramsay, John M. Lanicci, and Elisabeth Hope Murray* 197

5.1 Introduction 197

5.2 The Importance of Clear Definitions for Homeland, National, and Human Security 197

5.3 Using Environmental Security as a "Processor" in Strategy Development 198

5.3 Concluding Points: Better Integration of Environmental Security into National Security Strategic Planning Is Warranted and Necessary 202

Index 205

FOREWORD

On March 11, 2011, a massive earthquake hit off the coast of Japan. I was on assignment in London for the U.S. Air Force (USAF), and remember seeing the first U.S. Geological Survey tweet reporting the event early in the morning, followed by an avalanche of distressing and then catastrophic reports on the subsequent tsunami and nuclear disaster at Fukushima. The scale of the disaster was incredible, with nearly 16,000 dead and an energy sector in collapse. Within hours, the U.S. military began one of its largest peacetime disaster responses (Operation Tomodachi), highlighting the importance of allies and planning in responding to events.

The series of disasters that hit that day were a stark reminder of the power of environmental forces over even the most well-prepared and highly industrialized of countries. Critical vulnerabilities were overwhelmed, sparking a series of events at the Fukushima Daiichi nuclear plant and subsequent meltdown, whose political effects quickly cascaded around the globe. While the events following the Tohoku earthquake largely focused on the planning failures at Fukushima, they also highlighted the benefits of proper planning—namely, for the earthquake itself, and the military's ability to respond to natural hazards. But how does one plan in the face of such uncertainty of historically unique events? And why do military and security organizations continue to warn about the rising frequency and intensity of disasters?

I met John Lanicci in 2011 at Maxwell Air Force Base in Alabama, where we were trying to answer some of these questions for the U.S. Air Force. John had been commander of the Air Force Weather Agency, and had previously written about the need to better integrate environmental information into intelligence, surveillance, and reconnaissance as part of a growing concern over the potential strategic impacts of severe weather and climate. I had come from working with the intelligence community at the U.S. Department of Energy, and transferred to USAF in 2010 to lead their energy and environmental security research under the Minerva Initiative. As this book describes, there had been work done in the 1990s, but it didn't seem to fit with the newly emerging security threats we saw from wicked hazards like climate change. There were no journals for environmental security, no programs for teaching it, and very few courses on the subject. The problem was that no one person could know all the critical factors in assessing environmental security risks.

In preparing planning scenarios and wargames for USAF, we realized the need to reach out to experts from all areas, from civil engineering and hydrogeology, to transport planners and farmers. The sheer complexity of interacting hazards, especially with climate change shifting conditions in the background, made the task seem daunting. Somehow, the authors of this book (Drs. Lanicci, Murray, and Ramsay) have managed to accomplish this at last, covering subjects from the response to Hurricane Katrina, to the importance of the Ogallala Aquifer for American food security. Yet this also suggests that the book is not relevant only for a small sub-section of security studies students, but instead can apply to people from a wide variety of subjects. Whether people are siting a new powerplant or managing a hotel chain, these emerging environmental risks are becoming ever more important for understanding how to sustain our security and well-being.

We are facing disasters that appear more in slow-motion, and are more difficult to understand. At the time of writing, much of the United States is in the grips of unusually hot weather, from flash droughts and triple digit temperatures in the southern and eastern United States, to a mild fall and conspicuously missing sea ice in Alaska. The Bahamas are reeling from the impacts of Hurricane Dorian, while Puerto Rico is still attempting to recover from the 2017 Maria storm. Every week we receive new warnings from the military, from NASA, from scientists and even insurance corporations around the globe, but yet we continue to find it difficult to know what all this means.

This book provides useful frameworks and case studies for understanding the nature of emerging environmental security threats, and how organizations can plan for future risks. The authors even admit that they showed disagreement among themselves on how to interpret certain risks—that's how it should be. Ultimately, the only certainty is that environmental conditions are changing, but how we value what to protect, at what cost, remain questions about values and politics. What Drs. Lanicci, Murray and Ramsay provide is a valuable background to those discussions, to help prevent paralysis in the face of uncertainty.

To quote President Eisenhower, "Plans are worthless, but planning is everything. There is a very great distinction because when you are planning for an emergency you must start with this one thing: the very definition of 'emergency' is that it is unexpected, therefore it is not going to happen the way you are planning."

It's best to start here.

—*Chad M. Briggs*
University of Alaska Anchorage
October 2019

PREFACE

It is becoming increasingly clear that the traditional model of nation-state-based national security is incomplete, and purely military capabilities, though necessary, are insufficient to protect the United States and other democracies from the array of threats that challenge liberty and the free flow of people and commerce. While survival of the state is central to all national security models, security threats today are increasingly wicked in nature, complex, dynamic, and asymmetric. For example, not only are energy, water, gender, and food security core dimensions of human security, they are each related to climate change, and ultimately, each is related to environmental security as well. Consequently, a more complete picture of modern national security would seem to require a more complete integration of environmental security. Logically, for students of academic homeland security programs (and indeed other related degree programs in disciplines such as intelligence studies, international affairs, meteorology, conflict studies, peace studies, and political science), a more complete understanding of security and threats to security seems critical. The purpose of this text is to better address the many aspects of environmental security and represent this major area of academic research in an introductory text format that can be used in the rapidly growing number of (homeland) security studies programs as well as related degree programs. It is our hope that many such degree programs will find the concepts, challenges, and case studies in this text to be useful extensions to their curricula and that students will achieve a more robust and deeper appreciation for the vital role environmental security plays in overall state security, as well as in our nation, our way of life, and indeed for the human race.

ACKNOWLEDGMENTS

Many thanks are necessary upon the completion of this book. First, thanks to all of our contributing authors, without whose patience, scholarship, generosity, and understanding this text would not have been possible. Thanks as well to our reviewers and colleagues, whose suggestions have improved our chapters and have clarified this complex subject. We owe a significant debt of gratitude to the American Meteorological Society and their excellent publishing team, who have helped us at each stage of this project from conception to completion. We would like to thank our families and loved ones for their unending patience and support through the years. Finally, understanding that Earth is on the edge of a tipping point, we would like to thank all of those readers who endeavor to help educate students to understand the critical choices we must make to provide a more secure society for future generations.

—*John Lanicci, University of South Alabama*
—*Elisabeth Hope Murray, Embry-Riddle Aeronautical University*
—*James D. Ramsay, University of New Hampshire*

INTRODUCTION

This is not the first book ever written about environmental security. The authors are aware of nearly a dozen books on the subject published over the last 20 years. It is not our intention to describe or comment on any of these texts as they are all well written and provide a rich source of information about the topic. However, if one wants to *teach* a course on this subject, it is important to understand that potential students will likely come from a variety of disciplines, such as international studies, political science, geography, security studies, environmental science, atmospheric and climate science, etc., each with its own unique vernacular, body of research, and approaches to such research. Hence, there is a need for a way to "level the playing field" so that students coming from these various disciplines can attain a common level of understanding prior to tackling the weighty issues that environmental security attempts to address. Most of the texts written about environmental security provide some introduction prior to engaging the heart of their material, but none of them are written as textbooks specifically for use by either undergraduate or graduate students. We believe that environmental security will only grow in importance over time, especially as the impacts of climate change begin to play out on the global stage; thus, it is important for students (and faculty) to have a good foundation from which they can launch more complex, intertwined studies in this area.

We also want to point out that, as climate change is a security threat reaching across regional and state boundaries, so our authorship spans the globe. Indeed, some of the perspectives of other authors show the perspective held by their respective states. The most interesting example of this is found in unit 2, where our case study authors actually disagree with each other as to the level of risk our environment is under from increased energy demands and the fossil fuel industry. You will also see this in the chapter 1.2's presentation of the IPCC reports, which highlight not one but five possible global futures based on different greenhouse gas outputs and global temperature rise. These discrepancies are not worrisome; instead, they represent the flexibility of the environmental security paradigm. They also show that, despite differences in political affiliation, the responsibility for climate change is firmly in human hands.

With this in mind, we have organized this book into main sections (units), each containing 2–3 chapters:

- Unit 1—Introduction
  - What are the environment and security, and how should the concept of environmental security be defined?
  - Defining climate change: Causes, impacts, and institutions

- Unit 2—Natural resources and security
  - Food scarcity and conflict in an era of climate change
  - Energy security
  - Water security: Challenges and adaptations
- Unit 3—Disaster management and response
  - Natural disasters and disaster management
- Unit 4—Conflict: Sources and types
  - Environmental security and conflict

Unit 2 covers several security domains of concern to practitioners. Unit 3 covers those extreme events and climatic anomalies that produce natural disasters around the world that could destabilize fragile geopolitical stability in less-developed countries and threaten critical infrastructure and economic stability in well-developed countries. Unit 4 describes various types of conflicts that stress current stability structures around the world and introduces the concept of human security. A fifth unit is intended to provide a summary of the book from the policy-making perspective and offers a "Where do we go from here?" conclusion.

Each unit in the book begins with an overview intended to introduce students to the key concepts and questions necessary for understanding that major topic area. The overview is followed by individual case studies that provide real-world examples of these topic areas and illustrate the concepts in action. As the topics covered in unit 2 are so broad and crucial to the greater context of the book, there is a short preface, followed by several introductory chapters, followed by case studies. Thus, the book can be used several ways. One approach is to use the unit overviews as a traditional academic text without the case studies, which may be more appropriate for basic undergraduate courses without a high level of rigor. Another approach uses the overviews and case studies to introduce the major topics and examine them in more detail. This approach would be appropriate for senior-level "capstone" types of courses and beginning or intermediate graduate-level courses. Yet a third approach could use this book as a reference text for study of a subset of environmental security (e.g., food security). This approach would be most appropriate for an advanced graduate-level "reading" type of course in which students would be reading and discussing several articles from the peer-reviewed literature, in which our book provides a handy "desk reference." However the book is used, we hope that it provides a useful foundation and will act as a catalyst to learn more about this fascinating topic that is critical to our future.

1.1

WHAT ARE THE ENVIRONMENT AND SECURITY, AND HOW SHOULD THE CONCEPT OF ENVIRONMENTAL SECURITY BE DEFINED?

Jarrod Hayes
Elisabeth Hope Murray
John M. Lanicci
James D. Ramsay

KEY TERMS AND CONCEPTS

Homeland security Homeland security represents the intersection of evolving threats and hazards with traditional governmental and civic responsibilities for civil defense, emergency response, law enforcement, customs, border control, and immigration. In combining these responsibilities under one overarching concept, homeland security breaks down longstanding stovepipes of activity that have been and could still be exploited by those seeking to harm America. Homeland security also creates a greater emphasis on the need for joint actions and efforts across previously discrete elements of government and society (Department of Homeland Security 2010).

National security The art and science of developing policy and strategy actions, coordinating and applying all instruments of national power including diplomatic, informational/intelligence, military, and economic power in order to preserve the nation-state and defend the economy and citizenry.

Human security Human security is an emerging paradigm for understanding global vulnerabilities. Proponents challenge the traditional notion of national security by arguing that the proper referent for security should be the individual rather than the state. Human

security holds that a people-centered view of security is necessary for national, regional, and global stability. Human security typically includes several security subdimensions including environmental, political, economic, personal, community, food, and health security [adapted from Gómez and Gasper (2013)].

Environmental security Challenges to national or homeland security posture that result from extreme environmental or climatic events acting locally or transnationally to destabilize the countries or regions of the world, resulting in geopolitical instability, resource conflicts, vulnerabilities in critical infrastructure, or some combination of these impacts

Security strategy A coordinated plan to identify risks, threats, or hazards to a nation, organization, community, or individual including development of countermeasures designed to mitigate either the frequency or severity or both of identified risks, threats, or hazards.

Weather The U.S. National Weather Service defines weather as the "state of the atmosphere with respect to wind, temperature, cloudiness, moisture, pressure, etc. Weather refers to these conditions at a given point in time (e.g., today's high temperature)" (National Weather Service 2018).

Climate   Climate, in contrast to weather, is understood as the long-term pattern of weather in a particular region, including averages of "precipitation, temperature, humidity, sunshine, wind velocity, phenomena such as fog, frost, and hail storms, and other measures of the weather that occur over a long period in a particular place" (NASA 2017).

Climate change (aka anthropomorphic climate change)   According to the UN 1992 Framework Convention on Climate Change (UNFCC; United Nations 1992) "climate change" means a change of climate that is attributed directly or indirectly to human activity that alters the composition of the global atmosphere and that is in addition to natural climate variability observed over comparable time periods.

IPCC   The Intergovernmental Panel on Climate Change (IPCC) is part of the United Nations and is the foremost authority of peer-reviewed scholarship on climate science (see www.ipcc.ch). The IPCC is the leading international body for the assessment of climate change. It was established by the United Nations Environment Programme (UNEP) and the World Meteorological Organization (WMO) in 1988 to provide the world with a clear scientific view on the current state of knowledge in climate change and its potential environmental and socioeconomic impacts. In the same year, the UN General Assembly endorsed the action by the WMO and UNEP in jointly establishing the IPCC. It is composed of scholars and policy makers from 195 nations; however, the IPCC only reviews and assesses the most recent scientific, technical, and socioeconomic information produced worldwide that is relevant to the understanding of climate change. It does not conduct any research, nor does it monitor climate-related data or parameters.

Disaster (see Mach et al. 2014)   Severe alterations in the normal functioning of a community or a society due to hazardous physical events interacting with vulnerable social conditions, leading to widespread adverse human, material, economic, or environmental effects that require immediate emergency response to satisfy critical human needs and that may require external support for recovery.

Risk (see Mach et al. 2014)   "The potential for consequences where something of value is at stake and where the outcome is uncertain, recognizing the diversity of values. Risk is often represented as probability or likelihood of occurrence of hazardous events or trends multiplied by the impacts if these events or trends occur. . . . The term risk is often used to refer to the potential, when the outcome is uncertain, for adverse consequences on lives, livelihoods, health, ecosystems and species, economic, social and cultural assets, services (including environmental services) and infrastructure."

1.1.1. CREATING WORKING DEFINITIONS FOR ENVIRONMENT AND SECURITY

Weather and climate have always played important roles in human history. There are numerous historical examples of weather and climate resulting in widespread famine and mass migrations and influencing the start of hostilities between nations and within nations. However, the linkages among weather, climate, and security are complex and nonlinear. In many cases, the environment is not the sole cause of instability but may be a contributor to it, in combination with several other factors. While these factors are critically important to understanding the complex geopolitical situations that exist in many regions around the world, it is first necessary to discuss the concepts of *environment* and *security* and then define *environmental security* as it will be used in this textbook.

The American Meteorological Society (AMS) Glossary defines *environment* as "external conditions and surroundings, especially those that affect the quality of life of plants, animals, and human beings" (AMS 2018). A useful exercise that is often conducted at the start of environmental security courses is to require each student to write a term on the board that they think should be included in a list of features that characterize the environment. When the list was sufficiently lengthy, we would lead a guided discussion where the class would attempt to categorize these features. The categorizations could be natural vs human-made or they could be domain related (oceanic, land, atmosphere, etc.). Regardless of the categorization used, at the end of the exercise, the class had a working list that they could use throughout the course for evaluating environmental impacts as they relate to other factors, including security.

Once the list of environmental features has been created and the class has properly vetted them, compare them to the list we provide here as Table 1.1.1. (Do not look at these until the exercise is complete!) Examination of Table 1.1.1 shows that this list includes both natural and human-made features, and thus, the extent of the potential influence of the environment has become wide-ranging. How many of the items in Table 1.1.1 are consistent with the AMS Glossary definition of environment presented above?

Table 1.1.1. Features of environment as described by an environmental security class.

Water sources

Climate

Infrastructure

Natural resources (e.g., minerals)

Food

Ecosystems

Weather

Wildlife

Culture (socioeconomics)

Atmospheric structure

Population

Now we can conduct a similar exercise on the concept of *security*. In this case, we begin with an excerpt from a standard dictionary definition of security (*Merriam-Webster*, s.v. "security"):

1. The quality or state of being secure, such as freedom from danger (safety) and/or freedom from fear or anxiety
2. Something that secures protection, which can include measures taken to guard against espionage or sabotage, crime, attack, or escape
3. An organization or department whose task is security

Once the list of security features was created, we would again lead a guided discussion to have the class categorize them, this time leading them toward defining different types of security. The exercise of categorizing security into types, or realms, is important because it parallels some of the same deliberations that policy makers have on what should constitute security from a national policy perspective (national security being one of the security "realms"). As was done with environment,

compare the class's security list to the one we provide here as Table 1.1.2 (as before, do not look at these until the exercise is complete).

Table 1.1.2. Features of security as described by an environmental security class.

Information technology

Transportation

Intelligence, reconnaissance, surveillance (ISR)

Risk analysis

Geography

Natural resources

Population

Infrastructure

Borders

Emergency management

Food

Later in this book, we introduce the concept of *human security*, which draws its roots from the first definition in the *Merriam-Webster* description above. We will discuss its importance in comparison with more traditional types covered in this book.

Once these exercises are completed, the class should discuss whether any of the environmental features on their list could potentially impact any of the security areas they defined. In this way, the class can examine ways of combining the features of environment and security that they have developed. If taken to a logical conclusion, such a discussion should lead to the class developing its own definition of environmental security, providing a useful segue into examining the various definitions of environmental security that are explored in the rest of this unit.

Understood in terms of creating a political and social space that allows for a rapid, extraordinary policy response to environmental problems, the appeal of environmental security is obvious. Often, environmental problems may have a severe and acute impact on ecosystems and humans, pushing concerned actors to invoke security. It is also usually the case that environmental problems have emerged where normal political processes have failed over many years to produce policies that prevent detrimental outcomes. The ability to focus minds, generate policy urgency, and rise above

Figure 1.1.1. Displaced citizens after Hurricane Katrina. Photo by Ammar Abd Rabbo via Flickr Creative Commons.

the often-glacial pace of normal policy making makes framing environmental problems as matters of security appealing to those who want to act quickly. Indeed, those arguing that climate change is a matter of security in many ways seek to cut off a process of normal politics that, by all appearances, will produce an outcome detrimental to humanity and global ecosystems—if it has not already (Pal and Eltahir 2015). From this backdrop, let us examine a brief history of environmental security and look at various ways of defining it.

1.1.2. A BRIEF HISTORY OF THE ENVIRONMENTAL SECURITY DISCIPLINE

One does not have to look far these days to find media headlines that illustrate the intertwined nature of today's major crises: political unrest; shortages of food, water, and energy; natural disasters; terrorism; mass migration; disease outbreaks, etc. What is not obvious from a cursory look at these news stories is that environmental threads run through nearly all of them and, more impor-

tantly, that the interactions and connections among these threads have the potential to threaten every state as well as the individuals residing therein, no matter how prosperous or secure. These interactions and connections are at the core of environmental security.

The concept of environmental security has been around since the 1970s (Myers 2004), when researchers were exploring the connections between multidecadal drought, poor land-use management, and famine in the Sahel region of sub-Saharan Africa that led to a humanitarian disaster resulting in an estimated 100,000 deaths. The research focused on the climate, geography, people, and implications of these changes on the security of individuals or tribal groups living in the region. At this time within the U.S. policy community, the focus was on the Soviet Union and Warsaw Pact countries, so environment, though acknowledged as important, was not considered to be a component of national security. This changed when the Cold War ended.

In the years immediately following the collapse of the Soviet Union and dissolution of the Warsaw Pact, interest in the possibility of links between the natural environment and national security grew in the U.S. policy-making community. The idea was to examine environmental degradation from single-event disasters such as tropical cyclones or cumulative changes from climatic anomalies such as drought and their connection to the emergence of new or exacerbation of existing sustainability issues, resource contention, and geopolitical instability. This body of work took the form of a variety of research and pilot programs conducted by a combination of academic institutions, nongovernmental organizations (NGOs), and the U.S. federal government (primarily through the Departments of State and Defense).

During this period, seminal research on environmental security began to explore the complex linkages among environmental degradation, resource scarcity, and conflict in many regions of the world (e.g., Homer-Dixon 1999). While this research was taking place, a debate emerged within the U.S. policy-making community regarding the appropriateness of tying environment to security. On one side of the argument, proponents of environmental security argued that an increasingly complex multipolar world could only be understood by incorporating environmental issues and other nontraditional areas (e.g., social, economic) into a redefined concept of security (e.g., Tuchman Mathews 1989). On the other side of the argument, individuals acknowledged that environmental, health, and socioeconomic concerns have important *connections* to security but that these issues should *not* be characterized as security concerns (e.g., Deudney 1990). Specifically, Deudney warned that that environmental degradation is unlike traditional national security concerns for three reasons. First, environmental degradation has little in common with interstate violence—the traditional focus of national security. Second, trying to harness nationalist sentiment by invoking national security might undermine the globalist perspective necessary to address the collective action aspect of many environmental problems. Third, Deudney argued environmental problems are not likely to cause interstate wars.[1] The two sides of this debate have been described by Dabelko and Simmons (1997) and Mansfield (2004). Levy (1995) also provides an interesting discourse on

this debate, including some prescient views on potential security implications of global climate change, some 15 years before it became a mainstream consideration in national security planning.

According to Mansfield (2004), the U.S. policy community's interest level in environmental security peaked during the mid- to late 1990s when it became a part of the U.S. State Department's priority list, and a triagency memorandum of understanding among the Departments of State, Energy, and Defense resulted in dedicated resources being spent on environmental security. The relationships among environmental, socioeconomic, and security issues were viewed as important to understanding a multipolar world that contained much uncertainty. During this period, the U.S. military conducted a number of humanitarian relief operations, both domestic and abroad, that were linked to extreme environmental events of one kind or another. These are illustrated in Figure 1.1.2, which is a timeline of such operations conducted by U.S. Transportation Command over a 12-year period spanning from the end of the Cold War to the beginning of post–September 11 military operations. The significant expenditures on humanitarian relief by the Department of Defense (DoD) were taking place during a period of steep personnel and budgetary drawdowns driven by a perceived "peace dividend." However, despite the DoD budget cuts, several of the regional combatant commands saw environmental security as a constructive way to engage developing countries and establish "military to military" contacts with these nations. The belief was that these military and diplomatic contacts were a necessary investment that could become very important should the U.S. military become involved in stabilization or other types of operations in those regions [see, e.g., Henk (2006), who discusses these types of operations in Africa].

After the September 11 terrorist attacks, U.S. foreign policy was primarily directed towards what was known as the global war on terrorism. As a result, environmental security had a reduced emphasis in the U.S. policy-making community. However, in the late 2000s, possible connections between global climate change and national security rekindled interest in environmental security in the U.S. and European policy-making

---

1. The difficulty of accurately identifying the direct and indirect causes of conflict makes Deudney's case on this third point less convincing than on the first two, as there are some suggestions that climate change—acting through drought—played a hand in the twenty-first century conflicts in Sudan and Syria (Gleick 2014; Maystadt et al. 2015; Kelley and Michela 1980).

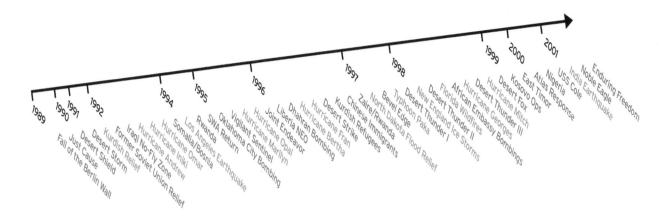

Figure 1.1.2. U.S. Transportation Command (USTRANSCOM) humanitarian relief operations timeline (red highlighting added by the authors to illustrate the fraction of these operations that were environmentally related). Graphic adapted from a USTRANSCOM presentation to the U.S. Air Force Air War College in 2002.

communities. This interest was catalyzed by several policy-type papers on the issue [e.g., Center for Naval Analyses (CNA) 2007; Busby 2007; Council of the European Union 2008]. Ultimately, the potential implications of climate change on national security made their way into U.S. foreign policy–planning documents such as the quadrennial defense review (Department of Defense 2014), quadrennial diplomacy and development review (Department of State 2015), and quadrennial homeland security review (Department of Homeland Security 2014). It should be pointed out that in these documents, climate change is not portrayed as a traditional threat but as a catalyst for exacerbating existing threats or creating new ones.

1.1.3. DEFINING ENVIRONMENTAL SECURITY

Unsurprisingly, the academic response to the term "environmental security" has been approached differently than in policy circles. King (2000) provided a thorough summary of the diverse definitions for environmental security that were found in the literature and in federal government agency regulations of that time. These ranged from environmental restoration, compliance, and conservation considerations to more security-focused definitions. King's (2000, 14–16) definition of environmental security is reproduced below:

Environmental security is a process for effectively responding to changing environmental conditions that

have the potential to reduce peace and stability in the world and thus affect U.S. national security.

King's definition of the environment focused on the natural components of Earth's atmosphere, land, soil, vegetation, and ocean areas, so it was a domain-related definition. In this way, it is somewhat limiting and unappreciative of the broader context within which we envision environmental security to reside today. For example, Ramsay and O'Sullivan described modern environmental security as a distinct security construct, juxtaposed to national security and international security. According to Ramsay and O'Sullivan (2013, p. 11),

There is no gold standard definition of ES [environmental security], just as there is none for HS [homeland security], but we believe good social scientific analysis of such a contested concept, as a sub-category of other theoretical constructs, should offer a working definition—rather than assume a term's meaning is well-known or well-established. . . . Environmental security is, in many regards, the ultimate *transnational security* problem since it addresses security challenges that are the result of a complex mixture of physical, economic and political eco-systems issues, as well as the dynamic and often unpredictable interplay between natural and human systems. As a result, ES is often not just a localized domestic security problem for one nation. Rather, ES more often involves complex global security policy issues, requiring the participation of several governments, industrial organizations and non-governmental organizations, as well as many other global, regional and local groups.

In this textbook, we present a definition for environmental security that is like King's, but which takes a broader approach such as in Ramsay and O'Sullivan. In addition, the working definition of environmental security for this text incorporates elements of the approach taken to outline the national security threat from global climate change as described in the CNA (2007) report on the subject. Hence, leveraging the definition of Ramsay and Kiltz (2014, 118–119), Ramsay and O'Sullivan (2013), and the CNA (2007) report, we offer the following working definition of ES:

Challenges to national or homeland security posture that result from extreme environmental or climatic events acting locally or transnationally to destabilize the countries or regions of the world, resulting in geopolitical instability, resource conflicts, vulnerabilities in critical infrastructure, or some combination of these impacts.

This definition preserves King's original linkage to national security and his characterization of the natural environment but goes further in two ways. First, it enhances King's definition by introducing a cause–effect argument involving changing environmental conditions and human activities that is applicable to both national and homeland security. Second, it links vulnerabilities in critical infrastructure to weather and climatic extremes, which can result in security challenges in more-developed countries. This incorporates the natural versus human-made categorization discussed in the last section.

1.1.4. DISAGGREGATING ENVIRONMENTAL SECURITY

Because the concept of environmental security actually encompasses multiple relationships between a perceived threat and referent (object of the threat), it is useful to disaggregate the concept of environmental security before addressing the political and social effects of environmental security claims. Table 1.1.3 below suggests some different security dynamics related to the environment but is not intended to be exhaustive.

Some trends should stand out. First, the actors usually empowered are governments. This is not unusual; intuition suggests that national governments are often considered the actors best positioned to address secu-

Table 1.1.3. Types of security and associated threats.

Security type	Threat	Referent	Empowered actors	Example
Ecological	Pollution, human alteration of biosphere	Ecosystems, species	Governments, NGOs	Widening and deepening of Suez Canal may increase flow of invasive species
National	Political/social unrest or violence caused by environmental changes	States	Governments	Syrian conflict sparked (in part) by climate change–induced drought
Common	Political/social unrest or violence caused by environmental changes	Communities of states, civilization, humanity	Governments	Rising sea levels caused by climate change
Human	Increased mortality/disadvantage caused by environmental changes	Individuals	Governments, NGOs	Poor access to clean water for individuals or communities
Economic	Disruption of economic activities by environmental changes	Economy, economic processes, jobs	Governments, corporations	Changes in climate drive migration of pests, damaging agricultural output
Climate	Human activity that changes the chemistry of the atmosphere, inducing climate instability	Ecosystems, states, societies	Governments	Bleaching of coral reefs, submersion of low-lying coral atolls

rity threats.[2] Second, environmental security is almost exclusively conceived of in reference to human welfare. That is, people rarely conceive of environmental security in terms of some inherent value of the environment or biodiversity. Rather, the value of the environment or biodiversity is usually understood in terms of their value to humans or human society. While the extinction of a species may elicit a momentary period of consciousness, it rarely elicits sustained concern unless the species is understood as important for human welfare. Thus, the collapse of cod fisheries in the North Atlantic prompted Canadian policy makers to impose a fishing moratorium in 1992 that continues to today even as global biodiversity losses continue unabated (Cardinale et al. 2012; Walsh 1992).

Identifying the varieties of security that inhabit the concept of environmental security also hints at the contestation over environmental security. When the nongovernmental environmental advocacy organization Greenpeace makes claims regarding "environmental security," they are likely very different from "environmental security" claims made by major manufacturing corporations or, in some cases, by national governments; nonetheless, the energy and power behind debates over environmental security tends to come from the political effects of security claims.

1.1.5. FITTING ENVIRONMENTAL SECURITY INTO A LARGER SECURITY STRATEGY IN THE UNITED STATES

Understanding this relationship between environmental security and power leads us to ask, how might environmental security fit in within a larger strategic context of national or homeland security? Broadly, as defined above, environmental security concerns both the domestic security of civilians within the United States or any other country and, at a minimum, the emergency management activities of the Federal Emergency Management Agency (FEMA). In addition to political violence/ terrorism, environmental security includes threats to the U.S. economy from large-scale environmental accidents (such as the BP *Deepwater Horizon* Gulf oil spill), geological events (i.e., tsunamis, earthquakes)[3] and climatic or weather extremes (such as Hurricane Katrina and even the 2011–2012 Western states' drought), strategic resource shortages (food, water, energy, etc.), and/or deficits to critical infrastructure (CI)—the mechanisms by which societies operate. In this sense, environmental security straddles the realms of transnational/transborder, traditional international, and national as well as human security problem sets. And because it addresses both the risks of natural disasters and even of precursors to political disruption that can lead to terrorism, environmental security should be considered a key element of "homeland" security as Figure 1.1.3 demonstrates.

1.1.6. THE MISSING LINK: HUMAN SECURITY

Figure 1.1.3 makes clear the inverse relationship between environmental *in*security and human security. Human security is the rationale behind environmental security in that keeping the environment secure for its own sake is a noble goal, but most states and organizations focus on the link between humanity and the environment in which we live; thus, keeping the environment secure can also keep humanity secure. Before going any further, however, let's look a little closer at human security. At its most basic level, we understand human security to mean security that prioritizes the individual over the security of the state (King and Murray 2001). Made popular by the 1994 UN human development report, human security thinking emphasizes that most if not all of the United Nations' 2030 sustainable development goals

---

2. In most cases, the state or government in the form of the national security complex—military and national intelligence agencies—is seen as the actor capable of marshaling the resources necessary to counter threats. Yet when it comes to environmental problems, it is far from clear that the military or other elements in the national security complex are capable of effectively addressing climate change. Where environmental degradation threatens human security (e.g., drought dries up water supplies or reduces crop yields), national security actors are well placed to provide emergency supplies, but it is not within their mission space to put in place the long-term measures required to ameliorate human suffering.

3. Japan's earthquake and tsunami were estimated to have cost well over $200 billion (U.S. dollars), *not* including the as-yet undetermined costs of the Fukushima Daishi nuclear plant disaster (*Tulsa World*, 8 January 2012; www.tulsaworld.com/business/ moneypower/japan-tsunami-pushes-into-record-for-insurance-losses/article_c70b4375-a9c8-50b7-a538-621069e1070a.html).

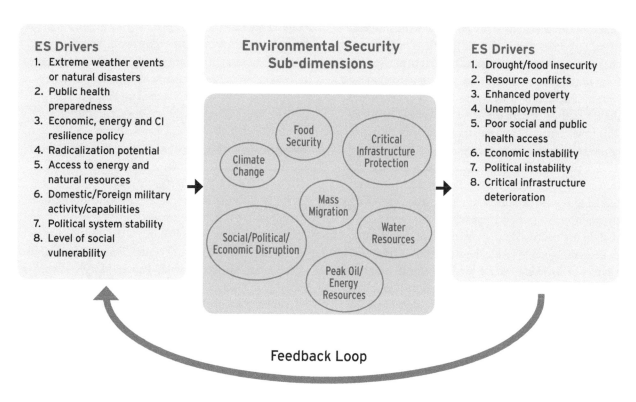

Figure 1.1.3. General structure of the environmental security construct, drivers, and consequences (Ramsay and O'Sullivan 2013).

are unachievable without a paradigm shift that focuses on sustainability at local levels rather than a prolonged focus on continuing to securitize the sovereignty of the modern state (United Nations 2016; United Nations Development Programme 1994). Thus, we understand human security to be a broad conceptual paradigm uniquely capable of assessing and responding to the demands of the pressing threats from global problems such as climate change. By failing to integrate a human security approach to these challenges, global security will continue to be under growing threat—particularly since the best scientific data continue to forecast that all American systems of governance will be taxed by increased global temperatures and other impacts of climatic shifts (IPCC 2014).

Indeed, though both the media and policy makers focus a great deal of time and attention on the threats American society faces from asymmetrical terrorism, climate change is arguably the most aggressive threat facing the globe today; equally, as we will see throughout this book, there is, of course, a link between asymmetrical terrorism and environmental insecurity. No single state is prepared to face the

challenges emerging from climate change, which include direct and indirect conflicts, heightened social and political tensions both in the United States and abroad, adverse effects on food prices and availability, drought and other impacts on water access, negative impacts on investments and economic competitiveness, increased risks to human health, and continued climate discontinuities, as well as other unforeseen consequences (National Intelligence Council 2016; Department of Defense 2016; IPCC 2007, 2014).

Most human security threats are complex and can sometimes take years (if not decades) to resolve; as with other such threats, climate change is not a problem that can be "fixed" within one election cycle. Indeed, changes in the climate can take many years to surface enough to see tangible change (IPCC 2016). However, the logic of security is oriented toward immediate action. Threat claims force constituencies to consider whether the referent is something they want to preserve and, if so, whether the claimed threat is credible. Of course, in the environmental context, acute crises like hurricanes can enhance the perceived need for urgent action, while slow changes like sea level rise can undermine it. Successful claims of threat also have the potential to tie into emotional responses like anxiety or fear that concentrate focus. Finally, the nature of threats also moves issues to the front of the queue because they are often accompanied by time constraints: if we do no act now/quickly, then the referent will disappear or be irrevocably damaged. This time constraint bolsters the urgency of the issue and empowers prompt response.

The problem, however, is that immediate, urgent action can create a short-term perspective that has the potential to reward "optical solutions"—policies that appear to produce change by addressing proximate causes but that do not address deeper, distal causes—rather than policies designed to tackle the structural or underlying sources of environmental degradation. This, in turn, has the potential to produce poorly considered policies as policy makers rush to provide solutions demanded by a concerned or fearful public. The short-term element of security is not unique to environmental security, but environmental problems make the short-term perspective particularly pernicious. Take, for example, climate change. It has been estimated that to adequately address the problem, some 80% of the known fossil fuel reserves need to remain unexploited (McGlade and Ekins 2015), necessitating a reconstruction of the entire energy foundation of modern human political economies away from carbon-based fuels to alternatives (solar, hydro, wind, hydrogen, nuclear). The need for this transition is urgent but complicated, requiring carefully constructed policies with clear attention to long-term consequences of decisions and durable policy commitments. These are not areas where the logic of security excels.

Thus, a democratic, two-party system with elections every two to six years that focuses almost solely on a national security approach to policy will struggle to convince the American public of the rightness of a human security approach to the climate change problem. This is heightened by the poor job politicians have done thus far and continue to do in appropriately informing the public about the dangers of climate change via the media,[4] due largely to campaign funding provided by fossil fuel companies and the strength of the various fossil fuel lobbies.

REFERENCES

AMS, 2018: "Environment." Glossary of Meteorology, http://glossary.ametsoc.org/wiki/Environment.

Busby, J., 2007: Climate change and national security: An agenda for action. Council on Foreign Relations Special Rep. 32, 40 pp., www.cfr.org/report/climate-change-and-national-security.

Cardinale, B. J., and Coauthors, 2012: Biodiversity loss and its impact on humanity. *Nature*, **486**, 59–67, https://doi.org/10.1038/nature11148.

CNA, 2007: National security and the threat of climate change. CNA Rep., 35 pp.

Council of the European Union, 2008: Climate change and international security. High Representative and the European Commission Paper S113/08, 11 pp.

Dabelko, D. G., and P. J. Simmons, 1997: Environment and security: Core ideas and US government initiatives. *SAIS Rev.*, **17** (1), 127–146, https://doi.org/10.1353/sais.1997.0008.

Department of Defense, 2014: Quadrennial defense review 2014. Office of the Secretary of Defense Rep., 64 pp., http://archive.defense.gov/pubs/2014_Quadrennial_Defense_Review.pdf.

——, 2016: Climate change adaptation and resilience. Department of Defense Directive 4715.21, 12 pp., http://www.esd.whs.mil/Portals/54/Documents/DD/issuances/dodd/471521p.pdf.

Department of Homeland Security, 2010: Quadrennial homeland security review: A strategic framework for a secure homeland. Office of the Secretary of Homeland Security Rep., 108 pp., https://www.dhs.gov/sites/default/files/publications/2010-qhsr-report.pdf.

——, 2014: The 2014 quadrennial homeland security review. Office of the Secretary of Homeland Security Rep., 103 pp., http://www.dhs.gov/sites/default/files/publications/2014-qhsr-final-508.pdf.

Department of State, 2015: Enduring leadership in a dynamic world: Quadrennial diplomacy and development review 2015. Office of the Secretary of State Rep., 90 pp., http://www.state.gov/documents/organization/241429.pdf.

4. President Trump has referred to climate change as a "hoax" in speeches, tweets, and in statements to the media both before and during his presidential campaign. According to PolitiFact, "while he hasn't necessarily repeated the charge that China 'invented' climate change, he has said as recently as Jan. 18, 2016, that action on climate change 'is done for the benefit of China'" (www.politifact.com/truth-o-meter/statements/2016/jan/24/bernie-s/yes-donald-trump-really-did-tweet-climate-change-h/).

Deudney, D., 1990: The case against linking environmental degradation and national security. *Millennium*, **19**, 461–476, https://doi.org/10.1177/03058298900190031001.

Gómez, O. A., and D. Gasper, 2013: Human security: A thematic guidance note for regional and national human development report teams. United Nations Development Programme Rep., 16 pp., http://hdr.undp.org/sites/default/files/human_security_guidance_note_r-nhdrs.pdf.

Gleick, P. H., 2014: Water, drought, climate change, and conflict in Syria. *Wea. Climate Soc.*, **6**, 331–340, https://doi.org/10.1175/WCAS-D-13-00059.1.

Henk, D., 2006: The environment, the US military, and southern Africa. *Parameters*, **36** (2), 98–117, https://ssi.armywarcollege.edu/pubs/parameters/articles/06summer/henk.pdf.

Homer-Dixon, T. E., 1999: *Environment, Scarcity, and Violence*. Princeton University Press, 253 pp.

IPCC, 2007: *Climate Change 2007: Impacts, Adaptation and Vulnerability*. Cambridge University Press, 976 pp.

——, 2014: *Climate Change 2014: Mitigation of Climate Change*. Cambridge University Press, 1465 pp., http://www.ipcc.ch/pdf/assessment-report/ar5/wg3/ipcc_wg3_ar5_full.pdf.

——, 2016: Fifth assessment report—Synthesis report. YouTube, www.youtube.com/watch?v=fGH0dAwM-QE.

Kelley, H. H., and J. L. Michela, 1980: Attribution theory and research. *Annu. Rev. Psychol.*, **31**, 457–501, https://doi.org/10.1146/annurev.ps.31.020180.002325.

King, G., and C. J. L. Murray, 2001: Rethinking human security. *Polit. Sci. Quart.*, **116**, 585–610, https://doi.org/10.2307/798222.

King, W. C., 2000: Understanding international environmental security: A strategic military perspective. U.S. Army Environmental Policy Institute Rep. AEPI-IFP-1100A, 32 pp., http://www.aepi.army.mil/publications/overseas-international/docs/king-a.pdf.

Levy, M., 1995: Is the environment a national security issue? *Int. Secur.*, **20**, (2), 35–62.

Mach, K. J., S. Planton, and C. von Stechow, Eds., 2014: Annex II: Glossary. *Climate Change 2014: Synthesis Report*, Cambridge University Press, 117–130.

Mansfield, W. H., 2004: The evolution of environmental security in a North American policy context. *Poverty and Environment Times*, No. 2, United Nations Environmental Programme, Arendal, Norway, www.grida.no/publications/265.

Maystadt, J.-F., M. Calderone, and L. You, 2015: Local warming and violent conflict in North and South Sudan. *J. Econ. Geogr.*, **15**, 649–671, https://doi.org/10.1093/jeg/lbu033.

McGlade, C., and P. Ekins, 2015: The geographical distribution of fossil fuels unused when limiting global warming to 2°C. *Nature*, **517**, 187–190, https://doi.org/10.1038/nature14016.

Myers, N., 2004: Environmental security: What's new and different? *Hague Conf. on Environment, Security and Sustainable Development*, The Hague, Netherlands, Institute for Environmental Security, http://www.envirosecurity.org/conference/working/newanddifferent.pdf.

NASA, 2017: Climate vs. weather. Joint Polar Satellite System, accessed 11 October 2018, https://jointmission.gsfc.nasa.gov/climate_vs_weather.html.

National Intelligence Council, 2016: Implications for US national security of anticipated climate change. Director of National Intelligence Rep., www.dni.gov/files/documents/Newsroom/Reports and Pubs/Implications_for_US_National_Security_of_Anticipated_Climate_Change.pdf.

National Weather Service, 2018: "Weather." Glossary, http://w1.weather.gov/glossary/index.php?word=WEATHER.

Pal, J. S., and E. A. B. Eltahir, 2016: Future temperature in southwest Asia projected to exceed a threshold for human adaptability. *Nat. Climate Change*, **6**, 197–200, https://doi.org/10.1038/nclimate2833.

Ramsay, J., and T. O'Sullivan, 2013: There's a pattern here: The case to integrate environmental security into homeland security strategy. *Homeland Secur. Aff.*, **9**, 6, https://www.hsaj.org/articles/246.

——, and L. Kiltz, Eds., 2014: *Critical Issues in Homeland Security: A Case Book*. Westview Press, 367 pp.

Tuchman Mathews, J., 1989: Redefining security. *Foreign Aff.*, 68 (2), 162–177, www.foreignaffairs.com/articles/1989-03-01/redefining-security.

United Nations, 1992: United Nations Framework Convention on Climate Change. United Nations Doc., 31 pp., https://unfccc.int/files/essential_background/background_publications_htmlpdf/application/pdf/conveng.pdf.

——, 2016: Sustainable development goals. United Nations, www.un.org/sustainabledevelopment/sustainable-development-goals/.

United Nations Development Programme, 1994: Human development report. United Nations Development Programme Rep., 136 pp., hdr.undp. org/sites/default/files/reports/255/hdr_1994_en_complete_nostats.pdf.

Walsh, M. W., 1992: Canada bans N. Atlantic cod fishing for 2 years. Los Angeles Times, 3 July, http://articles.latimes.com/1992-07-03/news/mn-1249_1_cod-fishing-ban.

ADDITIONAL RESOURCES

Ackerman, J. T., 2008: Climate change, national security, and the quadrennial defense review: Avoiding the perfect storm. *Strategic Studies Quart.*, **2** (1), 56–96, https://www.airuniversity.af.mil/Portals/10/SSQ/documents/Volume-02_Issue-1/ackerman.pdf.

Dodds, F., and T. Pippard, 2005: *Human and Environmental Security: An Agenda for Change.* Earthscan, 320 pp.

Easterling, W. E., 2007: Climate change and the adequacy of food and timber in the 21st century. *Proc. Natl. Acad. Sci. USA*, **104**, 192679, https://doi.org/10.1073/pnas.0710388104.

Elliott, L., 2015: Human security/environmental security. *Contemp. Polit.*, **21**, 11–24, https://doi.org/10.1080/13569775.2014.993905.

Everingham, J.-A., N. Collins, J. Cavaye, W. Rifkin, S. Vink, T. Baumgartl, and D. Rodriguez, 2016: Energy from the foodbowl: Associated land-use conflicts, risks and wicked problems. *Landscape Urban Plann.*, **154** (10), 68–80, https://doi.org/10.1016/j.landurbplan.2016.01.011.

Gerrard, M., 2015: America's forgotten nuclear waste dump in the Pacific. *SAIS Rev.*, **35** (1), 87–98, https://doi.org/10.1016/j.landurbplan.2016.01.011.

Harris, P. G., 2013: *What's Wrong with Climate Politics and How to Fix It.* Polity Press, 296 pp.

Howden, S. M., J.-F. Soussana, F. N. Tubiello, N. Chhetri, M. Dunlop, and H. Meinke, 2007: Adapting agriculture to climate change. *Proc. Natl. Acad. Sci. USA*, **104**, 192691–192696, https://doi.org/10.1073/pnas. 0701890104.

Means, A. J., 2014: Beyond the poverty of national security: Toward a critical human security perspective in educational policy. *J. Educ. Policy*, **29**, 719–741, https://doi.org/10.1080/02680939.2013.876674.

Morton, J. F., 2007: The impact of climate change on smallholder and subsistence agriculture. *Proc. Natl. Acad. Sci. USA*, **104**, 192680–192685, https://doi.org/10.1073/pnas.0701855104.

Schmidhuber, J., and F. N. Tubiello, 2007: Global food security under climate change. *Proc. Natl. Acad. Sci. USA*, **104**, 192703–192708, https://doi.org/10.1073/pnas.0701976104.

1.2

DEFINING CLIMATE CHANGE: CAUSES, IMPACTS, AND INSTITUTIONS

Elisabeth Hope Murray

1.2.1. INTRODUCTION TO CLIMATE CHANGE

Climate change is one of the key drivers of social, economic, military, and political change. It is the threat multiplier affecting every other point made throughout this book—food security, water security, environmental hazards, and conflict. It is one of the greatest challenges humanity has ever faced.

But before we go any further into discussing the causes, impacts, and institutions at the forefront of climate change policy and research, let's break down some basic terms. First, what do we mean when we use the term "climate"? To begin, we should point out that "climate" is not the same as "weather"; the weather today represents climate change as poorly as Napoleon represents France. Is there a relationship between weather and climate? Of course there is. But in this relationship, weather is only one aspect of climate change. The U.S. National Oceanic and Atmospheric Administration (NOAA) highlights this relationship, noting that weather is the "state of the atmosphere with respect to wind, temperature, cloudiness, moisture, pressure, etc. Weather refers to these conditions at a given point in time (e.g., today's high temperature), whereas climate refers to the 'average' weather conditions for an area over a long period of time (e.g., the average high temperature

for today's date)" (NOAA 2018). Climate, then, can be understood as the long-term pattern of weather in a particular region, including averages of "precipitation, temperature, humidity, sunshine, wind velocity, phenomena such as fog, frost, and hail storms, and other measures of the weather that occur over a long period in a particular place" (NASA 2017). Scientists study these changes for a number of reasons but largely to assess the impact changes in these averages will have on life here on Earth.

Of course, scientists and researchers don't only look at how these climate averages are changing over time; they also look at why they are changing over time. We know that climate change is a part of Earth's natural cycles. For example, we know that Earth's climate responds to changes in the distribution of sea surface temperatures in the equatorial Pacific Ocean, a phenomenon better known as the El Niño/Southern Oscillation (ENSO). This then leads to the logical question: If climate change is always happening and if it's part of a natural cycle, then why is climate change such a threat? What's all the doom and gloom about? Unfortunately, these "natural" changes in climate are not the problem. The problem lies with what is commonly known as *anthropogenic* climate change. Throughout this book, when we use the term "climate change," we mean anthropogenic climate change. In fact, most media outlets, politicians, researchers, and institutional leaders in the field do exactly the same thing, so it's important not to confuse the daily (or seasonal) changes in climate with anthropogenic climate change. "Anthropogenic" means simply "caused by humans." Thus, throughout this book, when we use the term climate change, we use the definition set forth by the United Nations 1992 Framework Convention on Climate Change (UNFCC), where climate change means a change of climate that is attributed directly or indirectly to human activity that alters the composition of the global atmosphere and that is in addition to natural climate variability observed over comparable time periods (United Nations 1992).

This climate change, attributed directly or indirectly to human activity, is the thing that is threatening food production, limiting water supply and access, increasing the risk of catastrophic flooding, causing sea level rise, and shifting weather patterns, just to name a few major challenges for our time. We want to be very clear: humans, and specifically a lifestyle enjoyed by individuals in industrialized, Western states, have created an environment of insecurity felt across the globe that will test all of our capabilities. This is largely happening through the production of greenhouse gases (GHGs). Greenhouse gases are understood to be the gases that absorb terrestrial radiation and contribute to the so-called greenhouse effect; the main greenhouse gases are water vapor, methane, carbon dioxide, and ozone (NOAA 2018). Most climate change science points to methane and carbon dioxide produced by and for humans as the worst offenders in climate change and its effects (IPCC 2016).

However, there is some good news here. If we created the situation, we also have the power to change the situation. Unlike catastrophic events in which humans take no part or have no influence, climate change is something we can actively prepare for and take action to prevent future aggression. We will talk more about this later in the book, but we bring this up here to emphasize that, though we have created a mess, humans have agency to actually impact our climate in a positive way.

The next logical question is, How do we know this is happening? How can we be sure humans are responsible? We can be sure because overwhelmingly the individuals who have dedicated their lives to the study of the climate agree that this is happening. Over 97% of climate scientists agree that climate change is occurring and that humans are responsible (see, e.g., Anderegg and Goldsmith 2014; Cook et al. 2016; Floyd 2015; Fritz 2013). To put that into perspective, approximately 40% more scientists have found that humans cause climate change than have found that flossing is good for your teeth (Berchier et al. 2008; Hujoel et al. 2006)! Indeed, much of the debate within the climate science community is not whether humans are responsible but is instead focused on exactly how bad the consequences of climate change are going to be and exactly what can be done to best support resilience. We will see this reflected in unit 2 regarding energy security and the situation with tar sands in Canada.

Much of these discussions take place within the boundaries of the UNFCC in the Intergovernmental Panel on Climate Change (IPCC). Though scientists have been highlighting changes in the global climate since the midcentury, the IPCC has been largely responsible for providing a mechanism for climate scientists to work together in an effort to educate the public about the facts of climate change. The IPCC is understood to be the leading body for the assessment and evaluation of climate change globally. As stated in Chapter 1.1, the IPCC was established in 1988 by the United Nations Environment Programme (UNEP) and the World Meteorological Organization (WMO); the establishment of the IPCC was endorsed by the UN General Assembly that same year. Currently, 195 states are members of the IPCC, including the United States, China, India, South Africa, Mexico, Japan, North Korea, South Korea, and Iran. Governments participate in the review process and plenary sessions, but individual, independent scientists are responsible for the production of research, providing the scientific, technical, and socioeconomic information. This separation of research and planning helps ensure that the information published by the IPCC remains unbiased by any individual state's propaganda or ideology regarding climate change (IPCC 2018). Thousands of scientists from across the globe participate in writing the peer-reviewed publications that make up the reports provided by the IPCC. The peer-review process, usually conducted through blind reviews of academic work by multiple scholars in the same academic field, is the highest academic standard and serves to provide an objective and complete assessment of the most current information.

The IPCC's main work comes from the production of reports, produced and reviewed over a series of years, often in conjunction with several international meetings. The following sections highlight the five current reports.

1.2.2. FIRST ASSESSMENT REPORT–1990 (AND SUPPLEMENTAL REPORTS–1992)

The first assessment report (FAR) and the supplemental reports largely established the science for climate change and suggested possible impacts and responses to these challenges. FAR is broken into three working groups: Working Group 1—The Scientific Assessment of Climate Change; Working Group 2—The Potential Impacts of Climate Change; and Working Group 3—The Formulation of Response Strategies. FAR also includes a report from the Special Committee on the Participation of Developing Countries. The final conclusions find that greenhouse gas emissions are impacting the global climate but to what extent yet remains unclear and "is not likely [to be clear] for a decade or more"; it also emphasizes the need for lessening the gap between less-developed countries (LDCs) and more-developed countries (MDCs)[1] in order to provide a global approach to combating global warming. Perhaps most importantly, FAR highlights the need for education (IPCC 1990, p. 60):

> Because climate change would affect, either directly or indirectly, almost every sector of society, broad global understanding of the issue will facilitate the adoption and the implementation of such response options as deemed necessary and appropriate. Further efforts to achieve such global understanding are urgently needed.

1.2.3. SECOND ASSESSMENT REPORT–1995

The second assessment report (SAR) built strongly on the findings of FAR, producing more substantial evidence for anthropogenic causes of climate change. Again, the report is broken down into three working groups: Working Group 1—The Science of Climate Change; Working Group 2—Impacts, Adaptations and Mitigation of Climate Change: Scientific-Technical Analyses; and Working Group 3—Economic and Social Dimensions of Climate Change. The titles of the three working groups give a feeling of the more nuanced approach to the research presented in the report. Overall, SAR highlights the continued increase in GHG concentrations, the impact of aerosols and their link to radioactivity, and the "discernible human influence on the global climate." Of particular interest is the fact that SAR consistently reinforces the expectation that the climate will continue to change in the future because of the lack of preventative action taken since FAR (IPCC 1995).

1.2.4. THIRD ASSESSMENT REPORT–2001

The third assessment report (TAR) provides an assessment of scientific data to inform policy makers about what constitutes "dangerous anthropogenic interference with the climate system" (IPCC 2001, p. 2), highlighting concerning rates of change in the climate system, the socioeconomic impacts of climate change, and the potential for mitigation. TAR also highlights areas of grave vulnerability from changes in temperature, precipitation, and extreme climate events (which we will cover more in unit 3) and links climate change to sustainable development in both MDCs and LDCs. TAR is also the first of the reports to emphasize the varying financial cost of climate change and to stress that early, preventative measures will be much more cost effective (IPCC 2001). Similar to the previous reports, TAR is separated into three working groups: Working Group 1—The Scientific Basis; Working Group 2—Impacts, Adaptation, and Vulnerability; and Working Group 3—Mitigation.

1.2.5. FOURTH ASSESSMENT REPORT–2007

The fourth assessment report (AR4) continues to be broken down into three different working groups: Working Group 1—The Physical Science Basis; Working Group 2—Impacts, Adaptation, and Vulnerability; and Working Group 3—Mitigation of Climate Change. AR4 is of particular interest for U.S. policy makers as, for the

---

1. The designation of a country as "more" or "less" developed uses criteria involving economies, institutions, and infrastructure and is often confusing. For the purposes of this textbook, we will adopt the terminology "more developed" and "less developed" countries. A useful summary of the different terminology and criteria used to define them appears online (www.harpercollege.edu/mhealy/g101ilec/intro/eco/ecomea/ecomeafr.htm). Additionally, formal definitions of MDC and LDC are given at the start of Unit 4.

first time, threats to U.S. domestic security are raised. AR4 is also able to test some of the findings proposed in FAR and SAR, highlighting the fact that of the previous 12 years (1995–2006), 11 rank among the warmest years in the instrumental record of global surface temperature (note that since AR4, temperatures have continued to rise, regularly surpassing this number). Both the rise in sea level and the decrease in snow and sea ice are noted, highlighting in particular the loss of approximately 7% of frozen ground in the Northern Hemisphere alone since 1900. AR4 points to the challenges of GHGs that are stored long term in the atmosphere. On a lighter note, the report does confidently point to the fact that sustainable development policies can enhance mitigative and adaptive capacities, reduce emissions, and reduce vulnerabilities if states can overcome barriers to their implementation (IPCC 2007a).

1.2.6. FIFTH ASSESSMENT REPORT–2013, 2014

The fifth assessment report's (AR5) Working Group 1— The Physical Science Basis was published in late 2013, while Working Groups 2 and 3 (Impacts, Adaptation, and Vulnerability and Mitigation of Climate Change, respectively) were published in early 2014. This report focuses on risk, a new element of the IPCC reports. Here, we see how climate change involves complex interactions and changing likelihoods of diverse impacts, providing a much more nuanced report than seen previously. The IPCC here projects five climate futures based on greenhouse gas expenditure; the lower the increase in GHGs, the better the climate future. Equally, compared to past reports, AR5 assesses a substantially larger knowledge base of relevant academic literature and provides a more comprehensive assessment across a broader set of topics. Working Group 2 in particular focuses on expanded coverage on human systems, adaptation, and the ocean.

AR5, particularly in Working Groups 2 and 3, is different in another way as well in that there is a stronger moral tone. Working Group 3, for instance, emphasizes that "effective mitigation will not be achieved if individual agents advance their own interests independently. . . . Issues of equity, justice, and fairness arise with respect to mitigation and adaptation" (IPCC 2014, p. 5).

As of publication, AR5 is the latest of the IPCC reports. The sixth assessment report (AR6) will be finalized in 2021 in time for the first UNFCC global climate "stocktake," when individual states will review their progress toward the goal of keeping global warming below 2°C.

As AR5 provides some excellent facts regarding the anthropogenic impact on climate change, let's look at some of the evidence gathered there:

- CO_2 emissions from fossil fuel combustion and industrial processes contributed about 78% of the total GHG emission increase from 1970 to 2010, with a similar percentage contribution for the period 2000–2010.
- About half of cumulative anthropogenic CO_2 emissions between 1750 and 2010 have occurred in the last 40 years.
- Annual anthropogenic GHG emissions have increased by 10 $GtCO_2eq$ between 2000 and 2010, with this increase directly coming from energy supply (47%), industry (30%), transport (11%), and buildings (3%) sectors.
- Globally, economic and population growth continue to be the most important drivers of increases in CO_2 emissions from fossil fuel combustion. The contribution of population growth between 2000 and 2010 remained roughly identical to the previous three decades, while the contribution of economic growth has risen sharply.
- Without additional efforts to reduce GHG emissions beyond those in place today, emissions growth is expected to persist, driven by growth in global population and economic activities. Baseline scenarios, those without additional mitigation, result in global mean surface temperature increases in 2100 from 3.7° to 4.8°C compared to preindustrial levels (IPCC 2014).

This is alarming evidence that key "points of no return" may have already been met; if this is true, we may already be seeing irreversible changes in major ecosystems, such as urban and rural areas, coastal areas, forestry, and all areas of food production (IPCC 2007b). Ecosystems such as the Arctic tundra, the Florida Everglades and the Amazon rainforest are under severe threat, while the Sahara and other deserts are growing, further challenging resource access. Indeed, according to Working Group 3, all aspects of food security are potentially affected by climate change, including food access, utilization, and price stability (IPCC 2014).

These summaries only scratch the surface of the danger climate change poses to our societies. Climate change is likely to result in increased poverty, migration, violent conflict, terrorism, displacement, and civil unrest, as we will see more fully in unit 4.

We no longer have the luxury of waiting to implement policies countering climate change. As we consider environmental security, we must first understand the threat climate change poses to each aspect of national, homeland, and human security and take responsibility on a personal and communal level to implement more sustainable living in order to counter the inevitabilities of climate change.

REFERENCES

Anderegg, W., and G. Goldsmith, 2014: Public interest in climate change over the past decade and the effects of the 'climategate' media event. *Environ. Res. Lett.*, **9**, 054005, https://doi.org/10.1088/1748-9326/9/5/054005.

Berchier, C., D. Slot, S. Haps, and G. Van der Weijden, 2008: The efficacy of dental floss in addition to a toothbrush on plaque and parameters of gingival inflammation: A systematic review. *Int. J. Dent. Hyg.*, **6**, 265–279, https://doi.org/10.1111/j.1601-5037.2008.00336.x.

Cook, J., and Coauthors, 2016: Consensus on consensus: A synthesis of consensus estimates on human-caused global warming. *Environ. Res. Lett.*, **11**, 048002, https://doi.org/10.1088/1748-9326/11/4/048002.

Floyd, D., 2015: Comment on 'Quantifying the consensus on anthropogenic global warming in the scientific literature.' *Environ. Res. Lett.*, **10**, 039001, https://doi.org/10.1088/1748-9326/10/3/039001.

Fritz, R., 2013: History and future of the scientific consensus on anthropogenic global warming. *Environ. Res. Lett.*, **8**, 031003, https://doi.org/10.1088/1748-9326/8/3/031003.

Hujoel, P., J. Cunha-Cruz, D. Banting, and W. Loesche, 2006: Dental flossing and interproximal caries: A systematic review. *J. Dent. Res.*, **85**, 298–305, https://doi.org/10.1177/154405910608500404.

IPCC, 1990: Overview. *Climate Change: The IPCC 1990 and 1992 Assessments*, IPCC, 51–62, https://www.ipcc.ch/ipccreports/1992%20IPCC%20Supplement/IPCC_1990_and_1992_Assessments/English/ipcc_90_92_assessments_far_overview.pdf.

——, 1995: *IPCC Second Assessment: Climate Change 1995.* Cambridge University Press, 572 pp., http://ipcc.ch/pdf/climate-changes-1995/ipcc-2nd-assessment/2nd-assessment-en.pdf.

——, 2001: *Climate Change 2001: Synthesis Report.* Cambridge University Press, 398 pp., www.grida.no/publications/267.

——, 2007a: *Climate Change 2007: Synthesis Report.* IPCC, 104 pp., www.ipcc.ch/publications_and_data/ar4/syr/en/contents.html.

——, 2007b: *Climate Change 2007: Impacts, Adaptation and Vulnerability.* Cambridge University Press, 976 pp., www.ipcc.ch/publications_and_data/publications_ipcc_fourth_assessment_report_wg2_report_impacts_adaptation_and_vulnerability.htm.

——, 2014: *Climate Change 2014: Mitigation of Climate Change.* Cambridge University Press, 1465 pp., www.ipcc.ch/pdf/assessment-report/ar5/wg3/ipcc_wg3_ar5_full.pdf.

——, 2016: Fifth assessment report—Synthesis report. YouTube, www.youtube.com/watch?v=fGH0dAwM-QE.

——, 2018: Organization. IPCC, http://ipcc.ch/organization/organization.shtml.

NASA, 2017: Climate vs. weather. Joint Polar Satellite System, https://jointmission.gsfc.nasa.gov/climate_vs_weather.html.

NOAA, 2018: "Weather." Glossary, http://w1.weather.gov/glossary/index.php?word=WEATHER.

United Nations, 1992: United Nations Framework Convention on Climate Change. United Nations Doc., 31 pp., https://unfccc.int/files/essential_background/background_publications_htmlpdf/application/pdf/conveng.pdf.

NATURAL RESOURCES: THEIR ACCESS AND RELATIONSHIP TO SECURITY

KEY TERMS AND CONCEPTS

Food security   A subdimension of the larger concept of human security. Food security is a situation that exists when all people, consistently, have physical, social, and economic access to sufficient, safe, and nutritious food that meets their dietary needs and food preferences for an active and healthy life (adapted from the FAO).

Carrying capacity   Carrying capacity pertains to the number of a species that an environment can sustain, considering the limiting factors at play (e.g., food, water, competition).

Biogeochemical   Biogeochemicals are groups of chemical elements (i.e., phosphorous) or molecules (i.e., water) that are essential to support life on Earth. The five essential biogeochemicals include carbon, nitrogen, sulfur, phosphorous, and water. Each has a cycle, and each cycle is mitigated by activities of human living. The existence, abundance, and distribution and chemical forms of each determine whether and to what degree life is supported or endangered.

Extreme weather event   An extreme weather event is an event that is rare within its statistical reference distribution at a particular geographic location. Definitions vary, but an extreme weather event would normally be as rare as or rarer than the 10th or 90th percentile. For example, the characteristics of what is called extreme weather may vary from place to place. An extreme climate event is an average of a number of weather events over a certain period of time, an average which is itself extreme (e.g., rainfall over a season).

Greenhouse gases   Greenhouse gases are those gaseous constituents of the atmosphere, both natural and anthropogenic, that absorb and emit radiation at specific wavelengths within the spectrum of infrared radiation emitted by Earth's surface, the atmosphere, and clouds. This property causes the greenhouse effect. Water vapor (H_2O), carbon dioxide (CO_2), nitrous oxide (N_2O), methane (CH_4), and ozone (O_3) are the primary greenhouse gases in Earth's atmosphere. Moreover, there are several entirely human-made greenhouse gases in the atmosphere, such as halocarbons and other chlorine- and bromine-containing substances, dealt with under the Montreal Protocol. Besides CO_2, N_2O, and CH_4, the Kyoto Protocol deals with the greenhouse gases sulphur hexafluoride (SF_6), hydrofluorocarbons (HFCs), and perfluorocarbons (PFCs).

Strong state   Typically used in reference to a "weak state." A strong state with effective institutions can dampen a given blow from resource scarcity and other environmental damage by providing relief and correcting structural scarcities. In contrast, "weak" or "weakened" states are notably less able to support their economies or people from the consequences of shocks such as political dissent, conflict, draught, or famine.

Energy security   The International Energy Agency defines energy security as "the uninterrupted availability of energy sources at an affordable price," that is, energy that is affordable, reliable, and accessible.

WTO   The World Trade Organization (WTO) is the only global international organization dealing with the rules of trade between nations. At its heart are the WTO agreements, negotiated and signed by the bulk of the world's trading nations and ratified in their parliaments. The goal is to ensure that trade flows as smoothly, predictably, and freely as possible (from www.wto.org/english/thewto_e/thewto_e.htm).

IEA   The International Energy Agency (IEA) works to ensure reliable, affordable, and clean energy for its 30 member countries and beyond. Their mission is guided by four main areas of focus: energy security, economic development, environmental awareness, and engagement worldwide (see www.iea.org/about/).

Renewable energy   Energy derived from natural processes (e.g., sunlight and wind) that are replenished at a faster rate than they are consumed. Solar, wind, geothermal, hydro, and some forms of biomass are common sources of renewable energy.

EROI   The energy return on investment (EROI) is a critical determinant of energy prices. For example, if a given energy sources can be produced relatively cheaply, it will allow the price to remain low. However, the ratio decreases when energy becomes scarcer and more difficult to extract or produce—especially as demand remains high, a trend seen in the oil market.

Political economy   Political economy is the interaction of economic and political structures or processes—the combined politics of economics and economic influences on politics and the fates of nations and humanity.

Water security   The capacity of a population to safeguard sustainable access to adequate quantities of acceptable-quality water for sustaining livelihoods, human well-being, and socioeconomic development; for ensuring protection against waterborne pollution and water-related disasters; and for preserving ecosystems in a climate of peace and political stability.

ISIS   The Islamic State in Iraq and Syria (ISIS) is an asymmetric transnational terrorist organization located primarily in Syria and Iraq. ISIS is also commonly known as the Islamic State in Iraq and the Levant (ISIL) or Da'esh.

Transnational corporations   According to the UN Conference on Trade and Development, transnational corporations (TNCs) are incorporated or unincorporated enterprises comprising parent enterprises and their foreign affiliates. A parent enterprise is defined as an enterprise that controls assets of other entities in countries other than its home country, usually by owning a certain equity capital stake.

Neoliberalism   Neoliberalism is a modified form of liberalism that favors free market capitalism.

Peak oil   Peak oil is the theorized point in time when the maximum rate of extraction of petroleum is reached, after which it is expected to enter terminal decline.

INTRODUCTION TO UNIT 2

The environments of security include a robust nexus between the natural environment and several aspects of human security such as food, environmental, economic, and water security. The center of gravity of human security is that individuals, not just nation states, need to be secure for peace and prosperity to be sustained. This unit presents a series of chapters that vary in their content and their direct relationship to domestic or national security. For example, chapter 2.1 will introduce the reader to the challenges presented by food, energy, and water security. Each chapter will explore how major natural resources, such as food, water, and energy, are related to security and conflict, including how human activities that mitigate, alter, or influence their supply in nature can subsequently add to insecurity.

In addition to the concepts of food, energy, and water and their relationship to security, this unit will offer three compelling case studies that provide specific examples of food, water, or energy security from around the world. These examples include case studies about the Islamic State in Iraq and Syria (ISIS) and control of oil in the Middle East, water security issues in the Jordan River basin, and finally, a look at how depletion of non-renewable energy sources, especially of oil and natural gas, could soon produce severe limits to growth for all nations.

STUDENT LEARNING OBJECTIVES

1. Discuss the aspects of food production and how vulnerabilities of food production can present challenges to U.S. national security.
2. Describe the connections between food, water, and energy security.
3. Discuss the aspects of energy production and how vulnerabilities to energy production can present challenges to economic prosperity and limit the growth of more developed nations.
4. Describe the components of the water cycle and how human activities mitigate access to potable water and how subsequent water shortages may incite conflict and subsequently present challenges to global and U.S. national security.
5. Describe examples of how constraints in the supply of or limited access to natural resources have led to or have sustained conflict.
6. Discuss the role climate change has in food, water, and energy insecurity.

FOOD SCARCITY AND CONFLICT IN AN ERA OF CLIMATE CHANGE

Linda Kiltz
James D. Ramsay

It can be mockery to tell someone they have the right to food when there is nobody with the duty to provide them with food. That is the risk with the rights rhetoric. What I like about choosing the counterpart, the active obligation of duties rather than the rights, you can't go on and on without addressing the question who has to do what, for whom, when.

—*Dr. Onora O'Neill*[1]

2.1.1. INTRODUCTION

In the spring of 2012, U.S. farmers planted over 96 million acres in corn, the most in 75 years (Brown 2012). An early spring marked by warm weather and plenty of rain got the nation's corn crop off to a great start. However, corn is a sensitive crop that is vulnerable to both extreme heat and drought. At elevated temperatures, the corn plant, which is normally productive, goes into thermal shock, thus impacting overall corn yield for the year (Wan et al. 2015). As spring turned to summer, the temperature climbed in late June and early July to 100° or higher 10 days in a row (Brown 2012). The entire Corn Belt[2] of the United States faced rising temperatures and low rainfall. At the beginning of the summer in early June, the U.S. Department of Agriculture reported that 72% of the U.S. corn crop was good to excellent (King 2013). However, one month later, only 40% of the corn crop in the United States rated good to excellent, while 60% was in fair to poor condition (King 2013). By August 2012, one half of the U.S corn crop was rated as poor to very poor (King 2013). Final 2012 numbers placed corn yield at 123.1 bushels per acre and 10.76 billion bushels—reductions of 26% and 27%, respectively (Rippey 2015).

The drought was so severe that Agriculture Secretary Tom Vilsack designated 2,245 counties in 39 states as disaster areas because of drought, or 71% of the United States (USDA 2013). In fact, by September 2012, nearly

---

1. This quotation comes from an answer to a question following the Second Reith Lecture, BBC Radio 4, 10 April 2002. Dr. O'Neill is also the author of *Faces of Hunger*, one of the few explorations by a philosopher of the ethical dimensions of the subject.

2. The U.S. Corn Belt is typically thought of as a region of the midwestern United States that has dominated corn production in the United States since the mid-1850s. More generally, the concept of the "Corn Belt" refers to the area of the Midwest dominated by agriculture.

two-thirds (65.45%) of the continental United States was covered by drought according to the U.S. Drought Monitor (Rippey 2015). As the prospect of a bumper corn crop evaporated, U.S. corn prices surged with predictions of increased food prices in 2013 throughout the world because America is the world's largest producer of corn, accounting for roughly 40% of the world corn production (Wan et al. 2015). Corn is also connected to many food items—such as feed for hogs, dairy cows, and beef cattle and as a component in many processed foods—as well as the production of ethanol. Thus, declining corn production in 2012 led to price increases in food and gasoline throughout the United States and had significant impacts on grain prices throughout the world (Cleetus 2012; Boyer et al. 2013).

Seemingly far removed from the bread basket of America, a violent riot at a platinum mine in South Africa that resulted in three deaths occurred at the height of the U.S. drought on 2 August 2012 (Bar-Yam and Lagi 2015). Additional civil unrest occurred throughout this platinum-mining region and included a particularly violent incident on 16 August at the Marikana mine, which resulted in 34 strikers killed and about 80 more injured—the most violent such incident since the end of apartheid in 1994 (McClenaghan 2012). The protests, taken up by gold miners and agricultural workers, resulted in the destruction of over 120 acres of crops (Bar-Yam and Lagi 2015).

Scholars contend that the interconnected environmental, political, social, and economic conditions that give rise to social violence and civil unrest are often poorly understood. In this case, however, Bar-Yam and Lagi (2015) showed a link between the violence in South Africa and the rapidly rising food prices that had affected many parts of the world, including triggering widespread food riots in 2007–08 and the Arab Spring uprisings in North Africa and the Middle East in 2010–11 (Bar-Yam and Lagi 2015). At the beginning of August 2012, when the labor riots started in South Africa, corn (maize) prices had risen to record highs, driven in part by a drought in the U.S. Midwest but also by other underlying causes that have increased food prices rapidly in recent years. In South Africa, corn is the staple grain. In 2009, the UN Food and Agricultural Organization reported that more than half of the per capita calorie intake was from grains, of which 57% was from maize and 32% from wheat [Food and Agriculture Organization (FAO) 2013]. Because poorer consumers are more dependent on corn and wheat, their ability to afford them is more sensitive to food prices than higher-income consumers. While the South African riots have been attributed to labor issues and corruption in both the government and union organizations, worker demands included significant wage increases amid claims that they were being paid "hunger wages" that did not cover necessities for their families (Bar-Yam, Y., and M. Lagi, 2015).

In recent years, climate change has increasingly been seen described as a security problem because there is growing evidence that climate change may increase the risk of violent conflict because it undermines human security (Adger et al. 2014; Barnett and Adger 2007).

These and many other examples begin to highlight the concept of food security, a commonly included subdimension of the larger notion of human security discussed in unit 1. According to the UN FAO, "Food security exists when all people, at all times, have physical, social and economic access to sufficient, safe and nutritious food which meets their dietary needs and food preferences for an active and healthy life. Household food security is the application of this concept to the family level, with individuals within households as the focus of concern. In contrast, Food insecurity occurs when people do not have adequate physical, social or economic access to food as defined above" (FAO 2013).

This chapter will look at the relationship between conflict, food production, and climate variability. First, there will be a discussion on the impact of climate change on agricultural production. Next, there will be a review of the environment–conflict literature. Finally, there will be a discussion of three possible pathways to conflict: 1) the resource scarcity pathway, 2) the weak state pathway, and 3) the migration pathway.

2.1.2. IMPACT OF CLIMATE CHANGE ON AGRICULTURE

The basic measure of any society's development and stability is agriculture. If a nation can produce enough food to feed its own population, it has developmental potential. If it cannot, it faces food insecurity and hunger, increased levels of conflict and violence, and population migration. Changes in the environment due to climate change can thereby destabilize a society and weaken nation-states. LeBlanc (2003) argues that no matter how clever societies are at managing their resources, over the long term, they must be able to maintain the population–resource balance so as to not outstrip the carrying capacities of their ecosystems. According to Galloway (1986), since often-rapid changes in climate can significantly alter this carrying capacity,[3] populations either accept reduced food supplies, migrate to nondegraded areas, or go to war to secure additional resources. Climate change, due to both increasing ambient air temperatures and altered timing and amounts of precipitation, will greatly affect food and water supplies in the future; thus, it is important to understand these effects on agricultural production and food security.

Landmark studies by Parry et al. (2004), Cline (2007), World Bank (2010), and others show that impacts of global climate change on food systems are expected to be geographically and temporally variable, widespread and complex, and influenced by preexisting and emerging social and economic conditions. Several historical studies show the impacts of climate trends on food systems (Lobell and Field 2007; Lobell et al. 2011a). For example, Lobell and Field (2007) showed that recent climate trends, attributable to human activity, had a discernible negative impact on global production of wheat, maize, and barley from the 1980s through 2002. In a global study on crop yields, Lobell et al. (2011a) showed warming trends were estimated to have lowered wheat and maize yields by roughly 6% and 4%, respectively, between 1980 and 2008.

Wheeler and Von Braun (2013, p. 512) write the following conclusion about these climate change impact studies:

> Specific projections vary with the climate model scenario used, the simulations methods, and the time scale over which the projections are done. However, the broad-scale pattern of climate change impacts on crop productivity and production has remained consistent across these global studies spanning almost 20 years of research. Crop yields are more negatively affected across most tropical areas than at higher latitudes, and

impacts become more severe with an increasing degree of climate change.

These observations and conclusions are highlighted in the numerous reports published by the Intergovernmental Panel on Climate Change (IPCC).

The scientific consensus established by the IPCC is that, generally, up to 2050, temperate regions will experience increased crop yields associated with anticipated mean temperature rises of 1°–3°C, whereas water-constrained tropical regions will undergo yield decreases (Smith et al. 2007; Vermeulen et al. 2012; IPCC 2014a). However, as temperatures increase beyond this, all areas see negative yields (Parry et al. 2007; IPCC 2014a). Current IPCC findings indicate that projected climate change will have potentially large negative impacts on food production in developing regions but only small changes in developed regions (IPCC 2014a). For example, across Europe, crop losses in the south are predicted to be offset with gains in the north, as temperature and precipitation levels suitable for growing shift upward (Ewert et al. 2005; IPCC 2014a).

In addition, regional assessments show high levels of uncertainty in specific findings, which underscores the possibility for significant negative impacts on agriculture even before 2050 (IPCC 2014b). These specific findings include lower long-term crop yields due to damage during specific development stages, production losses due to excessive soil moisture under scenarios of increased precipitation, increases in crop irrigation requirements by up to 20% due to increased atmospheric CO_2 concentrations, and increased water stress in the Middle East and Southeast Asia due to irrigation withdrawals from freshwater sources (IPCC 2014b). A recent systematic review of changes in the yields of the major crops grown across Africa and South Asia under climate change found that average crop yields may decline across both regions by 8% by the 2050s (Lobell et al. 2011a). Across Africa, yields are predicted to change by −17% (wheat), −5% (maize), −15% (sorghum), and −10% (millet) and, across South Asia, by −16% (maize) and −11% (sorghum) under climate change (Lobell et al. 2011b).

---

3. Carrying capacity pertains to the number of a species that an environment can sustain, considering the limiting factors at play (e.g., food, water, competition).

Additionally, extreme environmental events[4] affect agricultural output by damaging crops during specific development stages. Several studies show that climate change has led to quantifiable and discernable changes in the intensity and or frequency of some types of extreme events such as heavy precipitation and climatic anomalies such as drought (Donat et al. 2013; IPCC 2014c; Melillo et al. 2014; Seneviratne et al. 2012). Heavy precipitation, flood frequency, soil erosion, and salinization can reduce agricultural output, singly or combined. For example, researchers have shown how the increased occurrence and magnitude of adverse and extreme agroclimatic events based on the IPCC scenarios can impact key crops such as wheat, corn, and soybeans (Trnka et al. 2014; Deryng et al. 2014; Lesk et al. 2016).

Already, trends in precipitation have been observed between 1900 and 2015. More intense and more frequent extreme precipitation events have long been projected in a warming climate (Hartmann et al. 2013; Hirsch and Archfield 2015). Mean precipitation, especially at high latitudes, is predicted to increase with global warming, though this includes considerable spatial variation (IPCC 2014a). Significant increases in precipitation have been observed in eastern North and South America, northern Europe, and northern and central Asia (IPCC 2014a). For rain-fed crops, heavy precipitation could cause loss of crops because of excessive soil moisture; one study posited losses of $3 billion per year in the United States by 2030 (Rosenzweig et al. 2002).

Warming climate and more frequent extreme events will have significant impacts on crop production in the future, which will lead to greater food insecurity in many regions of the world. A. J. McMichael presages the IPCC's findings (McMichael 2003, p. 11):

> Allowing for future trends in trade and economic development, modeling studies have been used to estimate the impacts of climate change upon cereal grain yields (which account for two-thirds of world food energy). Globally, a slight downturn appears likely, but this would be greater in already food-insecure regions in south Asia, parts of Africa, and Central America. Such downturns would increase the number of malnourished people by several tens of millions in the world at large.

More specifically, Cline (2007) finds that global warming will have at the least a moderately negative effect on agriculture and possibly a severe negative effect if carbon fertilization and water constraints are present. Also, since greenhouse gas (GHG) emissions are likely to continue, the warming will not halt by 2080 but will continue into the next century (Cline 2007). By the end of this century, the effects of climate change on agriculture will be severe across many regions; these effects will not be felt uniformly across all agricultural areas but rather disproportionately in the developing countries, especially Africa, Latin America, and India, where populations are increasing and people are most socially vulnerable (Cline 2007; IPCC 2014a,b).

The world is in transition from an era of food abundance to one of scarcity. Over the last decade, the world grain reserve has fallen by one-third, and the population continues to grow, thus putting greater and greater demands on food supplies (Brown 2012). According to the FAO, world agricultural production growth is expected to fall by 1.5% per year to 2030, followed by a further reduction by 0.9% to 2050 (FAO 2013). This contrasts with past trends, where from 1962 to 2007, global agricultural production grew by more than 2% per year on average (Grafton et al. 2015). It is estimated that we will need to feed an additional 2.4 billion people by 2050 and to do so would require at least a 60% increase in food supplies (Grafton et al. 2015). To feed a population of 9 billion people by 2050, it is estimated that annual agricultural output must grow by at least 1.3% per year (Grafton et al. 2015). The ability to meet these food production goals while also facing severe soil erosion, deforestation, depleting aquifers, and rising temperatures seems nearly impossible unless radical changes are made in our global food production and distribution system. If more food is not produced, then it is highly probable that food prices and food insecurity will increase in many regions of the world and there will be greater civil unrest and conflict, as predicted by several scholars and witnessed in recent

---

4. Extreme environmental events are those weather-related events considered rare within a specific geographic location. Definitions vary, but an extreme weather event would normally be as rare as or rarer than the 10th or 90th percentile. For example, the characteristics of what is called extreme weather may vary from place to place. An extreme climate event is an average of several weather events over a certain period of time, an average that is itself extreme (e.g., rainfall over a season).

decades (Adger et al. 2014; Barnett et al. 2010; Barnett and Adger 2007; Homer-Dixon 1994).

2.1.3. ENVIRONMENTAL CHANGE AND SCARCITY-BASED CONFLICT

Numerous studies show that environmental stress and changes are catalysts that create social and political insecurity that may evolve into civil conflict within states or conflict between nation-states (Swain 1993; Gleditsch 1998; Nordås and Gleditsch 2007; Salehyan 2008; Swain et al. 2011; Hsiang and Burke 2014; Swain 2015).

Several scholars have conducted basic research examining the phenomena of climate change and conflict, including its causes and consequences and its ethical and political ramifications (Adano et al. 2012; Benjaminsen et al. 2012; McLeman 2013; Raleigh and Kniveton 2010; Scheffran and Battaglini 2011; Hsiang et al. 2011; Swain 2015). The dialog on the linkage among climate change, security, and conflict has been influenced by early research on environmental security, especially by the work of the Toronto Group (Homer-Dixon 1999, 1991, 1994).

A rapidly changing climate, food scarcity and access, and increased competition and conflict are main themes in the environmental security discourse (Barnett et al. 2010; Barrett 2013; Homer-Dixon 1999, 1991, 1994). Homer-Dixon's Toronto Project on Environmental Change and Acute Conflict (TPECAC) research group was one of the primary "pro" environment–conflict research groups. They assumed a tight linkage between environmental changes (especially those that resulted in natural resource shortages such as in food production) and conflict and conducted several qualitative studies to determine if their reasoning was correct (Homer-Dixon 1999, 1991, 1994). They also examined the standard Malthusian[5] drivers of population growth and resource distribution issues. TPECAC identified two potential pathways from environmental change to conflict. In the first, the overexploitation/degradation of natural resources force large-scale migrations, which in turn trigger ethnic strife between the new arrivals and established groups. In the second, resource scarcity causes economic hardship and undermines state capacity

and legitimacy, which in turn facilitates grievance-based rebellion. In a series of reports and articles that represent some of the most solid case-oriented work in the field, Homer-Dixon (1991, 1994) employed a very complex theoretical scheme, where four basic social effects of environmental disruption (decreased regional agricultural production, population displacement, decreased economic productivity, and disruption of institutions) may produce scarcity conflicts, group identity conflicts, and relative-deprivation conflicts.

However, despite their efforts, the TPECAC group was unable to identify a *direct* linkage between the environment and conflict. Instead, they argued that when taken in combination with political and socioeconomic factors, environmental change and natural resource scarcity could indeed contribute to the outbreak of violent intrastate conflict (Homer-Dixon 1994). More recently, Hsiang and Burke (2014) analyzed 50 quantitative studies that examined the association between violent conflict and changes in climatological variables. They found consistent support for a causal association between climatological changes and various conflict outcomes (Hsiang and Burke 2014). Despite these studies and cases, establishing a clear and direct relationship between environmental change (such as climate change) and violent conflict has proven to be very difficult (Nordås and Gleditsch 2007; Salehyan 2008; Barrett 2013; Adger et al. 2014). Most quantitative and/or empirical studies of climate change and conflict have yielded either inconclusive or contradictory results (with some forms of environmental degradation and change driving conflict and others dampening it) (Hauge and Ellingsen 1998). For example, Raleigh and Kniveton (2010) confirmed the trend of high rainfall leading to increased risk of localized communal conflict. However, their findings indicated that a combination of socioeconomic and political factors with climate change factors lead to conflict (Raleigh and Kniveton 2010).

Because of the difficulty to establish this direct linkage, some researchers have begun to look at more indirect mechanisms by which environmental change might drive conflict and how it might act as a threat multiplier rather than a direct source of conflict (Scheffran et

---

5. In Thomas Robert Malthus's (1766–1834) essay on the principle of population, he proposed that human populations grow exponentially (i.e., doubling with each cycle) while food production grows at an arithmetic rate (i.e., by the repeated addition of a uniform increment in each uniform interval of time).

al. 2012; Buhaug et al. 2008; Swain 2015). For example, Buhaug et al. (2008) assert that increasing scarcity and variability of renewable resources, sea level rise, and intensification of natural disasters are relevant in relation to armed conflict.

As a threat multiplier, climate change essentially leverages a society's existing weaknesses, pushing the state closer to conflict and or collapse; thus, climate change is an important part of the conflict equation and must be included in conflict models to better understand future conflict occurrences. The next section discusses how climate change may be a threat multiplier by triggering violent escalations in existing conflicts or through the pathways of resource scarcity, the weak state, and migration. As we've seen thus far, conflict can be a result of resource scarcity. Unit 4 of this book will explore the relationship between environmental security and conflict in more detail. What follows in this chapter are initial concepts behind the various pathways that lead to scarcity-based conflict

2.1.4. PATHWAYS TO CONFLICT

2.1.4.1. The Resource Scarcity Pathway
Scarcity-based conflicts—whether over dwindling food stores, disappearing water sources, or a dearth of arable land—are the sort of Malthusian-based climate change scenarios that have come to occupy the discourse of both national security scholars and policy makers (Swain 2015; Hayes and Knox-Hayes 2014). Can resource scarcities be a source of conflict? There is little consensus on the answer, with some scholars finding that resource scarcity has been and will continue to be an important driver of conflict (Hsiang and Burke 2013; Barnett and Adgar 2007; Matthew et al. 2010) while others question whether environmental factors of any kind can play a role at all (Hauss 2015; Gleditsch 1998).

Recent history (2007–14) provides several examples of, if not outright scarcity-driven conflict, scarcity-driven political instability. For example, between 2007 and the end of 2008, there were an unprecedented number of food riots in more than 25 countries. A combination of environmental and human factors—droughts and floods hitting several major crop-growing regions, the diverting of large amounts of corn for use in ethanol production in the United States, the climbing price of

oil, and shrinking stores of grain in many countries—all drove food prices to record highs. In 2007 alone, the world food stores declined by 11% while the FAO food price index rose by more than 40% (Rosenthal 2007; Schneider 2008; Bellemare 2015). In fact, Jacques Diouf, director general of the FAO, warned at the time that food shortages and soaring energy prices could trigger riots and instability because individuals in developing countries were spending between 60% and 65% of their national income for food imports, while in developed countries, the figure was only 10%–20% (Win 2009). In less than a year, the price of rice on the world market increased by 75% and wheat by 120% (Schneider 2008; Adam 2008). In Haiti, the high food prices led to a week of violent protests and riots that brought down the Haitian government as protestors clashed with Haitian police and even UN Peacekeepers (Schneider 2008). The unrest resulted in five deaths, the torching of cars, and the looting of businesses. In September 2010, rioting broke out in Mozambique (again) after high wheat prices forced the government to raise the price of bread by 30%. The rioting lasted for days and left 10 people dead and at least 300 wounded (Berazneva and Lee 2013).

Food protests and riots have occurred in recent years in Argentina (Auyero and Moran 2007; Rohter 2001), Mexico (BBC 2007; Bush 2010), India (Messer 2009; Wischnath and Buhaug 2014), Yemen (Gros et al. 2015), Pakistan, Indonesia, Brazil, Senegal, Egypt, and Mozambique (Bates and Carter 2015). These are summarized in Table 2.1.1.

Several researchers have shown that food prices and food availability affect sociopolitical stability and lead to increases in political violence (Bellemare 2015; Wischnath and Buhaug 2014). In the case of the 2008–09 and 2010–11 food price spikes, they have been associated with food riots (Barrett 2013; Berazneva and Lee 2013). For example, some researchers have found that the food riots that occurred in 2007–08 in Africa were due to high and rising international commodity prices as well as several other factors including higher levels of poverty, restricted food access and availability, urbanization, and more oppressive regimes (Hendrix and Birkman 2013; Berazneva and Lee 2013).

Though most of the time, food shortages do not lead to riots, if a large amount of the population lives on or near the subsistence line, they may not be able to pay higher prices for food, particularly if staple prices are

Table 2.1.1. Food price unrest around the world, September 2007–April 2008. Compiled by Frances Moore, Earth Policy Institute (www.earthpolicy.org), 16 April 2008 using "Clashes over food prices trouble political leaders," Reuters, 2 April 2008; Julian Borger, "Feed the world? We are fighting a losing battle, UN admits," *Guardian*, 26 February 2008; and other press reports. (For more information from the Earth Policy Institute, see www.earthpolicy.org.)

Location	Date	Description
Haiti	April 2008	Days of rioting left five people dead, including a UN Peacekeeper, and forced the resignation of Haiti's prime minister. Food prices in the country, the poorest in the Western Hemisphere, have increased by between 50% and 100% in the last year.
Thailand	April 2008	Rice has become so valuable that thieves have taken to stealing it out of fields at night; the army is now being used to prevent food theft.
Bangladesh	April 2008	Twenty-eight people were injured after ten thousand workers rioted in the capital, Dhaka, demanding higher pay to cover fast-increasing food costs. Rice prices in Bangladesh have doubled in the last year.
Trinidad and Tobago	April 2008	Bandits hijacked and looted two vans carrying flour, milk, and juice as prices rose in supermarkets across the country.
Egypt	March–April 2008	When rice prices in Egypt more than doubled, many people became dependent on state-subsidized bread, which sold for 20% of market price. Fights in the long bread lines killed six people, and the government called in the army to bake bread for the public.
Ivory Coast	March–April 2008	Protests against high food prices left 1 person dead and 20 wounded and prompted the government to temporarily suspend taxes on staple goods.
Ethiopia	March–April 2008	Prices of basic foods in Addis Ababa jumped between 30% and 70% within one year. As a result, the government banned cereal exports and subsidized wheat for low-income city dwellers.
United Arab Emirates	March 2008	Soaring food prices caused hundreds of workers to protest for higher wages in Sharjah, where cars and offices were set on fire.
Senegal	March 2008 and November 2007	Senegal's 18 unions marched in November 2007 to protest the spiraling cost of basic food. Further unrest the following spring led to clashes with police and at least 24 arrests.
Philippines	February–April 2008	In February 2008, the Philippines was the world's largest rice importer, and needed to make a direct appeal to Vietnam asking it to guarantee rice supplies. The following April, the government deployed troops to deliver grain to poor areas in the capital. Amid growing fears of shortages, the government asked fast-food restaurants to serve half portions of rice.
Afghanistan	February–March 2008	Wheat export restrictions by Pakistan caused prices to double over much of the country, which lead in turn to an increase in smuggling over the border. Continued high prices contributed to spreading social unrest.
Burkina Faso	February–March 2008	Three hundred protestors were arrested in food price riots. Unions marched demanding further cuts in taxes and prices. The government responded by suspending import duties on staple food imports for three months.
Morocco	February 2008 and September 2007	In February 2008, 34 people were sentenced to jail for taking part in food price riots. This followed rioting in September 2007 when protestors clashed with police after the government raised the price of bread 30%.

. . . .

Table 2.1.1. (*continued*)

Location	Date	Description
Cameroon	February 2008	At least 24 people were killed and over 1,500 arrested over riots caused by rising food and fuel costs in the worst unrest seen in over 15 years.
Yemen	February 2008	The prices of bread and other staple foods nearly doubled in only a four month period. This price spike provoked demonstrations and riots that killed at least a dozen people.
Pakistan	January–February 2008	Thousands demonstrated in January 2008 after the price of wheat flour doubled in less than a week. The army was used to guard grain supplies and to crack down on hoarding and smuggling into Afghanistan, and the government introduced ration cards for the first time since the 1980s.
Indonesia	January 2008	More than 10,000 people took to the streets in Jakarta on 14 January to protest soybean prices that more than doubled in less than a year, subsequently increasing the cost of the Indonesian soy-based staple, tempeh.
China	November 2007	Inflation in China was the worst it has been in more than a decade, and food inflation has reached 18.2%. Cooking oil became so expensive that three people were trampled to death in November 2007 in a stampede to grab bottles at a reduced price.
Mauritania	November 2007	A sudden rise in the price of staple foods triggered demonstrations across the country that left at least 2 people dead and 10 wounded. The government responded by raising civil service salaries by 10% and eliminating tariffs on rice.
Uzbekistan	September 2007	Protests took place in the heavily populated Ferghana Valley region after local bread prices rose 50% to 100%.

usually held artificially low by government regulation (Barrett 2013). However, if a rise in the price of staple crops puts food out of reach, then food riots become more likely (Barrett 2013; Lobell et al. 2011b; Bush 2010). While it is generally not possible to pinpoint when an agricultural shortage will generate food riots or protests, food shortages combined with sudden increases in domestic food prices increases the probability of urban unrest and food insecurity and be a threat multiplier (Hendrix and Birkman 2013).

Given that much hinges on the standard drivers of conflict and demand and structural-based scarcities, what role does this leave for environmental factors such as scarcity and/or degradation? Hauge and Ellingsen (1998) find that the states affected by environmental degradation (especially deforestation, land degradation, and water scarcity) are more likely to experience intrastate conflict overall, with land degradation being the single most aggravating factor. Land degradation and water scarcity are both significant when it comes to general armed conflict but again are not significant when

it comes to civil war. Despite this, Hauge and Ellingsen (1998) found state capacity and regime type were also drivers of conflict under conditions of environmental stress. As we discuss in the next section, governments and stable markets play a key role in mitigating the negative effects of climate change (Barnett and Adger 2007; Raleigh et al. 2015).

2.1.4.2. The "Weak State" Pathway

When it comes to climate change and conflict, state capacity, or strength, is an important intervening variable. Normally, a strong state with effective institutions can dampen a given blow from resource scarcity and other environmental damage by providing relief and correcting structural scarcities. In contrast, states or governments weakened by poverty, drought, war, political dissent, or some combination of these are notably less able to support their economy or people from the consequences of such intervening variables. Barnett and Adger (2007) and others describe the characteristics of strong states that include having effective administrative hierarchies, controlling the legitimate use of force, mediating impending conflicts before they turn violent, and having the capacity and ability to manage the impacts of environmental degradation and change (Hauge and Ellingsen 1998; Kahl 2006). Barnett and Adger (2007, p. 650) write, "In strong liberal-democratic states, both the structural conditions and livelihood factors that increase the risk of violent conflict are reduced. When states cannot provide all these functions, the risk of violent conflict increases." A strong state is able to not only utilize its own internal resources to mitigate climate change impacts but also bring in outside aid prior to disaster striking. These are some of the primary reasons why developed countries tend to be more resilient to extreme weather events than developing countries (Scheffran et al. 2012). In weak or fragile states, weak institutions and or corrupt practices result in an unfair distribution of resources and an inability to adequately compensate their people for lost resources; such failures can lead to growing grievances against the state and those elites seen to be hoarding resources for their own benefit (Kahl 2006; Wljeyaratne 2009; Scheffran et al. 2012). Kahl (2006) has argued that, in addition to civil disputes arising when political leaders seek to exploit environmental and social pressures for personal gain, environmental change can be a factor in state failures through its impacts on revenue, legitimacy, and social cohesion. Such grievances can combine with already existing ones and tip the balance toward conflict. The impacts of climate change can further stress an already fragile state by worsening environmental degradation, increasing pressure on all levels of society, and could worsen socioeconomic and political tensions, particularly in societies dependent on natural resources. Barnett et al. (2010) argue that environmental change can undermine a state's legitimacy in the eyes of its people when it is unable to correct or prevent damage done to economic livelihoods, human health, and food and water security. Whether a state can prevent such impacts, the state's own resources, capacity, and even military strength may be lessened, providing an opportunity for insurgents. An extra drain on resources also means less money going to other needy areas (Barnett et al. 2010; Swain 2015).

Bernauer et al. (2010) suggested that whether climate change leads to conflict hinges on the ability of the state to settle or moderate grievances before they lead to outright conflict and that democracy is an important intervening variable, as democratic systems are better able to avoid violence during economic downturns. They posit that climate change, by reducing a country's rate of economic growth, can reduce the amount of resources available to the government both to correct climate-related damages and to maintain general stability, thus weakening its capacity to provide for its people. Loss of legitimacy would follow quickly (Bernauer et al. 2010).

Climate change is likely to have significant economic impacts because of crop losses, land degradation, water shortages, damage caused by extreme weather events and sea level rise, damage and loss of critical infrastructure, and overall loss in economic output and productivity (Nordhaus 1991; Cline 1992; Bergholt and Lujala 2012; Stern 2013). Bergholt and Lujala (2012, p. 6) write, "Research indicates that economic growth is related to the occurrence of armed conflict. If sudden changes in economic growth increase the risk of armed conflict, and weather-related disasters cause negative growth shocks, a logical consequence would be that such disasters can cause armed conflict via their negative impact on growth."

Increasing economic damage from environmental and climate change impacts will sap a nation-state's ability to deal with the current crisis at hand and leave it less able to undertake further adaptive measures in the future as conditions worsen. And as the section on resource scarcity suggests, when a state is unable or unwilling to correct the scarcity or impacts by providing adequate recovery measures, subsidizing food costs after a massive crop loss or by relocating those who have lost their livelihoods and homes, it risks losing legitimacy in the eyes of its people. The heavy monsoon that hit Pakistan in July 2010 is a clear example of this. In this case, the monsoon caused floods that ravaged the country, bringing enormous damage to crop lands, critical infrastructure, homes, and businesses (Bergholt and Lujala 2012). The death toll was estimated at 2,000, while an estimated 10%, or 20.3 million, Pakistanis were affected [Office of U.S. Foreign Disaster Assistance (OFDA) 2010]. It is during such a crisis that people look to their national leaders for support and assistance. In Pakistan, however, Prime Minister Zardari continued his tour of Western countries as the disaster unfolded and as militant groups proved more effective than the government in delivering aid, thus increasing public anger toward the government and enhancing the public's view of the militant groups

(Shah 2010). Scarcity of resources in combination with the inability of weaker nation-states to effectively mitigate climate change impacts and to respond effectively to natural disasters and social unrest will likely induce population migration with states and across national boundaries that are likely to cause conflict.

2.1.4.3. The Migration Pathway

One of the impacts of climate change that is cited by scholars is the displacement of large numbers of people that some refer to as environmental migrants or refugees (Myers and Kent 1995; Castles 2002; Foresight 2011). Climate-induced migration is often discussed within a framework of national security in which such refugees are seen as threats to the host nation's national security (Myers 1989; Myers and Kent 1995; Oels 2012). For example, Myers and Kent (1995) argued that climate change would uproot (that is, displace) more than 180 million people by 2050 and that these refugees would pose a threat to national security. Myers (2002, p. 611) argued that the issue of environmental refugees[6] may be one of the "foremost human crises of our time." Such refugees are often the target of popular resentment by receiving communities because they are perceived as threats to social cohesion and national identity as well as competitors for scarce resources (Swain 1993; Salehyan 2008; Methmann and Oels 2015). For example, it is estimated that 1.5–2 million Zimbabweans have migrated to South Africa since 2000, and in May 2008, a spate of xenophobic attacks took place on migrants, leading to 65 deaths and the further displacement of 150,000 people (Gornall et al. 2010).

However, Nicholls and Tol (2006) argue that the nature and extent of migration in response to climate change are unknown, and whether such displacement will cause severe host–newcomer tensions is also open to debate. For example, Nordås and Gleditsch (2007) argued that the impact of environmental change on migration has not been subject to much rigorous, comparative analysis and there was a lack of systematic data. Studies by Reuveny (2007) that look at a nonrandom set of cases with out-migration in areas with severe environmental degradation provided evidence that climate change

could trigger more human mobility/displacement. For example, changes in crop yields due to climate change will occur over broad geographic areas and will likely lead to long-term population shifts (IPCC 2014a). This is especially relevant to developing countries with large rural populations that derive their living from agriculture. For example, research by Feng et al. (2010) found a significant effect of climate-driven changes in crop yields in Mexico on the rate of emigration of Mexicans to the United States. They estimated a 10% reduction in crop yields would lead to an additional 2% of the population of Mexico to emigrate to the United States; thus, by the year 2080, an estimated 1.4 to 6.7 million adult Mexicans would be induced to emigrate because of declines in agricultural productivity (Feng et al. 2010).

While the state of the research is too patchy to draw general conclusions about likely future implications of climate change on migration and conflict, the U.K. Foresight review on migration and global environmental change is one of the most comprehensive reports on the subject (Foresight 2011).

The Foresight (2011, p. 9) report stated, "The impact of environmental change on migration will increase in the future. Environmental change may threaten people's livelihoods, and a traditional response is to migrate. Environmental change will also alter populations' exposure to natural hazards, and migration is, in many cases, the only response to this. For example, 17 million people were displaced by natural hazards in 2009 and 42 million in 2010." The comprehensive Foresight (2011) report concluded that climate change will likely trigger out-migration from vulnerable regions and amplify current urbanization trends. However, the Foresight (2011) report has modest conclusions regarding conflict between environmental migrants and established residents. Other research has examined the possibility that climate-induced migration may increase the likelihood of violent conflict through many migration drivers (Reuveny 2007; Brown 2008).

The International Organization for Migration (IOM) organizes the effects of climate change into two sets of migration drivers: climate processes, where long-term changes in a region's environment change people's in-

---

6. Environmental refugees are those people who have been forced to leave their traditional homeland either temporarily or permanently because of a marked environmental disruption (natural or triggered by people) that jeopardizes their existence and/or seriously affects their quality of life.

centives (through income loss, loss of housing, increased scarcity, etc.) to remain in a location (Brown 2008), and extreme weather events, sudden cataclysmic events such as floods, glacial lake outbursts, and hurricanes that can displace large numbers of people in a short period of time. Clearly, if people's homes are destroyed and fields washed away, they may seek new livelihoods elsewhere. A person's ability to migrate depends on one's level of mobility, which is a function of one's access to resources, along with other forms of social and financial capital (Brown 2008).

Whether people choose to leave their homes or are driven from them, they tend to follow one of the four main types of migratory movement: international migration, internal displacement, rural-to-urban migration, or temporary migration. International migration is what most people think of when it comes to migration. In terms of environmental and climate migration, the crossing of international borders is rather rare despite the common conception of hordes of poor people moving to developed countries (Kolmannskog 2008). Those that do cross international borders tend to follow preexisting routes, especially to those places where they have familial and social ties. A vast majority of those uprooted by environmental and climactic changes move within their country of origin. While there are no reliable global estimates for the number of people uprooted each year because of food insecurity brought on by drought, severe flooding, or other climate-related disasters, there are numerous tragic examples of the propensity of climate change–related effects to displace significant numbers of poor and vulnerable people. In 2011, drought and famine in the eastern Horn of Africa killed an estimated 260,000 Somalis—half of them children—and drove a quarter of the country's population from their homes. Two factors specifically contributed to the drought's impacts on displacement: the underlying vulnerability of the country's rural poor, who were totally dependent on rain-fed agriculture to survive, and ongoing violence that made it harder for people in urgent need of food and water to access aid. When long-term changes like droughts set in, rural-to-urban movement becomes a commonplace response. When those who subsist on local agriculture for their livelihood can no longer make a living, they tend to head to the nearest urban center, looking for jobs.

The IOM outlines four major consequences of such forced migration. First, rural-to-urban population movements due to increasing food and water insecurity will put increased pressure on existing urban infrastructures and services, which in many cities of the developing world are already severely strained. The second major consequence is that economic and brain drains will occur in the countries of origin because of mass migration (i.e., displacement) further weakening the potential for future economic growth across the developing world. Third, the influx of large numbers of environmental refugees to new areas will result in increased ethnic tensions as different groups, once separated, mix and as the newcomers begin to compete with those already established for limited and in many cases decreasing resources. The fourth major consequence concerns human health and welfare. In general, as populations move, disease goes with them. But massive numbers of environmental refugees displaced in camps or crammed into urban slums represent a threat of increased disease activity as poor sanitary conditions combine with the difficulty of providing vaccinations and medical treatment to the displaced.

The research base surrounding the links between migration, environmental change, and conflict is fraught with controversy. Tracing out the complex circumstances that influence people's decision to leave their homes and embark on uncertain and potentially dangerous journeys can be extremely difficult, and the lack of systematic data on the phenomenon complicates matters. Motivations can be tied to diverse and interplaying factors, including economic opportunities, food scarcity, land degradation, political persecution, and overpopulation.

2.1.5. CONCLUSIONS

Robert Kaplan's article "The coming anarchy" (Kaplan 1994) posited that population growth and the degradation of renewable resources would lead to increased epidemics, massive refugee movements, and ultimately the breakdown of social relations into anarchy. He writes: "Nations break-up under the tidal wave of refugees from environmental and social disaster. As borders crumble, another type of boundary is erected—a wall of disease. Wars are fought over scarce resources, especially water, and war itself continues with crime, as armed bands of stateless murderers clash with private security forces of the elites."

While many may not agree with Kaplan's somewhat apocalyptic message, it is important to study the direct and indirect links between the scarcity of renewable resources and violence. This chapter has shown there are connections between precipitating factors and food security. Last, as you conduct your own study using this chapter and many other resources, you will undoubtedly come to your own conclusion about the relationship between food security and conflict.

REFERENCES

Adam, D., 2008: Food price rises threaten global security—UN. Guardian, www.theguardian.com/environment/2008/apr/09/food.unitednations.

Adano, W. R., T. Dietz, K. Witensburg, and F. Zaal, 2012: Climate change, violent conflict and local institutions in Kenya's drylands. *J. Peace Res.*, **49**, 65–80, https://doi.org/10.1177/0022343311427344.

Adger, W. N., and Coauthors, 2014: *Human security. Climate Change 2014: Impacts, Adaptation, and Vulnerability. Part A: Global and Sectoral Aspects*, Cambridge University Press, 755–791, www.ipcc.ch/pdf/assessment-report/ar5/wg2/WGIIAR5-Chap12_FINAL.pdf.

Auyero, J., and T. P. Moran, 2007: The dynamics of collective violence: Dissecting food riots in contemporary Argentina. *Soc. Forces*, **85**, 1341–1367, https://doi.org/10.1353/sof.2007.0030.

Barnett, J., and W. N. Adger, 2007: Climate change, human security and violent conflict. *Polit. Geogr.*, **26**, 639–655, https://doi.org/10.1016/j.polgeo.2007.03.003.

——, R. A. Matthew, and K. L. O'Brien, 2010: Global environmental change and human security: An introduction. *Global Environmental Change and Human Security*, R. Matthew, B. McDonald, and K. O'Brien, Eds., MIT Press, 3–31.

Barrett, C. B., 2013: *Food Security and Sociopolitical Stability*. Oxford University Press, 512 pp.

Bar-Yam, Y., and M. Lagi, 2015: South African riots: Repercussion of the global food crisis and US drought. *Conflict and Complexity*, Springer, 261–267.

BBC, 2007: Mexicans stage tortilla protest. BBC, http://news.bbc.co.uk/2/hi/6319093.stm.

Bellemare, M. F., 2015: Rising food prices, food price volatility, and social unrest. *Amer. J. Agric. Econ.*, **97**, 1–21, https://doi.org/10.1093/ajae/aau038.

Benjaminsen, T. A., K. Alinon, H. Buhaug, and J. T.

Buseth, 2012: Does climate change drive land-use conflicts in the Sahel? *J. Peace Res.*, **49**, 97–111, https://doi.org/10.1177/0022343311427343.

Berazneva, J., and D. R. Lee, 2013: Explaining the African food riots of 2007–2008: An empirical analysis. *Food Policy*, **39**, 28–39, https://doi.org/10.1016/j.foodpol.2012.12.007.

Bergholt, D., and P. Lujala, 2012: Climate-related natural disasters, economic growth, and armed civil conflict. *J. Peace Res.*, **49**, 147–162, https://doi.org/10.1177/0022343311426167.

Bernauer, T., A. Kalbhenn, V. Koubi, and G. Ruoff, 2010: Climate change, economic growth, and conflict. *Climate Change and Security*, Trondheim, Norway, Royal Norwegian Society of Sciences, 21–24.

Boyer, J. S., and Coauthors, 2013: The U.S. drought of 2012 in perspective: A call to action. *Global Food Secur.*, **2**, 139–143, https://doi.org/10.1016/j.gfs.2013.08.002.

Brown, L. R., 2012: *Full Planet, Empty Plates: The New Geopolitics of Food Scarcity*. W. W. Norton, 165 pp.

Brown, O., 2008: Climate change and migration. International Organization for Migration Migration Research Series Rep. 31, 64 pp., https://www.iom.cz/files/Migration_and_Climate_Change_-_IOM_Migration_Research_Series_No_31.pdf.

Buhaug, H., N. P. Gleditsch, and O. Theisen, 2008: Implications of climate change for armed conflict. World Bank Group Social Development Department Rep., 52 pp., http://siteresources.worldbank.org/INTRANETSOCIALDEVELOPMENT/Resources/SDCCWorkingPaper_Conflict.pdf.

Bush, R., 2010: Food riots: Poverty, power and protest. *J. Agrar. Change,* **10**, 119–129, https://doi.org/10.1111/j.1471-0366.2009.00253.x.

Carter, Brett, and Robert H. Bates. 2011. Public Policy, Price Shocks, and Conflict: Price Shocks and Civil War in Developing Countries. Working paper, Department of Government, Harvard University. Accessed 5 Nov 2018, https://dash.harvard.edu/handle/1/23674970.

Castles, S., 2002: Environmental change and induced migration: Making sense of the debate. United Nations High Commissioner for Refugees Working Paper 70, 16 pp., http://www.unhcr.org/en-us/research/working/3de344fd9/environmental-change-forced-migration-making-sense-debate-stephen-castles.html.

Cleetus, R., 2012: The enormous costs of the 2012 drought to American farmers and taxpayers. Union of Concerned Scientists, https://blog.ucsusa.org/rachel-cleetus/the-enormous-costs-of-the-2012-drought-to-american-farmers-and-taxpayers.

Cline, W. R., 1992: *The Economics of Global Warming.* Institute for International Economics, 416 pp.

——, 2007: *Global Warming and Agriculture: Impact Estimates by Country.* Center for Global Development, 250 pp.

Deryng, D., D. Conway, N. Ramankutty, J. Price, and R. Warren, 2014: Global crop yield response to extreme heat stress under multiple climate change futures. *Environ. Res. Lett.,* **9**, 034011, https://doi.org/10.1088/1748-9326/9/3/034011.

Donat, M. G., and Coauthors, 2013: Updated analyses of temperature and precipitation extreme indices since the beginning of the twentieth century: The HadEX2 dataset. *J. Geophys. Res. Atmos.,* **118**, 2098–2118, https://doi.org/10.1002/jgrd.50150.

Ewert, F. M., D. A. Rounsevell, I. Reginster, M. J. Metzger, and R. Leemans, 2005: Future scenarios of European agricultural land use: I. Estimating changes in crop productivity. *Agric. Ecosyst. Environ.,* **3**, 101–116, https://doi.org/10.1016/j.agee.2004.12.003.

FAO, 2013: FAOSTAT: Food and agriculture data. FAO, accessed 20 Aug 2018, http://faostat3.fao.org.

Feng, S., A. Krueger, and M. Oppenheimer, 2010: Linkages among climate change, crop yields and Mexico–US cross-border migration. *Proc. Natl. Acad. Sci. USA,* **107**, 142257–142262, https://doi.org/10.1073/pnas.1002632107.

Foresight, 2011: Migration and global environmental change: Final project report. Government Office for Science Rep., 234 pp., www.gov.uk/government/publications/migration-and-global-environmental-change-future-challenges-and-opportunities.

Galloway, P. R., 1986: Long-term fluctuation in climate and population in the preindustrial era. *Popul. Dev. Rev.,* **12**, 1–24.

Gleditsch, N. P., 1998: Armed conflict and the environment: A critique of the literature. *J. Peace Res.,* **35**, 381–400, https://doi.org/10.1177/0022343398035003007.

Gornall, J., R. Betts, E. Burke, R. Clark, J. Camp, K. Willett, and A. Wiltshire, 2010: Implications of climate change for agricultural productivity in the early twenty-first century. *Philos. Trans. Roy. Soc.,* **365B**, 2973–2989, https://doi.org/10.1098/rstb.2010.0158.

Grafton, R. Q., C. Daugbjerg, and M. E. Qureshi, 2015: Towards food security by 2050. *Food Secur.,* **7**, 179–183, https://doi.org/10.1007/s12571-015-0445-x.

Gros, A., A. S. Gard-Murray, and Y. Bar-Yam, 2015: Conflict in Yemen: From ethnic fighting to food riots. *Conflict and Complexity*, P. V. Fellman, Y. Bar-Yam, and A. A. Minai, Eds., Springer, 269–280.

Hartmann, D. L., and Coauthors, 2013: Observations: Atmosphere and surface. *Climate Change 2013: The Physical Science Basis*, T. F. Stocker et al., Eds., Cambridge University Press, 159–254.

Hauge, W., and T. Ellingsen, 1998: Beyond environmental scarcity: Causal pathways to conflict. *J. Peace Res.,* **35**, 299–317, https://doi.org/10.1177/0022343398035003003.

Hayes, J., and J. Knox-Hayes, 2014: Security in climate change discourse: Analyzing the divergence between US and EU approaches to policy. *Global Environ. Polit.,* **14** (2), 82–101, https://doi.org/10.1162/GLEP_a_00230.

Hendrix, C., and H.-J. Birkman, 2013: Food insecurity and conflict dynamics: Causal linkages and complex feedbacks. *Stability,* **2**, 26, https://doi.org/10.5334/sta.bm.

Hirsch, R. M., and S. A. Archfield, 2015: Flood trends: Not higher but more often. *Nat. Climate Change,* **5**, 198–199, https://doi.org/10.1038/nclimate2551.

Homer-Dixon, T. F., 1991: On the threshold: Environmental changes as causes of acute conflict. *Int. Secur.,* **16** (2), 76–116.

——, 1994: Environmental scarcities and violent conflict: Evidence from cases. *Int. Secur.,* **19** (1), 5–40.

——, 1999: *Environment, Scarcity, and Violence.* Princeton University Press, 272 pp.

Hsiang, S. M., and M. Burke, 2014: Climate, conflict, and social stability: What does the evidence say? *Climatic Change,* **123**, 39–55, https://doi.org/10.1007/s10584-013-0868-3.

——, K. C. Meng, and M. A. Cane, 2011: Civil conflicts are associated with the global climate. *Nature,* **476**, 438–331, https://doi.org/10.1038/nature10311.

IPCC, 2014a: *Climate Change 2014: Impacts, Adaptation, and Vulnerability. Part A: Global and Sectoral Aspects.* Cambridge University Press, 1132 pp., www.ipcc.ch/pdf/assessment-report/ar5/wg2/WGIIAR5-PartA_FINAL.pdf.

——, 2014b: *Climate Change 2014: Impacts, Adaptation, and Vulnerability: Part B: Regional Aspects.* Cambridge University Press, 688 pp., www.ipcc.ch/pdf/assessment-report/ar5/wg2/WGIIAR5-PartB_FINAL.pdf.

——, 2014c: *Climate Change 2014: Synthesis Report.* R. K. Pachauri and L. A. Meyer, Eds., IPCC, 151 pp.

Kahl, C., 2006: *States, Scarcity, and Civil Strife in the Developing World.* Princeton University Press, 333 pp.

Kaplan, R., 1994: The coming anarchy. *Atlantic Monthly*, February, accessed 30 June 2018, https://www.theatlantic.com/magazine/archive/1994/02/the-coming-anarchy/304670/.

King, S., 2013: Crop production down in 2012 due to drought, USDA reports. USDA, accessed 30 November 2017, https://www.nass.usda.gov/Newsroom/archive/2013/01_11_2013.php.

Kolmannskog, V., 2008: Future floods of refugees: A comment on climate change, conflict and forced migration. Norwegian Refugee Council Rep., 44 pp., https://www.nrc.no/resources/reports/future-floods-of-refugees/.

Lagi, M., K. Z. Bertrand, and Y. Bar-Yam, 2011: The food crises and political instability in North Africa and the Middle East. New England Complex Systems Institute Rep., 15 pp., http://necsi.edu/research/social/food_crises.pdf.

LeBlanc, S. A., 2003: *Constant Battles: The Myth of the Peaceful, Noble Savage.* St. Martin's Press, 294 pp.

Lesk, C., P. Rowhani, and N. Ramankutty, 2016: Influence of extreme weather disasters on global crop production. *Nature*, **529**, 84–87, https://doi.org/10.1038/nature16467.

Lobell, D. B., and C. B. Field, 2007: Global scale climate—Crop yield relationships and the impacts of recent warming. *Environ. Res. Lett.*, **2**, 014002, https://doi.org/10.1088/1748-9326/2/1/014002.

——, M. Bänziger, C. Magorokosho, and B. Vivek, 2011a: Nonlinear heat effects on African maize as evidenced by historical yield trials. *Nat. Climate Change*, **1**, 42–45, https://doi.org/10.1038/nclimate1043.

——, W. Schlenker, and J. Costa-Roberts, 2011b: Climate trends and global crop production since 1980. *Science*, **333**, 616–620, https://doi.org/10.1126/science.1204531.

Matthew, R. A., J. Barnett, B. McDonald, and K. L. O'Brien, 2010: *Global Environmental Change and Human Security.* MIT Press, 328 pp.

McClenaghan, M., 2012: South African massacre was the tip of an iceberg. Bureau of Investigative Journalism, www.thebureauinvestigates.com/2012/10/18/south-african-massacre-was-the-tip-of-an-iceberg/.

McLeman, R., 2013: *Climate and Human Migration: Past Experiences, Future Challenges.* Cambridge University Press, 294 pp.

McMichael, A. J., 2003: Global climate change and health: An old story writ large. *Climate Change and Human Health: Risks and Responses*, A. J. McMichael et al., Eds., World Health Organization, 1–17.

Melillo, J. M., T. C. Richmond, and G. W. Yohe, Eds., 2014: *Climate Change Impacts in the United States: The Third National Climate Assessment.* U.S. Global Change Research Program, 841 pp., https://doi.org/10.7930/J0Z31WJ2.

Messer, E., 2009: Rising food prices, social mobilizations, and violence: Conceptual issues in understanding and responding to the connections linking hunger and conflict. *Napa Bull.*, **32**, 12–22, https://doi.org/10.1111/j.1556-4797.2009.01025.x.

——, 2010: Climate change and violent conflict: A critical literature review. Oxfam Rep., 133 pp., www.oxfamamerica.org/static/oa3/files/climate-change-and-violent-conflict.pdf.

Methmann, C., and A. Oels, 2015: From 'fearing' to 'empowering' climate refugees: Governing climate-induced migration in the name of resilience. *Secur. Dialogue*, **46**, 51–68, https://doi.org/10.1177/0967010614552548.

Myers, N., 1989: Environment and security. *Foreign Policy*, **74** (1), 23–41.

——, 2002: Environmental refugees: A growing phenomenon of the 21st century. *Philos. Trans. Roy. Soc.*, **357B**, 609–613, https://doi.org/10.1098/rstb.2001.0953.

——, and J. Kent, 1995: Environmental exodus: An emergent crisis in the global arena climate institute. Climate Institute Rep., 246 pp., http://climate.org/archive/PDF/Environmental%20Exodus.pdf.

Nicholls, R. J., and R. S. Tol, 2006: Impacts and responses to sea-level rise: A global analysis of the SRES scenarios over the 21st century. *Philos. Trans. Roy. Soc. London*, **361A**, 1073–1095, https://doi.org/10.1098/rsta.2006.1754.

Nordås, R., and N. P. Gleditsch, 2007: Climate change and conflict. *Polit. Geogr.*, **26**, 627–638, https://doi.org/10.1016/j.polgeo.2007.06.003.

Nordhaus, W. D., 1991: A sketch of the economics of the greenhouse effect. *Amer. Econ. Rev.*, **81** (2), 146–150.

Oels, A., 2012: From 'securitization' of climate change to 'climatization' of the security field: Comparing three theoretical perspectives. *Climate Change, Human Security and Violent Conflict*, Springer, 185–205.

OFDA, 2010: Pakistan–Floods. OFDA Fact Sheet 3, 4 pp., https://www.usaid.gov/sites/default/files/documents/1866/Pakistan%20Floods%20and%20Complex%20Emergency%20Fact%20Sheet%20%232.pdf

Parry, M. L., C. Rosenzweig, A. Iglesias, M. Livermore, and G. Fischer, 2004: Effects of climate change on global food production under SRES emissions and socio-economic scenarios. *Global Environ. Change*, **14**, 53–67, https://doi.org/10.1016/j.gloenvcha.2003.10.008.

——, and Coauthors, 2007: Technical summary. *Climate Change 2007: Impacts, Adaptation and Vulnerability*, M. L. Parry et al., Eds., Cambridge University Press, 23–78.

Raleigh, C; D Kniveton, 2010: Chronic Communal Conflict and Environmental Pressures, Paper presented at the Climate Change and Security Conference Trondheim, Norway, 21–24 June 2010; at: (28 October 2010).

Reuveny, R., 2007: Climate change-induced migration and violent conflict. *Polit. Geogr.*, **26**, 656–673, https://doi.org/10.1016/j.polgeo.2007.05.001.

Rippey, B. R., 2015: The U.S. drought of 2012. *Wea. Climate Extremes*, **10**, 57–64, https://doi.org/10.1016/j.wace.2015.10.004.

Rohter, L., 2001: Argentine food riots end, but hunger doesn't. *New York Times*, 24 December 1st ed., A6.

Rosenthal, E., 2007: UN agency warns world food supply dwindling. *New York Times* acNov 2018 https://www.nytimes.com/2007/12/18/business/worldbusiness/18supply.html.

Rosenzweig, C., F. N. Tubiello, R. Goldberg, E. Mills, and J. Bloomfield, 2002: Increased crop damage in the U.S. From excess precipitation under climate change. *Global Environ. Change*, **12**, 197–202, https://doi.org/10.1016/S0959-3780(02)00008-0.

Salehyan, I., 2008: From climate change to conflict? No consensus yet. *J. Peace Res.*, **45**, 315–326, https://doi.org/10.1177/0022343308088812.

Scheffran, J., and A. Battaglini, 2011: Climate and conflict: The security risks of global warming. *Reg. Environ. Change*, **11** (Suppl.), 27–39, https://doi.org/10.1007/s10113-010-0175-8.

——, M. Brzoska, H. G. Brauch, P. M. Link, and J. Schilling, Eds., 2012: *Climate Change, Human Security and Violent Conflict: Challenges for Societal Stability*. Hexagon Series on Human and Environmental Security and Peace, Vol. 8, Springer Science and Business Media, 873 pp.

Schneider, M., 2008: We are hungry! A summary report of food riots, government responses, and states of democracy in 2008. Cornell University Dept. of Development Sociology Rep., 51 pp.

Schwartz, P., and D. Randall, 2003: An abrupt climate change scenario and its implications for United States national security. Pentagon Rep., 23 pp.

Seneviratne, S. I., and Coauthors, 2012: Changes in climate extremes and their impacts on the natural physical environment. *Managing the Risks of Extreme Events and Disasters to Advance Climate Change Adaptation*, C. B. Field et al., Eds., Cambridge University Press, 109–230.

Shah, S., 2010: Pakistan floods: Army steps into breach as anger grows at Zardari. Guardian, www.theguardian.com/world/2010/aug/08/pakistan-floods-army-popular-zardari-anger.

Smith, P., and Coauthors, 2007: Agriculture. *Climate Change 2007: Mitigation of Climate Change*, B. Metz et al., Eds., Cambridge University Press, 497–540.

Stern, N., 2013: The structure of economic modeling of the potential impacts of climate change: Grafting gross underestimation of risk onto already narrow science models. *J. Econ. Lit.*, **51**, 838–859, https://doi.org/10.1257/jel.51.3.838.

Swain, A., 1993: Environment and conflict: Analysing the developing world. Uppsala University Department of Peace and Conflict Research Rep. 37, 50 pp.

——, 2015: Climate change: Threat to national security. *Encyclopedia of Public Administration and Public Policy*, CRC Press, Editors: Melvin J. Dubnick, Domonic A. Bearfield, DOI: 10.1081/E-EPAP3-120053262.

——, R. B. Swain, and A. Themnér, 2011: *Climate Change and the Risk of Violent Conflicts in Southern Africa*. Uppsala University Center for Sustainable Development and Global Crisis Solutions Rep., 118 pp.

Trnka, M., R. P. Rötter, M. Ruiz-Ramos, K. C. Kersebaum, J. E. Olesen, Z. Žalud, and M. A. Semenov, 2014: Adverse weather conditions for European wheat production will become more frequent with climate change. *Nat. Climate Change*, **4**, 637–643, https://doi.org/10.1038/nclimate2242.

USDA, 2013: USDA designates 597 counties in 2013 as disaster areas due to drought. USDA, https://www.usda.gov/media/press-releases/2013/01/09/usda-designates-597-counties-2013-disaster-areas-due-drought.

Vermeulen, S. J., B. M. Campbell, and J. S. Ingram, 2012: Climate change and food systems. *Annu. Rev. Environ. Resour.*, **37**, 195–222, https://doi.org/10.1146/annurev-environ-020411-130608.

Wan, J., M. Qu, X. Hao, R. Motha, and J. J. Qu, 2015: Assessing the impact of year 2012 drought on corn yield in the US Corn Belt using precipitation data. *J. Earth Sci. Eng.*, **5**, 333–337, https://doi.org/10.17265/2159-581X/2015.06.001.

Warner, K., C. Ehrhart, A. de Sherbinin, S. Adamo, and T. Chai-Onn, 2009: In search of shelter: Mapping the effects of climate change on human migration and displacement. United Nations University–Cooperative for Assistance and Relief Everywhere–Center for International Earth Science Information Network–Columbia University Rep., 36 pp.

Wheeler, T., and J. Von Braun, 2013: Climate change impacts on global food security. *Science*, **341**, 508–513, 10.1126/science.1239402.

Win, TL 2009: Food security still a problem as hunger rises. Reuters accessed 5 Nov 2018, https://www.reuters.com/article/us-food-security/food-security-still-a-problem-as-hunger-rises-fao-idUSTRE52T2R720090330

Wischnath, G., and H. Buhaug, 2014: Rice or riots: On food production and conflict severity across India. *Polit. Geogr.*, **43**, 6–15, https://doi.org/10.1016/j.polgeo.2014.07.004.

Wljeyaratne, S., 2009: Fragile environment, fragile state: What role for conflict-sensitivity and peace-building? Canadian Council for International Cooperation Discussion Paper, 12 pp.

World Bank, 2008: Adaptation and mitigation of climate change in agriculture. World development report 2008: Agriculture for development, World Bank Rep., 200–201.

——, 2010: World development report 2010: Development and climate change. World Bank Rep., 444 pp., https://openknowledge.worldbank.org/handle/10986/4387.

ENERGY SECURITY

Terrence M. O'Sullivan

These advances have become too significant for the oil and gas industry to ignore. In the first three months of this year, the heads of some of the world's largest oil companies have spoken of a "global transformation" (Saudi Aramco) that is "unstoppable" (Royal Dutch Shell) and "reshaping the energy industry" (Statoil). Isabelle Kocher, chief executive of French power and gas group Engie, calls it a new "industrial revolution" that will "bring about a profound change in the way we behave." —*Pilita Clark (2017)*

The prognosis for the IOCs [international oil companies] was already grim before governments became serious about climate change and the oil price collapsed . . . their old business model is dying. . . . In this new world, the only realistic option . . . lies in restructuring and realizing (selling) many of their current assets to provide cash for their shareholders. —*Paul Stephens, international oil analyst (Macalister 2016a)*

2.2.1. INTRODUCTION

In September 2017, after more than 100 years of fossil fuels vehicle manufacturing, U.S. automobile giant General Motors, long considered emblematic of American manufacturing greatness in the twentieth century,[1] announced that it would stop making gasoline and diesel vehicles by 2023. This followed on the heels of similar announcements by several European auto firms, including Volvo, Jaguar Land Rover, and Aston Martin, making similar pledges for complete transition to emissions-free automobiles and away from fossil fuels–powered engines. Great Britain, France, the Netherlands, and Norway plan to phase out and eventually ban gas and diesel vehicle sales, with China and India preparing to join them in the coming decades (Davies 2017). Electric vehicle (EV) sales grew by 42% from 2015 to 2016 alone—more than 8 times the rate of the overall car market (Clark 2017). These developments will eventually be a substantial blow to the oil industry, given that most of its product is used for transportation [Institute for Energy Research (IER) 2017a,b].[2]

---

1. Though significantly diminished by the twenty-first century, General Motors Corporation (GMC) was still the number one U.S. car manufacturer by 2016 (Edmunds 2016).

2. Of U.S. oil consumed, 71% is used in transportation, via gasoline, diesel, and jet fuel. An additional 24% is used in industry and manufacturing, 5% is used in the commercial and residential sectors, and under 1% in electricity generation (EIA 2016b).

The world stands poised on the brink of nothing short of a new energy revolution—one that will transform how the global political economy[3] operates. Energy has been the central driving force behind almost all human progress and civilization, from the Stone Age harnessing of fire and early Industrial Revolution coal-driven steam engines to the twentieth century oil and gas era. Renewable energy will revolutionize not just the oil-driven transportation sector but overall energy-generation and energy-use models (changing grid-level energy utility models, with a rise in microgrid independent power generation) and even the century-old model of geopolitics and war that has long driven global fortunes and imperial conquest.

By 2017, solar energy was, on average, cheaper than any other form of power in the world. The cost of renewable solar and wind energy fell to at or below the cost of fossil fuels energy (coal, oil, and natural gas) in most markets. This trend shows no signs of reversing, and now, related technology improvements (in battery and other energy storage, electricity transmission and electric device efficiencies, electric charging speed, etc.) and the spread of renewables infrastructure (charging stations, home and business microgrid solar and wind energy generation, etc.) are accelerating the transition from old energy models to new.

Energy security presents a complex, uncertain, and game-changing environmental and strategic security dilemma for the twenty-first century. On the one hand, both national security and domestic "homeland security" are tied to the economic well-being of the nation, including continued commerce, transportation, manufacturing, agriculture, services, government operations, national defense, etc.—all of which rely on energy, the majority of which currently comes from relatively easy access to cheap fossil fuels. In addition, an increasingly energy-intensive U.S. consumer economy, heavily meat-oriented diet, and automobile- and home ownership–oriented cultural/consumption habits emerged and deepened in the prosperous decades after World War II. This was magnified by free trade–oriented *globalization*, coordinated by the World Trade Organization (WTO), which emerged as the dominant international economic model.

The potential (or partial) sacrifice of those ways of life in the interest of reducing greenhouse gases (GHGs) is unpalatable to many Americans, and U.S. foreign and domestic policy and global security strategies continue to be heavily predicated on protecting and securing easy sources of (dirty) fossil fuels energy. But as discussed in this chapter, energy consumption has become decoupled from economic growth, as energy prices have dropped for a variety of reasons, including technology that has improved energy efficiency, and the *supply* of fossil fuels and cheap renewable energy has increased (solar, wind, etc.), all of which has decreased the growth in *demand* for energy.

On the other hand, energy security in the current Earth-changing "Anthropocene" era[4] of history is intimately tied to critical *environmental security*. The virtually unimpeded extraction and burning of GHG pollution–producing fossil fuels for energy up to now poses an *existential threat* to humanity from *climate disruption* that is a dire threat to the overall sustainable security of all nations. While energy is fundamentally necessary for short- and long-term political and economic stability, the process of transitioning toward energy conservation and sustainable, renewable, independent sources of energy (solar, wind, biomass, etc.) may have beneficial influences on both economic development and international security and stability. From an economic standpoint, there is a growing, real risk for investors that the oil and gas markets will collapse in the next few decades because of rapidly advancing, increasingly competitive renewable energy technologies and the shifting political will of the global community in transitioning away from fossil fuels. Many energy analysts have been warning large energy companies and investors, buffeted by low crude oil and gas prices (and the near collapse of coal), climate change regulations, and their own arrogant, shortsighted corporate strategies, that they must transform their business models or face a "nasty, short, brutish end" within 15 years or less (by 2025 or 2030) (Macalister 2016a).

Fighting climate change with renewable energy is now profitable for businesses and private individuals, and the market will shift—and is just a matter of how fast

---

3. "Political economy" is the interaction of economic and political structures or processes—the combined politics of economics and economic influences on politics and the fates of nations and humanity.

4. See discussion of the so-called Anthropocene era elsewhere in this book.

and where this revolutionary transition occurs. Energy security in the context of climate change currently had until very recently represented something of a *collective action problem*—a scenario where there is conflict between individual nation's and corporations'/industries' economic interests and the interests of humanity and the planet. Like other for-profit industries, it has been in the interests of oil and gas (and coal) companies to extract and produce as much of their product as they can. It had been a choice to be "selfish," in the same ways that wealthier developed nations have been for generations, and to continue to build dirty coal-powered electricity plants rather than cooperate in collective action to save the planet. It is clearly in humanity's collective interest to significantly cut back (or eliminate) fossil fuels energy emissions. But what has changed radically now is that one need not be altruistic to begin to transition from dirty energy (current or planned) to cleaner, renewable energy. The price is becoming unbeatable.

To better frame the concepts around energy security, the next section illustrates the energy pyramid and law of tolerance.

2.2.2. THE ENERGY PYRAMID AND THE LAW OF TOLERANCE

As represented in Figure 2.2.1, the traditional *energy pyramid* is one essential way to demonstrate nature's

consumption relationships (what eats what to live) and the flow of energy through any ecosystem. Aside from volcanic/geothermal heat, energy on Earth's surface originates from the sun, and the species that use the most available solar energy are called producers. These are primarily plants and other organisms that derive growth from photosynthesis and thus produce food that forms the base that's used by the rest of those up at higher *trophic levels* on the pyramid. Energy is transferred up at each level to other organisms that consume those below it, but because of the laws of thermodynamics, there exists a necessary loss of energy in the transfer to each successive (higher) trophic level. Thus, each successive trophic level possesses only 10% of the energy of the level directly below it. Subsequently, each successively higher level can support fewer species or individuals. Hence, at the top are carnivores and peak predators, the smallest number of species, and the least amount of stored energy. The farther away from the primary producers at the base, the less energy available. Figure 2.2.1 shows the energy transfer pyramid and the inescapable loss of 90% of available energy moving up each trophic level from producers to consumers.

Conceived in 1931, Shelford's "law of tolerance" assumes there are harmful or fatal effects of a small change in environmental conditions of biological organisms that go beyond the limits of tolerance of that species (Pörtner 2001). Similarly, the law of tolerance

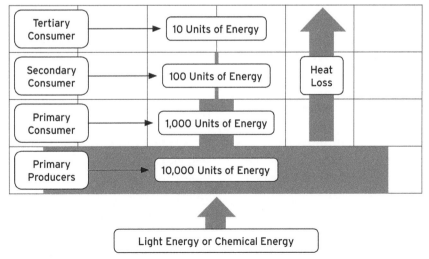

Figure 2.2.1. The energy pyramid.

can be applied as a metaphor for not just organisms and ecosystems, but for human society as well. With degradation of the natural environment because of climate disruption, small changes to the conditions (such as rising temperatures and ocean acidification from carbon emissions) of lower-order producer organisms like plankton and other sea creatures have the potential to cause catastrophic cascading failures at the levels above them (Pörtner et al. 2001).

Similarly, even small changes in the availability and energy return on investment of human energy sources have the potential to be highly disruptive to the modern economic and even political systems.

2.2.3. DEFINING AND (RE)FRAMING ENERGY SECURITY

Human development is limited by the material world, despite the failure of central prevailing economic development models to account for this basic, commonsense fact. Much as we now know that the human mind and body are intimately connected, it is interesting to note that economic prosperity and civilization are intimately connected to our natural environment as well (Cottrell 2009). Energy is a common thread that connects all critical infrastructures, including government, private sector commerce and services, transportation, electricity, food production, water use, manufacturing, communications, national defense, and virtually every aspect of modern society. Without relatively easy energy sources, societies throughout history have experienced severe energy insecurity and often catastrophically collapsed. Yet that very easy energy is currently causing *all* of humanity to barrel toward catastrophe.

Energy security can be defined in a variety of ways but centers on the need for and availability of energy for a nation's economic well-being. The International Energy Agency (IEA) defines energy security as "the uninterrupted availability of energy sources at an affordable price" (IEA 2016)—that is, energy that's *reliable, affordable,* and *accessible.* This framing is subjective and even controversial, however—particularly in the context of competing environmental security interests directly linked to greenhouse gas pollution externalities from fossil fuels

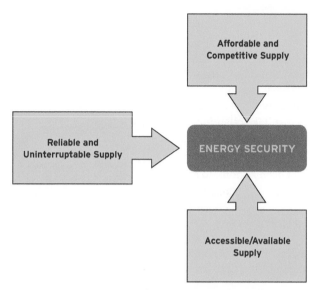

Figure 2.2.2. Components of energy security, adapted from the IEA (2016).

energy consumption. The IEA also notes two other important dimensions to account for: *long-* and *short-term* energy security—in which long-term security deals more with energy investments that fit with a nation's economic development goals (and even environmental sustainability priorities) and short term with the mitigation of energy disruption risks and supply–demand price shocks (IEA 2016).

The challenge with definitions of any complex social construct, however, is how to best accommodate both the meaning and the reality of short-term versus sustainable, longer-term economic development goals. Indeed, even the wealth of the United States (or any nation) will not be enough save it from many of the catastrophic future global disruptions that are estimated to derive from climate change/global warming if the fossil fuels economy continues to operate at its current rate.[5]

Energy security can be diminished for many inter-related, mutually magnifying reasons. Author Jared Diamond highlights overexploitation of natural resources, loss of trade, societal conflicts and war, climate change, and societal inability to adapt to changing conditions as among the most important. Environmental degradation from pollution, population growth, habitat loss, declining overexploited ecosystems and water sources, combined with the many growing effects of GHGs leading to cli-

---

5. Interestingly, the case study to follow in unit 2 on "limits of growth" will directly address this notion.

mate change/global warming (soil degradation, extreme weather events, sea level and sea temperature rise, ocean acidification, etc.) have combined with other converging factors (Diamond 2005).

2.2.4. SOURCES OF ENERGY USED IN THE U.S. (AND GLOBAL) ECONOMY

In the United States, petroleum, natural gas, coal, renewable energy, and nuclear electric power are the essential energy sources, while electricity, a secondary energy source, is produced by the others. In 2016, the shares of total primary energy consumption for the five energy-consuming sectors were [from U.S. Energy Information Administration (EIA) 2017b] as follows:

- Electric power—39%
- Transportation—29%
- Industrial—22%
- Residential—6%
- Commercial—4%

In the United States, the electric power–generation sector—primarily large utility companies—generates most of the electricity consumed by the other four sectors, and sectors' fuel use patterns vary widely. For instance, 92% of the transportation sector (energy used for transportation) is supplied by oil and oil products; only 1% of the oil energy is used to generate electricity. By contrast, the electrical power sector gets most of its energy from natural gas and coal despite the fact that renewables are the fastest-growing sector for new capacity and the fastest-growing energy jobs sector.

Petroleum, natural gas, and coal have been the kings of U.S. energy use for the entire twentieth century. Nevertheless, since the turn of this century, there have been significant changes in U.S. energy production and consumption (EIA 2017b):

- Coal is a dying industry in the United States, and is set to decline worldwide as well, because of efforts by American, Chinese, and Western governments to rein in electricity generation by the dirtiest of fossil fuels. U.S. coal production peaked in 2008 and by 2016 was

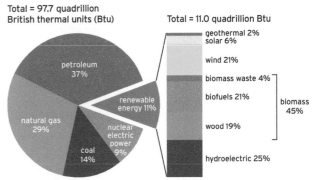

U.S. energy consumption by energy source, 2017

Note: Sum of components may not equal 100% because of independent rounding.
Source: U.S. Energy Information Administration. *Monthly Energy Review*, Table 1.3 and 10.1, April 2018, preliminary data

Figure 2.2.3. The 2017 U.S. energy consumption by source (EIA 2017b).

so low (down to 1980 levels) that some of the biggest coal companies were on the verge of bankruptcy.

- Natural gas production soared, however—much of it taking the place of coal in electricity generation. Touted as a dubious (now largely debunked) "bridge fuel" toward sustainability (DeSmogBlog 2010), gas production, primarily through hydraulic fracturing (fracking) in U.S. shale formations, and consumption have risen to historic levels. Nevertheless, the collapse of oil and other energy prices led to significant losses by fracking companies, and by 2015, the clear majority were operating in the red (Rowell 2015).
- New methods of shale oil extraction also led to a boom in U.S. crude oil production in Texas and North Dakota's Bakken oil fields after 2008. Nevertheless, like gas fracking operations, the boom had turned to bust by 2015 because global oil prices—which had been at a 70-year high of $150 per barrel in 2008—had dropped below $50 per barrel by 2016 (Macrotrends 2016), making the energy return on investment (EROI)[6] for expensive fracked shale oil financially untenable for most operations.
- Energy production from renewable wind and solar energy reached record highs by 2016. In 2016, international solar power–generating capability increased by 30% and overall renewable energy power by 9%. By 2017, renewable energy represented over half of all new global power-generation capacity (Clark 2017).

---

6. The EROI is a key determinant of the price of energy, as sources of energy that can be tapped relatively cheaply will allow the price to remain low. The ratio decreases when energy becomes scarcer and more difficult to extract or produce.

2.2.5. SLOUCHING TOWARD THE RENEWABLES FUTURE

The EIA (2016a) defines renewable energy as "resources that are replenished in a relatively short period of time." Renewable energy is any natural source that is not finite and depletable, including solar, wind, geothermal, tidal (lunar gravity), and photosynthesis-related biomass. In the United States, around 12% of all energy—including 14% of its electricity—consumed by 2016 was derived from renewable sources (EIA 2016b). Although among the lowest as a percentage of Western nations, the overall consumption of renewable energy in the United States is among the largest.

In 2016, in the wake of the United Nations (UN) 21st Conference of the Parties (COP21)[7] climate agreement, lawsuits against Exxon Mobil Corporation for hiding its knowledge about the effects of greenhouse gas pollution for 30-plus years, and overall declining confidence in oil, gas, and coal investments, even the world's most powerful fossil fuels companies were tentatively beginning to get on the renewable energy bandwagon. Shell, Total,[8] Statoil, even Exxon were hedging their bets with announcements of various "green" investments, as even Saudi Arabia, the world's biggest oil-exporting nation, announced it would sell off portions of its national oil company and diversify its economy beyond petroleum (Macalister 2016b).

Although the clear majority of overall U.S. energy still comes from nonrenewable fossil fuels, the fastest-growing energy sector in the United States, with 20% annual growth rates, is *renewables*—particularly wind and solar power (each growing at almost 30% per year as of 2016) (EIA 2016b). Globally, meanwhile, many countries are now far exceeding these percentages, generating vast amounts of electric power from renewables, and the trend lines have been very strong for this transition. By 2017, it had become common to read about European nations such as Germany and the Netherlands exceeding their daily electric power generation needs through renewable energy alone. Also, the attendant technologies that will be important for the revolutionary transition from fossil fuels to renewables are improving every year at a rapid pace. Large-capacity lithium-ion battery efficiency and storage rose over 50% from 2016 to 2017, for instance (Clark 2017), enabling the creation of grid-level batteries (vs smaller microgrid or vehicle batteries) that could store massive amounts of energy, capable of supplying towns and even cities.

Our ancestors used renewable wood and other biomass energy for thousands of years—and these resources were considered *renewable* because the human population was small enough not to stress (or threaten) the natural energy supplies, that is, until the rise and collapse of early civilizations such as the Rapa Nui on Easter Island. But modern technology and the explosion of human populations around the world have made both energy resources once considered renewable extremely finite and contributed to the growing destruction of the natural environment in the process.

By 2016, *total* U.S. *renewable energy* distribution and consumption was approximately (EIA 2017b) as follows:

- Hydroelectric power—25%
- Biomass wood—21%
- Biomass biofuels—22%
- Wind—19%
- Solar—5%
- Biomass waste—5%
- Geothermal—2%

In the United States, the combination of dropping prices, including near- or actual solar and wind parity price or below with coal, oil, and even gas in some regions, and the prospect of enforcement of the Environmental Protection Agency's Clean Power Plan to reduce carbon, including coal-fired power, emissions

---

7. COP21 is part of the global negotiating framework for climate change within the UN. In 2015, COP21, also known as the 2015 Paris Climate Conference, set out to, for the first time in over 20 years of UN negotiations, achieve a legally binding and universal agreement on climate, with the aim of keeping global warming below 2°C.

8. Total of France announced in May 2016 that it planned to spend almost EUR 1 billion to buy the battery manufacturer Saft, saying the deal would "allow us to complement our portfolio with electricity storage solutions, a key component of the future growth of renewable energy." Total also paid $1.4 billion (U.S. dollars) in 2011 for SunPower, then among the largest U.S. solar panel makers, and subsequently set up New Energies, its low-carbon technologies arm. Shell also established a similar green division around the same time (Macalister 2016b).

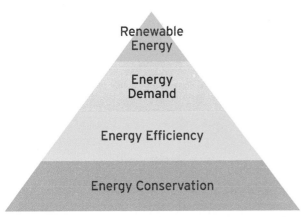

Figure 2.2.4. The pyramid of energy conservation. The base of our social demand for energy should be conservation oriented, as this figure shows, which is the greenest way to manage energy demand, while saving consumers money and reducing pollution.

has convinced even large U.S. utility companies to begin hedging their bets on investing in renewables [Union of Concerned Scientists (UCS) 2017]. Renewable energy remains a minority of U.S. energy generation, but achievement of parity price is increasingly making it competitive with even the cheapest fossil fuels.

One 2017 study showed that the elimination of tens of billions of dollars in U.S. federal and state tax preferences and other subsidies to crude oil producers would lead to almost 50% of as-yet-undeveloped oil investments to be unprofitable, given the then-current $50 (U.S. dollars) per barrel oil prices. This confirms the environmental movement's beliefs that most untapped fossil fuels reserves could be "kept in the ground" economically, allowing the United States to meet its carbon emissions commitments under the 2015 Paris Accord. But it also represents a threat to the stock values and long-range prospects of the global oil industry (Erickson et al. 2017).

As the 2015 COP21 global climate negotiations highlighted, the world needs a revolutionary transformation from dirty fossil fuels to lower-polluting renewables, while acknowledging energy security needs of member countries, if it is to have a chance to reach the goal of keeping global average temperature increases below 2°C (Erickson et al. 2017). To have a chance at reaching this goal while maintaining energy security, there must be at least a 50% reduction of global CO_2 emissions relative to current levels by 2050. Among the critical components required to meet this goal will be further progress on wind and solar capacity and related energy storage,

energy efficiency (currently one of the most important and easiest for progress), "smart grid" and microgrid electricity generation advances, and innovations in transportation technology and greater mass transit. Though controversial, nuclear power and as-yet-unproven carbon capture and storage (CCS) may also factor into the strategy.

One way of framing the concept of energy security in the age of climate disruption is as a pyramid, as illustrated in Figure 2.2.4.

Typically, both cost and complexity increase as you move from conservation activities toward efficiency activities toward renewables—that is, as you travel up the pyramid. Hence, as the social demand for energy increases, the basis of the demand and the policies governing its production, transmission, and storage should be to maximize conservation and minimize negative externalities of energy production. The ultimate societal destination should become maximal use of renewable energy.

2.2.6. SUSTAINABLE/RENEWABLE ENERGY AS SECURITY: THE METHODS

2.2.6.1. Wind Power

Wind energy supplied roughly 8% of electricity generation in the United States in 2016. Larger *utility-scale* and smaller local *distributed* wind power have both been helping revolutionize renewable energy generation. Utility-scale wind often comes from vast "farms" of very large wind turbines, on land or offshore, that generate and transfer (like any power plant would) energy to where it is needed. The largest of these turbines can generate as much as 4 megawatts (MW) of energy, though most fall into the 1–2-MW range. Distributed wind generation involves much smaller-scale wind energy at individual homes or businesses, which is then distributed over a local area. As a comparison, most home wind turbines generally produce under 10 kilowatts (kW) of power, while smaller business-scale turbines can produce 11 to 100 kW. These turbines may or may not be connected to an electrical grid (i.e., the power utilities), but in places where they are, any excess electricity that is not used might be sold to the local utility and distributed for more widespread use [U.S. Department of Energy (DOE) 2017].

2.2.6.2. Solar Power

Solar power has become competitive (price parity) with fossil fuels, per kilowatt hour of power, in many major markets and with wind power is threatening to disrupt the comparative monopoly of the traditional giant utility companies. Solar can be divided into three major sub-categories: 1) solar thermal power at utility scale, 2) solar photovoltaic power at utility scale, and 3) distributed solar capacity. Solar electric energy is generated by two main means: thermal (heat) and photovoltaic (PV; solar panels, etc.), which can be done at either larger utility scales or in smaller *distributed systems* (such as business or home rooftop arrays) that could be independent of or integrated into the broader electrical grid.

Utility-grade solar electrical–generation systems involve either large-array PV systems or large systems that focus reflected heat from mirrors on a central point that generates steam to power turbines. Meanwhile, distributed systems are decentralized micropower-generation points that are not measured or controlled by any central organization, regardless of whether they are connected to a central energy grid.

2.2.6.3. Solar Thermal Power on Utility Scale

Solar thermal power–generation systems focus sunlight to produce intense heat that is converted to electricity. All solar thermal power systems have solar energy collectors with two main components: *reflectors* (mirrors) that capture and focus sunlight onto a *receiver*. In most types of systems, some type of heat-transfer fluid is heated and circulated in the receiver, producing steam, which is then converted to energy via an electricity-generating turbine. These systems track sunlight to keep it focused toward receivers as the sun moves throughout the day. Solar thermal power systems may also have heat energy storage systems that allow solar energy concentration and collector systems to heat an energy storage during the day, allowing the storage system heat to be used to produce electricity at night or during cloudy weather. In some cases, solar thermal power plants are designed as hybrid energy-generation systems, capable of using other energy sources such as natural gas to backup or supplement the solar energy in the event of low solar radiation. There are three main types of concentrating solar thermal power systems: linear concentrating systems (parabolic troughs and reflectors), solar power towers, and solar dish/engine systems (EIA 2016a).

2.2.6.4. Solar PV Power on Utility Scale

The efficiency of solar energy collectors (amount of sun that can be converted to energy) is continually improving, just as the overall cost per kilowatt hour of PV continues to plummet to levels beyond the most optimistic ones of only a few years ago. Among the main issues that traditionally limited solar PV power has been the reliability of the sun, which only shines part of the day, and thus requires either alternatives for nighttime or efficient storage. Until recently, both of those were lacking cost-effective solutions. But the rapid advances in storage batteries and other methods (gravity storage) are making utility (large-)scale solar energy practical.

Central to this breakthrough is the steady decline in the cost of lithium-ion battery storage. Battery technology is reliant on breakthroughs and efficiencies in chemistry and materials science and the many specific uses for different battery designs.[9] Recent projections suggest battery technology is still in its infancy but that the cost of batteries might fall from 1990 levels of $10,000 per kWh to as low as $100 per kWh by 2019 (Kittner et al. 2017). If so, it would make renewable wind, solar, and other storage competitive with even coal and natural gas as 24-hour energy sources and significantly reduce the complexity of integrating such systems into energy grids. One study concluded that "There may be room for a number of different battery chemistries that all provide different services on an evolving grid, some providing voltage regulation and frequency control, and others serving long-duration outages and providing backup for buildings and communities" (Kittner et al. 2017).

2.2.6.5. Distributed Solar Capacity

In addition to larger grid-level power, there is significant promise in distributed, microgrid power that would emerge from rooftop solar arrays on businesses and homes. As with other solar power generation, the cost versus benefits of this type of power are now also reaching or surpassing fossil fuels energy, even for residential installations in many parts of the United States and

---

9. For instance, an EV battery must be able to have high output and be recharged quickly, thousands of times, whereas other battery types would have less rigorous performance demands.

around the world. These systems hold the promise of not just supplementing standard electric utility power but circumventing it "off grid"—and allowing power year-round energy independent of often fragile regional and national grids, including in times of major power outages from disasters such as hurricanes. The value of this type of distributed PV power was shown in 2017's devastating Hurricanes Irma (which caused the largest power outages in U.S. history in Florida and Georgia) and Maria (which knocked out power to over 95% of Puerto Rico).

2.2.7. THE ECONOMICS OF ENERGY SECURITY: THE CALCULUS OF ENERGY RETURN ON INVESTMENT

Many less-developed countries (LDCs) suffer from perpetual energy insecurity, since their ability to produce energy domestically or to buy it on the international market (often using precious foreign exchange—or "forex"[10]—currency) may be highly limited. Historic examples of relative energy insecurity for the most-developed, wealthy postindustrial countries have usually involved disruptions caused by or which lead to war or other political conflict or by price spikes that relate to deliberate or accidental supply constrictions, such as oil embargos, pipeline disruptions, natural disasters (hurricanes, earthquakes), etc.

Added to each of these problems is a declining availability of "easy energy," as the energy return on investment (EROI)—the ratio of a particular source of energy required to extract *new* energy—also declines. Examples of EROI can range from the simple caloric food energy investment it would take our primitive ancestors to search for and gather wood for their fires to the substantial energy in manufacture of equipment, storage facilities, transportation, extraction (exploration, drilling, pumping, etc.), and refinery processing to produce fuel oil and gasoline. Homer-Dixon (2007), Hall et al. (2009), Turner (2012), Klein (2015), and others have proposed variations on an economic EROI model. Collectively, they posit modern capitalist society is in decline in large

measure because of diminishing energy return on energy invested, worsened by an unsustainable global economic growth model that relies on accelerating expansion and (over)consumption—that in the end is threatening not only economic collapse but the very survival of human civilization.

Tainter (2011) reinforces this idea that societies/empires accelerate toward unsustainable collapse because they are unable (or unwilling) to adapt their prevailing complex social and economic models—once very successful—to population growth; overall diminishing rates of return; declining energy, food, water, and other resources; and catastrophic environmental degradation.

2.2.8. A TIDY LINKAGE BETWEEN ENERGY AND FOOD SECURITY

Globally, there is a steadily increasing connection between modern industrial food production and fossil fuels production, inasmuch as both are reliant on many of the same unsustainable and diminishing sets of resources, and because large-scale farming relies heavily on chemical fertilizers, herbicides, and pesticides derived from fossil fuels (Alom et al. 2013). During energy commodity price increase shocks such as the 1973 Organization of the Petroleum Exporting Countries (OPEC) oil crisis, staple food prices soared to more than twice what they were before the crisis. In contrast, when energy prices plummeted between 2014 and 2016, food commodity prices also dropped—often to the detriment of producers of both.

This energy and food price volatility—both up and down—can be destabilizing, especially to countries dependent on EROI calculations for either or both commodity categories. Such variations in oil and gas price significantly impact economies such as Russia's, for whom, as of 2016, energy exports represented half their foreign trade revenues, or Venezuela (95% of revenues are from exported oil), as well as Saudi Arabia and Azerbaijan, among others. In some cases, those governments were faced with food and other import commodity price increases and political instability.

---

10. Foreign exchange currencies are traded in the very large and highly "liquid" over-the-counter global forex market. Even though technically all nations' currencies are traded, not all currencies are accepted by sellers as payment for foreign trade in oil, gas, and other commodities. Thus, a country's available supply of higher-value dollar, pound, euro, yen, and other forex currencies can limit its ability to import foreign goods, including fuel, if its own currency is unwanted by sellers. (See, e.g., www.investopedia.com/terms/f/forex.asp.)

Cheap fossil fuels EROIs have enabled most of the world's nations to go from being predominately rural and agricultural before the Industrial Revolution to majority urban now with only 4% of humanity now employed in agriculture worldwide. Decreasing energy returns on investment in energy production can cause food price spikes and political instability to the point of overthrown governments. Over time, growing energy costs could even require a return of more people to food production in developing countries.

2.2.9. CLIMATE, ENERGY, AND FOOD ECONOMICS

Increasingly, the diets of wealthy postindustrial societies and rising economies alike have become the focus of energy security, food security, and climate change mitigation socioeconomics. To put it in the simplest terms, the current global diet and food economics models overall have been making substantial damaging contributions to the rise in disruptive GHS emissions. The amount of rising energy-intensive global meat consumption alone has also had a major impact on agricultural GHG emission's contributions to global warming—making dietary patterns a significant matter for both energy security and climate security (Tilman and Clark 2014).

2.2.10. ENERGY, FOOD AND WATER RESOURCE INSTABILITY, AND WAR

Energy has been a common historical pretext for war, as politics and events in the volatile Middle Eastern oil region have attested, and has been arguably the biggest driver of global growth and prosperity—particularly through coal and then oil and gas—since the Industrial Revolution in the 1700s (Ayres et al. 2013). Without adequate energy, economies suffer, and militaries cannot deploy for national defense.

During the 1973 Arab–Israeli War, OPEC imposed a retaliatory oil trade embargo against Israel's ally, the United States, and other supporters, in response to its resupply of the Israeli military and to flex its economic and political muscle in anticipation of peace negotiations. Aside from the embargo, the Arabic OPEC nations also introduced cuts in oil production, all of which significantly raised petroleum/gas prices in the United States and destabilized global energy, food, and other prices overall (Chand 2008).

Climate changes have historically contributed to substantial geopolitical upheaval in regions such as the Middle East—as one of the key causal variables for the 2010–11 so-called Arab Spring, the Syrian civil war, and even the rise of the murderous terrorist army, the Islamic State in Iraq and Syria (ISIS), or "Da'esh" (Breisinger et al. 2011; Werrell and Femia 2013; Kelley et al. 2015). The Middle East and North Africa region had previously been extremely reliant on global food imports and thus particularly sensitive to global food supply and price fluctuations, given how poor the region was in fertile land and water resources. In sum, extreme weather events driven by climate change in both major food-producing countries and energy-producing regions such as the Middle East can increase food prices significantly and lead to further political unrest, war, and disruption of global supplies (Perez and Stecker 2013).

2.2.11. U.S. ENERGY POLICY: TWO STEPS FORWARD, ONE STEP BACK?

Every science- and security-related institution within the U.S. federal government's executive branch had, at least up to the 2016 election, thoroughly assessed and analyzed the threat from climate change and incorporated policy and mission statements highlighting the dire need for prevention and response.

Yet as of this writing, the Trump White House has brought in the most fossil fuels–friendly administration in recent history. The policies and statements of the president and his officials have sent a combination of mixed messages; promoted highly contradictory positions; or outright declared that environmental regulations were a burden, that climate change did not exist, and that fossil fuels had received an unjust assessment by the scientific community. They vowed to abolish the Environmental Protection Agency (EPA) (Neslen 2017), have withdrawn U.S. participation in the Paris Climate Agreement (Zhang et al. 2017), and cut environmental programs and regulations, including the Obama administration's Clean Power Plan (Rott 2018), and those for renewable energy.

These significant shifts were occurring even as the administration touted, for example, achieving a milestone initiated by the previous White House. The Trump DOE in September 2017 bragged about the U.S. solar industry achieving a 2020 utility-scale solar cost target set by the 2011 SunShot Initiative, which sought to reduce solar system energy costs to 6¢ per kWh. This goal had been met three years early. In contrast, the White House budget was slashing DOE's renewable energy and energy efficiency program budget by 70% (Chow 2017).

President Trump's predecessor, Barack Obama, who came into office in 2009, continued (at least through 2013) a decidedly mixed set of climate-related policies. Despite some obvious proenvironmental speeches and initiatives, such as the 2013 Obama Georgetown climate address and the June Climate Action Plan (White House 2013), these policies had not addressed many core issues needed for substantial GHG emission reductions. Clearly, some White House domestic climate and environmental policies (such as the Clean Power Plan, which increased regulation of coal-fired power plants) were positive. But many administration actions worsened global GHG emissions and domestic environmental damage.

In contrast to his second-term environmental initiatives, in late 2013, in Cushing, Oklahoma, President Obama gave a speech (McKibben 2013):

> Over the last three years, I've directed my administration to open up millions of acres for gas and oil exploration across 23 different states. We're opening up more than 75 percent of our potential oil resources offshore. We've quadrupled the number of operating rigs to a record high. We've added enough new oil and gas pipeline to encircle the Earth, and then some. . . . In fact, the problem . . . is that we're actually producing so much oil and gas . . . that we don't have enough pipeline capacity to transport all of it where it needs to go.

Other U.S. policies that either continued the trend of increasing rather than decreasing U.S. fossil fuels production or that added new capacities in fossil fuel production include the following:

- Giving Shell Oil authority to drill in the Alaska's Beaufort Sea. Obama said, "Our pioneering spirit is naturally drawn to this region, for the economic opportunities it presents" (McKibben 2013).
- Continued financial subsidies of fossil fuel industry. These subsidies were significant enough that if eliminated, wind power would then be competitive per kilowatt hour (Goossens 2013) and solar cheaper.

Since then, of course, even unsubsidized solar has become as cheap or cheaper than fossil fuel energy.
- Fracking of shale gas and oil is increasingly being shown to be both environmentally destructive and unhealthy to nearby residents, as a 2013 U.S. Institute of Medicine workshop summary report illustrates (Coussens and Martinez 2013).
- The proposed Trans-Pacific Partnership, which did not pass under Obama, would have stripped national and local environmental regulation ability, just as the North American Free Trade Agreement (NAFTA) did before it, to a lesser extent—allowing governments to be sued for trade violations by private corporations simply for efforts to tighten their environmental policies (Smith 2013).

As climate policy activist Bill McKibben lamented in 2013, "Building more renewable energy is not a useful task if you're also digging more carbon energy—it's like eating a pan of Weight Watchers brownies after you've already gobbled a quart of Ben and Jerry's" (McKibben 2012, 2013). The math of climate change clearly indicates that most of the current known reserves of global fossil fuels must remain in the ground, undeveloped and unburned, for any hope of averting calamity.

2.2.11.1. Current Energy Policy

President Trump's administration's energy policies are unabashedly favorable to the fossil fuels industry and related (extractive) industries such as coal. Such energy policies seem counter to those of the previous administration, which clearly emphasized renewable energy sources development and integration as well as other green initiatives. These policies are said to promote energy independence and security based on aggressive exploitation of oil, coal, and natural gas and range from skepticism to outright hostility toward renewable energy generation. Indeed, they have made their way into the current U.S. national security strategy (White House 2017). Among the central early initiatives were proposals to end the federal moratorium on coal mining leases; expedited fossil fuels exploration and infrastructure, including in places such as East and West Coast offshore drilling and the Alaska National Refuge; and elimination of the Obama Clean Power Plan (UCS 2017) and rollback of other even more long-running environmental regulations such as the Clean Water (aka Federal Water

Pollution Control) [U.S. Fish and Wildlife Service (FWS) 2018a] and Clear Air Acts (EPA 2018), the Endangered Species Act (FWS 2018b), and others. The 2018 budget proposals scheduled major cuts in renewable energy and efficiency programs.

2.2.12. CONCLUSIONS

Energy security is about ensuring the provision of safe, clean, and reliable sources of energy desired by (needed by) a nation. The competition for energy resources has fueled (literally) some of the biggest geopolitical clashes in history—making energy-rich regions such as the Middle East flashpoints of power struggles and war.

Energy is certainly the linchpin of modern human civilization. Energy not only connects all economic infrastructures critical to national security, but also drives virtually every major human advance in history, from the burning of peat and wood for the prehistoric Iron Age to the Industrial Revolution's (soon to be waning) era of fossil fuels (oil, gas, and coal) extraction and consumption. A lack of energy security has contributed to the decline and fall of civilizations and empires and losses of nations in war. Without fuel to power transportation, light, industry, agriculture, communication, and every other aspect of modern civilization, life as most people know it would cease to exist.

The world's energy paradigm is in major transition, regardless of U.S. federal policies designed to forestall those changes. The central reason for this is that, for the first time in history, a milestone has been reached and surpassed in many instances: renewable solar and wind energy is now cheaper than coal and as cheap or cheaper than oil or natural gas energy in increasing numbers of countries and markets. This is unlikely to ever change, given the comparative EROI advantage that major renewables have on increasingly expensive extraction techniques for fossil fuels, and the markets respond to the cheaper energy. Renewable energy is the fastest-growing job sector and energy-generation infrastructure in the world.

As Jared Diamond (2005, p. 420) notes, in relation to threats to energy, food, water, and other resource-related collapse potential,

> When people are desperate, undernourished and without hope, they blame their governments, which they see as responsible for or unable to solve their problems.

They try to emigrate at any cost. They fight each other over land. They kill each other. They start civil wars. They figure that they have nothing to lose, so they become terrorists, or they support or tolerate terrorism.

Nevertheless, the global politics and economics of energy security have become even more difficult and complicated since the 1970s. The very resources that helped create the comparatively affluent (at least for most nations) globalized world we live in have caused an existential climate emergency that threatens to destroy human civilization—and the climate that has existed for most of recorded human history.

REFERENCES

Alom, F., B. D. Ward, and B. Hu, 2013: Macroeconomic effects of world oil and food price shocks in Asia and Pacific economies: Application of SVAR models. *OPEC Energy Rev.*, **37**, 327–372, https://doi.org/10.1111/opec.12015.

Ayres, R. U., J. C. J. M. van den Bergh, D. Lindenberger, and B. Warr, 2013: The underestimated contribution of energy to economic growth. *Struct. Change Econ. Dyn.*, **27**, 79–88, https://doi.org/10.1016/j.strueco.2013.07.004.

Breisinger, C., O. Ecker, and P. Al-Riffai, 2011: Economics of the Arab awakening. International Food Policy Research Institute Policy Brief 18, 4 pp., www.ifpri.org/publication/economics-arab-awakening.

Chand, R., 2008: The global food crisis: Causes, severity and outlook. *Economic and Political Weekly*, Vol. 43, No. 26, 115–122.

Chow, L., 2017: Trump Energy Dept. boasts about reaching Obama's solar cost reduction goal. Ecowatch, www.ecowatch.com/doe-solar-cost-2484800774.html.

Clark, P., 2017: The Big Green Bang: How renewable energy became unstoppable. *Financial Times*, 18 May, www.ft.com/content/44ed7e90-3960-11e7-ac89-b01cc67cfeec?mhq5j=e7.

Cottrell, F., 2009: *Energy and Society: The Relation between Energy, Social Change, and Economic Development.* AuthorHouse, 484 pp.

Coussens, C., and R. M. Martinez, 2013: *Health Impact Assessment of Shale Gas Extraction: Workshop Summary.* National Academies Press, 154 pp., https://doi.org/10.17226/18376.

Davies, A., 2017: General Motors is going all electric. Wired, www.wired.com/story/general-motors-electric-cars-plan-gm/.

DeSmogBlog, 2010: The myth that gas is "clean energy." Fracking the future: How unconventional gas threatens our water, health, and climate, DeSmogBlog Rep., 5–13, https://www.desmogblog.com/fracking-the-future/desmog-fracking-the-future.pdf.

Diamond, J., 2005: *Collapse: How Societies Choose to Fail or Succeed.* Penguin, 575 pp.

DOE, 2017: Utility-scale wind energy. WINDExchange, https://windexchange.energy.gov/markets/utility-scale.

Edmunds, 2016: Automobile market share by manufacturer. Edmunds, www.edmunds.com/industry-center/data/market-share-by-manufacturer.html.

Erickson, P., A. Down, M. Lazarus, and D. Koplow, 2017: Effect of subsidies to fossil fuel companies on United States crude oil production. *Nat. Energy*, **2**, 891–898, https://doi.org/10.1038/s41560-017-0009-8.

EIA, 2016a: Solar explained: Solar thermal power plants. EIA, www.eia.gov/energyexplained/?page=solar_thermal_power_plants.

——, 2016b: Monthly energy review. EIA Rep., 235 pp., https://www.eia.gov/totalenergy/data/monthly/archive/00351603.pdf.

——, 2017a: Monthly energy review. EIA Rep., 243 pp., www.eia.gov/totalenergy/data/monthly/archive/00351704.pdf.

——, 2017b: U.S. energy facts explained. EIA, accessed 19 May 2017, www.eia.gov/energyexplained/index.cfm?page=us_energy_home.

EPA, 2018: Clean Air Act of 1990 amendment summary. EPA, accessed 5 April 2018, www.epa.gov/clean-air-act-overview/1990-clean-air-act-amendment-summary.

FWS, 2018a: Digest of federal resource laws of interest to the U.S. Fish and Wildlife Service. FWS, accessed 5 April 2018, www.fws.gov/laws/lawsdigest/fwatrpo.HTML.

——, 2018b: Endangered Species Act: Overview. FWS, accessed 5 April 2018, www.fws.gov/endangered/laws-policies/.

Goossens, E., 2013: Wind power rivals coal with $1 billion order from Buffett. Bloomberg, www.bloomberg.com/news/print/2013-12-17/wind-power-rivals-coal-with-1-billion-order-from-buffett.html.

Hall, C. A. S., S. Balogh, and D. J. R. Murphy, 2009: What is the minimum EROI that a sustainable society must have? *Energies*, **2**, 25–47, https://doi.org/10.3390/en20100025.

Homer-Dixon, T., 2007: *The Upside of Down: Catastrophe, Creativity, and the Renewal of Civilization.* Knopf, 448 pp.

IEA, 2016: What is energy security? IEA, accessed 11 June 2016, www.iea.org/topics/energysecurity//whatisenergysecurity/.

IER, 2017a: Petroleum (oil). IER, www.instituteforenergyresearch.org/?encyclopedia=petroluem-oil.

——, 2017b: Renewable energy. IER, www.instituteforenergyresearch.org/?encyclopedia=renewable-energy.

Kelley, C. P., S. Mohtadi, M. A. Cane, R. Seager, and Y. Kushnir, 2015: Climate change in the Fertile Crescent and implications of the recent Syrian drought. *Proc. Natl. Acad. Sci. USA*, **112**, 3241–3246, https://doi.org/10.1073/pnas.1421533112.

Kittner, N., F. Lill, and D. M. Kammen, 2017: Energy storage deployment and innovation for the clean energy transition. *Nature*, **2**, 17125, https://doi.org/10.1038/nenergy.2017.125.

Klein, N., 2015: *This Changes Everything: Capitalism vs. the Climate.* Simon and Schuster, 576 pp.

Macalister, T., 2016a: Oil firms have 10 years to change strategy or face 'short, brutish end.' Guardian, www.theguardian.com/business/2016/may/05/oil-firms-environment-energy-climate-change.

——, 2016b: Green really is the new black as Big Oil gets a taste for renewables. Guardian, www.theguardian.com/business/2016/may/21/oil-majors-investments-renewable-energy-solar-wind.

Macrotrends, 2016: Crude oil prices—70 year historical chart. Macrotrends, accessed 5 July 2016, www.macrotrends.net/1369/crude-oil-price-history-chart.

McKibben, B., 2012: Global warming's terrifying new math: Three simple numbers that add up to global catastrophe—And that make clear who the real enemy is. *Rolling Stone*, 19 July, https://www.rollingstone.com/politics/politics-news/global-warmings-terrifying-new-math-188550/

——, 2013: Obama and climate change: The real story. *Rolling Stone*, 17 December, www.rollingstone.com/politics/news/obama-and-climate-change-the-real-story-20131217.

Neslen, A., 2017: Donald Trump 'taking steps to abolish Environmental Protection Agency.' Guardian, www.theguardian.com/us-news/2017/feb/02/donald-trump-plans-to-abolish-environmental-protection-agency.

Perez, I., and T. Stecker, 2013: Climate change and rising food prices heightened Arab Spring. Scientific American, https://www.scientificamerican.com/article/climate-change-and-rising-food-prices-heightened-arab-spring/.

Pörtner, H., 2001: Climate change and temperature-dependent biogeography: Oxygen limitation of thermal tolerance in animals. *Naturwissenschaften*, **88**, 137–146, https://doi.org/10.1007/s001140100216.

——, and Coauthors, 2001: Climate induced temperature effects on growth performance, fecundity and recruitment in marine fish: Developing a hypothesis for cause and effect relationships in Atlantic cod (*Gadus morhua*) and common eelpout (*Zoarces viviparus*). *Cont. Shelf Res.*, **21**, 1975–1997, https://doi.org/10.1016/S0278-4343(01)00038-3.

Rott, N., 2018: Trump moves to let states regulate coal plant emissions. National Public Radio, www.npr.org/2018/08/21/639396683/trump-moves-to-let-states-regulate-coal-plant-emissions.

Rowell, A., 2015: Fracking boom bursts in face of low oil prices. EcoWatch, http://ecowatch.com/2015/09/15/fracking-boom-bust-opec/.

Smith, H., 2013: Happily ever NAFTA: New trade pact could boost corporations and harm environment. Grist, http://grist.org/politics/free-trades-just-another-word-for-secret-lawsuits-the-tpp-the-environment-and-you/?utm_source=newsletter&utm_medium=email&utm_term=Daily%2520Dec%25206&utm_campaign=daily.

Tainter, J. A., 2011: Energy, complexity, and sustainability: A historical perspective. *Environ. Innovation Soc. Transitions*, **1**, 89–95, https://doi.org/10.1016/j.eist.2010.12.001.

Tilman, D., and M. Clark, 2014: Global diets link environmental sustainability and human health. *Nature*, **515**, 518–522, https://doi.org/10.1038/nature13959.

Turner, G. M., 2012: On the cusp of global collapse? Updated comparison of *The Limits to Growth* with historical data. *GAIA*, **21**, 116–124, https://doi.org/10.14512/gaia.21.2.10.

UCS, 2017: The clean power plan. UCS, www.ucsusa.org/our-work/global-warming/reduce-emissions/what-is-the-clean-power-plan#.V3qEZ47WRvo.

Werrell, C. E., and F. Femia, 2013: The Arab Spring and climate change: A climate and security correlations series. The Center for American Progress, Stimson, and The Center for Climate and Security Rep., 62 pp., https://climateandsecurity.files.wordpress.com/2018/07/the-arab-spring-and-climate-change_2013_02.pdf.

White House, 2013: Fact sheet: President Obama's climate action plan. White House, https://obamawhitehouse.archives.gov/the-press-office/2013/06/25/fact-sheet-president-obama-s-climate-action-plan.

——, 2017: National security strategy of the United States of America. White House Rep., 68 pp., www.whitehouse.gov/wp-content/uploads/2017/12/NSS-Final-12-18-2017-0905.pdf.

Zhang, H.-B., H.-C. Dai, H.-X. Lai, and W.-T. Wang, 2017: U.S. withdrawal from the Paris Agreement: Reasons, impacts, and China's response. *Adv. Climate Change Res.*, **8**, 220–225, https://doi.org/10.1016/j.accre.2017.09.002.

2.3

WATER SECURITY: CHALLENGES AND ADAPTATIONS

Terrence M. O'Sullivan
Elisabeth Hope Murray
John M. Lanicci
James D. Ramsay

2.3.1. INTRODUCTION

Humans can survive, most of us, for weeks without food but only for days without water. All interconnected human and natural ecosystems are reliant on, and vulnerable to, disruptions to the *water cycle* (aka hydrologic cycle). The water cycle is the collection of processes by which water moves among Earth's land, ocean, and atmospheric systems as rain, snow, ice, water vapor, etc. and is subsequently available in the chemical forms plants, animals, and humans require for life.

Water access seems to be an increasing security phenomenon. For example, in 2018, Capetown, South Africa, became the world's first major city to face the prospect of running entirely out of water. This dilemma arose from the combination of increased demand from population growth and development and an unprecedented 3-year regional drought directly linked to climate change; the drier, hotter weather, decreased winter rainfall, and lower stream flows caused the city's reservoirs to almost dry out (Mulligan 2018). Many major geographic regions around the world, including North and South America, Asia, and Australia in particular, face similar short- to long-range threats of severe water shortages by midcentury.

Capetown is not alone in its struggle to secure enough potable water. Multiple climate change models, many of which are presented in the Intergovernmental Panel on Climate Change (IPCC) reports discussed in unit 1, have predicted the trend toward water scarcity. Widespread water scarcity is increasingly common and particularly troubling when one considers that water is one of the most pivotal components of life on Earth.

Water has become perhaps the most important variable in the Anthropocene, both as a critical human need and a source of disruption, making water access a central security issue for most states. "Anthropocene" is a term many scientists and policy makers use to indicate the current epoch of history, characterized by population growth, industrialization, and climate change. Over the last 100 years, the increase in global water usage has been double the rate of the population growth, more rapidly depleting both surface and underground water sources (Barbier 2015). Although water-related resource poverty has always been a problem throughout history, it has become exacerbated as climate change has acted to widen impacts on the most vulnerable demographics and communities that are already living in poverty.

As we've seen in earlier chapters, climate change is a significant threat multiplier. It is not surprising then that among the greatest threat variables of all in our era is the supply of water—either too little water or too much

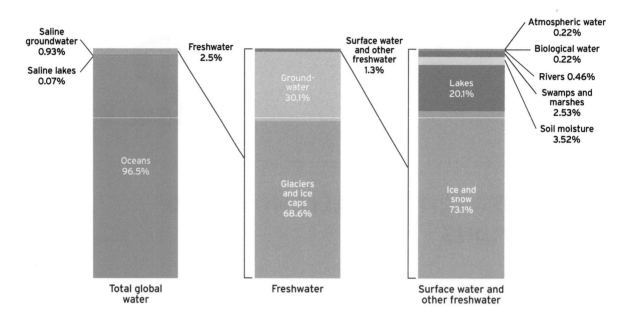

Figure 2.3.1. Distribution of Earth's water. Source: Igor Shiklomanov's chapter "World fresh water resources" in Peter H. Gleick (editor), 1993, *Water in Crisis: A Guide to the World's Fresh Water Resources*.

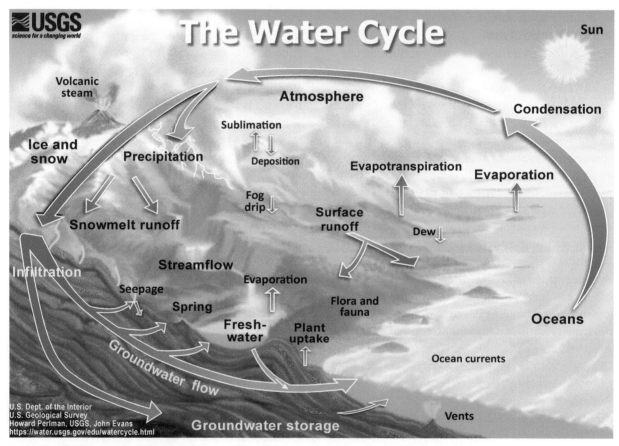

Figure 2.3.2. The water (hydrologic) cycle.

water in the form of storms, floods, and rising ocean levels. Subsequent to inconsistency in water supply is disrupted food production—the importance of which will continue to be discussed throughout this unit and which was thoroughly discussed in chapter 2.1. For example, Figure 2.3.2 depicts the water (or hydrologic) cycle and how Earth's water continuously moves through the atmosphere, into and out of the oceans, over the land surface, and underground, while Figure 2.3.1 depicts how water is distributed on Earth. [According to the U.S. Geological Survey, of the world's total water supply of about 332.5 million cubic miles of water, over 96% is saline. And, of the total freshwater, over 68% is locked up in ice and glaciers. Another 30% of freshwater is in the ground. Fresh surface-water sources, such as rivers and lakes, only constitute about 22,300 cubic miles (93,100 cubic kilometers), which is about 1/150th of 1% of total water. Yet rivers and lakes are the sources of most of the water people use every day.] In Figure 2.3.2, we can see the many places in the water cycle that human activity can impact the otherwise natural connections within and between all aspects of the cycle; for example, land-use policies and overpopulation can influence runoff and infiltration. Among the issues addressed in this chapter are the nature of water as a cyclic biogeochemical that is regularly disrupted by activities of human living; rising demand and declining availability of water through drought, access restrictions, and overconsumption; and the ruination of usable supplies through pollution, contamination, overfertilization, and either inefficient—or nonexistent—comprehensive water management systems and policies in many parts of the planet.

2.3.2. BIOGEOCHEMICAL CYCLING AND THE ROLE OF WATER

To help place the significance and uniqueness of water, which is key to understanding its role in security, it is first important to realize that potable, accessible water represents a very small portion of the total water on Earth. Indeed, as seen in Figure 2.3.1, potable, accessible water is about 2.5% of the total water supply. Water is one of five essential biogeochemicals critical to human survival. Although water is just one of five essential biogeochemicals, it is likely one of the most critical as it connects the other biogeochemicals to each other as well as to all activities of human living.

Biogeochemical cycling is an essential component of life on Earth. The term "biogeochemical" refers to the fact that each element has a biological, chemical, and geological component to its cycle. The five essential biogeochemicals are carbon, nitrogen, sulfur, phosphorus, and water. Each of these chemicals has a distinct cycle where it exists in either gaseous (airborne) or sedimentary (geological) reservoirs. Each of the five essential biogeochemicals exists in a cycle that moves through both biotic and abiotic environments, and each can be and is mitigated by human activities. The fact that each element cycles is critical as it leads directly to the ability of each chemical to be available and—perhaps most importantly—connects each chemical to human influence. Figure 2.3.2 shows the water cycle. Notice the portions of the water cycle that can be easily mitigated by human activities.

Like all biogeochemicals, the hydrologic cycle is sensitive to the influence (mitigation) of human activities. Extraordinary disturbances such as anthropogenic (i.e., human-caused) climate change, concentrated and sustained mitigation by human activity (development, mining, etc.), wildfires, or major storms can each affect the capacity of the water cycle to self-adjust its availability. Subsequently, an impaired ability to self-adjust can in turn lead to relative shortages. For example, even though a cyclic biogeochemical like water naturally regenerates its supplies and has subterranean reservoirs, those supplies can shrink over time when the natural rate of recharge is smaller than the rate of extraction due to human activities such as the rapid growth of metropolitan areas or large-scale commercial agriculture. Indeed, the largest aquifer in the world, the Ogallala in the southwest of the United States (see Figure 2.3.3a), is shrinking since the rate of extraction has been greater than the rate of regeneration for several decades, as shown in Figure 2.3.3b. In other regions of the world, prolonged water shortages have led to drought, crop failure, and migration and ultimately facilitate governmental failure and the rise of radicalized terrorist organizations. Domestically, the economic and agricultural viability of several U.S. states is imperiled because of the lack of adequate supplies of freshwater [U.S. Department of Agriculture Natural Resources Conservation Service (USDA NRCS) 2018]. In this way, and to some degree ironically, a renewable and essential resource tends to be in chronic short supply in many U.S. states and in many nations.

Figure 2.3.3a. The Ogallala Aquifer.

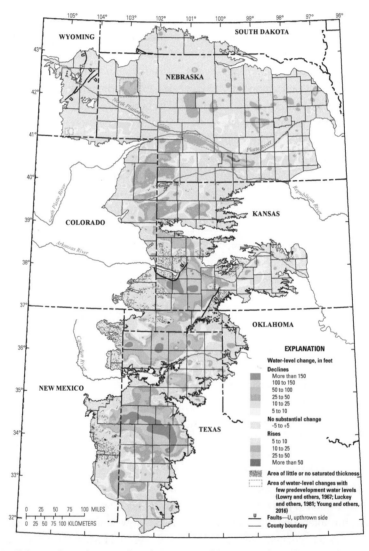

Figure 2.3.3b. The Ogallala Aquifer under stress (2015). Courtesy of the U.S. Geological Survey (https://www.usgs.gov/water).

To exemplify the precious nature of water as one of the five essential biogeochemicals, let us consider the water cycle. Around 99% of the world's water is not usable for human consumption; 96.5% is ocean saltwater, and only 2.5% is freshwater. Of this freshwater, less than half is accessible to humans, with the majority of that frozen in glaciers and the rest beneath the earth in deep water aquifers. Ultimately, and quite extraordinarily, only approximately *0.3%* of the world's freshwater is accessible in surface lakes, rivers, and marshlands [U.S. Geological Survey (USGS) 2016].

2.3.2.1. Water Use

Knowledge of the water cycle helps us to better understand how human activities might mitigate it. Precise breakdowns of how much water is consumed by which sector of the economy are difficult to measure. However, there is general agreement that agricultural consumption accounts for about 70% of the freshwater used today; the remaining 30% is all that remains to meet the increasing demand from domestic household consumption, energy extraction, and industries. It is estimated that agricultural water requirements will increase by almost 20% by 2050 because of a growing population and the subsequent need for crop production, which requires irrigation. This trend line is concerning when one considers that around 40% of the world's food is currently grown in artificially irrigated areas (Kiers et al. 2008). Water usage trends present different concerns in various regions of Earth. For example, in places such as East Asia, agricultural usage presents concerns because of the combination of rapidly growing populations and poor irrigation practices such as large-scale irrigation systems that lead to depleted surface and groundwater resources (Kiers et al. 2008).

Water is a vexing resource. Recall that although 70% of Earth is covered in water, potable, usable, drinkable water is a minor fraction of Earth's overall supply. It is easy to understand why, as population grows, the need to grow more crops increases. Growing more crops to feed more people is a complex interaction of cultural norms (i.e., eating higher vs lower on the food chain: more meat vs more grains); social investments in water-saving irrigation practices; use of fertilizers, herbicides, and pesticides; and local climate (among other factors as well). Whether in more-developed or less-developed nations, considerable challenges to accessing adequate supplies of freshwater remain, as Figure 2.3.4 shows.

2.3.3. WHAT IS WATER SECURITY?

We've established how vital water is to life. It follows that scarcity of a critical resource is inherently a security issue. We've also discussed how water cycles in nature and how human activities can mitigate that cycle. It does not seem like water access challenges are then directly related to security issues. We will use the term water security to refer to an array of local, regional, and global security challenges that are based on water access and availability. Water security can be defined in various ways, but, for the purposes of this text, we use the UN's definition, which defines water security as "the capacity of a population to safeguard sustainable access to adequate quantities of acceptable quality water for sustaining livelihoods, human well-being, and socio-economic development, for ensuring protection against water-borne pollution and water-related disasters, and for preserving ecosystems in a climate of peace and political stability" (Bigas 2013; UN-Water 2013). Figure 2.3.5 shows projected water scarcity in 2040 by country, and Figure 2.3.6 shows projected areas of global of physical and economic water scarcity by 2025.

The UN definition of water security seems to capture important complexity as well as the interrelatedness of the water usage–based variables, including water consumption scarcity due to drought, pollution, or disasters, each of which affects potability, agriculture/food, industry, energy, construction, services, transportation, and broad environmental stability, while still highlighting the potential for flood damage, deluge rainfall, and superstorms. The UN definition also captures the sometimes-overlooked socioeconomic aspects of fair, efficient distribution and policies impacting access to clean, sustainable supplies of water. In addition, the World Bank estimates that 4.5 billion people lack safely managed sanitation services and another 2.1 billion people lack daily access to safely managed drinking water (World Bank 2017). Further, water-related hazards of excess water, such as storms and floods, as well as hazards due to deficiency, such as droughts, are responsible for 9 out of 10 natural disasters (World Bank 2017). And as indicated above, climate change is acting as a major disturbance to the world's water supply and is subsequently expected to increase this risk as well as reduce the world's supply of freshwater (World Bank 2017).

Water scarcity develops from a wide variety of factors. Deteriorating water infrastructures, deforestation,

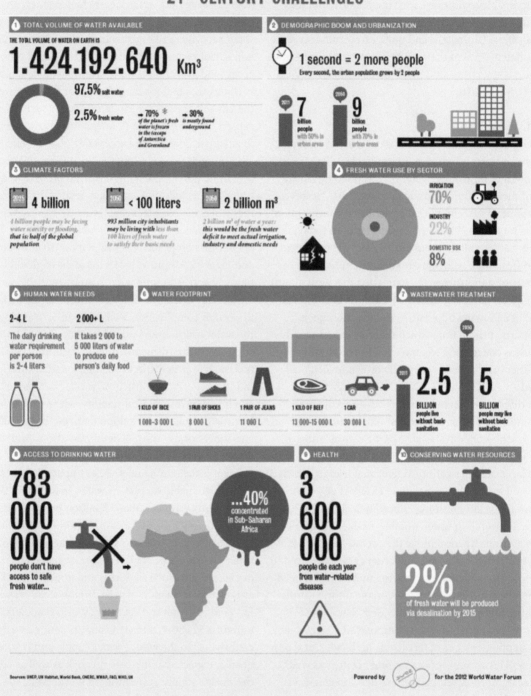

Figure 2.3.4. Water challenges in the twenty-first century.

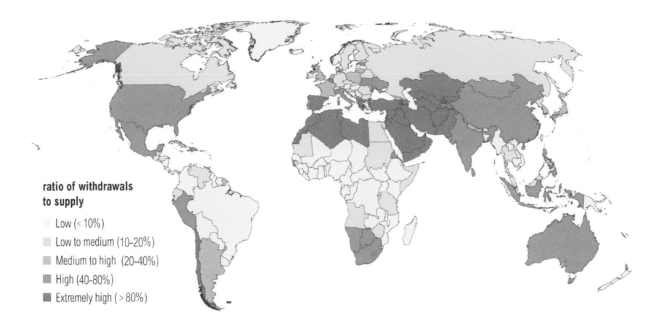

ratio of withdrawals
to supply

Low (< 10%)
Low to medium (10-20%)
Medium to high (20-40%)
High (40-80%)
Extremely high (> 80%)

NOTE: Projections are based on a business-as-usual scenario using SSP2 and RCP8.5.

Figure 2.3.5. Projected water scarcity in 2040 by country.

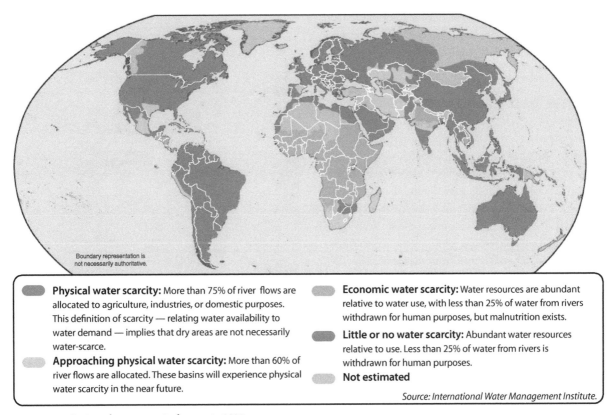

Physical water scarcity: More than 75% of river flows are allocated to agriculture, industries, or domestic purposes. This definition of scarcity — relating water availability to water demand — implies that dry areas are not necessarily water-scarce.

Approaching physical water scarcity: More than 60% of river flows are allocated. These basins will experience physical water scarcity in the near future.

Economic water scarcity: Water resources are abundant relative to water use, with less than 25% of water from rivers withdrawn for human purposes, but malnutrition exists.

Little or no water scarcity: Abundant water resources relative to use. Less than 25% of water from rivers is withdrawn for human purposes.

Not estimated

Source: International Water Management Institute.

Figure 2.3.6. Projected water scarcity by type in 2025.

privatization of water resources, freshwater salinization, overuse of underground aquifers, drought, and climate change all cause depletion in usable water supply. Further, climate change is increasingly implicated as a cause of severe storm-related flooding, deluge rainfall, landslides, erosion, and waterborne diseases. In addition, global warming is increasing the water vapor content of the atmosphere, which in turn acts as a warming "amplifier" (Science X 2014), thus reinforcing the warming cycle and exacerbating aspects of the water cycle that lead to water scarcity. Clearly, as mentioned earlier, water scarcity is directly linked to population increases as well. Counterintuitively, the relative rates of population growth are not reflected in the rates of change of water usage. For example, the world's population has tripled in the last 100 years, but water use has increased six fold. Part of this irregularity can be explained by how water is used by modern and modernizing society. Agriculture now consumes roughly 70% of the potable water used worldwide, while industrial use accounts for approximately 20%, but personal consumption only accounts for about 10%. As a result, predictably, as Earth's population continues to grow in the next 100 years, a disproportionate amount of water will be needed if we are to feed the world's growing population and support increasing industry and personal consumption.

2.3.4. THE WATER-POPULATION-FOOD-ENERGY NEXUS

Among the most important complex interrelationships with water issues is the nexus of population, food, and energy. This nexus highlights the need to address issues like family planning, social/cultural and religious ideology, diet, climate change, and water security at the same time. Even a cursory consideration of these topics reveals that food production is intimately tied to water access. Given that agriculture accounts for almost 70% of all water usage, as Earth's population grows, demand for potable water increases as well. Moreover, within the world of agriculture, raising plants and animals requires vastly different supplies of water.

As seen in Figure 2.3.7, water use seems very unevenly distributed across population centers, between the more-developed nations (such as the United States, Europe, Canada, Japan, South Korea, Australia) as well as between more- and less-developed nations (such as

Malawi, North Korea, Somalia, Ethiopia, Eritrea). Just like energy, Americans are by far the largest consumers. Water consumption is expected to soar further as less-developed populations seek to emulate a Western lifestyle of diet, travel, heating and cooling, etc. Exemplifying this point, consider that one kilogram of grain-fed beef needs at least 15 cubic meters of water, while a kilogram of cereals needs less than 3 cubic meters (Leon 2013). Hence, the more beef intensive a culture's diet, that is, the higher on the food chain a culture lives, the more water intensive the dietary demands are.

In addition, extraction of fossil fuel–based energy resources is increasingly water and energy intensive. Newer oil and gas techniques such as hydraulic fracturing (fracking) and tar sands extraction are extremely water intensive, depleting groundwater in places plagued by drought and water shortages already (in the United States, the Southwest and California, for instance). We will delve into this further in the following case study on tar sands later in this unit. For now, it is key to emphasize that

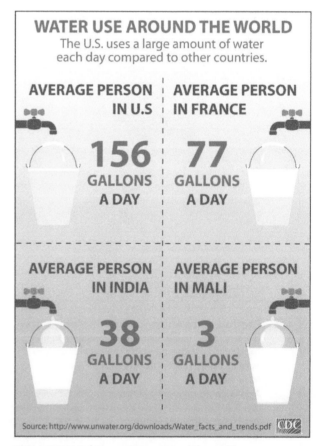

Figure 2.3.7. Relative water use around the world.

the drive to transition to sustainable renewable energy such as wind and solar will have positive effects on water security, since it will both reduce climate-disrupting greenhouse gas emissions from fossil fuels extraction and burning and also more sustainably reduce water usage and contamination in an era where water insecurity from that very climate change is rapidly worsening.

2.3.5. ISSUES RELATED TO WATER SECURITY

There are many significant issues that are related to the provision of water in developing societies. For example, growing urban populations are often most affected by water insecurity, and countries around the world are struggling to meet the increasing and competing needs of urban citizens, commerce, industry, energy production, and, of course, agriculture. In the process, natural environments are also being significantly impacted from pollution and human resource exploitation, damaging forests, grasslands, and other freshwater sinks, as well as fresh- and saltwater fisheries and ecosystems.

Part of the challenge of improving water security is that these systems are increasingly fragile, even as the number of people globally who are water insecure continues to grow. This is compounded by the fact that governmental policy responses "are slow, uneven and largely inadequate to address the nature and scale of the global challenges" even as "there is evidence to demonstrate that risks to drinking water security can be reduced even in the most difficult and challenging contexts" (Hope and Rouse 2013).

As mentioned throughout this chapter, agriculture uses more water than any other sector worldwide. Increased urbanization—in both the more- and less-developed nations—has been built on valuable agricultural land that has also intensified the need for irrigation and use of fertilizers, pesticides, and herbicides and the use of genetically altered seed stocks needed to increase yield per hectare. Increased yield per hectare is required as the amount of arable land has diminished with urbanization. As with all we have seen with water usage generally, climate change has disrupted water

cycles and has subsequently enhanced global food shortages and price spikes that have destabilized the economies and governments of less-developed countries where food represents a larger part of the incomes for most of the population.

Analysts note that both irrigated and rain-fed agricultural water sources will continue to be affected, disrupting the livelihoods of poor rural farmers, as well as urban populations' food security. Especially in less-developed countries, adaptation measures that build upon improved land and water management practices will be fundamental in boosting overall resilience to climate change. And this is not just to maintain food security: as we know from the water cycle, the continued integrity of land and water systems is essential for all economic uses of water (Turral et al. 2011). One study found approximately "5.7% of the global total land area has shifted toward warmer and drier climate types from 1950–2010, and significant changes include expansion of arid and high-latitude continental climate zones, shrinkage in polar and midlatitude continental climates" (Chan and Wu 2015).

Land use and development patterns have also had a major impact (recall the water cycle diagram in Figure 2.3.2). In cities such as Houston, Texas, and Bangalore, India,[1] resource-planning failures have reduced previously available water storage and increased the likelihood of damaging flood runoff. There is a great need for better rural and urban land- and water-use planning to increase supplies when possible but also to manage water resources more efficiently and fairly across all areas of demand.

Various industries, including construction and fossil fuels energy extraction (as noted), can be water intensive. In areas such as California, there were very public debates about water use for fracking (Cohen 2017), including controversies over contaminated fracking waste injection wells near aquifers that supplied freshwater for cities and agriculture. The bottled water industry has precipitated numerous policy conflicts and political protests around the world as it secured water rights (sometimes even monopolies) on various water sources

---

1. For example, in Bangalore, the center of India's tech industry, water is so scarce that water delivery cartels have emerged, drawing ever-diminishing aquifer supplies from the ground to supply businesses and residences.

that were otherwise used as city or regional public water systems. Well-publicized cases have emerged in Bolivia,[2] India, and Michigan, among others.

Other uses for water are for transportation of people and goods—as with canals, river systems, etc. Specifically, drought can severely impact these water sources and systems, and major waterways are likely to be disrupted by future climate-related changes. The Mississippi River, the Great Lakes shipping lanes, and other water transportation routes are each part of the water security for regions that rely on them for commerce, agricultural irrigation, drinking water, and other water uses. Europe has been the center of increasingly impacted river systems, particularly as both populations and water-use demands grow, and climate change portends significant changes in regional riverine ecosystems (Iglesias and Garrote 2015).

Often overlooked is the fact that most natural ecosystems need to have at least a minimum allowance of water to function. Humans rely on these ecosystems; excess water harvesting and/or land-use methods can have a detrimental effect on sensitive environmental systems such as wetlands and rivers. In drought-impacted western United States, the demands of agriculture and urban water have competed with allowing adequate flow in rivers and lakes,[3] affecting other water-use priorities, such as the lucrative recreational salmon migration, and the river systems overall. In coastal areas such as Florida, the excessive use of freshwater aquifers has encouraged saltwater intrusion. Conflicts between human and natural environmental water needs vary widely but are increasingly having unintended effects on other important systems besides water (see, e.g., Grantham et al. 2014).

2.3.6. THE GROWING CONFLUENCE OF CLIMATE CHANGE, ENVIRONMENTAL STRESSES, AND FOOD AND WATER INSECURITY

Climate change research indicates a very sobering reality in recent years: it is increasingly clear that Earth's ecological and biological systems are far more sensitive to the influence of greenhouse gases and other human-caused environmental perturbations than previously thought, such that the existence of human civilization is now in jeopardy [National Research Council (NRC) 2013; Durack et al. 2014; Mann 2014; Stanton et al. 2015]. Water access and security will be among the most important challenges for human climate adaptation and, by extension, global security among nations. Further, water security will continue to be influenced by alterations of natural ecosystems that are influenced by climate change, population growth, land use, resource exploitation, pollution patterns, globalization of capitalism, and other variables [Department of Defense (DoD) 2014a; IPCC 2014; NRC 2013].

The World Bank's conservative estimation is that by midcentury there could be a 20% global reduction in water availability because of climate change, and by 2100, absent climate mitigation activities, changes that could help prevent a disastrous global average temperature rise of 4°C, available freshwater could catastrophically decline by as much as 50% (World Bank 2014) even as the global population climbs to a projected 9 billion. The combination of water stresses and damage from (persistent) extreme weather could exacerbate risk of worldwide famine—especially if multiple regional crop failures from weather disasters coincide with water shortages. In the last decade, modeling projections by economic development analysts about both global warming and water pollution (from nitrogen and phosphorus fertilizer runoff into lakes, rivers, and oceans, in particular) have become more pessimistic. In addition, as floods that contaminate water supplies and destroy food crops and droughts increase in frequency and severity, many developing nations are facing major water shortages for consumption, agriculture, industry, and hydropower generation. Already in countries such as India, there are signs of looming water and food crisis; during the June and July dry months, that nation experiences frequent power outages and water shortages (Bhalla 2015).

The 2014 Department of Defense quadrennial defense review emphasized the threat-multiplying elements of human-caused environmental stressors (DoD 2014b, p. 8):

---

2. Most notably, the 1999–2000 "Cochabamba Water War," in Bolivia's third largest city, in which the municipal government ceded the city's water rights to a private corporation, which raised water rates significantly—leading to large-scale protests and eventual rescinding of the agreement.

3. Examples include the Colorado River basin, a major source of water for several western U.S. states (Castle 2014).

These changes, coupled with other global dynamics, including growing, urbanizing, more affluent populations, and substantial economic growth in India, China, Brazil, and other nations, will devastate homes, land, and infrastructure. Climate change may exacerbate water scarcity and lead to sharp increases in food costs. The pressures caused by climate change will influence resource competition while placing additional burdens on economies, societies, and governance institutions around the world. These effects can act collectively as threat multipliers. That is, they act to aggravate stressors abroad such as poverty, environmental degradation, political instability, and social tensions—conditions that can enable terrorist activity and other forms of violence.

2.3.7. WATER: ACCESS AND SECURITY

While not all flood disasters can be linked to climate change, examples of such include the 2010 floods in Pakistan, which covered 20% of the Pakistani state at its highest point, and the massive flood devastation from 2017's Hurricane Harvey on the U.S. Gulf Coast.

Water scarcity is a global threat multiplier. A prime example is the ongoing Syrian civil conflict, whose origins are directly linked to massive regional drought (Werrell et al. 2015). Indeed, global drought-related increases in food prices have substantially contributed to the civil disruption, creating one of the greatest refugee crises since World War II. Environmentally triggered social, economic, and political instability will be increasingly driven by locked-in water-related trends. In turn, water scarcity will continue to drive mass migration and displacement that has so clearly created havoc and hardship across the Middle East and Europe. Indeed, such chaos is expected even if climate change mitigation efforts succeed in keeping global average temperatures to 2°C below preindustrial levels in the next 80 years as expressed in the Paris Agreement [UN Framework Convention on Climate Change (UNFCCC) 2015]. We will discuss the devastation of emerging weather hazards further in unit 3; for now, suffice it to say that the links between security (food and energy), water, and climate change are clear.

2.3.8. CONCLUSIONS

Water is critical to human welfare. As a biogeochemical, water circulates through our biosphere, it connects all essential geochemicals and impacts essentially every aspect of modern living. As a result, water access is tied directly to (mitigated by) extraordinary events such as population, land use, food and energy production, and climate change. Critical food and water supply chain systems are increasingly prone to damage by climate change and extreme weather events. In turn, factors that perturb water access threaten food access and can cause widespread famine and ultimately can cause massive displacement of populations that become environmental refugees. The combination of the weather and climate disaster variables and human population dynamics will affect even the wealthiest countries' populations and imperil domestic and international security in multiple ways. In contrast, as water access improves, sources of conflict are expected to decline.

Water security is arguably the most important part of any future sustainable (and therefore peaceful) world. A water-secure world values—indeed requires—mindful and comprehensive management of critical supplies for consumption, agriculture, industry, recreation, and other positive uses and mitigates and adapts to the potential destructive power of water in the form of severe weather. Climate change, pollution, and rising water demand due to increased population and dietary changes all demand integrated water resource management on every continent and in every sector, including finance, health, energy, industry, urban and regional planning, agroindustry, tourism, and education.

As the Global Water Partnership (2017) notes, "A water secure world reduces poverty, advances education, and increases living standards. It is a world where there is an improved quality of life for all, especially for the most vulnerable—usually women and children—who benefit most from good water governance."

REFERENCES

Barbier, E., 2015: Water and growth in developing countries. *Handbook of Water Economics*., A. Dinar and K. Schwabe, Eds., Edward Elgar, 500–512.

Bhalla, N., 2015: World has not woken up to water crisis caused by climate change: IPCC head. Reuters, www.reuters.com/article/us-india-climatechange-water/world-has-not-woken-up-to-water-crisis-caused-by-climate-change-ipcc-head-idUSKBN0L71A420150203.

Bhattacharyya, A., and M. Werz, 2012: Climate change, migration, and conflict in southern Asia: Rising tensions and policy options across the subcontinent. Center for American Progress Rep., 84 pp., https://cdn.americanprogress.org/wp-content/uploads/2012/11/ClimateMigrationSubContinentReport_small.pdf.

Bigas, H., 2013: Water security and the global water agenda: A UN-Water analytical brief. UN-Water Rep., 47 pp., www.unwater.org/publications/water-security-global-water-agenda/.

Bradshaw, C. J. A., and B. W. Brook, 2014: Human population reduction is not a quick fix for environmental problems. *Proc. Natl. Acad. Sci. USA*, **111**, 162610–162615, https://doi.org/10.1073/pnas.1410465111.

Castle, S. L., B. F. Thomas, J. T. Reager, M. Rodell, S. C. Swenson, and J. S. Famiglietti, 2014: Groundwater depletion during drought threatens future water security of the Colorado River basin. *Geophys. Res. Lett.*, **41**, 5904–5911, https://doi.org/10.1002/2014GL061055.

Chan, D., and Q. Wu, 2015: Significant anthropogenic-induced changes of climate classes since 1950. *Sci. Rep.*, **5**, 13487, https://doi.org/10.1038/srep13487.

Cohen, J., 2017: The fracking debate. University of California, Santa Barbara, accessed, 4 April 2018, www.news.ucsb.edu/2017/017822/fracking-debate.

DoD, 2014a: DoD releases 2014 climate change adaptation roadmap. DoD, www.defense.gov/News/News-Releases/News-Release-View/Article/605221/.

——, 2014b: Quadrennial defense review 2014. DoD Rep., 88 pp., http://archive.defense.gov/pubs/2014_Quadrennial_Defense_Review.pdf.

Durack, P. J., P. J. Gleckler, F. W. Landerer, and K. E. Taylor, 2014: Quantifying underestimates of long-term upper-ocean warming. *Nat. Climate Change*, **4**, 999–1005, https://doi.org/10.1038/nclimate2389.

Foreign Policy, 2014: 2014 fragile states index. Foreign Policy, http://foreignpolicy.com/fragile-states-2014/.

Gledhill, R., D. Hamza-Goodacre, and P. L. Low, 2013: Business not as usual: Tackling the impact of climate change on supply chain risk. Resilience, PwC Rep., 15–20, www.pwc.com/gx/en/governance-risk-compliance-consulting-services/resilience/publications/pdfs/issue3/business_not_as_usual.pdf.

Global Water Partnership, 2017: The water challenge. Global Water Partnership, https://www.gwp.org/en/About/why/the-water-challenge.

Grantham, T. E., M. Mezzatesta, D. A. Newburn, and A. M. Merenlender, 2014 Evaluating tradeoffs between environmental flow protections and agricultural water security. *River Res. Appl.*, **30**, 315–328, https://doi.org/10.1002/rra.2637.

Halligan, L., 2013: Rising food prices will reap a bitter harvest. Telegraph, accessed 26 March 2013, www.telegraph.co.uk/finance/comment/liamhalligan/9782815/Rising-food-prices-will-reap-a-bitter-harvest.html.

Harden, J. D., 2017: Weather service confirms a new record of 64 inches of rain fell during Harvey. Houston Chronicle, www.chron.com/about/article/Weather-service-confirms-64-inches-of-rain-fell-12233072.php.

Hope, R., and M. Rouse, 2013: Risks and responses to universal drinking water security. *Philos. Trans. Roy. Soc.*, **371A**, 20120417, https://doi.org/10.1098/rsta.2012.0417.

Iglesias, A., and L. Garrote, 2015: Adaptation strategies for agricultural water management under climate change in Europe. *Agric. Water Manage.*, **155**, 113–124, https://doi.org/10.1016/j.agwat.2015.03.014.

IPCC, 2014: *Climate Change 2014: Synthesis Report.* IPCC, 151 pp.

Kiers, E. T., R. R. Leakey, A.-M. Izac, J. A. Heinemann, E. Rosenthal, D. Nathan, and J. Jiggins, 2008: Agriculture at a crossroads. *Science*, **320**, 320–321, https://doi.org/10.1126/science.1158390.

Kug, J.-S., J.-H. Jeong, Y.-S. Jang, B.-M. Kim, C. K. Folland, S.-K. Min, and S.-W. Son, 2015: Two distinct influences of Arctic warming on cold winters over North America and East Asia. *Nat. Geosci.*, **8**, 759–762, https://doi.org/10.1038/ngeo2517.

Lelieveld, J., Y. Proestos, P. Hadjinicolaou, M. Tanarhte, E. Tyrlis, and G. Zittis, 2016: Strongly increasing heat extremes in the Middle East and North Africa (MENA) in the 21st century. *Climatic Change*, **137**, 245–260, https://doi.org/10.1007/s10584-016-1665-6.

Leon, S. M., 2013: *Sustainability in Supply Chain Management Casebook: Applications in SCM.* Pearson Education, 316 pp.

Maddocks, A., R. S. Young, and P. Reig, 2015: Ranking the world's most water-stressed countries in 2040. World Resources Institute, www.wri.org/blog/2015/08/ranking-world%E2%80%99s-most-water-stressed-countries-2040.

Mann, M. E., 2014: Earth will cross the danger threshold by 2036. Scientific American, accessed 4 April 2018, www.scientificamerican.com/article/earth-will-cross-the-climate-danger-threshold-by-2036/.

Mulligan, G., 2018: Will Cape Town be the first city to run out of water? BBC, www.bbc.com/news/business-42626790.

National Intelligence Council, 2012: Global trends 2030: Alternative worlds. National Intelligence Council Rep., 160 pp., https://www.dni.gov/files/documents/GlobalTrends_2030.pdf.

NRC, 2013: Abrupt impacts of climate change: Anticipating surprises. National Academy of Sciences Rep., 4 pp., http://dels.nas.edu/resources/static-assets/materials-based-on-reports/reports-in-brief/abrupt-climate-change-brief-FINAL-web.pdf.

Perez, I., and T. Stecker, 2013: Climate change and rising food prices heightened Arab Spring. Scientific American, https://www.scientificamerican.com/article/climate-change-and-rising-food-prices-heightened-arab-spring/.

Rice, D., 2015: Intolerable' heat waves forecast for Persian Gulf. USA Today, www.usatoday.com/story/weather/2015/10/26/heat-waves-persian-gulf-climate-change-global-warming/74625754/.

Risky Business Project, 2015: Heat in the heartland: Climate change and economic risk in the Midwest. Risky Business Project Rep., 58 pp., https://riskybusiness.org/site/assets/uploads/2015/09/RBP-Midwest-Report-WEB-1-26-15.pdf.

Science X, 2014: New study confirms water vapor as global warming amplifier. Phys.org, accessed 6 April 2018, https://phys.org/news/2014-07-vapor-global-amplifier.html.

Sly, L., 2015: As tragedies shock Europe, a bigger refugee crisis looms in the Middle East. Washington Post, 29 August, www.washingtonpost.com/world/middle_east/as-tragedies-shock-europe-a-bigger-refugee-crisis-looms-in-the-middle-east/2015/08/29/3858b284-9c15-11e4-86a3-1b56f64925f6_story.html?utm_term=.d4dcc75200bb.

Stanton, J. C., K. T. Shoemaker, R. G. Pearson, and H. R. Akçakaya, 2015: Warning times for species extinctions due to climate change. Global Change Biol., 21, 1066–1077, https://doi.org/10.1111/gcb.12721.

Steinbruner, J. D., P. C. Stern, and J. L. Husbands, Eds., 2013: Climate and Social Stress: Implications for Security Analysis. National Academies Press, 252 pp., https://doi.org/10.17226/14682.

Turral, H., J. J. Burke, and J.-M. Faurès, 2011: Climate change, water and food security. Food and Agriculture Organization Water Rep. 36, 200 pp.

UNFCCC, 2015: Adoption of the Paris Agreement. UNFCCC Rep., 32 pp.

UNHCR, 2009: Climate change could become the biggest driver of displacement: UNHCR chief. UNHCR, www.unhcr.org/news/latest/2009/12/4b2910239/climate-change-become-biggest-driver-displacement-unhcr-chief.html.

UN-Water, 2013: Water security and the global water agenda: A UN-Water analytical brief. UN University Rep., 47 pp., www.unwater.org/publications/water-security-global-water-agenda/.

USDA NRCS, 2018: Ogallala Aquifer initiative. USDA NRCS, www.nrcs.usda.gov/wps/portal/nrcs/detailfull/national/programs/initiatives/?cid=stelprdb1048809.

USGS, 2016: The water cycle: Freshwater storage. USGS, https://water.usgs.gov/edu/watercyclefreshstorage.html.

Werrell, C. E., and F. Femia, Eds., and T. Sternberg, 2015: Did we see it coming? State fragility, climate vulnerability, and the uprisings in Syria and Egypt. SAIS Rev. Int. Aff., 35 (1), 29–46.

Wirsing, R. G., 2013: The Brahmaputra: Water hotspot in Himalayan Asia. Global Water Forum, www.globalwaterforum.org/2012/06/02/the-brahmaputra-water-hotspot-in-himalayan-asia/.

Woo, S. H., B. M. Kim, and J. S. Kug, 2015: Temperature variation over East Asia during the lifecycle of weak stratospheric polar vortex. J. Climate, 28, 5857–5872, https://doi.org/10.1175/JCLI-D-14-00790.1.

World Bank, 2014: Turn down the heat: Confronting the new climate normal. World Bank Rep., pp. 1–34.

——, 2017: Water: Overview. World Bank, 4 April 2018, www.worldbank.org/en/topic/water/overview.

2.4

CASE STUDY: ISIS OIL LOOTING AND ENVIRONMENTAL SECURITY IN IRAQ AND SYRIA

Melinda Negrón-Gonzales

2.4.1. OIL AS ESSENTIAL

Oil was coined the "black gold" that enabled the so-called Islamic State [or Islamic State in Iraq and Syria (ISIS) or Islamic State in Iraq and the Levant (ISIL)] to become one of the wealthiest insurgent groups in modern history. Oil products have been the backbone of the war economy in Syria, and ISIS capitalized on this by strategically capturing key areas with oil resources in Syria and also Iraq. By 2015, the group was reportedly generating about $40 million per month from oil sales (Faulconbridge and Saul 2015), though estimates varied widely. This sizable and steady revenue stream allowed ISIS to pay its fighters well, which in turn served as a valuable recruitment tool.

As such, by 2015 there was an international chorus of analysts and policy makers who argued that disrupting ISIS's ability to extract and sell oil was a necessary step to ultimately defeating the group. These experts presented different ways to accomplish this objective, including sealing the Turkish border to curtail cross-border sales and conducting airstrikes on oil infrastructure in Iraq and Syria. After initial hesitation to bomb oil wells, refineries, and transport vehicles, in late 2015, the U.S.-led international coalition stepped up its bombing campaign against these targets. Critics warned, however, that bombing oil

installations could have dire long-term consequences on the environment, people's health, and postconflict reconstruction efforts (Kirkpatrick and Al-Jawoshy 2014). That is, the cure could be worse than the disease, posing grave long-term threats to the well-being of the local population and to the likelihood of building a durable peace. Conversely, proponents of bombing underscored the need to defeat ISIS as quickly as possible to prevent further bloodshed, displacement, and ISIS-caused ecological destruction. For proponents, any environmental collateral damage that resulted from airstrikes was a necessary price to pay to ultimately crush the group.

This chapter explores the dynamics surrounding ISIS's booming oil industry, especially during the height of its territorial conquest in Syria and Iraq between 2014 and 2017. It examines the efforts by the U.S.-led international coalition and other actors to strike a balance between preventing ISIS from extracting and selling oil by bombing oil facilities on the one hand while trying to avoid widespread environmental destruction on the other. The chapter begins with a look at the scope and impact of ISIS looting and smuggling of oil, followed by a discussion of the measures taken by the international community to stop these activities and the dearth of international laws to guide these efforts. Although ISIS was militarily defeated in Iraq by 2018, it still hangs on to small pockets of territory in Syria. As such, it has been exceedingly difficult for analysts to assess the environmental impact of ISIS's activities in Syria, where most of the group's oil resources were located and where most bombings by the U.S.-led coalition against such targets were conducted. What is clear, however, is that the sheer number of ISIS-controlled energy resources, coupled with its practice of setting fire to oil wells as it has retreated, will have a lasting impact on the long-term environmental and human security of people in and around Syria and Iraq.

2.4.2. ISIS OIL LOOTING AND SMUGGLING

During times of war, the capture of areas rich in natural resources enables militant groups to grow and expand territorial control. ISIS is merely the latest in a long line of militant groups that have generated enormous sums of money through the pillaging and trafficking of natural resources during wartime. Other examples include Charles Taylor's rebel forces of the National Patriotic Front of Liberia, which controlled timber and mineral resources in both Liberia and Sierra Leone (UN Security Council 2005), and various rebel groups in the Democratic Republic of Congo, which hijacked control over the diamond trade. In fact, according to the United Nations Environment Program (UNEP), 40% of all intrastate conflicts in the last 60 years were linked to the appropriation or control of natural resources (UNEP 2015a).[1] Moreover, the presence of oil and gas reserves, specifically, tends to prolong armed conflict (Lujala 2010). Although neither Iraq's nor Syria's civil war was caused by a scramble to control oil resources, it is clear that militants' ability to capture these resources strengthened these groups, especially ISIS, thereby prolonging the conflicts in both countries.

Different estimates place oil as the biggest or second biggest revenue base for ISIS. In mid-2015, the U.S. Treasury Department estimated revenue from oil to be $40 million per month, a figure that fell to $4 million per month by late 2017 as the group lost much of its oil-rich territory (Johnston 2017). The group captured its first oil field in Syria in 2013 when it strategically withdrew from northwest Syria to the oil-rich eastern region. By 2014, it controlled 60% of the oil-producing resources in eastern Syria (Al-Khatteeb and Gordts 2014). Although Syria was not a major oil exporter before the outbreak of civil war in 2011, petroleum products composed about 45% of its exports and about 25% of government revenues (Humud et al. 2015). Consequently, the Islamic State's capture of these resources dealt a major blow to the Syrian government's revenue base. This was not the case in Iraq, however. Despite ISIS's capture of Mosul and nearby oilfields, it was never able to control a significant portion of Iraq's oil infrastructure. Iraq has the world's second largest oil reserves and most of the state's oil assets are in the southern region beyond the reach of ISIS, which was only able to control swaths of territory in the northern region. Hence, even at its peak, ISIS controlled only a negligible amount of Iraq's overall oil output. Likewise, ISIS-directed trafficking had only a minor impact on international markets (Marcel 2014).

Over time, ISIS has trafficked different types of oil. Refined oil has been sold and used to power vehicles and generators in ISIS territory, and crude oil has been sold locally and across borders, especially in Turkey. Smuggling across the Syria–Turkey border and Iraq–Turkey border has long been done by trucks, donkeys, or makeshift pipelines through desolate areas of desert or mountainous terrain as well as through legal crossings. In fact, Turkey's border with Iraq has been a site for illicit cross-border oil sales by Iraqi Kurds and by Saddam Hussein's government since the 1990s when it

---

1. Much of the scholarship on the relationship between natural resources and conflicts has focused on questions of causality: Does resource scarcity contribute to the outbreak of violent conflict? Or does resource abundance contribute to the occurrence of armed conflict?—the so-called resource curse. Scholars have also addressed the management of resources during violent conflicts and post conflict reconstruction. See Conca, K and Wallace, J. 2009: Environment and Peacebuilding in War-torn Societies: Lessons from the UN Environment Programme's Experience with Post conflict Assessment, in *Global Governance: A Review of Multilateralism and International Organizations*: Vol. 15, No. 4, pp. 485–504.; Collier, P and Hoeffler, A. 2012: High-value natural resources, development, and conflict: Channels of causation, in *High-Value Natural Resources and Peacebuilding*, ed. P. Lujala and S. A. Rustad. London: Earthscan.; De Koning, R. 2008: Resource-Conflict Links in Sierra Leone and the Democratic Republic of Congo. Stockholm: Stockholm International Peace Research Institute.

used Turkey as a conduit to circumvent international sanctions. These preexisting and well-established smuggling networks in Iraq and Syria have served ISIS well. Seasoned middlemen of the illicit oil trade know how to avoid detection and use hubs in Turkey to transport oil destined for international markets to Ceyhan, a major tanker shipping port on the Turkish coast (RadioFree Europe 2015).

As ISIS's power grew in 2014, Turkey received the brunt of global opprobrium, from friends and foes, for not doing enough to block oil smuggling across its border. By mid-2014, Washington's frustration over Turkey's seemingly half-hearted attempts to staunch the flow of illegal oil was clearly visible, though the Obama administration was careful to avoid linking Turkish officials to ISIS smuggling operations. The Russians were not as remissive. After Turkey shot down a Russian jet in Syria, the Russian Defense Ministry not only claimed to have clear evidence of ISIS "trade routes" running through Turkey, it also implicated Turkish officials, including President Erdogan, of collusion with ISIS oil smugglers. Nevertheless, the Brookings Institution had already reported a year prior that cross-border flows through Turkey were exaggerated and that ISIS was actually selling most of its product in Iraq and Syria (Lister 2014). Moreover, despite strong allegations against Turkey, clear evidence of collusion between the Turkish state and ISIS never materialized, although numerous journalistic investigations revealed rampant corruption among Turkish border guards who were indeed allowing a wide range of illegal goods (and people) to cross in and out of Turkey. By mid- to late 2015, persistent international pressure (and a spate of ISIS attacks in Turkey) led to an uptick in Turkish border patrol agents, random searches, and aerial patrols (Arango and Schmitt 2015).

Turkey's enhanced border security may have reduced sales to external actors but did little to prevent ISIS from selling to local clients, and there have been plenty willing to do business with ISIS. ISIS has sold much of its oil to other rebel groups and even to the Syrian government. Indeed, before Syrian government forces were able to win back large swaths of territory in 2017, much of Syria's energy infrastructure was controlled by rebel groups, forcing the Syrian government to procure deals with militants, including ISIS, in order to meet its energy

needs (RadioFree Europe 2015). Accordingly, as reported by the Financial Action Task Force (FATF),[2] the Assad regime has permitted banks to continue servicing their branches in rebel-held cities because those branches are used by the Syrian government to transfer payment for oil and gas to rebels. Moreover, the Assad regime, like ISIS, has also run oil and gas smuggling networks around the country. This differs considerably from the Iraqi government's approach before ISIS was defeated in Iraq. Because much less of Iraq's energy infrastructure was controlled by ISIS even at its peak, Baghdad did not need to make deals with militants and instructed banks in ISIS-held areas to cease operations (FATF 2015).

As noted, ISIS has taken advantage of historic smuggling routes between Tukey, Iraq, and Syria and has exploited local actors' needs for energy resources. It has also benefited greatly from the sheer desperation of ordinary citizens who have participated, mostly as transporters and refiners, in the illicit oil trade. This includes veteran smugglers as well as newcomers who have relied on the income after the collapse of the formal Syrian economy. Because the black market for oil forms the backbone of the complex war economy in Syria (less so in Iraq), it is integral to the survival and well-being of not only rebel forces and Syrian government loyalists, but also Syrians caught in the middle. Indeed, insofar as the ISIS caliphate was a de facto state, it controlled the fate of millions of innocent civilians for whom it provided public goods for several years. A robust black market in energy resources was not only inevitable but necessary to ensure the survival of captured peoples. Even as pro-government and anti-government forces have captured almost all ISIS territory in Syria, the lucrative sale of stolen oil continues under various state and non-state actors.

2.4.3. IMPACT ON ENVIRONMENTAL AND HUMAN SECURITY

Armed conflicts inevitably have deleterious effects on the environment and often threaten people's livelihoods, health, and security long after fighting has ceased. The situation is worse, however, when state or non-state actors deliberately use environmental destruction as a weapon of war, as ISIS has. The environmental foot-

---

2. FATF is the multinational body that develops and promotes policies to counter illicit financial activities.

print of the ongoing conflicts in Iraq and Syria, when examined narrowly to focus on ISIS oil extraction and trafficking as well as airstrikes to curb extraction and trafficking, is difficult to assess while hostilities continue in Syria (there is more information on Iraq). Still, it is abundantly clear that ISIS activities and anti-ISIS operations have negatively impacted the environmental and human security of people in the region. Specifically, ISIS's primitive oil extraction methods, mismanagement of refineries, creation of ad hoc refineries, and burning of oil wells have exposed individuals and the environment to numerous toxins, threatening long-term ecological vitality and public health (Relief Web 2018).

Conditions in Syria make it nearly impossible to adequately evaluate the status on the ground, though preliminary reports are bleak. Whereas Syrian oil export facilities have remained largely under state control, oil-producing areas have been held mostly by rebel groups, especially ISIS during its heyday. Because international oil companies evacuated personnel at petroleum installations, there was a shortage of trained workers. Despite having its own tankers and developing relationships with locals to help with extraction (Solomon et al. 2016), the lack of knowledgeable personnel in ISIS-held territories led to messy extraction of crude oil, especially before ISIS was able to recruit engineers. This caused the release of toxins into the atmosphere and soil, endangering groundwater. One of the biggest problems has been the refinement of crude oil in regular and improvised refineries. Burning crude oil in open pits that produce limited yields of poor-quality product has left ISIS territory, according to one observer, looking like an "alien planet" (Thompson 2015). Both primitive oil refining and airstrikes against ISIS-controlled refineries release pollutants that are heavily regulated during peacetime.

A report titled "Amidst the debris" written by analysts at PAX organization attempted to estimate the scope of damage to critical infrastructure, such as oil refineries and installations, and approximate environmental damage (data were sparse, so the study was more hypothetical than empirical). Generally, it is well established that primitive oil extraction, refinement, and airstrikes generate significant air pollution and contaminate soil and water, thereby producing long-term negative health consequences. The fires that ensue and their toxic fumes further contribute to air pollution, landscape degradation, and the depletion of arable land. The report also under-

scores the more dangerous effects of Syria's heavy crude, which unlike Iraq's light crude, has a higher proportion of potentially hazardous contaminants, such as heavy metals. The density of heavy crude and its toxic constituents make it a particularly problematic soil and aquifer contaminant. Moreover, according to the report, doctors in Syria reported widespread symptoms associated with exposure to noxious gases (Zwijnenburg and Pas 2015).

To make matters worse, ISIS has followed a scorched-earth policy, setting off explosives to torch oil wells, as it has retreated in both Iraq and Syria. For example, in early 2016, UNOSAT (the operational satellite application program of the UN Institute for Training and Research) detected fires at several oil wells around Qayyarah, Iraq (which ISIS had captured in 2014). Later that year as Iraqi armed forces advanced to retake the oil field, ISIS set fire to 20 oil wells. Three other oil-producing areas in Iraq experienced the same tactic as ISIS retreated: the Hamrin Mountains, Baiji oil refinery, and Kirkuk. Such fires can last for months—and these did. ISIS fighters also filled trenches with crude oil and set them on fire to block the visibility of anti-ISIS forces. These fires emit black carbon and toxic fumes into the atmosphere, and the gas that lingers even after the flames have been extinguished can be deadly (Thomas 2017). Specifically, according to researchers at PAX,

> Oil fires release harmful substances into the air, such as sulphur dioxide, nitrogen dioxide, carbon monoxide, polycyclic aromatic hydrocarbons (PAHs), particulate matter and metals such as nickel, vanadium and lead. The nitrogen and sulphur compounds are associated with acid rain, which can have a negative impact on vegetation and lead to the acidification of soils. Furthermore, these substances can cause severe short-term health effects, especially for people with pre-existing respiratory problems (Zwijnenburg and Postma 2017, p. 9).

The effects of burning of oil fields in Kuwait and Iraq in the 1991 Gulf War illustrated how these tactics can have dire long-term consequences on human security. Indeed, after decades of war, Iraq has become one of the world's most contaminated countries (Yakupitiyage 2015). ISIS has repeated these tactics in Syria, too, where it has lost most of its territory.

Anti-ISIS forces (U.S. and Russia coalitions), in their attempt to degrade and defeat ISIS, have destroyed or damaged hundreds of oil targets, including modular refineries and transport vehicles. This has also contributed to high levels of pollution. The biggest challenge for anti-ISIS coalitions has been to strike at the heart of ISIS's financial assets without further destabilizing the lives of the millions trapped in ISIS-held territory, or completely obliterating Iraq's and Syria's energy infrastructure, or creating environmental catastrophes that will endanger people for years to come. Anti-ISIS airstrikes on oil installations, such as mobile refineries, rather than oil fields have mitigated the harmful effects of the bombings, although it depends on where the mobile refineries are located. Some mobile refineries are located near agricultural areas or residential neighborhoods. Moreover, even precision attacks on regular refineries that leave intact some parts to reduce harmful effects can result in contamination.

There is another, nonenvironmental, negative impact of anti-ISIS airstrikes—the reality is that black market oil not only profits ISIS and other rebel groups but also keeps civilians alive. For example, diesel is widely used for generators that power civilians' homes and local businesses and is used by farmers to power agricultural machinery. Targeting and destroying or compromising makeshift refineries reduces oil supply and subsequently could cause the local price of diesel to skyrocket, which makes it even more difficult for civilians to afford it.

The effects of ISIS's scorched-earth policy and anti-ISIS airstrikes may also determine the success or failure of postconflict efforts. Severe environmental damage and the destruction of natural resource infrastructure make postconflict stabilization and reconstruction efforts extremely challenging. Public health crises and ecological damage to residential and agricultural areas are very costly to governments in postconflict countries. An added concern is that, in the haste to rebuild damaged oil infrastructure after conflict has ended, shoddy reconstruction may further damage the environment, which may serve as a catalyst for even more health and financial crises down the road, and that could in turn facilitate more armed conflict. In short, as stated in a UNEP report on protecting the environment during armed conflict, "There can be no durable peace if the natural resources that sustain livelihoods are damaged, degraded, and destroyed" (Mrema et al. 2009, p. 4).

2.4.4. INTERNATIONAL EFFORTS TO STOP ISIS'S OIL LOOTING AND SMUGGLING

There have been several nonmilitary methods proffered for disrupting ISIS's ability to profit from oil. Enhanced border security has been seen as paramount to curb smuggling. Turkey's and Jordan's measures to better patrol their borders not only reduced the flow of illicit oil, they also diminished opportunities for ISIS to levy taxes on commercial truck traffic (U.S. Department of the Treasury 2016). Another method to prevent ISIS from profiting from oil has been to raise international awareness and set guidelines and binding resolutions to which states must comply. Accordingly, the UN Security Council (UNSC) has addressed the problem of ISIS financing, including its ability to amass millions through oil sales, by passing several binding resolutions. For example, in 2014 UN Security Council Resolution S/RES/2195 called upon member states, "to collect, analyze and exchange information, including law enforcement and intelligence information" to "prevent terrorism benefiting from transnational organized crime" and to share information as appropriate. However, the unanimous adoption of UNSC Resolution 2253 (2015) the following year was a response to inadequate compliance with previous resolutions—1267 (1999), 1989 (2011), and 2199 (2015)—and suggests these rules have not been as impactful as anticipated (UN 2015). Another measure taken by the international community was the creation in January 2015 of the Counter-ISIL Finance Group (CIFG; which the United States co-chairs with Italy and Saudi Arabia). Its historic joint meeting in February 2016 with the Financial Action Task Force aimed to develop a greater understanding of how ISIS raises and moves funds, with the goal of devising more effective measures to dry up its revenue streams (Glaser 2016).[3]

Despite these efforts to address transnational transactions, it was the *internal* demand for oil in Syria and Iraq that fed ISIS coffers during its peak years and that continues to buttress the robust black market for natural

---

3. For a comprehensive index of international and regional efforts to combat terrorism, see Harvard Law School Program on International Law and Armed Conflict (PILAC; at https://pilac.law.harvard.edu/international-counterterrorism-efforts-index#international-counterterrorism-efforts-welcome).

resources. This reality culminated in heightened pressure in 2015 to use armed force to curtail looting and smuggling inside Iraq and Syria. The anti-ISIS, U.S.-led coalition responded to pressure by ramping up airstrikes against ISIS oil targets and, following the 2015 downing of a Russian passenger airliner by an ISIS sympathizer, so did the Russians. In December 2015, Russia's defense ministry reported that it destroyed dozens of refineries and hundreds of transport vehicles, particularly along the Iraq–Syria border controlled by ISIS (Russia Ministry of Defense 2015; Telegraph 2015). Russia, like the United States, has continually targeted ISIS oil production, storage, processing, and transportation hubs for several years although not nearly as much as the U.S.-led coalition, which has been the leading force against the group (Ciziri 2017).

Though some of the earliest U.S. airstrikes against ISIS oil installations took place in the Deir ez Zor region of eastern Syria in 2014, it was not until 2015, as ISIS expanded its territory and began to increase attacks against Western targets, that the U.S.-led international coalition began to take more aggressive action against the group's energy assets, including key elements of its oil supply chain such as oil tanker trucks. Operation Tidal Wave II, which stepped up attacks on oil targets, was launched on 21 October and by November 2015, coalition airstrikes had destroyed hundreds of oil refineries and oil tankers along the Syria–Iraq border and elsewhere (Miklaszewski 2015).[4] Obama administration officials were careful to explain early on that the primary objective was to prevent ISIS from utilizing these refineries to make money; hence, refineries were not completely destroyed. In the words of one U.S. Defense Department official during a postoperation briefing (U.S. Department of Defense 2014):

> We're trying real hard to be precise in these attacks. It wasn't about obliterating the refineries off the face of the map. It was about degrading their [ISIS's] ability to use these refineries, them themselves. . . . These refineries were in place before ISIL came along. And assuming that Syria gets to a point where it's better governed, you know, we'd like to preserve the flexibility for those refineries to still contribute to a stable economy in what we hope will be a stable country when the Assad regime is not in control anymore.

The briefing underscores the Department's concern over Syria's energy security in the postconflict period. However, the official's response when probed to explain the environmental impact of the airstrikes was rather vague and circumspect.

In addition to wreaking havoc on the environment, some analysts argued before and during the uptick in anti-ISIS airstrikes that this method was ineffectual and often led to even more dangerous refinement methods. Chris Harmer, senior analyst with the Institute for the Study of War, asserted that the airstrikes, while "tactically spectacular" were "strategically insignificant" because they cannot change the fact that ISIS controls the oil fields and the destruction of small oil refineries will simply culminate in more microrefineries located in residential neighborhoods (Collard and Whitlock 2014). The Financial Action Task Force reached a similar conclusion in a 2015 report (FATF 2015), and a subsequent investigation by the Financial Times also suggested the group began to rely more heavily on even more rudimentary refineries created by locals (Solomon et al. 2016).

These criticisms notwithstanding, many policy makers and analysts have concluded the bombing campaigns considerably disrupted ISIS's ability to refine and sell oil products. Meanwhile debates about environmental damage have receded into the background, eclipsed by discussions about refugee flows, among other things. By July 2016, U.S. officials noted ISIS's near collapse of its oil smuggling in Iraq, forcing the group to cut salaries and services. In fact, its smuggling in Iraq was reduced by at least 90% by 2016, according to security and municipal officials (Rasheed 2016). It is important, however, to once again distinguish between conditions on the ground in Syria and Iraq. The situation in Iraq has differed because there have been fewer ISIS-controlled wells and refineries and because the U.S. footprint in Iraq has been significantly greater than in Syria. By May 2016, the United States estimated that ISIS revenue in Iraq and Syria had been reduced to $250 million a year (Rasheed 2016). Analysts who predicted that disabling its capacity to amass a small fortune from oil pillaging and smuggling would be a critical component of victory against ISIS have been vindicated as the group struggles in 2018 to hold onto the shrinking vestiges of its short-lived proto-state.

---

4. For up-to-date accounts on airstrikes, see U.S. Department of Defense (www.defense.gov/OIR/Airstrikes/).

The bombing campaigns against ISIS's energy assets have indeed successfully destroyed sources of revenue and have disrupted smuggling networks, but at what cost? Environmental nongovernmental organizations have drawn attention to the harmful effects of bombing oil resources and called on the U.S.-led coalition to limit airstrikes against oil infrastructure. Nevertheless, ISIS's barbaric attacks hardened convictions that ISIS needed to be defeated as soon as possible, whatever the costs. In addition, despite the detrimental long-term effects of airstrikes against petroleum installations, there exist few legal constraints to limit the use of airstrikes on such targets. Hence, at the heart of the debate about how to prevent ISIS oil pillaging and smuggling is a more general debate about how to prevent rebels in any conflict from engaging in environmentally calamitous activities without further threatening environmental security.

There is a range of international law that covers protection of the environment during conflict—international humanitarian law (IHL), international criminal law (ICL), international environmental law (IEL), and international human rights law (HRL). These, in theory, could have been applied to the conflicts in Iraq and Syria. There are, however, some caveats which explain why these international regimes have served as rather weak disincentives to anti-ISIS forces (of course, international laws have absolutely no deterrent effect over ISIS, which does not perceive itself to be beholden to any international laws). Some of these legal frameworks are quite underdeveloped, and there is a dearth of pertinent case law because there have been so few cases tried on environmental protection during conflict. Moreover, monitoring conditions during war is exceedingly difficult and enforcement of international law is a perennial problem. Indeed, the international community has been woefully ineffectual when it comes to holding states accountable for environmental damage incurred during conflict, not to mention other serious war crimes. Holding non-state actors, such as ISIS, accountable for environmental destruction is even more problematic and less likely. After all, even individual accountability for specific ISIS leaders accused of committing atrocity crimes committed (genocide, ethnic cleansing, crimes against humanity and war crimes) would require a UN Security Council referral to the International Criminal Court. If the international community has not yet pursued a referral to the ICC for genocidal acts against

the Yazidi, for example, it is highly unlikely that it would attempt to go after ISIS for environmental destruction.

Moreover, ISIS and other rebel groups are not the only entities that tend to escape accountability for ecological destruction during war. The likelihood of the United States or another great power being held responsible for environmental damage due to airstrikes on oil targets, or something else, is perhaps even lower than the prospect of ISIS leaders facing penalties for ecological destruction. Great powers' veto power in the UN Security Council shields them and their allies from international scrutiny and legal action. Lastly, most international laws that cover environmental protection were written for international rather than internal conflicts, resulting in a legal vacuum for civil wars such as Syria's (Mrema et al. 2009). In short, it is unlikely that either ISIS, other rebels or even state actors will be held accountable in international courts for environmental damage that occurred during the conflicts in Iraq or Syria. Despite vociferous calls for environmental justice from some environmentalists, there simply is not a permanent international mechanism to monitor legal infringements and address compensation claims for environmental damage incurred during an international armed conflict.

Moreover, there has been inadequate study of the existing rules of armed conflict and how they relate to environmental security. This is this gradually changing. For instance, a 2009 UNEP report provided an inventory of international law protecting the environment during armed conflict. It concluded that,

> Articles 35 and 55 of Additional Protocol I to the 1949 Geneva Conventions do not effectively protect the environment during armed conflict due to the stringent and imprecise threshold required to demonstrate damage: While these two articles prohibit "widespread, long-term and severe" damage to the environment, all three conditions must be proven for a violation to occur. In practice, this triple cumulative standard is nearly impossible to achieve, particularly given the imprecise definitions for the terms "widespread," "long-term" and "severe" (UNEP 2009, p. 5).

In addition, the report stated, "[T]here is no standard UN definition of what constitutes a "conflict resource" and when sanctions should be applied to stop illegal exploitation and trade of such resources." (UNEP 2009, p. 5).

Another UN study was conducted as ISIS tore across Iraq and Syria. The International Law Commission (ILC) assigned a special rapporteur in 2013 to coordinate a 4-year study to identify and examine international legal frameworks directly relevant to environmental protection before, during, and after armed conflict (International Law Commission 2017). Moreover, since 2010, the United Nations Environment Program has formed partnerships with various research institutes and universities to establish the largest global research program on renewable and nonrenewable natural resources and postconflict peacebuilding. The UNEP's work culminated in reports spanning 150 case studies from 67 conflicts (UNEP 2015b). This trove of data can aid in subsequent postconflict peacebuilding efforts, including Iraq and Syria, as Iraq engages in reconstruction and the Syrian civil war nears its end. As these lacunae in the international legal infrastructure are increasingly discussed, the international community will devise instruments and mechanisms to fill extant gaps. However, it will take time to strengthen international legal and organizational instruments to monitor and enforce international laws governing environmental protection during conflict.

2.4.5. CONCLUSIONS

ISIS became a powerful insurgent group by capturing oil-producing areas in Syria and Iraq, which enabled it to become one of the wealthiest militant groups in modern history. Capitalizing on its control of oil-producing regions and the energy needs of state and non-state actors, ISIS dominated the war economies in portions of Iraq and Syria for several years. The U.S. Treasury's estimate of the revenue it generated from oil products over the course of several years stands at a staggering $500 million. International and local organizations have only recently been able to assess the vast environmental effects of ISIS's reign of terror in Iraq and Syria, but it is clear that ISIS's reckless management of oil resources has caused untold environmental damage. Its scorched-earth policy of burning oil fields and its destruction of everything in its path as it has withdrawn from territory will deprive Iraqis and Syrians of their natural resources, including already-scarce arable land, and will also cause public health crises for years to come.

The international community, especially anti-ISIS armed forces led by the United States, diligently pursued ISIS in Iraq and Syria, culminating in the group's military defeat in Iraq by 2018 and its precipitous demise and near-defeat in Syria. This has been accomplished in part by striking one of the core sources of its revenue: oil. Accordingly, anti-ISIS forces have conducted hundreds of airstrikes against ISIS's oil infrastructure, including modular refineries. These anti-ISIS operations have successfully diminished ISIS's capacity to profit from Iraq's and Syria's oil. Yet these operations have also inevitably culminated in collateral damage to people and places, further threatening the environmental and human security of people in the region.

2.4.6. DISCUSSION QUESTIONS

1. Describe what ISIS has been trying to accomplish, and how ISIS became a powerful and influential sub state actor in the region.
2. Discuss the various ways the "West" has attempted to try and halt or slow the looting of oil by ISIS—and, have these been successful? Why or why not?
3. Reflect on the armed conflict in Syria and discuss some of the impacts on human security in the region. What in your view can/should be done about such insecurities? Include in your discussion energy, political, gender, and economic security.
4. Imagine you are the foreign minister of Turkey. How might you engage in the ISIS conflict and what might you do to eliminate it and to prevent another armed insurgency?

REFERENCES

Al-Khatteeb, L., and E. Gordts, 2014: How ISIS uses oil to fund terror. Brookings Institution, www.brookings.edu/on-the-record/how-isis-uses-oil-to-fund-terror/.

Arango, T., and E. Schmitt, 2015: A path to ISIS through a porous Turkish border. *New York Times*, 10 March 1st ed., A1, www.nytimes.com/2015/03/10/world/europe/despite-crackdown-path-to-join-isis-often-winds-through-porous-turkish-border.html.

Ciziri, E., 2017: Russian jets strike ISIS oil facilities east Syria. ARA News, accessed 1 June 2017, http://aranews.net/2017/02/russian-jets-strike-isis-oil-facilities-east-syria/.

Collard, R., and C. Whitlock, 2014: U.S. says airstrikes crippled most of small oil refineries held by Islamic State in Syria. *Washington Post Middle East Section*, 25 September, www.washingtonpost.com/world/us-led-airstrikes-could-open-new-fronts-for-syrian-battles-against-islamic-state/2014/09/25/bedc3176-449c-11e4-b437-1a7368204804_story.html?utm_term=.305adf907cff.

FATF, 2015: Financing of the terrorist organization Islamic State in Iraq and the Levant (ISIL). Financial Action Task Force Rep., 48 pp., www.fatf- http://www.fatf-gafi.org/media/fatf/documents/reports/Financing-of-the-terrorist-organisation-ISIL.pdf.

Faulconbridge, G., and J. Saul, 2015: Islamic State oil is going to Assad, some to Turkey, U.S. official says. Reuters, accessed 15 May 2017, www.reuters.com/article/us-mideast-crisis-syria-usa-oil/islamic-state-oil-is-going-to-assad-some-to-turkey-u-s-official-says-idUSKBN0TT2O120151210.

Glaser, D., 2016: The sixth counter ISIL finance meeting convenes in Kuwait. U.S. Department of the Treasury, accessed 30 May 2017, www.treasury.gov/connect/blog/Pages/The-Sixth-Counter-ISIL-Finance-Meeting-Convenes-in-Kuwait.aspx.

Humud, C., R. Pirog, and L. Rosen, 2015: Islamic State financing and U.S. policy approaches. Congressional Research Service Rep. R43980, 32 pp., https://fas.org/sgp/crs/terror/R43980.pdf.

International Law Commission, 2017: Summaries of the work of the International Law Commission: Protection of the environment in relation to armed conflicts. International Law Commission, accessed 7 June 2017, http://legal.un.org/ilc/summaries/8_7.shtml.

Johnston, P., 2017: Oil, Extortion Still Paying Off for ISIS. The RAND Blog, https://www.rand.org/blog/2017/10/oil-extortion-still-paying-off-for-isis.html

Kirkpatrick, D. D., and O. Al-Jawoshy, 2014: Weeks of U.S. airstrikes fail to dislodge ISIS in Iraq. *New York Times*, 23 September 1st ed., A12, www.nytimes.com/2014/09/23/world/middleeast/isis-iraq-airstrikes.html?action=click&contentCollection=Middle%20East&module=RelatedCoverage&region=EndOfArticle&pgtype=article.

Lister, C., 2014: Cutting off ISIS' cash flow. Brookings Institution, accessed 7 June 2017, www.brookings.edu/blog/markaz/2014/10/24/cutting-off-isis-cash-flow/.

Lujala, P., 2010: The spoils of nature: Armed civil conflict and rebel access to natural resources. *J. Peace Res.*, **47**, 15–28, https://doi.org/10.1177/0022343309350015.

Marcel, V., 2014: ISIS and the dangers of black market oil. Chatham House, accessed 25 May 2017, www.chathamhouse.org/expert/comment/15203.

Miklaszewski, J., 2015: U.S. destroys 280 ISIS oil trucks in Syrian city of Deir ez-Zor. NBC News, accessed 30 May 2017, www.nbcnews.com/storyline/isis-terror/u-s-destroys-280-isis-oil-trucks-syrian-city-deir-n468126.

Mrema, E. M., C. Bruch, and J. Diamond, 2009: Protecting the environment during armed conflict: An inventory and analysis of international law. UNEP Rep., 88 pp., https://postconflict.unep.ch/publications/int_law.pdf.

RadioFree Europe, 2015: Interview: Turkey's crackdown on IS's oil trade, and Russia's evolving strategy in Syria. RadioFree Europe, accessed 14 June 2017, www.rferl.org/a/russia-turkey-syria-islamic-state-oil-trade/27405175.html.

Rasheed, A., 2016: ISIS suffers near collapse in oil revenue as it loses territory in Iraq. Business Insider, accessed 15 June 2017, www.businessinsider.com/isis-loses-oil-revenue-as-it-loses-territory-in-iraq-2016-7.

Relief Web, 2018: Iraq's toxic conflict. Relief Web, accessed 8 April 2018, https://reliefweb.int/report/iraq/iraq-s-toxic-conflict.

Russia Ministry of Defense, 2015: Speech by the chief of the Main Operations Directorate of the General Staff of the Russian Armed Forces—Deputy Chief of the General Staff of the Russian Federation Sergey Rudskoi lieutenant general of the armed forces. Russian Ministry of Defense, accessed 15 June 2017, http://syria.mil.ru/news/more.htm?id=12070708@cmsArticle.

Sayigh, Y., 2015: The war over Syria's gas fields. Carnegie Middle East Center, http://carnegie-mec.org/diwan/60316.

Solomon, E., R. Kwong, and S. Bernard, 2016: Inside Isis Inc: The journey of a barrel of oil. Financial Times, accessed 13 June 2017, http://ig.ft.com/sites/2015/isis-oil/.

Telegraph, 2015: Dramatic video of Russian air strikes 'on Islamic State oil empire.' Telegraph, www.telegraph.co.uk/news/worldnews/europe/russia/12070100/Russia-releases-dramatic-pictures-of-air-strikes-on-Islamic-State-oil-empire.html.

Thomas, C., 2017: Fighting the flames of ISIL in Iraq. al Jazeera, accessed 20 June 2017, www.aljazeera.com/indepth/inpictures/2017/01/fighting-flames-isil-iraq-170121081713478.html.

Thompson, M., 2015: U.S. bombing of ISIS oil facilities showing progress. Time, accessed 28 May 2017, http://time.com/4145903/islamic-state-oil-syria/.

UN, 2015: Unanimously adopting Resolution 2253 (2015), Security Council expands sanctions framework to include Islamic State in Iraq and Levant. United Nations un.org, accessed 18 June 2017, www.un.org/press/en/2015/sc12168.doc.htm.

UNEP, 2015a: Environmental rule of law: Critical to sustainable development. UNEP Rep., 2 pp., https://wedocs.unep.org/bitstream/handle/20.500.11822/10664/issue-brief-erol.pdf?sequence=1&isAllowed=y.

——, 2015b: Addressing the role of natural resources in conflict and peacebuilding: A summary of progress from UNEP's Environmental Cooperation for Peacebuilding Programme—2008–2015. UNEP Rep., 52 pp., http://postconflict.unep.ch/publications/ECP/ECP_progress_report_2015.pdf, June 30, 2017.

UN Security Council, 2005: Resolution S/2005/176. UNSC, 9 pp.

——, 2014: Resolution S/RES/2195. UNSC, 6 pp.

U.S. Department of Defense, 2014: Department of Defense press briefing by Rear Adm. Kirby in the Pentagon briefing room. U.S. Department of Defense, accessed 2 June 2017, www.defense.gov/News/Transcripts/Transcript-View/Article/606932/.

U.S. Department of the Treasury, 2016: United States, Italy, and the Kingdom of Saudi Arabia hold fourth plenary of the Counter-ISIL Finance Group in Rome. U.S. Department of the Treasury, accessed 28 May 2017, www.treasury.gov/press-center/press-releases/Pages/jl0416.aspx.

Yakupitiyage, T., 2015: Environment: A silent victim of the Syrian conflict. Inter Press Service, accessed 15 May 2017, www.ipsnews.net/2015/11/environment-a-silent-victim-of-the-syrian-conflict/.

Zwijnenburg, W., and K. Pas, 2015: Amidst the debris . . . : A desktop study on the environmental and public health impact of Syria's conflict. PAX Rep., 84 pp., www.paxforpeace.nl/publications/all-publications/amidst-the-debris.

Zwijnenburg, W. and Postma, F. 2017: Living Under a Black Sky: Conflict pollution and environmental health concerns in Iraq. PAX Rep., 34 pp., https://www.paxforpeace.nl/publications/all-publications/living-under-a-black-sky.

CASE STUDY: WATER AND POWER– INTERNATIONAL AND SUBSTATE WATER ALLOCATION CONFLICTS

Christiane J. Fröhlich

2.5.1. INTRODUCTION

As we learned in chapter 2.2, water is an existential resource. It is essential for all life and the subsistence and development of any political economy and thus for the overall standard of living. Consistent and sustained access to adequate and potable water supplies is essential to peace and stability. In contrast, the shortage of adequate freshwater can often be the impetus for migration, hunger, and regional conflict. The global water usage is estimated at 4,200 km^3 per year,[1] of which roughly one-third comes from global drinking water reservoirs that are relatively easy to access (13,000 km^3 of so-called blue water[2] as opposed to water that is bound up in glaciers as perpetual ice or in soil moisture and rain that does not run off or recharge groundwater supplies; such water stores are referred to as "green water"). While the world's population has tripled over the last 100 years, water usage has increased eightfold, according to Wissenschaftlicher Beirat der Bundesregierung Globale Umweltveränderungen (WBGU 2007, p. 83); it is also growing by approximately 10% per decade. Industrialization, growing environmental overuse, and degradation as well as the consequences of global warming have put increasing pressure on the global freshwater resources. The list of regions that suffer from insufficient water supply is therefore continually growing.

2.5.2. THE FALKENMARK WATER STRESS INDEX

The Falkenmark index is perhaps the most widely used measure of water stress. It is defined as the fraction of the total annual runoff available for human use. Falkenmark surveyed multiple countries and calculated the water usage per person in each economy. Based on the per capita usage, Table 2.5.1 shows that water conditions in an area can be categorized as no stress, stress, scarcity, and absolute scarcity.

In the case of increasing water scarcity, regardless of whether it is caused by overuse, degradation, or for political reasons, a society's overall standard of living can suffer considerably. According to UN-Water, 85% of the world population lives in the driest half of the planet, 783 million people do not have access to clean water, nearly 1

This text is a translation from Fröhlich (2015) by the author.

1. The figure 4,200 km^3 may not be the easiest to comprehend. Essentially, 4,200 km^3 converts to over 4.2 trillion cubic meters.

2. Blue water is water from fresh surface and groundwater, that is, from rivers, lakes, streams, or aquifers.

out of every 5 deaths under the age of 5 worldwide is due to a water-related disease, and in developing countries, as much as 80% of illnesses are linked to poor water and sanitation conditions.[3]

Table 2.5.1. Water scarcity index proposed by Falkenmark (1989).

Index (m³ per capita)	Category/condition
>1,700	No stress
1,000–1,700	Stress
500–1,000	Scarcity
<500	Absolute scarcity

Considering these numbers, it may seem rather logical that violent conflict over water will become more likely every day. However, it is crucial to carefully distinguish between international and substate water conflicts. Adding to the complexity of the matter, the fact is that water is more than just the chemical molecule H_2O; it does not only signify the mentioned "objective" data but also social, material, and symbolic communication processes and the related stakeholder interests. Water management and allocation arguably more often reflect existing power relations than actual water scarcity. Therefore, to fully understand and solve water allocation conflicts, it is key to take into account not only "objective" data, such as water quantity and quality, but also political, social, and symbolical connotations of the resource that add to water being perceived as a matter of conflict.

This chapter will address several aspects of the myth of international, violent "water wars," including the issue of water-related conflicts on the substate level, and illustrate their characteristics by analyzing one of the most famous international water basins: the Jordan basin. Finally, we will formulate recommendations for the future treatment of water conflicts and pose several relevant questions for discussion.

2.5.3. THE MYTH OF THE "WATER WAR"

The question of violent conflict escalation is particularly pressing regarding international water basins, which cover approximately half of Earth's surface, are home to 40% of the global population, and have been the subject of extensive research. Researchers agree that these parts of the world will see increasing conflicts, since neighboring states often have different interests about water utilization and allocation.

The risk of conflict is usually considered to be particularly high in regions where water scarcity combines with preexisting violence between societal groups. That is, the risk of conflict seems higher where the political atmosphere is characterized by confrontation, and where water (or its scarcity) can be utilized to acquire or sustain political power. In such a political climate, economic independence and self-sufficiency are considered key elements of national security as well as a means to reduce the dependence on potentially hostile neighbors to an absolute minimum. Therefore, it may seem plausible to assume that opposing claims to limited and shared water resources between different states constitute a zero-sum game, which in turn could lead to international violent conflict. That is, water access could be directly tied to conflict, which gives rise to "water wars."

Accordingly, it is a common and often-repeated claim that, for instance, "the next war in the Middle East will be about water" (propagated for example by the former UN Secretary General Boutros Boutros-Ghali). The neo-Malthusian[4] logic behind this perspective—that population growth plus scarce and decreasing water resources equals violent conflict—has proven to be politically influential but empirically unsound. It is one of the central findings of international water conflict research of the last 30 years that international water wars and resulting global consequences are very unlikely. To illustrate, we cite Barnaby (2009, p. 282): "Countries do not go to war over water, they solve their water shortages through trade and international agreements." She explains that it is the global trade with "virtual water"—the water that is needed for producing foodstuffs as well as other products—that allows states suffering from either an arid or semiarid climate, like those in the Middle East and North Africa (MENA) region, to cover their water

---

3. https://thewaterproject.org/water-scarcity/water_stats, last accessed 9 November 2018.

4. Robert Malthus (1766–1834), in his "Essay on population" (1798), explained that a growing population requires growing amounts of food to survive, while the space available for food production is limited. The logical consequences, according to Malthus, are food scarcity, hunger, and malnutrition.

needs and solve their water conflicts without violence. Already in 1988, Avraham Tamir posed the question, "Why go to war over water? For the price of a week's fighting, you could build five desalination plants. No loss of life, no internal pressure, and a reliable supply you don't have to defend in hostile territory" (Tamir 1988, p. 56; quoted in Lonergan 2001, p. 120).

These utterances are substantiated by large-scale empirical datasets. The International Freshwater Treaties database[5] lists more than 400 water agreements, 100 of them after 1945. Of 1,831 documented interactions between different neighbors of international water basins, the overwhelming majority—1,228—were cooperative in nature. Moreover, water treaties are usually very stable: even military conflicts often cannot harm them. One example of this is the water agreement between India and Pakistan with regard to the Indus, which has survived despite several sometimes-violent clashes between the two parties (Institute for Water and Watersheds 2014).

Does this mean, then, that water and conflict have nothing to do with each other? Absolutely not. Water allocation conflicts create suffering and pain in several parts of the world but, contrary to the common belief, mainly held on the substate level. To name only a few examples, southern Iraqi farmers are being forced into overpopulated urban centers because large-scale dams in Iraq, Syria, and Turkey considerably reduce the flow rate of the Euphrates River (Montenegro 2009). Syrian farmers from the north of the country—today the area controlled by the barbaric Islamic State (IS) or Da'esh—have suffered from an exceedingly long drought period between 2006 and 2010 without any assistance by the government led by Bashar al-Assad. The drought led to increased desertification and put growing pressure on the country's already-scarce water resources (see Worth 2010; Werrell et al. 2013). It contributed to internal migration movements (rural to urban and rural to rural) and may even have played a role in preparing the ground for the Syrian version of the Arab revolutions (Fröhlich 2018). In the occupied Palestinian territories, farmers are dependent on increasingly volatile precipitation patterns for their rain-fed agriculture, while the industrialized Israeli agriculture in the Israeli settlements receives heavily subsidized water for irrigation.

Thus, today's most urgent questions about water are typically concerned with the frequency of substate, local water conflicts, the reduction of risks contributing to them, and possible solutions to conflicts that have already broken out. However, the center of gravity of the overall debate on water conflicts is still grounded mainly on the interstate level. One example of this imbalance in addressing international and substate water issues is the Middle East. The next section will present the water issues in the Jordan basin as a good example of this.

2.5.4. THE JORDAN BASIN: WATER AS AN INSTRUMENT OF POWER

Climate and geography together with the political situation in the region have rendered the Jordan basin as one of the most heavily cited examples for international water resources with potential for (violent) conflict. Usable water stems from the Jordan River with its headwater and tributaries (Hasbani and Banyas in the Golan Heights, Dan in Israel, and Yarmuk in Jordan) and the Sea of Galilee and the different aquifers, and specifically its groundwater reservoirs. The last of these consists mainly of the mountain aquifer below the West Bank, the coastal aquifer below the Gaza Strip and along the Israeli coast as well as several other smaller and less developed aquifers. Ever since the June War of 1967 and the ensuing occupation of the West Bank, the Gaza Strip, and the Golan Heights, the majority of the regional water resources (ca. 80%) are controlled by Israel.

Today, the stakeholders in the Jordan basin consist of Israel, Syria, Jordan, and the Palestinian Authority, as well as—indirectly—Lebanon. Despite the recurring state of war between Israel and several of its neighbors, the probability of international violent conflict over water between the states surrounding the Jordan basin is low. The conflict between Jordan and Israel over the water in the Jordan River was regulated in a detailed peace agreement in 1994. The conflict between Syria and Israel over the Jordan River's tributaries Banyas and Hasbani is mainly seen as part of the political dispute over the Golan Heights and less about the actual water allocation—Syria depends much more on the water in the Euphrates–Tigris basin than on the water it lays claims to in the south, so a water war remains very unlikely here, too (see Daoudy 2004).

---

5. www.transboundarywaters.orst.edu, last accessed 9 December 2015.

However, substate water allocation conflicts are increasing rather than decreasing. The conflict between Israel and the Palestinians over access to the natural water resources is far from solved despite the oft-praised Oslo peace process. The dispute also cannot be separated from the overall political conflict between the two adversaries. The current water access patterns clearly mirror the asymmetric distribution of power between Israel and the Palestinians: while Palestinians have access to about 84 litres per head and day for household use, Israeli citizens, including Israeli settlers, consume approximately 250 litres per head and day. The abovementioned peace treaty between Israel and Jordan, which includes extremely detailed regulations concerning the allocation of water from the Jordan and Yarmuk Rivers to the two parties of the contract, does not once mention the Palestinians even though they are direct neighbors to the basin. This is mainly due to the weak bargaining power of Palestinian organizations and agencies.

While the supply of water in Israel and the Israeli settlements equals Western standards, many Palestinian families have to make do with an intermittent water supply. About 25%–30% of the Palestinian population are not connected to the water supply system at all. The population therefore has to rely on water brought by tankers, which is very expensive (between 2.35 and 4.91 U.S. dollars per cubic meter; see Nasser 2003, p. 107). The Palestinians pay the highest water prices in the region, as even tap water can cost 1 to 1.5 U.S. dollars per cubic meter.

It is true that during the Oslo peace negotiations, bilateral bodies with regard to water were created that—different from many other institutions—remained in effect even during the second intifada. However, these so-called Joint Water Committees nevertheless illustrate the asymmetrical nature of the Israeli–Palestinian conflict. While, in theory, both Palestinian and Israeli committee members have the same rights and duties, including the right to veto water-related infrastructural and other projects of the respective other, it is de facto only Israel that can effectively exercise that right. This obvious and continuing inequality perpetuates conflict structures that have developed over the last 70 years ad infinitum. Thus, the problem of an equitable and adequate water allocation is far from solved, since one conflict party is much more powerful than the other. The numerous existing solutions to the conflict are not being implemented for political reasons, because both sides give national interests and questions of political identity precedence over a sustainable and thus by definition cooperative water management.

Tensions in the Israeli–Palestinian conflict could, of course, be considerably reduced if Israel gave up control over at least part of the natural water resources in favor of the Palestinian people. But among others, this would entail reducing the water supply of certain Israeli user groups, such as the agricultural sector, in favor of Palestinian water consumers. Even if the political will to implement such a measure existed, this would pose considerable difficulties for the Israeli government. After all, the influential agricultural lobby holds strong ties to the Israeli settler movement and has dominated the Israeli water management sector and institutions for decades; they would hardly accept a massive increase in water prices or similar effects of such politics. Equally, a downsizing of the agricultural sector would be met with considerable domestic resistance because of the strong symbolic value of Israeli agriculture, especially for the settler movement. Moreover, in the eyes of many Israelis, relinquishing control over the water resources below the West Bank equals giving up territorial control: controlling the natural water resources is considered a matter of national security in a hostile environment. Security can, to an Israeli, only be ensured by continuous and ideally undivided Israeli control over and supervision of all natural water resources.

Instead, Israel has offered to provide the Palestinians with desalinated water from the Mediterranean coast. This way, Israeli discourse would argue that the natural resources remain untouched, domestic tensions could be reduced to a minimum, and Palestinian water supply would still be relieved. However, this is met with outright rejection by the Palestinian Authority (PA). Invoking international law, the PA insists that both the groundwater reservoirs under Palestinian territory and at least part of the Jordan River are rightfully theirs to control. The PA's main goal is clearly the creation of an autonomous, independent (i.e., possessing their own water resources) Palestinian state. Water is so important to all aspects of life in the Jordan basin that, to an average Palestinian, accepting such an offer would be regarded as an implicit acceptance of Israeli occupation of Palestinian territtiory. Moreover, most Palestinians would not be able to afford to pay for desalinated water, which would frustratingly increase the level of dependence on external assistance.

Thus, the Israeli–Palestinian water conflict illustrates the same entrenched positions and asymmetrical power relations dominating the overall political conflict. Two characteristics have proven to be particularly detrimental for the numerous attempts to solve the conflict. On the one hand, political and environmental issues are still often treated as independent from each other, one dealing with "hard politics," the other belonging in the realm of "soft issues," which could be dealt with by technocrats independent from any political issues. Accordingly, the abovementioned Joint Water Committee was deliberately not staffed with political decision-makers but with technocrats and academics, who, it can be argued, stood outside of the actual conflict decision-making. While this most certainly contributed to the fact that the committee continued to cooperate even during the second intifada, this depoliticization of the water issue unfortunately also contributed to the fact that every attempt to solve the conflict has failed up to now. So far, all actors involved lack the necessary political will to implement the proposed solutions.

On the other hand, the overwhelmingly bi-, or, even worse, unilateral approach to the water issue in the Middle East has contributed to perpetuating the conflict both by ignoring the cross-border nature of water resources as well as by continuously and repeatedly excluding legitimate stakeholders. The Palestinians have suffered from this the most, since their interests have been ignored more often than not because of their weak bargaining power; the Israeli–Jordanian peace treaty from 1994 is a case in point. It includes extensive regulations of the allocation of water from both the Jordan River and its tributary, the Jordanian Yarmuk, but does not in any way address the Palestinians' claims to this water.

In a nutshell, even though a water war between Israel and its neighbors is unlikely, a solution to the outlined obstacles remains one of the central challenges for those who want to solve the water conflict in the Jordan basin and, indeed, the larger Israeli–Palestinian core conflict.

2.5.5. CONCLUSIONS: WHAT MUST BE DONE

As shown above, international "water wars" are unlikely even in a difficult political climate. Internal water conflicts, however, have developed into urgent issues that demand a solution to avoid social unrest and human suffering. It is therefore high time for the international community to focus their efforts on the internal, local level instead of directing all efforts toward interstate water conflicts. The most pressing question is not whether the next war in the Middle East will be fought over water but how the risk of conflict at the substate level can be reduced and how acute conflicts can be solved.

First, preventive strategies for water allocation conflicts must be implemented in all places where high population growth is met with water scarcity. These include measures to increase water utilization efficiency (supply management) as well as measures to strengthen a society's adaptive capacity and resilience (demand management), with a particular focus on such societal groups that are already marginalized and taking into account intersectional categories such as gender, age, and socioeconomic status. Women and girls are an important target group for such measures, as noted in the 1992 Declaration of Rio: "Women have a vital role in environmental management and development. Their full participation is therefore essential to achieve sustainable development." In many regions of the world, women are responsible for water supply and crop production. Based on tradition and experience, they choose crops and irrigation techniques; moreover, they suffer the most from dried-up wells and increasing distances to the next water source. Many girls and women do not attend schools or training opportunities regularly because of the often time-intensive and dangerous task of providing a sufficient water supply for their family. Educating them about strategies to increase water efficiency and productivity as well as using local knowledge about traditional cultivation techniques (which are often more sustainable than modern industrialized agriculture) could help to minimize the effects of water stress.

In addition, the blatant lack of adequate legal instruments regarding water allocation and management on an international level exacerbates the existing difficult conditions. An international, cooperative effort is necessary to establish a legal framework that codifies the right of each human being to a sufficient water supply. The UN Watercourses Convention of 1997 is a step in the right direction; however, it has only recently been ratified (in August 2014), so we have yet to gauge its effectiveness.

What is more, to solve acute, protracted water conflicts and to prevent future water conflicts, it is necessary to better understand how water is being manipulated for political ends. Conflictive discourse structures need to be uncovered that perpetuate water conflicts by reinscribing contesting perspectives following a predominantly nationalist logic (see Fröhlich and Ide 2015). It will not suffice to continue to base hydropolitical decision-making on static political borders. Negotiations about water allocation also should not focus on supply management alone; demand management is direly needed. When such negotiations are contested, the author considers it to be particularly important to analyze domestic economic structures, especially the size and structure of the respective agricultural sectors. The water–food nexus needs to be addressed in a more proactive manner, especially by helping agricultural sectors adapt to a warming, increasingly water-scarce world, and by promoting and increasing affordable, small-scale irrigation agriculture to achieve greater food security. In the end, rising food prices and escalating undernourishment and starvation carry a high risk of destabilization in an increasingly water-scarce world.

2.5.6. WHAT YOU SHOULD KNOW FROM HERE

Empirical research has shown that the risk of violent interstate water conflicts is very low to nonexistent—the mechanisms of diplomacy and negotiation have proven to be efficient and established enough to minimize the risk of an outbreak of violence. However, this does not mean that water is not an issue of conflict. On the contrary, water allocation conflicts on the substate level, even violent ones, have become commonplace. The ever-increasing global demand for freshwater contributes to the competition between urban and rural spaces, between the state and the county/governorate level, and between different ethnic groups, as well as different economic interests. Intrastate and substate conflicts about water already threaten the livelihood of millions of people and therefore merit the diplomatic, academic, and financial attention of the international community.

2.5.7. DISCUSSION QUESTIONS

1. Relate how water access impacts other aspects of human security (for example, food, energy, economic, political, and gender security).
2. Is there such a thing as a "water war"? Why or why not?
3. How has water been used in Jordan as a weapon?

4. Identify and describe at least three things that must be accomplished to alleviate the water-access-based conflicts in the region.

SUGGESTED FURTHER READING

Earle, A., A. Jägerskog, and J. Ojendal, 2010: *Transboundary Water Management: Principles and Practice.* Earthscan, 261 pp.

Diehl, P. F., and N. P. Gleditsch, Eds., 2000: *Environmental Conflict: An Anthology.* Westview Press, 352 pp.

Lankford, B., K. Bakker, M. Zeitoun, and D. Conway, Eds., 2013: *Water Security: Principles, Perspectives and Practices.* Routledge, 376 pp.

Selby, J., 2003: *Water, Power and Politics in the Middle East: The Other Israeli–Palestinian Conflict.* IB Tauris, 275 pp.

Wolf, A. T., Ed., 2002: *Conflict Prevention and Resolution in Water Systems.* Elgar, 848 pp.

REFERENCES

Barnaby, W., 2009: Do nations go to war over water? *Nature*, **458**, 282–283, https://doi.org/10.1038/458282a.

Daoudy, M., 2004: Syria and Turkey in water diplomacy (1962–2003). *Water in the Middle East and in North Africa: Resources, Protection and Management*, F. Zereini and W. Jaeschke, Eds., Springer, 319–332.

Falkenmark, M., 1989: The massive water scarcity threatening Africa: Why isn't it being addressed? *Ambio*, **18**, 112–118.

Fröhlich, C. J., 2012a: Security and discourse: The Israeli–Palestinian water conflict. *Conflict Secur. Dev.*, **12**, 123– 148, https://doi.org/10.1080/14678802.2012.688290.

——, 2015: Wasser als Machtinstrument: Internationale und sub-staatliche Konflikte um Wasser. *Handbuch Sicherheitsgefahren*, T. Jaeger, Ed., VS Verlag, 75–82.

——, 2016. Climate Migrants as Protestors? Dispelling Misconceptions about Global Environmental Change in Pre-Revolutionary Syria. *Contemporary Levant* 1:1, 38-50, DOI: 10.1080/20581831.2016.1149355.

——, and T. Ide, 2015: Socio-environmental cooperation and conflict? A discursive understanding and its application to the case of Israel and Palestine. *Earth Syst. Dyn.*, **6**, 659–671, https://doi.org/10.5194/esd-6-659-2015.

Institute for Water and Watersheds, 2014: International freshwater treaties database. Oregon State University, accessed 3 December 2015, https://transboundarywaters.science.oregonstate.edu/content/international-freshwater-treaties-database.

Lonergan, S. C., 2001: Water and conflict: Rhetoric and reality. *Environmental Conflict: An Anthology*, P. F. Diehl and N. P. Gleditsch, Eds., Westview Press, 109–124.

Montenegro, M., 2009: The truth about water wars. Seed, accessed 13 November 2015, http://seedmagazine.com/content/article/the_truth_about_water_wars/.

Nasser, Y., 2003: Palestinian water needs and rights in the context of past and future development. *Water in Palestine: Problems–Politics–Prospects*, F. Daibes, Ed., Passia 85–123.

Tamir, A., 1988: *A Soldier in Search of Peace: An Inside Look at Israel's Strategy.* Harper and Row, 259 pp.

UN, 1987: Our common future. UN General Assembly Doc. A/42/427.

WBGU, 2007: *Welt im Wandel. Sicherheitsrisiko Klimawandel.* Springer, 291 pp.

Werrell, C., F. Femia, and A. M. Slaughter, 2013: The Arab Spring and climate change. Center for American Progress, accessed 13 November 2015, www.americanprogress.org/issues/security/report/2013/02/28/54579/the-arab-spring-and-climate-change/.

Worth, R. F., 2010: Earth is parched where Syrian farms thrived. *New York Times*, 14 October 1st ed., A1, www.nytimes.com/2010/10/14/world/middleeast/14syria.html?_r=0.

CASE STUDY: LIMITS TO GROWTH AND INSECURITY

Damien Short

2.6.1. INTRODUCTION

The 1972 Club of Rome report *The Limits to Growth* (Meadows et al. 1972) utilized a system dynamics computer model to simulate the interactions of five global economic subsystems, namely, population, food production, industrial production, pollution, and consumption of nonrenewable natural resources, the results of which posed serious challenges for global sustainability. A recent study (Turner 2007) collated historical data for 1970–2000 and compared them with scenarios presented in *The Limits to Growth*. The analysis shows that 30 years of historical data compare favourably with key features of the "standard run" scenario, which

results in collapse of the global system midway through the twenty-first century. The key driver behind the "limits to growth" prediction—and arguably the one most poised to quickly cause global economic collapse—is the depletion of non-renewable energy sources, especially of oil and natural gas.[1] Despite the best efforts of the fossil fuel industry to propagate a paradigm of energy abundance, especially in the United States (Heinberg 2014), global production of conventional oil has already peaked and—barring incredibly unlikely huge new discoveries of easily extracted oil—must soon decline as predicted in *The Limits to Growth* (Murray and Hansen 2013). New discoveries of oil and natural

---

1. As oil and natural gas production peak and decline, coal becomes increasingly pivotal in maintaining global energy consumption rates; however, this renewed focus on coal, seen in the "record rate" of coal gasification and coal-to-liquid plant construction of the last decade, will only further exacerbate strained coal resources. Indeed, world coal production continues to increase annually, with an overall increase of over 67% between 1990 and 2013. Even with more conservative estimates of coal production growth and the most opportunistic estimates of global coal reserves—relying on the World Coal Association's production growth rate of 0.4% between 2012 and 2013 remaining constant and the German Federal Institute for Geosciences and Natural Resources' estimate of 1,052 billion tons of reserves—the world will "run out" of coal in just over a century. As that figure assumes no "updates" to reserve figures (despite nearly every state with "significant coal resources" reporting a "substantial downward revision" in reserve estimates made since 1986) or increase in production rate (despite the sharp decreases in available oil and natural gas during the upcoming decades), it is reasonable to conclude that the limits to coal-dependent growth will also soon be reached (Heinberg 2007; World Coal Association 2015).

gas liquids[2] have dropped dramatically since their peak in the 1960s, and the world now consumes four to five barrels of oil for every one discovered (Mobbs 2008; Heinberg 2014, p. 25). Because oil production from conventional fields tend to drop globally by 5% each year, it is thus assured that such fields will eventually "run out."[3]

This downward global trend in oil discovery and supply has not gone unnoticed by the major international actors, namely, states and multi- and transnational corporations, who have taken various actions since the end of the Cold War to secure access to remaining conventional oil supplies. An examination of major international conflicts in the Persian Gulf region alone since 1990 demonstrates the determination of countries such as the United States to maintain control of conventional energy resources. Indeed, conventional energy supplies have become so precious to many states that "energy security" (Barnett 2001) is now an overriding objective within which foreign and domestic policies situate the procurement of oil (and other energy sources) as a matter of national security. Such a discourse often elevates concern for the global fossil fuel market over other considerations such as the environment and human rights (see White House 1998).

This change in rhetoric to boost the perceived necessity of fossil fuels is furthered by the influence of major energy corporations upon state governments (Short et al. 2015). As numerous corporations with international reach, such as Exxon Mobil and ConocoPhillips, have developed larger economies than many sizeable states.[4] Predictably, their power has correspondingly grown. Since such companies' business models center on fossil fuels, examples of corporate–state collaboration to further nonrenewable energy use may be found in varying arenas, from the more than $50 million Koch Industries spent on lobbying the U.S. government between 1998 and 2010 (Mayer 2010) and the formation of the American Legislative Exchange Council (which brings private corporations together with elected U.S. state officials to draft new legislation; Bedell 2014) to direct connections between advisors to the U.K. Cabinet Office and energy sector companies such as Centrica and Riverstone (Mobbs 2013). As the 200 largest listed fossil fuel companies spent $674 billion on developing new energy reserves (5 times as much as they spent returning money to shareholders) in 2012 (Economist 2013), the energy industry remains invested in pushing the "limits" as far as they can go.[5]

Though corporations may lobby otherwise,[6] resource limitations to growth are not the only significant, impending ecological threats to humanity and ecosystems worldwide. Carbon dioxide atmospheric concentrations "have increased by 40% since pre-industrial times", with concentrations of carbon dioxide, methane, and nitrous oxide at the highest in at least 800,000 years [Intergovernmental Panel on Climate Change (IPCC) 2013a], and the rate of carbon dioxide release is unprecedented, at least in the last 300 million years. The result of this level of pollution—inherently tied to an insistence on using and depleting nonrenewable energy sources (Hönisch et al. 2012)—is the phenomenon of climate change, in this context represented by the anthropogenic increase in Earth's surface temperature. Since 1880, the average global temperature has increased by roughly 0.85°C, with most of the increase—0.72°C—occurring in the past 50 years (IPCC 2013b). The effects of this global warming are diverse and range from shrinking glaciers and ice sheets to the highest rate of sea level rise in the past 2,000 years and increasingly frequent extreme weather events, all of which clearly result from "human influence on the climate system" (IPCC 2013a).

Knowing that these two consequences of persistent and exclusive use of fossil fuels are imminently approaching, one could reasonably argue that global use

2. Natural gas liquids (NGLs) are "hydrocarbons with longer molecular chains," such as propane and butane, within natural gas that are captured and used for heating and industrial purposes (Heinberg 2014, p. 25).

3. Conventional natural gas production follows a similar peak and decline bell curve and is expected to reach its plateau before the mid-twenty-first century (see Mobbs 2008; Maggio and Cacciola 2012).

4. Exxon's revenue is greater than the gross domestic product (GDP) of Thailand, for instance (Trivett 2011).

5. For more on corporate–state connections, see Chomsky (2013) and Palast (2002).

6. For example, the American Enterprise Institute, which receives funding from Exxon Mobil and other companies in the energy sector, "offered a $10,000 incentive to scientists and economists to write papers challenging the IPCC findings" after the Intergovernmental Panel on Climate Change released its fourth assessment report in 2007 (Jones and Levy 2009).

of oil, natural gas, and coal should be immediately curbed. At present, however, fossil fuels still remain the world's main source of energy, accounting for around 81% of global primary energy use (International Energy Agency 2011). This is undoubtedly due, at least in part, to a Western-propagated, neoliberal economic model, wherein corporations, being legally bound to pursue profit above all other considerations, continuously lobby for favourable legislation, deregulation, and tax incentives. As Bakan noted in his seminal text, *The Corporation: The Pathological Pursuit of Profit and Power* (Bakan 2005), under corporate law, the primary legal duty of the corporation is "simply to make money for shareholders" and failing to pursue this end "can leave directors and officers open to being sued" (Hinkley 2002; Bakan 2005).[7] Thus, the multitude of multibillion dollar companies that depend upon the continued global use of fossil fuels have not only a vested interest in advocating for further non-renewable energy extraction but, arguably, in the current energy market, a legal duty to do so—and at the very least an obligation to continue pursuing oil, coal, and natural gas extraction as long as it is profitable and legal to do so. Thus, while the use of renewable energy sources is growing (Energy Information Administration 2018), they are forced to compete with an established and highly subsidized[8] non-renewable market rather than be allowed to replace it.[9]

2.6.2. EXTREME ENERGY

The law of supply and demand would suggest that as conventional reserves are depleted (Carrington 2014; Grose 2013) and as demand for energy continues or rises, there is increasing pressure to exploit unconventional energy sources to meet supply [United Nations Environment Programme (UNEP) 2011a,b]. Klare (2011) first coined the term "extreme energy" to describe

a range of relatively new, higher-risk, non-renewable resource extraction processes that have become more attractive to the conventional energy industry as the more easily accessible supplies dwindle. Edward Lloyd-Davies points out, however, that this definition of extreme energy as a category is highly problematic as it is dependent upon specific examples; it lacks "explanatory or predictive power" (Lloyd-Davies 2013), and leaves open the question of who decides which extractive techniques qualify. A conceptual understanding would suggest that extreme energy is a "process whereby extraction methods grow more intense over time, as easier to extract resources are depleted." The foundation of this conception is the simple fact that those energy sources that require the least amount of effort to extract will be used first, and only once those are dwindling will more effort be exerted to gain similar resources. Extreme energy, in this sense, is evident in the history of energy extraction—in the change from gathering "sea coal" from British beaches and exploiting "natural oil seeps" to opencast mining and deep-water oil drilling. Viewed in this light, the concept of extreme energy becomes a lens through which current energy extraction efforts can be explained and the future of the energy industry predicted. Using this extreme energy lens necessitates an understanding of "the amount of energy that is needed to obtain energy," as in this process it is that value that is continually rising. This value may be calculated as either "net energy" or "energy return on investment" (EROI) whereby net energy is the available energy for use after subtracting the energy required for extraction and EROI is the percentage of energy produced divided by the amount required for extraction. When charted together, the net energy available to society is seen to decrease along with EROI in a curved mathematical relationship, which forms the "energy cliff"—that is, the point at which EROI becomes increasingly low and net energy drops to zero.

---

7. For further reading on the economic model and psychology under which corporations operate, see Elson (2002) and Connolly (2012). Notably, even privately held companies, such as Koch Industries, have a monetary interest in maintaining global fossil fuel use as long as nonrenewable energy sources continue to generate profit.

8. For example, in 2009, approximately $43–$46 billion were provided to renewable and biofuel technologies, projects, and companies by the governments of the world, compared with the $577 billion spent on fossil fuel subsidies in 2008 (Bloomberg 2010).

9. This concept is perhaps best illustrated by the insistence from both industry and governments that hydraulic fracturing will allow natural gas to replace the use of coal and thus reduce the emission of greenhouse gases, when in actuality, the abundance of hydraulic fracturing in the United State has simply lowered the price of U.S. coal and driven up exports (Carrington 2014; Grose 2013).

In the extreme energy process, the economic system can be conceptualized as consisting of two distinct segments: 1) the part that is extracting, refining, and producing energy (the energy industry) and 2) everything else that just consumes energy. What needs to be clearly understood is that the energy industry is in the rare position where the commodity that it produces is also the main resource it consumes. Therefore, as energy extraction becomes more extreme, and while the rest of the economy will be squeezed by decreasing energy availability and rising prices,[10] the energy industry's rising costs will be offset by the rising revenues it receives because of supply and demand. The net result will be a reallocation (through the market or otherwise) of resources from the rest of society to the energy industry to allow the energy industry to target evermore difficult-to-extract resources. This process intensifies as easier-to-extract resources are depleted, and data from recent extraction methods, such as hydraulic fracturing and tar sands extraction, show that industry is increasingly lurching toward the net energy cliff. Such action on the part of some of the largest and most commercially successful transnational corporations may only be understood as the logical result of the extreme energy process (Murphy and Hall 2011)—there simply are not enough easier-to-extract resources available [on this point, see also Heinberg (2014)].

2.6.3. THE ROLE OF NEOLIBERAL CAPITALISM

Despite the obvious negative implications of these developments, the process shows no sign of stopping but continues toward the precipice at an ever-increasing rate, fuelled by ever-increasing levels of energy consumption. Perpetuated by the global economic "growth" fixation (Purdey 2010), increasing amounts of energy are consumed each year (International Energy Agency 2013), driving the process over the edge. Of course, industry is not willing to halt the process (Lloyd-Davies 2013) as intense demand further pushes up the price of energy,[11] allowing extraction to remain economical—as long as enough resource is extracted at each site and the price stays high. The ironic result is that higher energy consumption leads to faster resource depletion, which

in turn results in the acceleration of the extreme energy process. Within this neoliberal economic context of increasing demand and profit potential, the results of extreme extraction techniques (Heinberg 2014) and the consequences of continuing the process are easily trumped in the interest of short-term profiteering and "energy security." Indeed, as Stephanie Malin notes, neoliberal "normalization" of unconventional energy extraction emerges most saliently regarding environmental outcomes and economic development (Malin 2014). Despite the prospective consequences of reaching our limits to growth, and with considerable evidence demonstrating a strong correlation between extraction effort and damage to both society and the environment, the extreme energy process continues to accelerate, with potentially disastrous consequences (Lloyd-Davies 2013; Huseman and Short 2012; Humphreys 2008).

The depth of connections already established between the extreme energy process and the "minimally good life" illustrates the otherwise overlooked insidious nature of this insistence upon striving toward the energy precipice. Human rights violations due to climate change and the release of pollutants are yet another side effect of humanity's dependence on fossil fuels that grows in magnitude with each decade. The tropics and subtropics have seen droughts increase in intensity and duration since the 1970s (IPCC 2007a), and diseases such as malaria are affecting larger portions of the population (Patz et al. 2005). Each year, approximately 200,000 deaths in the United States result from air pollution (Laboratory for Aviation and the Environment 2013), while a heat wave across Europe in 2003 (most likely resulting from global climate change; Stott et al. 2004) left roughly 30,000 people dead (Jha 2006). There is strong evidence to suggest that the worst consequences of anthropogenic climate change on human rights have not yet been felt. As predicted in *The Limits to Growth* (Meadows et al. 1972), the effects of climate degradation will rapidly increase with temperature throughout the twenty-first century (IPCC 2007b), resulting in large-scale deaths across Europe due to heat stroke [World Health Organization (WHO) 2009], worsening droughts across continents (IPCC 2007b), further loss of food and water, and a

---

10. At the time of writing, oil prices were in decline, but the finite nature of the resource guarantees that prices will again rise.

11. Notwithstanding the current, inevitably temporary, geopolitically induced price reduction, prices will undoubtedly rise over time as supply declines (see Mobbs 2015).

potential, eventual, extinction-level event for humanity if global emissions are not reduced in accordance with the latest climate science modelling. Such events, along with resulting unrest, wars, and mass migrations (IPCC 2014), threaten people's rights to life and health worldwide.

The rush to scrape the bottom of the fossil fuel barrel is thus creating a veritable perfect storm for current and future human rights abuses and ecocidal and geno-cidal consequences. As resources become scarcer, our scramble to use them grows, increasing the political prioritization of fossil fuel extraction over ecosystems, human health, and security, while increasing demand also ensures that such resources will run out sooner, which in turn will result in further conflict and human rights violations as food, health care, and other basic needs are no longer met, to say nothing of the abuses to human security that would also necessarily increase. These violations will most likely increase exponentially as resources are depleted—at least, that is, until the sharp population decline predicted in *The Limits to Growth* oc-curs (see Barry and Woods 2009; Ahmed 2014; Human Rights Council 2011).

In a recent paper, Martin Crook and I show how Karl Marx's classic critique of political economy, and his value analysis more specifically, helps explain the ecologically destructive forces unleashed by capitalist extractive and farming industries. Capitalism is structurally geared toward the social production of commodities in accordance with the imperatives of capital accumulation and exchange value and not in harmony with nature's laws of conservation, sustainability, and natural metabolic cycles.

2.6.4. THE ATHABASCA TAR SANDS EXAMPLE

In a separate study, the Athabasca "tar sands" [see Huseman and Short (2012) for a full definition of this extraction process] is a prime example of the artificial division and fragmentation of the local ecosystem in an attempt to extract oil, with no regard for the antiecological effects this unnatural throughput and transfer of energy and materials has on the local environment and critically downstream indigenous peoples. Figure 2.6.1 shows the Athabasca tar sands location.

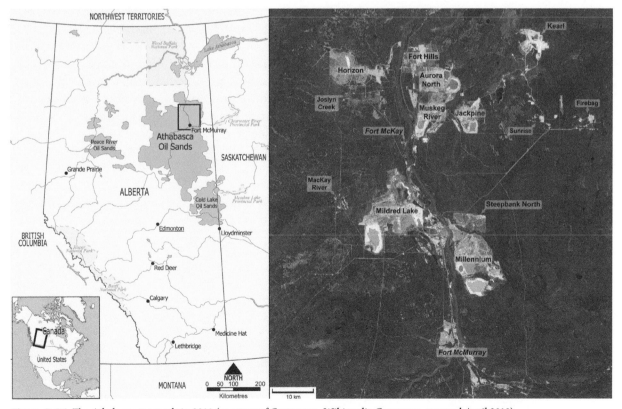

Figure 2.6.1. The Athabasca tar sands in 2011 (courtesy of Gretarsson, Wikimedia Commons, accessed April 2018).

One of the central ecological contradictions of capitalism is the exponential increase in the throughput of materials and energy needed by the relentless need for "growth" and the natural limits of production. Disequilibrium exists between capitals' ferocious pace in the throughput of energy and materials and nature's laws, temporal rhythms, and metabolic cycles, which eventually provokes an inevitable shortage of materials and an accumulation crisis (see Crook and Short 2014).[12] The result is that the price of the relevant raw material will go up as the amount of socially necessary labor time objectified in each individual product or use value rises in relative terms. This process is exemplified by extreme energy as the supply of fossil fuels begins to run up against natural limits, thus raising the relative amount of objectified labor in a given quantity of fossil fuel, leading, in the medium to long term, to a rise in the average price of fossil fuels. Indeed, within the process of extreme energy, where more complex and costly techniques are required for the extraction of ever-scarcer sources, the very same process unfolds (see Crook and Short 2014). So extreme energy "as a process" can be seen as both an expression of material shortages and a competitive market response in an attempt to correct the imbalance through the extraction of evermore extreme substitutes. The net effect is to put further pressure both on local ecosystems and the biosphere more generally.

Thus, capitalism sets in motion a rampant process of accumulation, which carves up nature and increases the material throughput of production to evermore ecologically unsustainable levels, disturbing the social metabolism of human civilization and leading to a "metabolic rift" of man from nature (see Crook and Short 2014). The process of extreme energy, and the role of extractive industries within it, are manifestations of the antiecological imperatives of capital accumulation, and the drive toward "unconventional" extraction techniques are a particularly virulent expression of the metabolic rift and the antiecological nature of the capitalist value–nature contradiction. The resort to costlier and more environmentally destructive forms of energy extraction within the extreme energy process signifies a particular form of environmental crisis under capitalism caused by material shortages and the natural limits of production.

In recent years, the demand for plentiful and "secure" energy resources has resulted in "the single largest energy policy shift in North America since . . . production peaked in 1971" (Crook and Short 2014, p. 89). As Macdonald Stainsby writes, "Having failed to pacify Iraq and having engendered new regional opposition in Africa, South America, and the Middle East, the U.S. empire has driven oil prices up to new heights—a trend which will continue into the future. Though peak oil[13] has profound implications for the U.S. dollar and the militarized global economy, these prices have, in the short-term, been masterfully recast as U.S. imperialism's latest and greatest asset: *the creation of massive new oil 'reserves' in a politically friendly region which can feed the U.S. domestic oil market*" (Crook and Short 2014, p. 89).[14] Namely, the tar sands[15] in northern Alberta, Canada,[16] which is widely considered to be the most destructive industrial project on Earth by environmental, human rights, and indigenous activists alike.[17] "Tar sands" is a colloquial term used to describe sands that constitute a naturally

---

12. Marx's analysis of accumulation crisis brought on by materials-supplies disturbances operates on two levels: the first focuses on the conditions of crisis caused by fluctuations in the value of the materials in question brought on by shortages and the second relates to the indirect fluctuations in "prices" brought on by the resultant competition and speculation and the credit system (see Marx 1968, p. 515). For further elaboration of the contradiction between "nature's time" and "labor's time," see Marx and Engels (1967, p. 118).

13. Peak oil is the theorized point in time when the maximum rate of extraction of petroleum is reached, after which it is expected to enter terminal decline.

14. Here, with peak oil and the creation of massive new oil reserves, we see again the operation of the law of value as delineated by Marx. The former being an expression of materials-supplies disturbances and the latter the utilization of *previously unused substitutes* (see Marx and Engels 1967, 118–119).

15. For a discussion of the term "tar sands" versus "oil sands," see Huseman and Short (2012).

16. "The recoverable oil reserves in Alberta's tar sands are so bountiful that they vie with oil reserves in Saudi Arabia and Venezuela for top status" (Petersen 2007, p. 12).

17. The Natural Resources Defense Fund (NDRC). "Tar Sands Crude Oil: Health Effects of a Dirty and Destructive Fuel," https://www.nrdc.org/sites/default/files/tar-sands-health-effects-IB.pdf.

occurring mixture of sand, clay, water, and bitumen—an exceptionally viscous and dense form of petroleum—which has, since the late nineteenth and early twentieth centuries, been referred to as "tar" because of its similar viscosity, odor, and color. Once again, this desired energy resource lies almost entirely within the traditional territories of native North Americans and as such is another example of the acute threat to indigenous peoples posed by the process of extreme energy, which brings with it large-scale dispossession and the "externalities" of pollution and environmental degradation.

Canada initiated oil production in the tar sands in 1967—"after decades of research and development that began in the early 1900s" (Humphries 2008)—with Suncor Energy, Inc., generating roughly 12,000 barrels per day. Even so, the tar sands were not regarded as a significant player in North America's bid to prolong the life of its petroleum-based economy until 2003—around the time of the American invasion of Iraq. Prior to this period, the extremely difficult extraction and production processes of tar sands development was considered too expensive to be economically viable, but with oil prices heading toward $150 per barrel, the tar sands not only became viable but the basis for a shift to American reliance on North American petroleum as a source of fuel (Black 2008), and yet again, the lives and lands of native peoples would be sacrificed to the "needs" of the dominant European–North American capitalist society.[18] The tar sands have not only seriously affected indigenous lands but are producing horrendous environmental destruction that is impacting indigenous physical and cultural health (Huseman and Short 2012). Indeed, environmental pollution from the tar sands[19] has been linked to high levels of deadly diseases such as leukemia, lymphoma, and colon cancer (Petersen 2007) in indigenous communities (e.g., the Dene, Cree, and Metis communities in Treaty 8 and Treaty 11 territories). For George Poitras, a Mikisew Cree First Nation member affected by tar sands mining in Fort Chipewyan, Alberta, the battle with industrial mining over land and resources comes down to the fundamental right to exist: "If we don't have land and we don't have anywhere to carry out our traditional lifestyle, we lose who we are as a people. So,

if there's no land, then it's equivalent in our estimation to genocide of a people" (Petersen 2007). And as Chief Roxanne Marcel (Mikisew Cree First Nation) states, "Our message to both levels of government, to Albertans, to Canadians and to the world who may depend on oil sands for their energy solutions, is that we can no longer be sacrificed."

In addition to the infamous tar sands (see Huseman and Short 2012) in Alberta, the march toward the net energy cliff is arguably spearheaded in the West by the most recently developed family of extreme energy extraction methods known as "fracking," a colloquial expression that usually refers to the extraction of shale gas, coal-bed methane (CBM)—termed coal seam gas (CSG) in Australia—and "tight oil." Exploitation of unconventional oil and gas is a new, more extreme form of fossil fuel extraction, targeting much less permeable rock formations than previous conventional oil and gas extraction. It is characterized by the drilling of dense patterns of, usually horizontal, wells (up to eight per square mile or more) in conjunction with other more intense processes such as hydraulic fracturing and dewatering. Different rock formations can be targeted, such as shale (shale gas and oil) and coal (coal-bed methane), but the negative impacts on the environment and society are very similar. For many local people affected, fracking has come to mean petroleum extraction companies turning up where they live and coating the area in hundreds or thousands of well pads, compressor stations, and pipelines alongside large volumes of truck traffic, with some likening it to an "invasion" and "occupation" (Perry 2012, p. 81) bringing with it a large variety of negative consequences for them and their environment.

2.6.5. CONCLUDING THOUGHTS

In an era of peaked conventional supplies (see Heinberg 2014), extractive industries are principally concerned with finding new fossil fuels to extract to ensure continued profits, the cumulative impacts of which are likely to be little more than simple "externalities" for the companies involved. Focused as they are on getting gas and oil out of the ground regardless, the industry and

---

18. Peak oil and the attendant rise in the price of oil is here understood as an expression of the contradiction between the natural limits of production and the treadmill of accumulation, what Marx called materials-supplies shortages, as argued above.

19. Timoney (2007) is a damning report on waterway pollution, highlighting arsenic among other highly toxic substances.

their government supporters are concerned to utilize the technologies that can be used to do just that. Moreover, they work on a drilling-site-by-drilling-site basis, and the cumulative impact of the whole process seems to be of little concern.

In the countries where fracking development has taken place, it has been controversial and divisive. Supporters of unconventional gas development often claim that it reduces gas prices, creates employment opportunities, and provides "energy security," all the while producing lower carbon emissions than coal. Its detractors often contest all such claims, usually pointing to contrary data emerging from the United States and Australia. Indeed, in numerous studies from both countries, local communities most affected by developments often cite considerable negative impacts on the environment and human health, including groundwater contamination, air pollution, radioactive and toxic waste, water usage, earthquakes, methane migration, and the industrialization of rural landscapes,[20] the cumulative effect of which has led to calls for the United Nations Human Rights Council (HRC; Environment and Human Rights Advisory 2011) to condemn fracking as a threat to basic human rights, particularly the rights to water and health. Fracking development is fast becoming a human rights issue (see Short et al. 2014; Elliot and Short 2014; Grear 2014; Grear et al. 2014). The United Nations Environment Programme (UNEP) has issued a "global alert" (UNEP 2012) on the issue of fracking development, warning of significant environmental risks to the air, soil, and water (contamination and usage competition); ecosystem damage; habitat and biodiversity impacts; and fugitive gas emissions—which will endanger carbon reduction targets. In terms of public health, UNEP (2012, 6–7) warned of risks of pipeline explosions; release of toxins into air, soil, and water; and competition for land and water resources needed for food production and that unconventional gas would likely be used "in addition to coal rather than being a substitute" (UNEP 2012, 7–9, 12) and would thus pose a threat to the development of sustainable economies. In a recent paper, de Rijke noted, "the extraordinary expansion of the unconventional gas industry has . . . led to questions about social power and the rights of individuals and local communities, the role of multinational corporations in politics and rural service provision, as well as related questions regarding fundamental processes of democracy, capitalist economies and social justice" (de Rijke 2013, p. 15), while the "close relationship between governments and powerful multinational corporations brings to the fore questions about political influence and human rights" (de Rijke 2013, p. 17).

Modern-day neoliberal capitalism[21] is the vital structural context to these issues, because the "problem is capitalism" (Lynch et al. 2013, p. 1011). It may be obvious to some, but growth-driven capitalism is antithetical to a physical reality of finite resources. As the natural world is finite, capitalism is inherently ecologically unsustainable and "sustainable development" an oxymoron. Planetary boundaries, "the limits to growth," and the *process* of extreme energy" are factors that will likely create a perfect storm for current and future human insecurity if policy makers continue to refuse to accept the realities and implications of these phenomena.

REFERENCES

Ahmed, N., 2014: Are you opposed to fracking? Then you might just be a terrorist. *Guardian*, 21 January, www.theguardian.com/environment/earth-insight/2014/jan/21/fracking-activism-protest-terrorist-oil-corporate-spies.

Anderson, B. J., and G. L. Theodori, 2009: Local leaders' perceptions of energy development in the Barnett shale. *South. Rural Sociol.*, **24** (1),113–129.

Apple, B. E., 2014: Mapping fracking: An analysis of law, power, and regional distribution in the United States. *Harv. Environ. Law Rev.*, **38**, 217–244.

Bakan, J., 2005: *The Corporation: The Pathological Pursuit of Profit and Power.* Constable and Robinson, 240 pp.

---

20. Reports of considerable negative impacts go well beyond the anecdotal realm; see, for example, environmental and health studies such as Brown (2014), McDermott-Levy et al. (2013), Moore et al. (2014), Osborn et al. (2011), and Vengosh et al. (2014) and social scientific enquiries such as Perry (2012), Anderson and Theodori (2009), Apple (2014), Beach (2013), Gramling and Freudenburg (1992), and Fleming and Measham (2014).

21. Neoliberal capitalism is a policy-oriented school of thought that redirects control of economic factors from the public sector to the private sector, a return to the laissez-faire economic liberalism of the nineteenth century.

Barnett, J., 2001: Environmental security and U.S. foreign policy. *The Environment, International Relations, and U.S. Foreign Policy*, P. G. Harris, Ed., Georgetown University Press, 288 pp.

Barry, J., and K. Woods, 2009: The environment. *Human Rights: Politics and Practice*, M. Goodhart, Ed., Oxford University Press, 380–395.

Beach, D., 2013: How the fracking boom impacts rural Ohio. EcoWatch, http://ecowatch.com/2013/09/16/fracking-boom-impacting-rural-ohio/.

Bedell, F., 2014: Economic injustice as an understanding of the existence of two Americas—Wealth and poverty. *Open J. Polit. Sci.*, **4**, 101–108, https://doi.org/10.4236/ojps.2014.43011.

Black, E., 2008: America with no plan for oil interruption: Ironically, as price per barrel drops, American oil supply from Canada imperiled. Cutting Edge News, www.thecuttingedgenews.com/index.php?article=896.

Bloomberg, 2010: Subsidies for renewables, biofuels dwarfed by supports for fossil fuels. Bloomberg, www.bloomberg.com/company/announcements/subsidies-for-renewables-biofuels-dwarfed-by-supports-for-2/.

Brown, V. J., 2014: Radionuclides in fracking wastewater: Managing a toxic blend. *Environ. Health Perspect.*, **122**, A50–A55, https://doi.org/10.1289/ehp.122-A50.

Carrington, D., 2014: Fracking boom will not tackle global warming, analysis warns. *Guardian*, 15 October, www.theguardian.com/environment/2014/oct/15/gas-boom-from-unrestrained-fracking-linked-to-emissions-rise.

Chomsky, N., 2013: Can civilization survive capitalism? AlterNet, www.alternet.org/noam-chomsky-can-civilization-survive-capitalism.

Connolly, N., 2012: Corporate social responsibility: A duplicitous distraction? *Int. J. Hum. Rights*, **16**, 1228–1249, https://doi.org/10.1080/13642987.2012.731193.

Crook, M., and D. Short, 2014: Marx, Lemkin and the genocide–ecocide nexus. *Int. J. Hum. Rights*, **18**, 298–319, https://doi.org/10.1080/13642987.2014.914703.

de Rijke, K., 2013: Hydraulically fractured: Unconventional gas and anthropology. *Anthropol. Today*, **29** (2), 13–17, https://doi.org/10.1111/1467-8322.12017.

Economist, 2013: Energy firms and climate change: Unburnable fuel. *Economist*, 4 May, www.economist.com/news/business/21577097-either-governments-are-not-serious-about-climate-change-or-fossil-fuel-firms-are.

Elliot, J., and D. Short, 2014: Fracking is driving UK civil and political rights violations. Ecologist, https://theecologist.org/2014/oct/30/fracking-driving-uk-civil-and-political-rights-violations.

Elson, D., 2002: Human rights and corporate profits: the UN Global Compact—Part of the solution or part of the problem? *Global Tensions: Challenges and Opportunities in the Global Economy*, L. Bernia and S. Bisnath, Eds., Routledge, 36–53.

Energy Information Administration, 2018: Renewable and alternative fuels. Energy Information Administration, https://www.eia.gov/totalenergy/data/browser/?tbl=T10.01#/?f=M&start=200001

Environment and Human Rights Advisory, 2011: A human rights assessment of hydraulic fracturing for natural gas. Environment and Human Rights Advisory Rep., 36 pp., https://earthworks.org/publications/a_human_rights_assessment_of_hydraulic_fracturing_for_natural_gas/.

Fleming, D. A., and T. G. Measham, 2014: Local economic impacts of an unconventional energy boom: The coal seam gas industry in Australia. *Aust. J. Agric. Resour. Econ.*, **59**, 78–94, https://doi.org/10.1111/1467-8489.12043.

Gramling, R., and W. Freudenburg, 1992: Opportunity-threat, development, and adaptation: Toward a comprehensive framework for social impact assessment. *Rural Sociol.*, **57**, 216–234, https://doi.org/10.1111/j.1549-0831.1992.tb00464.x.

Grear, A., 2014: Fracking—Human rights must not be ignored! Ecologist, https://theecologist.org/2014/oct/30/fracking-human-rights-must-not-be-ignored.

——, T. Kerns, E. Grant, K. Morrow, and D. Short, 2014: A human rights assessment of hydraulic fracturing and other unconventional gas development in the United Kingdom. Extreme Energy Initiative Rep., 125 pp.

Grose, T. K., 2013: As U.S. cleans its energy mix, it ships coal problems abroad. National Geographic, http://news.nationalgeographic.com/news/energy/2013/03/130315-us-coal-exports/.

Heinberg, R., 2007: Peak coal: Sooner than you think. On Line Opinion, www.onlineopinion.com.au/view.asp?article=5869.

——, 2014: *Snake Oil: How Fracking's False Promises of Plenty Imperils Our Future*. Clairview Books, 160 pp.

Hinkley, R. C., 2002: How corporate law inhibits social responsibility. *Humanist*, March/April, 26.

Hönisch, B., and Coauthors, 2012: The geological record of ocean acidification science. *Science*, **335**, 1058–1063, https://doi.org/10.1126/science.1208277.

Human Rights Council, 2011: Report of the special rapporteur on the human right to safe drinking water and sanitation. UN Rep. A/HRC/18/33/Add.4, 21 pp.

Humphreys, S., 2008: Climate change and human rights: A rough guide. International Council on Human Rights Policy Rep., 127 pp.

Humphries, M., 2008: North American oil sands: History of development, prospects for the future. Congressional Research Service Rep. RL34258, 30 pp., www.fas.org/sgp/crs/misc/RL34258.pdf.

Huseman, J., and D. Short, 2012: A slow industrial genocide: Tar sands and the indigenous peoples of northern Alberta. *Int. J. Hum. Rights*, **16**, 216–237, https://doi.org/10.1080/13642987.2011.649593.

International Energy Agency, 2011: World energy outlook: 2011. International Energy Agency Rep., 660 pp.

——, 2013: Key world energy statistics. International Energy Agency Rep., 82 pp.

IPCC, 2007a: Summary for policymakers. *Climate Change 2007: The Physical Science Basis*, S. Solomon et al., Eds., Cambridge University Press, 1–18.

——, 2007b: Projections of future changes in climate. *Climate Change 2007: The Physical Science Basis*, S. Solomon et al., Eds., Cambridge University Press, 12–17.

——, 2013a: Summary for policymakers. *Climate Change 2013: The Physical Science Basis*, T. F. Stocker et. al., Eds., Cambridge University Press, 1–29.

——, 2013b: *Climate Change 2013: The Physical Science Basis*. Cambridge University Press, 1535 pp., https://doi.org/10.1017/CBO9781107415324.

——, 2014: *Climate Change 2014: Impacts, Adaptation, and Vulnerability. Part A: Global and Sectoral Aspects*. Cambridge University Press, 1132 pp., http://www.ipcc.ch/pdf/assessment-report/ar5/wg2/WGIIAR5-PartA_FINAL.pdf.

Jha, A., 2006: Boiled alive. *Guardian*, 26 July, www.theguardian.com/environment/2006/jul/26/science.g2.

Jones, C. A., and D. L. Levy, 2009: Business strategies and climate change. *Changing Climates in North American Politics*, H. Selin and S. D. VanDeveer. Eds., MIT Press, 219–240.

Klare, M., 2011: The era of extreme energy: Life after the age of oil. Huffington Post, www.huffingtonpost.com/michael-t-klare/the-era-of-xtreme-energy_b_295304.html.

Laboratory for Aviation and the Environment, 2013: Air pollution causes 200,000 early deaths each year in the U.S. Massachusetts Institute of Technology, http://lae.mit.edu/?p=2821.

Lloyd-Davies, E., 2013: Defining extreme energy: A process not a category. Extreme Energy Initiative, http://extremeenergy.org/2013/07/25/defining-extreme-energy-a-process-not-a-category/.

Lynch, M., M. Long, K. Barrett, and P. Stretesky, 2013: Is it a crime to produce ecological disorganization? Why green criminology and political economy matter in the analysis of global ecological harms. *Br. J. Criminol.*, **53**, 997–1016, https://doi.org/10.1093/bjc/azt051.

Maggio, G., and G. Cacciola, 2012: When will oil, natural gas, and coal peak? *Fuel*, **98**, 111–123, https://doi.org/10.1016/j.fuel.2012.03.021.

Malin, S., 2014: There's no real choice but to sign: Neoliberalization and normalization of hydraulic fracturing on Pennsylvania farmland. *J. Environ. Stud. Sci.*, **4**, 17–27, https://doi.org/10.1007/s13412-013-0115-2.

Marx, K., 1968: *Theories of Surplus Value*. Vol. II. Progress Publishers, 661 pp.

——, and F. Engels, 1967: *Capital*. Vol. III. International Publishers, 992 pp.

Mayer, J., 2010: Covert operations: The billionaire brothers who are waging a war against Obama. *New Yorker*, 30 August, www.newyorker.com/magazine/2010/08/30/covert-operations.

McDermott-Levy, R., N. Kaktins, and B. Sattler, 2013: Fracking, the environment, and health: New energy practices may threaten public health. *Amer. J. Nurs.*, **113** (6), 45–51, https://doi.org/10.1097/01.NAJ.0000431272.83277.f4.

Meadows, D. H., D. L. Meadows, J. Randers, and W. W. Behrens, 1972: *The Limits to Growth: A Report for the Club of Rome's Project on the Predicament of Mankind*. Universe Books, 205 pp.

Mobbs, P., 2008: Sheet E1. Peak energy: The limits to oil and gas production. Free Range Activism, http://www.fraw.org.uk/mei/archive/handouts/e-series/e01/e01-peak_energy.html.

——, 2013: Economically and politically fracked: "Behind every picture lies a story"—Statistical reality versus PR-hype within the political project of unconventional gas in Britain. Free Range Activism, www.fraw.org.uk/mei/musings/2013/20130725-behind_every_picture_lies_a_story.html.

——, 2015: Environmentalists' oil price panic reflects their own existential crisis. Ecologist, www.theecologist.org/blogs_and_comments/commentators/2703420/environmentalists_oil_price_panic_reflects_their_own_existential_crisis.html.

Moore, C. W., B. Zielinska, G. Petron, and R. B. Jackson, 2014: Air impacts of increased natural gas acquisition, processing, and use: A critical review. *Environ. Sci. Technol.*, **48**, 8349–8359, https://doi.org/10.1021/es4053472.

Murphy, David J. and Charles A. S. Hall. 2011. Energy return on investment, peak oil, and the end of economic growth in "Ecological Economics Reviews." Robert Costanza, Karin Limburg & Ida Kubiszewski, Eds. Ann. N.Y. Acad. Sci. 1219: 52–72

Murray, J., and J. Hansen, 2013: Peak oil and energy independence: Myths and reality. *Eos, Trans. Amer. Geophys. Union*, **94**, 245–252, https://doi.org/10.1002/2013EO280001.

Natural Resources Defense Fund (2014). "Tar Sands Crude Oil: Health Effects of a Dirty and Destructive Fuel" NDRC IB 14-02-B 2. https://www.nrdc.org/sites/default/files/tar-sands-health-effects-IB.pdf.

Osborn, S. G., A. Vengosh, N. R. Warner, and R. B. Jackson, 2011: Methane contamination of drinking water accompanying gas-well drilling and hydraulic fracturing. *Proc. Natl. Acad. Sci. USA*, **108**, 8172–8176, https://doi.org/10.1073/pnas.1100682108.

Palast, G., 2002: *The Best Democracy Money Can Buy*. Pluto Press, 224 pp.

Patz, J. A., D. Campbell-Lendrum, T. Holloway, and J. A. Foley, 2005: Impact of regional climate change on human health. *Nature*, **438**, 310–317, https://doi.org/10.1038/nature04188.

Perry, S. L., 2012: Development, land use, and collective trauma: The Marcellus shale gas boom in rural Pennsylvania. *Cult. Agric. Food Environ.*, **34**, 81–92, https://doi.org/10.1111/j.2153-9561.2012.01066.x.

Petersen, K., 2007: Oil versus water: Toxic water poses threat to Alberta's indigenous communities. *Dominion*, Autumn, 12, 31, http://www.dominionpaper.ca/articles/1429.

Purdey, S. J., 2010: *Economic Growth, the Environment and International Relations: The Growth Paradigm*. Routledge, 192 pp.

Short, D., K. Hulme, and S. Bohm, 2014: Don't let human rights fall to wayside in fracking debate. Conversation, http://theconversation.com/dont-let-human-rights-fall-to-wayside-in-fracking-debate-24652.

——, J. Elliot, K. Norder, E. Lloyd-Davies, and J. Morley, 2015: Extreme energy, 'fracking' and human rights: A new field for human rights impact assessments? Extreme Energy Initiative, http://extremeenergy.org/2015/02/09/extreme-energy-fracking-and-human-rights-a-new-field-for-human-rights-impact-assessments/.

Stott, P., D. Stone, and M. Allen, 2004: Human contribution to the European heatwave of 2003. *Nature*, **432**, 610–614, https://doi.org/10.1038/nature03089.

Timoney, K. P., 2007: A study of water and sediment quality as related to public health issues. Treeline Ecological Research Rep., 83 pp.

Trivett, V., 2011: 25 US mega corporations: Where they rank if they were countries. Business Insider, www.businessinsider.com/25-corporations-bigger-tan-countries-2011-6?op=1.

Turner, G., 2007: A comparison of *The Limits to Growth* with thirty years of reality. CSIRO Working Paper Series 2008-09, 52 pp.

UNEP, 2011a: Athabasca oil sands, require massive investments and energy and produce massive amounts of oil and CO_2—Alberta, Canada. United Nations Environment Programme Global Environment Alert Service Rep. 54, 5 pp.

——, 2011b: Oil palm plantations: Threats and opportunities for tropical ecosystems. United Nations Environment Programme Global Environment Alert Service Rep. 73, 8 pp.

——, 2012: Gas fracking: Can we safely squeeze the rocks? United Nations Environment Programme Global Environment Alert Service Rep., 15 pp.

Vengosh, A. R. B. Jackson, N. Warner, T. H. Darrah, and A. Kondash, 2014: A critical review of the risks to water resources from unconventional shale gas development and hydraulic fracturing in the United States. *Environ. Sci. Technol.*, **48**, 8334–8348, https://doi.org/10.1021/es405118y.

White House, 1998: A national security strategy for a new century. White House Rep., 61 pp.

WHO, 2009: Euroheat: Improving public health responses to extreme weather heat-waves—Summary for policy-makers. WHO Regional Office for Europe Rep., 7 pp.

World Coal Association, 2015: Coal statistics. World Coal Association, www.worldcoal.org/resources/coal-statistics.

3

NATURAL DISASTERS AND ENVIRONMENTAL SECURITY

INTRODUCTION TO UNIT 3

This unit introduces the environmental security challenges posed by natural disasters. In order to understand the connections between natural disasters, their management, and environmental security, it is necessary to briefly introduce the concept of environmental and security cascading effects as first described in the report "National security and the threat of climate change" (CNA 2007). The authors of that report, a team of retired senior military officers, postulated that environmental hazards/threats, whether single-event natural disasters or long-term climatic anomalies, can put additional stress an already degraded natural environment and may contribute to geopolitical destabilization. They went on to describe how that destabilization might manifest itself from a U.S. national security perspective. Lanicci and Ramsay (2010) and Lanicci and Thropp (2014) presented two conceptualizations of this idea, one for less-developed and one for more-developed nations, respectively, reproduced here as Figure 3.1.

The premise of Figure 3.1 is that the same type of natural disaster may have differing effects and impacts depending on the governance, institutions, and prosperity of the affected country. Note that the primary differences between the figures appear at the end of the

"destabilizing effects" tier and throughout the "security impacts" tier. Lanicci and Thropp (2014) argued that for more-developed countries, damage to or loss of critical infrastructure from a natural disaster can be a significant security issue compared to the other effects shown along that tier and lead to loss of economic power and weakened national security posture in these countries. Along the third tier, the differences in security impacts are more notable, with the potential for failed states/radicalization and resource-based conflicts being an issue in the less-developed countries. The relationship between natural disasters, their management, and environmental security is presented within this context, and we invite you to use these conceptualizations as a means to evaluate the connections among environmental events, their immediate impacts, and their security implications.

In chapters 3.1 and 3.2, we define the concepts of *hazards* and *vulnerability* in order to set the stage for discussion of natural disasters. To facilitate understanding of the relationships between natural hazards and population vulnerability, we introduce two conceptual models for determining the vulnerability of a region and its population to natural disasters. One model is at a basic level and allows you to perform a cursory analysis of a

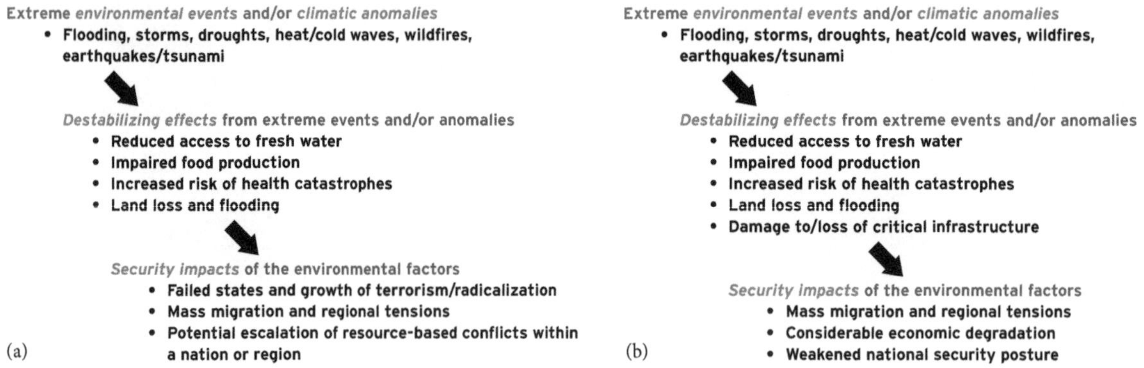

Extreme *environmental events* **and/or** *climatic anomalies*
- **Flooding, storms, droughts, heat/cold waves, wildfires, earthquakes/tsunami**

Destabilizing effects **from extreme events and/or anomalies**
- **Reduced access to fresh water**
- **Impaired food production**
- **Increased risk of health catastrophes**
- **Land loss and flooding**

Security impacts **of the environmental factors**
- **Failed states and growth of terrorism/radicalization**
- **Mass migration and regional tensions**
- **Potential escalation of resource-based conflicts within a nation or region**

(a)

Extreme *environmental events* **and/or** *climatic anomalies*
- **Flooding, storms, droughts, heat/cold waves, wildfires, earthquakes/tsunami**

Destabilizing effects **from extreme events and/or anomalies**
- **Reduced access to fresh water**
- **Impaired food production**
- **Increased risk of health catastrophes**
- **Land loss and flooding**
- **Damage to/loss of critical infrastructure**

Security impacts **of the environmental factors**
- **Mass migration and regional tensions**
- **Considerable economic degradation**
- **Weakened national security posture**

(b)

Figure 3.1. (a) CNA environment-to-security flow as described by Lanicci and Ramsay (2010) for less-developed countries; (b) environment-to-security flow as described by Lanicci and Thropp (2014) for more-developed countries.

population's vulnerability from data that can be gathered from a number of suitable websites; this model is used in chapter 3.3, which examines the vulnerability of the U.S. Gulf Coast region prior to the landfall of Hurricane Katrina in August 2005. The second model, known as Pressure and Release (PAR), is more complex because it requires you to gather the hazards and vulnerability data and also analyze the viability of a nation's institutions and governance practices in order to arrive at a more comprehensive assessment of natural disaster vulnerability.

Analyzing the disaster vulnerability of a region allows you to determine the environmental threats posed to the population and their ability to anticipate, react to, and recover from a natural disaster and, thus, evaluate potential impacts on regional security. For more advanced classes, the PAR model can be used as the primary means to trace the origins of population vulnerability to a set of root causes that may be far removed in time and space from the disaster event itself. And as we will see later in this unit, more-developed countries tend to deal with natural disasters differently than less-developed countries, based to a large extent on the degree to which the country has the economic foundation, robust institutions, and resilient infrastructure that can anticipate, react to, and learn from natural disasters. In chapter 3.3, we will see that even in more-developed countries such as the United States, if the natural-hazard event is powerful enough, it will overwhelm the government's ability to deal with its impacts. More-developed countries may be able to enact policies that improve disaster management as a result of lessons learned from a previous event; this topic will be examined in chapter 3.4. In countries without well-developed infrastructure and functioning political and social institutions, the impacts of natural-hazard events have the potential to destabilize not only the affected states or provinces but also the entire country, as we will see in chapter 3.5.

STUDENT LEARNING OBJECTIVES

1. Describe the different types of natural hazards and technological hazards and explain how natural hazards can cause technological hazards, and vice versa.
2. Distinguish between natural hazards that are manifested as single extreme events and those that are associated with climatic anomalies.
3. Describe the concept of vulnerability and provide examples using either the simplified disaster vulnerability model, the PAR model, or both.
4. Explain how hazards and vulnerabilities come together to cause a disaster, using an example from the unit chapters or another source.
5. Explain how disasters affect less-developed countries differently than more-developed countries, using an example from the unit chapters or another source.

KEY TERMS AND CONCEPTS

Hazard An event or physical condition that has the potential to cause fatalities, injuries, property damage, infrastructure damage, agricultural loss, damage to the environment, interruption of business, and other types of harm or loss

Natural hazard A hazard that originates in the natural environment

Technological hazard A hazard that is associated with a human-built entity

Extreme weather event Weather phenomena that are at the extremes of the historical distribution, especially severe or unseasonal weather

Climatic anomaly The difference between the average climate over a period of several decades or more and the climate during a particular month or season

Vulnerability The characteristics of a person or group and their situation that influence their capacity to anticipate, cope with, resist, and recover from the impact of a natural hazard

Disaster The outcome resulting when hazards and vulnerability collide

Traditional media Any form of mass communication available before the advent of digital media; this includes television, radio, newspapers, books, and magazines

Social media A group of Internet-based applications that build on the ideological and technological foundations of Web 2.0 and that allow the creation and exchange of user-generated content

Return period The average time (usually expressed in years) until the next occurrence of a specific event; this is also known as a recurrence interval

QUESTIONS FOR ANALYSIS AND DISCUSSION

Evaluate the utility of the two environment-to-security cascading effects concept models presented in Figure 3.1 as you read through the case studies in chapters 3.3 and 3.5. Did the models provide you with an effective construct for thinking about the progression of events associated with Hurricane Katrina and the Balkans flooding? Would you change the concept models? If so, how?

REFERENCES

CNA, 2007: National security and the threat of climate change. CNA Rep., 63 pp.

Lanicci, J. M., and J. Ramsay, 2010: Environmental security: Exploring relationships between the natural environment, national security, and homeland security. *Fifth Symp. on Policy and Socio-Economic Research*, Atlanta, GA, Amer. Meteor. Soc., PD.1.

——, and J. E. Thropp, 2014: Guaranteed access to space, Kennedy Space Center/Cape Canaveral, and climate change. *Fifth Conf. on Environment and Health*, Atlanta, GA, Amer. Meteor. Soc., 4.5, https://ams.confex.com/ams/94Annual/webprogram/Paper241731.html.

NATURAL HAZARDS OVERVIEW

John M. Lanicci

3.1.1. INTRODUCTION

The International Risk Management Institute (IRMI) defines a *hazard* as "conditions that increase the probability of loss" (IRMI 2018), while the U.S. Federal Emergency Management Agency (FEMA) defines it as "an event or physical condition that has the potential to cause fatalities, injuries, property damage, infrastructure damage, agricultural loss, damage to the environment, interruption of business and other types of harm or loss" (FEMA 1997).

Hazards are generally classified into two broad categories: *natural* and *technological* (or human-made). For the purposes of this unit, we adopt the taxonomy used by the Centre for Research on the Epidemiology of Disasters (CRED; www.emdat.be), with some modifications, shown in Table 3.1.1. Natural hazards, which originate within the natural environment, can be classified into

geophysical, hydrological, meteorological, climatological, biological, and *extraterrestrial*. Within the CRED taxonomy, we modify the definitions of meteorological and climatological hazards in order to distinguish between those that operate on short time scales as an individual extreme weather event[1] (e.g., tropical cyclone) and those that operate on longer time scales as a climatic anomaly[2] (e.g., drought). Both time scales are important to environmental security practitioners. We also modify the extraterrestrial hazard definition to emphasize solar disturbances (space weather) that can affect navigation, communication, and energy production and distribution systems. For the technological hazards, we adopt the CRED categories of *industrial, transport,* and *miscellaneous accidents* but add a fourth one for *infrastructure failure,* since critical infrastructure vulnerability is a very

---

1. According to the Met Office, extreme weather events are defined as "weather phenomena that are at the extremes of the historical distribution, especially severe or unseasonal weather" (UKMO 2018a). For the purposes of this textbook, an extreme weather event does not have to be record setting in terms of meteorological variables (e.g., pressure, temperature, precipitation) but unusual enough to cause casualties, damage to property, and/or disruption of business and normal human activities. Later in the chapter, we discuss the determination of thresholds for several of these impact categories.

2. According to the American Meteorological Society Glossary, a climate anomaly is defined as "the difference between the average climate over a period of several decades or more, and the climate during a particular month or season" (AMS 2018). Note that this definition does not provide a *threshold* for determining an anomaly.

Table 3.1.1. Hazard categories used in this chapter.

Hazard category (major)	Hazard subcategory	Definition [from Emergency Events Database (EM-DAT) classification used directly or modified for this unit]
Natural	Geophysical	A hazard originating from the solid earth
	Hydrological	A hazard caused by the occurrence, movement, and distribution of surface and subsurface freshwater and saltwater
	Meteorological	A hazard caused by extreme weather events lasting from minutes to days
	Climatological	A hazard caused by departures from long-term climatic normals, with time scales ranging from weeks to years
	Biological	A hazard caused by the exposure to living organisms and their toxic substances (e.g., venom, mold) or vectorborne diseases that they may carry
	Extraterrestrial	A hazard caused by solar disturbances that affect Earth's magnetosphere, ionosphere, and thermosphere; also includes effects and impacts from asteroids, meteoroids, and comets as they pass near Earth, enter Earth's atmosphere, and/or strike Earth
Technological	Industrial accident	A hazard caused by accidental release of chemicals, radiation, or other hazardous substances/materials or caused by explosion, fire, gas leak, or poisoning
	Transport accident	A hazard produced as the result of an air, road, rail, or water transport accident
	Infrastructure failure	A hazard produced as the result of a catastrophic failure of critical infrastructure such as transportation, energy, water, or other type
	Miscellaneous accident	A hazard produced as the result of an accident that is not included in the other categories above

important concept in environmental security, especially in more-developed countries.

A discussion of every hazard listed in Table 3.1.1 is beyond the scope of this unit. Instead, we select three natural hazards (tropical cyclones, floods, and drought), and for each, we provide a physical description, associated effects and impacts, and geographic distribution. Note that a tropical cyclone can be considered an extreme weather event, while a drought is a longer-term hazard from a climatic anomaly, and a flood can be caused *either* by a single extreme weather event (e.g., flash flood) or a climatic anomaly (e.g., excessive seasonal flood).

3.1.2. TROPICAL CYCLONES

The Met Office (UKMO) describes a *tropical cyclone* as a low-pressure system located over tropical or subtropical waters, with organized deep moist convection and winds circulating around a well-defined center (counter-clockwise in the northern hemisphere and clockwise in the southern hemisphere) (UKMO 2018b). A tropical

cyclone can extend to depths of 15 km (over 49,000 feet) in the atmosphere. While there is no "typical" diameter for a tropical cyclone, they can vary from less than 4° of latitude (444 km, 240 nautical miles) to greater than 16° of latitude (1778 km, 960 nautical miles) (Joint Typhoon Warning Center 2015). Its speed of movement is typically 9–14 kt (10–16 mph) but can be as high as 35 kt (40 mph) (UKMO 2018b). The tropical cyclone is usually identified early in its life cycle as a *tropical depression*, and when its maximum sustained winds reach 34 kt (39 mph) or higher, it becomes a *tropical storm*. Once the maximum sustained winds reach 64 kt (74 mph) or higher, the tropical cyclone is called a *hurricane* in the Atlantic and the eastern North Pacific Oceans or a *typhoon* in the western North Pacific Ocean. Depending on the size and intensity of the cyclone, hurricane-force winds can extend 80 km (43 nautical miles) or more from the storm's center (University Center for Atmospheric Research 2010). In contrast to the extratropical cyclone more commonly seen in midlatitudes (especially in winter) that draws its energy from thermal contrasts associated with cold and warm

Figure 3.1.1. Tropical cyclone damage examples: (a) the Treasure Bay Casino in Biloxi, Mississippi, completely moved off its moorings by Hurricane Katrina's storm surge (www.stormsurge.noaa.gov); (b) flooding in the Houston area from Tropical Storm Allison (https://texashurricane.files.wordpress.com/2011/06/20010609_houstonfloodallison.jpg); (c) wind damage in a Fijian village from Severe Tropical Cyclone Winston, as photographed by the New Zealand Defense Force (www.newsweek.com/fiji-tropical-cyclone-winston-photos-429070); and (d) dashcam video of tornado that formed during Typhoon Soudelor's transit through southern Taiwan (www.washingtonpost.com/news/capital-weather-gang/wp/2015/08/10/dashcam-records-terrifying-video-of-typhoon-soudelor-tornado-in-taiwan/?utm_term=.8cf18063569f).

fronts, a tropical cyclone draws its energy from a core of warm, moist air that circulates about its center and from the warm sea surface temperatures in its environment [National Hurricane Center (NHC) 2018a].

Tropical cyclones are categorized as a meteorological hazard in Table 3.1.1. However, they can be responsible for causing such hydrological hazards as flooding and biological hazards such as water contamination (this occurred in New Orleans, Louisiana, in the aftermath of Hurricane Katrina). It is also possible for a tropical cyclone to cause one or more of the technological hazards listed in Table 3.1.1. The primary physical effects and impacts from the tropical cyclone itself are *storm surge* and *storm tide, heavy rainfall* and *inland flooding, high winds, rip currents,* and *tornadoes* (NHC 2018b), which are described below.

Storm surge occurs when water is continuously pushed shoreward by the winds circulating around the cyclone. The intensity of the surge is dependent upon many factors, such as changes in the cyclone's strength and movement speed, the interaction between the cyclone's track and the geometry of the shoreline, the cyclone's radius of maximum winds, and characteristics of the coastline itself, such as depths of bays and estuaries and their configuration (NHC 2018b). *Storm tide* is water rise due to the combination of storm surge and astronomical high tide (NHC 2018b). Figure 3.1.1a shows an example of the effects of storm surge from Hurricane Katrina.

Heavy rains and *flooding* are another dangerous effect from tropical cyclones. According to the U.S. National Weather Service (NWS), nearly 60% of the flood-associated deaths from tropical cyclones occur

Table 3.1.2. Saffir–Simpson hurricane scale (courtesy of NHC).

Category	Sustained winds	Types of damage due to hurricane winds
1	74–95 mph 64–82 kt 33–42 m s^{-1}	Very dangerous winds will produce some damage: Well-constructed frame homes could have damage to roof, shingles, vinyl siding, and gutters. Large branches of trees will snap, and shallowly rooted trees may be toppled. Extensive damage to power lines and poles likely will result in power outages that could last a few to several days.
2	96–110 mph 83–95 kt 43–49 m s^{-1}	Extremely dangerous winds will cause extensive damage: Well-constructed frame homes could sustain major roof and siding damage. Many shallowly rooted trees will be snapped or uprooted and block numerous roads. Near-total power loss is expected with outages that could last from several days to weeks.
3 (major)	111–129 mph 96–112 kt 49–58 m s^{-1}	Devastating damage will occur: Well-built framed homes may incur major damage or removal of roof decking and gable ends. Many trees will be snapped or uprooted, blocking numerous roads. Electricity and water will be unavailable for several days to weeks after the storm passes.
4 (major)	130–156 mph 113–136 kt 58–70 m s^{-1}	Catastrophic damage will occur: Well-built framed homes can sustain severe damage with loss of most of the roof structure and/or some exterior walls. Most trees will be snapped or uprooted and power poles downed. Fallen trees and power poles will isolate residential areas. Power outages will last weeks to possibly months. Most of the area will be uninhabitable for weeks or months.
5 (major)	157 mph or higher 137 kt or higher 71 m s^{-1} or higher	Catastrophic damage will occur: A high percentage of framed homes will be destroyed, with total roof failure and wall collapse. Fallen trees and power poles will isolate residential areas. Power outages will last for weeks to possibly months. Most of the area will be uninhabitable for weeks or months.

inland from the storm's landfall (NWS 2018a). In many cases, the amount of rainfall from a tropical cyclone is a function of the storm's speed of movement, not just its intensity. A good example is Tropical Storm Allison, which struck Houston, Texas, in June 2001. This weak but slow-moving tropical cyclone made landfall southwest of Galveston, Texas, on 5 June then tracked slowly northward across western portions of the Houston area over the next 18 hours. Despite weakening to a tropical depression over the next four days, it produced as much as 36 inches (914 mm) of rainfall over southeast Texas, with the highest totals to the north and east of Houston. The record-setting rainfall[3] was mainly due to its slow progression before becoming stationary over eastern Texas. After several days, it finally began to move southward and exited the Texas coast over nearly the same location where it made landfall five days earlier (Stewart 2011). Figure 3.1.1b shows a photograph of the extensive flooding from this system.

High winds are a well-known tropical cyclone effect. In fact, the Saffir–Simpson hurricane intensity scale is based on maximum sustained winds (see Table 3.1.2). However, it is important to point out that wind speeds can be considerably higher in gusts or squalls. There are two primary ways in which a tropical cyclone's winds cause damage and destruction. First is when the winds lift the roofs from buildings, and second is when the debris picked up by the high winds becomes projectiles that subsequently damage other structures (NWS 2018a). An animation illustrating wind damage as a function of the Saffir–Simpson scale intensity can be found online (at www.nhc.noaa.gov/aboutsshws.php). Figure 3.1.1c shows an example of wide-scale wind damage over Fiji from Severe Tropical Cyclone[4] Winston in February 2016.

Tropical cyclones can produce *tornadoes* upon making landfall. These are most likely to occur in the cyclone's right-front quadrant relative to its motion. They

---

3. In 2017, these records were largely eclipsed by Hurricane Harvey, which produced 36 to 48 inches (914–1219 mm) in the Houston metro area (Blake and Zelinsky 2018).

4. Equivalent to a hurricane or typhoon, using the sustained wind speed definition presented earlier.

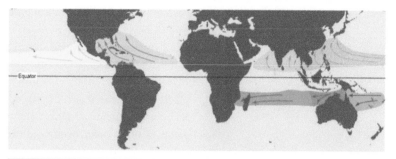

North Atlantic Ocean, the Gulf of Mexico, and the Caribbean Sea

The Hurricane season is "officially" from 1 June to 30 November. Peak activity is in early to mid-September. Once in a few years there may be a tropical cyclone occurring in May or December.

Northeast Pacific basin (Mexico to about the dateline)

A broad peak with activity beginning in late May or early June and going until late October or early November with a peak in storminess in late August/early September.

Northwest Pacific basin (From the dateline to Asia including the South China Sea)

Occur all year round regularly though there is a distinct minimum in February and the first half of March. The main season goes from July to November with a peak in late August/early September.

North Indian basin (Including the Bay of Bengal and the Arabian Sea)

A double peak of activity in May and November though tropical cyclones are seen from April to December. The severe cyclonic storms (>74 mph / 119 km/h winds) occur almost exclusively from April to June and again in late September to early December.

Southwest Indian basin (From Africa to about 100°E)

Beginning in late October/early November, reaching a double peak in activity—one in mid-January and one in mid-February to early March, and then ending in May.

Southeast Indian/Australian basin (100°E to 142°E)

Beginning in late October/early November, reaching a double peak in activity—one in mid-January and one in mid-February to early March, and then ending in May. The Australian/Southeast Indian basin February lull in activity is a bit more pronounced than the Southwest Indian basin's lull.

Australian/Southwest Pacific basin (142°E to about 120°W)

Begins in late October/early November, reaches a single peak in late February/early March, and then fades out in early May.

Figure 3.1.2. Tropical cyclone formation by regions and time of year [figure courtesy of NWS (2018b)].

can also occur within the cyclone's rainbands, sometimes far from the center of circulation (NWS 2018a). Figure 3.1.1d is a dashboard camera (dashcam) photograph taken from a tornado produced within Typhoon Soudelor in August 2015.

Figure 3.1.2 provides a geographic and temporal reference for tropical cyclone occurrence around the world. The hazards from tropical cyclones can cause casualties to people, pets, and livestock; damage and destruction to property, critical infrastructure, and the environment; and disruption to business and normal activities of a community.

3.1.3. FLOODS

The American Meteorological Society (AMS) Glossary of Meteorology defines a flood as "the overflowing of the normal confines of a stream or other body of water, or the accumulation of water over areas that are not normally submerged" (AMS 2018a). There are multiple ways a flood can develop, but generally, it is associated with one or more of the following phenomena: 1) excess precipitation, 2) storm surges, 3) seasonal flooding, 4) tsunami.

Precipitation that exceeds the amount that a geographic area can contain can cause a flood. The amount of rainfall that an area can contain is based on multiple

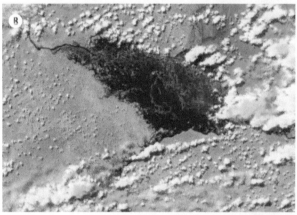

Figure 3.1.3. Flood types: (a) Nashville after two-day excess rainfall event in May 2010 (Camill 2010); (b) satellite view of seasonal flooding of the Zambezi River basin in Zambia in 2004 [false color image displays flooded area as black; image courtesy of Jesse Allen based on data from the Moderate Resolution Imaging Spectroradiometer (MODIS) Rapid Response Team at NASA Goddard Space Flight Center (GSFC)]; (c) aerial photo from U.S. Navy helicopter over Sendai, Japan, in the aftermath of the March 2011 tsunami [courtesy of U.S. Navy (www.navy.mil/view_image. asp?id=98323)].

factors such as soil/vegetation type, terrain elevation and slope, presence of buildings, stormwater drainage structures, and rainfall rate. A 2-inch rainfall may not sound like a large amount, but if it falls within 20 minutes (equivalent to an hourly rate of 6 inches), it can easily overwhelm storm drainage and other diversion structures, causing a rapid rise of water known as a *flash flood*. In other cases, prolonged excess precipitation can cause a flood that gradually develops over a period of days. Figure 3.1.3a shows an example of multiday excess rainfall that produced flooding in Nashville, Tennessee, in May 2010. During this event, some areas received two-day rainfall exceeding 19 inches (480 mm).

Seasonal flooding occurs when certain recurring phenomena such as ice/snowmelt cause water levels to rise above flood stage and periodically inundate areas that are prone to flooding, such as the flood plains that surround rivers. Many areas around the world experience seasonal flooding; in some cases the floods benefit local agriculture by bringing nutrients to the soils in the floodplain. However, when a departure from climatically normal precipitation occurs, seasonal floods can exceed the region's ability to absorb and divert the water away, and the results are often catastrophic. Figure 3.1.3b shows an example of excessive seasonal flooding in April 2004 over Zambia.

A *tsunami* is a series of waves created when a body of water, such as an ocean, is rapidly displaced on a massive spatial scale. Earthquakes, mass movements above or below water, volcanic eruptions and other underwater explosions, landslides, large meteorite impacts, and nuclear weapons testing at sea all have the potential to generate a tsunami. As the displaced water approaches the shoreline, the magnitude of the wave increases, and the resulting flooding can extend for many kilometers inland [National Institute of Water and Atmospheric Research (NIWA) 2018]. Figure 3.1.3c is a wide-area photograph of the flooding from the Japanese tsunami in March 2011.

Based on the previous discussion, floods can be categorized as a meteorological, hydrological, climatological, or even a geophysical hazard in Table 3.1.1. As with tropical cyclones, floods can cause casualties to people, pets, and livestock; damage and destruction to property, critical infrastructure, and the environment; and disruption to business and normal activities of a community. Additionally, floods can result in biological hazards or cause one or more of the technological hazards in Table

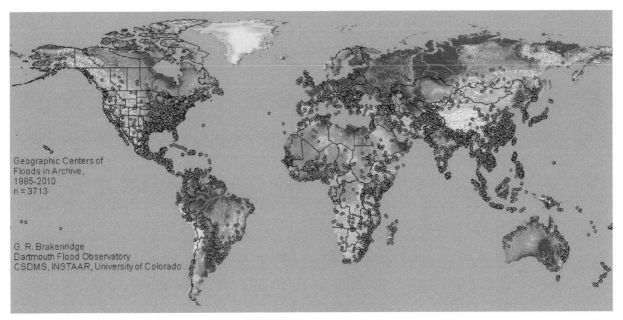

Geographic Centers of
Floods in Archive,
1985-2010
n = 3713

G. R. Brakenridge
Dartmouth Flood Observatory
CSDMS, INSTAAR, University of Colorado

Figure 3.1.4. Geographic locations of floods in the Dartmouth Flood Observatory archive, 1985–2010 (obtained from http://floodobservatory.colorado.edu).

3.1.1. Perhaps the most significant example in recent history was the Japanese tsunami in 2011.[5] The tsunami (a natural hazard) triggered the failure of the Fukushima Daiichi nuclear plant, resulting in a technological hazard (release of radioactive material into the atmosphere), whose track and intensity were subsequently influenced by atmospheric flow patterns along the Japanese coast and in the northwestern Pacific Ocean. Like tropical cyclones, floods are another natural hazard that can seriously affect both more-developed and less-developed countries. The geographic frequency of floods is illustrated in Figure 3.1.4, which is a worldwide flood archive map covering the period 1985–2010.

3.1.4. DROUGHTS

According to the AMS (2018b), a drought is "a period of abnormally dry weather sufficiently long enough to cause a serious hydrological imbalance." According to Wilhite and Glantz (1985), droughts can be categorized into four main types: 1) meteorological, 2) agricultural, 3) hydrologic, and 4) socioeconomic. The categories are defined primarily by the ways in which their effects and impacts are felt in a region. *Meteorological drought* is usually defined based on a departure of rainfall from the climatic normal for a period of time (weeks to months or longer) [National Drought Mitigation Center (NDMC) 2018]. *Agricultural drought* connects characteristics of drought to agricultural impacts. These can include precipitation deficits, abnormal evapotranspiration,[6] and deficits in soil moisture, groundwater, or reservoirs (NDMC 2018). A photograph of the effects of a 2012 agricultural drought on crops in Oklahoma is shown in Figure 3.1.5a. *Hydrological drought* occurs when water reserves available in aquifers, lakes, and reservoirs fall below the climatological average (NDMC 2018). Figures 3.1.5b and 3.1.5c are photographs of Lake Oroville, California, taken during periods of normal precipitation

---

5. A well-documented account of the tsunami can be found on the Natural Hazards web page of the National Centers for Environmental Information (see www.ngdc.noaa.gov/hazard/11mar2011.html). This web page also contains links to reports on the Fukushima Daiichi nuclear plant disaster.

6. Evapotranspiration is the process by which water is transferred from Earth's surface to the atmosphere, through a combination of liquid water *evaporation* (i.e., changing to water vapor) from water surfaces and bare soil and the *transpiration* of water from plants.

Figure 3.1.5. Drought type examples: (a) effects of a 2012 agricultural drought on the corn crop in Oklahoma (Tolman 2012); photographs of Lake Oroville, from (b) 20 July 2011 and (c) 5 September 2014, illustrating a hydrological drought (photos courtesy of California Department of Water Resources).

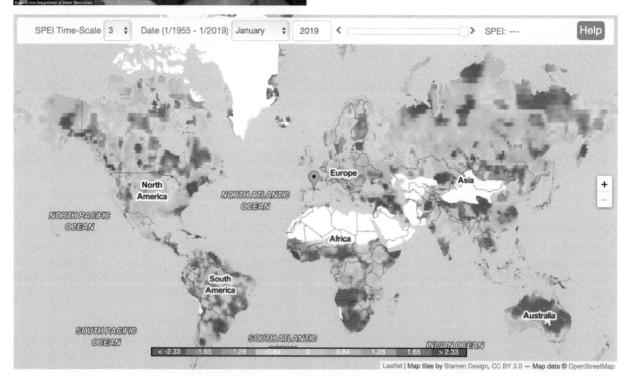

Figure 3.1.6. Three-month SPEI global drought monitor analysis for Nov 2018–Jan 2019. Deficit values are shown as shades of yellow, orange, and red, while surplus values are shown by green to blue shades (courtesy of http://sac.csic.es/spei/map/maps.html).

and hydrological drought, respectively. *Socioeconomic drought* is associated with the impacts of meteorological, agricultural, and hydrological drought on the supply and demand of an economic good or set of goods (NDMC 2018). It includes economic measures in addition to the physical and agricultural science–based measures featured in the other definitions.

Droughts can be considered climatological and hydrologic hazards using the definitions in Table 3.1.1. As with the previously described hazards, droughts affect more-developed and less-developed countries. The hazards from drought are primarily linked to agriculture and quality-of-life issues such as potable water for people, pets, and livestock. Drought can exacerbate or instigate other natural hazards, such as heat waves and wildfires. A good example comes from Russia during the summer of 2010, when this combination was responsible for total economic losses in excess of $3.6 billion (U.S. dollars), and an estimated 56,000 fatalities (determined by the increase in mortality over the rate from the previous year) (Munich Re 2015).

A number of agencies monitor the status of droughts around the world using different types of indices that account for surpluses and deficits in available groundwater. Figure 3.1.6 presents an example of one such measure, the standardized precipitation evapotranspiration index (SPEI; Vicente-Serrano et al. 2015). A relatively new index, the SPEI captures the primary impact on water demand from increased temperatures, which makes it valuable for monitoring the effects of climate change over different regions. Drought monitors such as the SPEI can be used in conjunction with other databases (e.g., food security) in order to identify at-risk regions in the world for humanitarian and/or other assistance.

Now that we have defined natural and technological hazards and described some examples of the former, the next logical step is to examine the ways in which natural hazards can act over a period of time to place populations at risk of harm and damage. This is done in the next chapter, which will introduce you to the concepts of vulnerability and natural disaster and the principles of disaster management.

REFERENCES

AMS, 2018a: Flood. Glossary of Meteorology, http://glossary.ametsoc.org/wiki/flood.

AMS, 2018b: Drought. Glossary of Meteorology, http://glossary.ametsoc.org/wiki/drought.

Blake, E. S., and D. A. Zelinsky, 2018: National Hurricane Center tropical cyclone report: Hurricane Harvey (AL092017). National Hurricane Center Rep., 77 pp., www.nhc.noaa.gov/data/tcr/AL092017_Harvey.pdf.

Camill, P., 2010: Global change: An overview. Nature Education Knowledge Project, www.nature.com/scitable/knowledge/library/global-change-an-overview-13255365.

FEMA, 1997: Multi Hazard Identification and Risk Assessment A Cornerstone of the National Mitigation Strategy. FEMA Rep., 34 pp., https://www.fema.gov/media-library-data/20130726-1545-20490-4487/mhira_in.pdf.

IRMI, 2018: Hazard. Glossary of Insurance and Risk Management Terms, www.irmi.com/term/insurance-definitions/hazard.

Joint Typhoon Warning Center, 2015: What is the average size of a tropical cyclone? Naval Oceanography Portal, www.usno.navy.mil/JTWC/product-information/frequently-asked-questions#tcsize.

Munich Re, 2015: Heat wave, drought, wildfires in Russia (Summer 2010). Munich Re Rep., 1 p., www.munichre.com/site/touch-naturalhazards/get/documents_ E-132629599/mr/assetpool.shared/Documents/5_Touch/_NatCatService/Catastrophe_portraits/event-report-hw-dr-wf-russia-touch-en-update.pdf.

NDMC, 2018: Types of drought. NDMC, https://drought.unl.edu/Education/DroughtIn-depth/TypesofDrought.aspx.

NHC, 2018a: Tropical cyclone. Glossary of NHC Terms, www.nhc.noaa.gov/aboutgloss.shtml#t.

——, 2018b: Hurricane preparedness—Hazards. NHC, www.nhc.noaa.gov/prepare/hazards.php.

National Institute of Water and Atmospheric Research, 2018: Tsuami. NIWA, https://www.niwa.co.nz/natural-hazards/hazards/tsunami.

NWS, 2018a: Tropical cyclone hazards. NWS, www.weather.gov/jetstream/tc_hazards.

——, 2018b: Tropical cyclone introduction. NWS, www.weather.gov/jetstream/tc.

Stewart, S. R., 2011: Tropical cyclone report: Tropical Storm Allison—5-17 June 2001. National Hurricane Center Rep., 19 pp., www.nhc.noaa.gov/data/tcr/AL012001_Allison.pdf.

Tolman, R., 2012: Is there a silver lining in the drought of 2012? Oklahoma Farm Report, http://oklahomafarmreport.com/wire/news/2012/09/00292_SilverLining09072012_114156.php.

UKMO, 2018a: Extreme weather events. Glossary, http://ukclimateprojections.metoffice.gov.uk/23146.

——, 2018b: Tropical cyclone facts. UKMO, www.metoffice.gov.uk/weather/tropicalcyclone/facts#what.

University Center for Atmospheric Research, 2010: Hurricanes, typhoons, cyclones—Background on the science, people, and issues involved in hurricane research. University Center for Atmospheric Research, https://news.ucar.edu/1438/hurricanes-typhoons-cyclones.

Vicente-Serrano, S. M., and Coauthors, Eds., 2015: Standardized precipitation evapotranspiration index (SPEI). Climate Data Guide, https://climatedataguide.ucar.edu/climate-data/standardized-precipitation-evapotranspiration-index-spei.

Wilhite, D. A., and M. H. Glantz, 1985: Understanding the drought phenomenon: The role of definitions. Drought Mitigation Center Faculty Paper 20, 16 pp., http://digitalcommons.unl.edu/droughtfacpub/20.

VULNERABILITY, NATURAL DISASTER, AND DISASTER MANAGEMENT

John M. Lanicci

3.2.1. INTRODUCTION

Wisner et al. (2004) define *vulnerability* as "the characteristics of a person or group and their situation that influence their capacity to anticipate, cope with, resist and recover from the impact of a natural hazard." The "characteristics" in the Wisner et al. definition are often described in terms of multiple socioeconomic and political factors that can influence the vulnerability of a country or region with respect to natural hazards. These factors are often difficult to quantify, especially if access to data about a country's social, economic, and political situation is either restricted by the government or is not well known. Additionally, these factors often do not remain static with time as changes to a population's socioeconomic and political factors could occur, while the natural hazards themselves could also be changing as a result of natural climatic variations (e.g., El Niño/La Niña) or those attributable to human activities (e.g., global warming from increasing greenhouse gases; environmental impacts from deforestation or poor agricultural practices). As a result, it is often difficult to determine a population's vulnerability to a natural hazard until after a disaster event has already taken place.

3.2.2. A SIMPLIFIED MODEL OF NATURAL HAZARDS VULNERABILITY

A vulnerability analysis can reveal the conditions prior to the onset of a disaster event. These can be quite complex since certain socioeconomic and political factors may be more important in some countries but not so in others. While there are many different approaches to such an analysis, for the purposes of this chapter, we leverage the Wisner et al. (2004) vulnerability definition, the Federal Emergency Management Agency (FEMA) (1997) hazard definition, and the hazard categories from Table 3.1.1 to build a simple model for evaluating hazards and vulnerability in a population, shown here as Figure 3.2.1. Note that we show hazards and their analysis as a separate entity from vulnerability and its analysis. This is not meant to imply that a region's natural hazards and a population's socioeconomic and political factors should be viewed in isolation from one another. Rather, we approach the analysis of each in a different way and then consider how they may interact or influence each other by means of the two-headed arrows connecting the two in the figure. To an extent, the diagram reflects the reality that analyses conducted by physical scientists and social scientists are quite different in terms of methodology and data. It has only

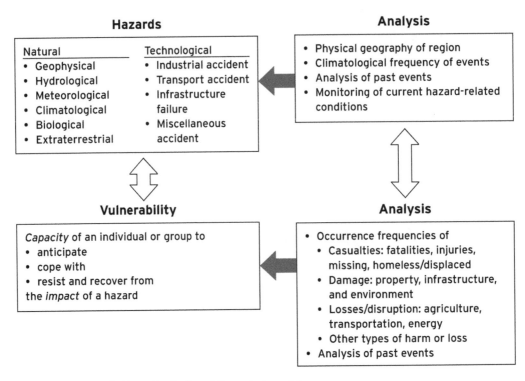

Figure 3.2.1. Simplified hazard and vulnerability analysis model.

been within the last 15 years that these communities have begun collaborating, an example of which is the increased interest by the atmospheric and climate science community in the integration of social scientists into the profession [e.g., American Meteorological Society (AMS) 2014].

To begin a hazards vulnerability analysis using Figure 3.2.1, we recommend first determining the geographic region and population to study. For the natural hazards portion of the analysis, search through a list of authoritative sources to obtain accurate descriptions of the physical geography, natural hazards and their geographic/temporal frequencies, any pertinent case studies of past occurrences of the hazard(s), and information on current monitoring of the hazard(s). For the physical geography portion, important details such as elevation, vegetation, and locations of important water bodies should be noted. Next comes the climatological frequencies of the natural hazard(s) endemic to the region; there are a number of authoritative sites from which to collect reliable data, and we include some in this chapter. Case studies can provide valuable insights into how a region/population has dealt with similar occurrences of the hazard(s) in the past, but we caution against drawing too many conclusions about the *present*

vulnerability of the region/population from these historical studies. It is also vitally important to know how the hazard is monitored at present; this can range from monitoring of specific types of hazards (e.g., U.S. National Hurricane Center) to more all-hazards/disaster-focused monitoring (e.g., Pacific Disaster Center).

For examining a region's/population's exposure to natural hazards and disasters (an important component in evaluating vulnerability), there are a number of good resources. To obtain disaster data and statistics, the UN PreventionWeb contains global reports and risk profiles that are available by country or region (www. preventionweb.net). The National Oceanic and Atmospheric Administration (NOAA) National Centers for Environmental Information natural hazards site contains links to information about tsunamis, earthquakes, volcanoes, and wildfires (www.ngdc.noaa.gov/hazard/hazards.shtml). Some sites, such as the Dartmouth Flood Observatory, the standardized precipitation evapotranspiration index (both mentioned in section 3.1.2), and the Global Fire Monitoring Center (www.fire.uni-freiburg.de) concentrate on only one hazard. These are just a few of the sites with accessible data that can be used for hazards and vulnerability research.

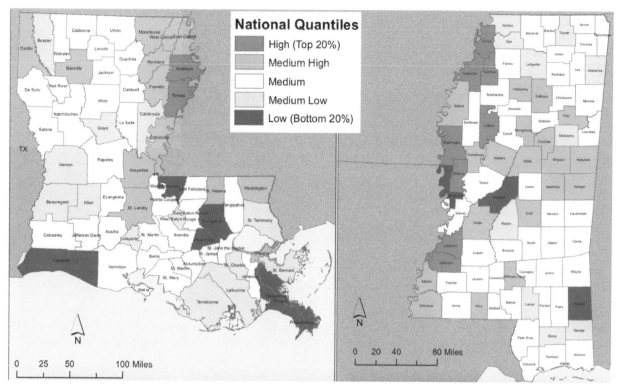

Figure 3.2.2. SoVI 2010–2014 for the Louisiana and Mississippi (adapted from http://artsandsciences.sc.edu/geog/hvri/ sovi®-2010-2014-state-maps).

There are also databases available that take a more direct approach to determining natural hazards vulnerability by considering social and economic factors (lower-left portion of Figure 3.2.1). One U.S.-based example is the Cutter et al. (2003) geographic information systems (GIS)-based comprehensive vulnerability-to-environmental-hazards index using socioeconomic and demographic data. Known as the social vulnerability index (SoVI®), their statistical approach began with 42 different variables, which were subsequently reduced to 11 independent factors that explain 76% of the variance in their data. The SoVI has been modified multiple times since the original version. The latest version, the 2010–2014 SoVI, uses eight significant components that explain 78% of the variance in their current data (see http://artsandsciences.sc.edu/ geog/hvri/sovi®-0 for details about the current version). These eight components, ranging from highest- to lowest-percent variance explained are 1) wealth, 2) race (Black) and social status, 3) age (elderly), 4) ethnicity (Hispanic) and lack of health insurance, 5) special needs populations, 6) service sector employment, 7) race

(Native American), and 8) gender (female). Since these components are derived from U.S. Census data, it is highly likely that these factors would not be translatable to a vulnerability analysis of another country and its population. The information from the SoVI is usually presented in map format as either a numerical score or a color-coded scheme that encapsulates multiple score intervals such as quantiles; an example of the latter is shown in Figure 3.2.2.

Another example of a U.S.-based comprehensive natural hazards vulnerability database is the Hazards U.S. Multi-Hazard (HAZUS-MH), which is a FEMA-operated GIS-based analysis tool (www.fema.gov/hazus; www.hazus.org). In contrast to the SoVI, which looks at natural hazards vulnerability based on statistically determined socioeconomic and demographic factors, HAZUS-MH estimates potential losses from four specific hazards (earthquakes, hurricane winds, floods, and tsunamis) using a combination of techniques based on information from seven categories: 1) general building stock, 2) essential facilities, 3) hazardous material facilities, 4) high potential loss facilities,

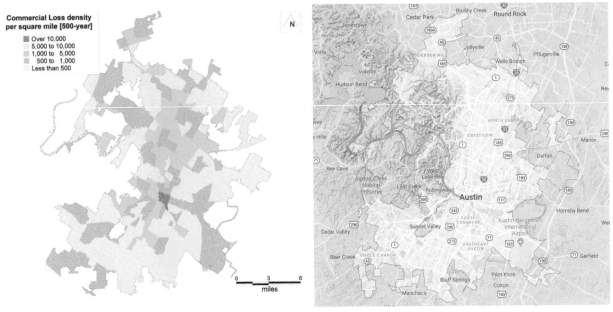

Figure 3.2.3. (left) HAZUS-MH "what if" estimate of commercial building value losses for a hypothetical once-in-500-year hurricane event in Austin, Texas, expressed in dollars per square mile (figure taken from FEMA 2004). (right) A map of Austin for geographic reference.

5) transportation "lifeline" systems, 6) utility "lifeline" systems, and 7) population demographics (https://www.fema.gov/pdf/plan/prevent/hazus/fema433_step3.pdf). Notice that the primary focus on HAZUS-MH is infrastructure. This is likely because HAZUS-MH was developed under contract by the National Institute of Building Sciences. An example of HAZUS-MH output for one of these hypothetical scenarios is shown in Figure 3.2.3. Since both HAZUS-MH and SoVI "drill down" to the county and census-tract levels, it is conceivable that they could be used together for developing "what if" scenarios for specific hazards and regions (e.g., Burton and Cutter 2008).

3.2.3. THE PRESSURE AND RELEASE DISASTER ONSET MODEL

The Pressure and Release (PAR) disaster onset model of Wisner et al. (2004) was developed to examine the socioeconomic and political conditions leading to a natural disaster in addition to the endemic natural hazards. The concept behind PAR is that natural disasters are not isolated incidents that just happen to a population but occur as a result of relationships among three important factors that can increase or decrease a population's vulnerability: 1) *root causes*, 2) *dynamic*

pressures, and 3) *unsafe conditions*. A diagram of the PAR model is shown in Figure 3.2.4. A unique aspect of the PAR model is how the relationships among the vulnerability factors change over time, as implied by the temporal flow on the left-hand side of Figure 3.2.4. For the purposes of this chapter, we will concentrate on this portion of the model.

The factors influencing vulnerability begin with the root causes, which define the "baseline" conditions for a country or region in terms of its access to resources, its structures, and its power, as well as its political and economic systems. According to Wisner et al. (2004), limited access to basic services (e.g., health, education), whether due to socioeconomic conditions, a restrictive political system, or a combination, will eventually lead to dynamic pressures on the population, such as inadequate education and training, a lack of effective institutions for assistance, and/or a lack of investment in the region. Macroforces such as rapid population changes, urbanization, and degradation of the natural environment also contribute to the dynamic pressures on a population. Wisner et al. (2004) explain that the "pressure and release" terminology refers to the pressures that the aforementioned conditions put on a population and that improvements to these conditions can "release" some of the pressure and actually decrease the population's

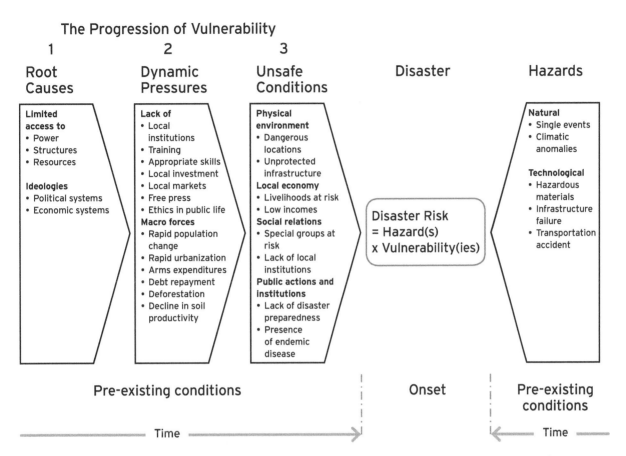

The Progression of Vulnerability

1	2	3		
Root Causes	**Dynamic Pressures**	**Unsafe Conditions**	**Disaster**	**Hazards**

Limited access to
- Power
- Structures
- Resources

Ideologies
- Political systems
- Economic systems

Lack of
- Local institutions
- Training
- Appropriate skills
- Local investment
- Local markets
- Free press
- Ethics in public life

Macro forces
- Rapid population change
- Rapid urbanization
- Arms expenditures
- Debt repayment
- Deforestation
- Decline in soil productivity

Physical environment
- Dangerous locations
- Unprotected infrastructure

Local economy
- Livelihoods at risk
- Low incomes

Social relations
- Special groups at risk
- Lack of local institutions

Public actions and institutions
- Lack of disaster preparedness
- Presence of endemic disease

Disaster Risk = Hazard(s) x Vulnerability(ies)

Natural
- Single events
- Climatic anomalies

Technological
- Hazardous materials
- Infrastructure failure
- Transportation accident

Pre-existing conditions ← Time → | Onset | Pre-existing conditions ← Time →

Figure 3.2.4. Conceptual flow diagram of the PAR model, illustrating how a disaster can occur when one or more hazards come into contact with a vulnerable population [adapted from Figure 2.1 in Wisner et al. (2004)].

vulnerability. If left unchecked, however, the dynamic pressures translate the effects of root causes into unsafe conditions. The diagram in Figure 3.2.4 shows a number of ways in which these unsafe conditions manifest themselves, such as poor living environments, poor economic conditions, a lack of necessary social and physical infrastructure to ensure safety of the population, and an overall lack of preparedness for coping with the impacts of natural hazards.

We can apply the principles shown in the PAR model to examine how an extended drought combined with poor agricultural practices and an inefficient, authoritarian government to produce a humanitarian crisis that contributed to the onset of the current (as of this textbook's publication) civil war in Syria. Using the vulnerability side of the PAR model in Figure 3.2.4, root causes included a governmental agricultural subsidy program that encouraged production of water-intensive crops in a region that receives less than

250 mm (10 inches) of annual precipitation (Gleick 2014). These policies resulted in the overpumping of groundwater systems used for irrigation. In the dynamic pressures portion of the PAR model, these policies and the outdated agricultural practices of Syrian farmers exposed weaknesses in education and training and a lack of knowledge about modern irrigation techniques. Meanwhile, the impacts of the longevity of the drought (a climatological natural hazard) were operating on the right-hand side of Figure 3.2.4. Figure 3.2.5 shows a timeline of SPEI averaged over Syria. Note that negative SPEI values began to appear in the time series as early as mid-1998 and remained negative for the next 18 years. As the conditions of the multiyear drought persisted, a significant decline in productivity and farm income resulted. As the dynamic pressures built on the left-hand side of the PAR model, unsafe physical, economic, social, and institutional conditions were manifested by a mass migration of more than 1.5 million people

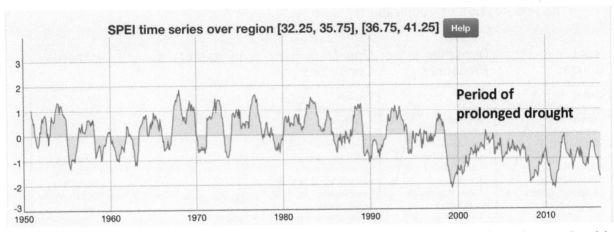

Figure 3.2.5. SPEI time series over region encompassing Syria. Areas of the curve above zero denote times of groundwater surplus, while those below zero denote times of deficit. Time series calculated using a 12-month running mean (source: http://sac.csic.es/spei/map/maps.html).

(mostly farmers and their families) from the rural areas to Syria's major cities by 2011 (Gleick 2014). The timing of the mass migration coincided with unrest against Syria's authoritarian government during the first half of 2011 and the outbreak of the civil war in the spring and summer of that year.

3.2.4. DISASTER: WHEN HAZARD MEETS VULNERABILITY

Detailed representations of vulnerability such as the PAR model show how it can be influenced by a number of factors. Using the previous discussion of hazards and vulnerability, Wisner et al. (2004) defined a disaster as *the outcome resulting when hazards and vulnerability collide*. While developing a suitable definition of natural disaster may seem like the end of the story, there are further nuances that need explanation before moving into the case studies. First, while the natural disaster definition refers to vulnerable communities, it does not mean that only populations with poor socioeconomic conditions are vulnerable to natural hazards. Even if the socioeconomic status of a region's population is above the median of the general population, their capacity to respond can still be exceeded by a natural event of significant enough magnitude. One example (among many in the more-developed world) is the occurrence of wildfires in Southern California. In this case, the natural hazard is the predisposition of the region to wildfires, especially during the dry summer months. Where such

events occur, many of the affected geographic regions have affluent populations, but when the sheer number of homes, property, and livelihoods destroyed and people displaced exceeds the capacity of the affected communities to respond, the event becomes a natural disaster.

The wildfire example provides segue to the next issue, which is that of defining an appropriate *threshold* for declaring a natural disaster. Recall from FEMA (1997) that potential impacts to a region from natural hazards can include casualties; damage to property, infrastructure, and the environment; agricultural loss; interruption of business, etc. So how many of these aforementioned elements need to be met, and to what degree, before the event can be declared as a natural disaster? There is no set answer to this question. According to FEMA's disaster declaration procedures (www.fema.gov/disaster-declaration-process), there are guidelines for preparing the declaration request, defined categories of declaration (i.e., emergency and major disaster declarations, which are defined in the next section), and monetary limits on the amount of aid provided for emergency declarations. However, there are no specific thresholds in terms of impacts to population, resources, and livelihood.

While there is a high degree of subjectivity involved in classifying an event as a natural disaster, many agencies collect data about natural and technological events around the world and try to determine if they qualify as disasters. The Centre for Research on the Epidemiology of Disasters (CRED) (discussed in section 3.1.1) is one such organization. They maintain a worldwide database of some 21,000 natural and technological disasters that have occurred since 1900, known as the Emergency Events Database (EM-DAT; CRED 1988). Their casualty, damage, and impact criteria for listing an event as a disaster are summarized below (www.emdat.be/guidelines):

- 10 or more deaths
- 100 or more people affected, injured, or homeless
- The affected country declares a state of emergency and/or appeals for international aid
- When figures are missing, EM-DAT will consider qualitative statements from the affected country: for example, "significant disaster/significant damage (i.e., 'worst disasters in the decade' and/or 'it was the disaster with the heaviest damage for the country')"

Lanicci et al. (2017) used the EM-DAT to document the ways in which natural disasters affected different countries in 2010. That year, the countries with the highest natural disaster–related *fatalities* were Haiti, Russia, China, and Pakistan, while those with the highest *economic damages* were Chile, China, Pakistan, Haiti, and New Zealand. Note that in this example, three countries were affected in terms of *both* casualties and economic/infrastructure damage. In an environmental security analysis, this would be a "red flag" to more closely monitor conditions in those countries in order to anticipate problems requiring humanitarian or other assistance. The Integrated Research on Disaster Risk (IRDR) program estimates that there are approximately 55 databases with national loss information as opposed to a handful that are global in coverage (IRDR 2014). While international efforts to collect and document disaster events are improving, significant limitations persist in temporal and spatial coverage, loss estimate accuracy, and inconsistency in loss indicator data across events (IRDR 2014).

Before moving into a discussion of emergency/disaster management, it is useful to summarize what has been discussed so far. First, there are several ways in which natural disaster vulnerability can be estimated. Some of these are more comprehensive than others, and

it is best to examine multiple sources when creating an assessment. Second, when we discuss natural disaster vulnerability of a population in terms of socioeconomic status and structure, we remind the reader that vulnerable communities are not limited to those with poor socioeconomic conditions. Third, a universally agreed-upon set of thresholds for classifying or declaring a natural disaster does not exist, although numerous databases collect data and document such events around the world. Finally, if one is trying to determine "where we are" on either of the environment-to-security cascade models from Figure 3.2.1 at this point in the unit, we literally have not even started using the model—all of the considerations covered in this chapter so far only set the baseline conditions prior to the natural disaster event's occurrence.

3.2.5. DISASTER MANAGEMENT[1]

This section outlines some basic principles of disaster management, which are taken from the four phases of emergency management (EM): 1) mitigation, 2) preparation, 3) response, and 4) recovery. According to Baird (2010), the four phases of EM can be traced to a seminal study on federal and state EM coordination commissioned by the U.S. National Governors Association (NGA) in the late 1970s. The results of the study were published by NGA (1979) and recommended that federal and state efforts should be extended to include mitigation and recovery activities and that natural and technological hazards (the latter including enemy attack) should be dealt with as part of a comprehensive, "all hazards" approach to EM. The primary reason for including a discussion of disaster management in this section is to provide a context for examining the degree to which a country or region is able to anticipate, cope with, respond to, and recover from the impacts of natural and/or technological hazards (second and third tiers of the environment-to-security cascade models in Figure 3.2.1). Thus, we can say that the four phases of disaster management can complement either our simplified vulnerability analysis model or the more complex PAR model by noting that the ability of a community, nation, or region

---

1. Since we are using the same reference system (four phases) for emergency management and disaster management, we will use them interchangeably in this discussion. Keep in mind, however, that emergency and disaster management are not identical (www.un-spider.org/risks-and-disasters/emergency-and-disaster-management).

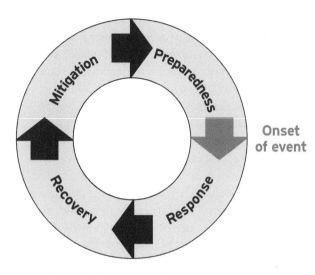

Figure 3.2.6. The four phases of disaster management.

to *mitigate* and *prepare* for hazards is definitely influenced by various socioeconomic and political factors that contribute to the vulnerability of the population. A representation of the four disaster management phases (with the onset of a disaster event included) is shown in Figure 3.2.6; these will be described in detail below.

3.2.5.1. Mitigation

In addition to being one of the four phases of disaster management, mitigation is one of four long-term risk management strategies available to individuals and communities. Mitigation is defined by FEMA (2008) as "Activities providing a critical foundation in the effort to reduce the loss of life and property from natural and/or manmade disasters by avoiding or lessening the impact of a disaster and providing value to the public by creating safer communities." The other three strategies are *avoidance*, *retention*, and *transfer*. Avoidance includes not performing an activity that could carry risk. A natural hazards example would be to permanently relocate away from a specific hazard-prone area (this is not always possible). Retention (also known as tolerance) is to accept/live with the level of risk and its consequences. A natural hazards example would be to live near the coast with no home protection or flood insurance. This strategy would most likely be used by a population with no choice but

to live where they do and who cannot afford to purchase insurance or other protection. Transfer reassigns the risk of loss by causing another party to accept the risk, typically by contract or by hedging.[2] Insurance is one type of risk transfer that uses contracts. A natural hazards example would be to live near the coast and purchase flood insurance.

Mitigation involves taking precautionary actions and/or enacting controls or countermeasures to reduce potential losses from the hazard. While mitigation does not eliminate the risk from the hazard, it can reduce the potential losses from it. Two examples of natural hazard mitigation are 1) constructing a levee system to mitigate flood damage and 2) enacting legislation to mandate standards for building construction in hurricane- or earthquake-prone areas. A good example of the latter comes from the aftermath of Hurricane Andrew in 1992, which devastated south Florida and was (at the time) the most destructive hurricane in U.S. history, causing $26.5 billion in damage (1992 dollars) and killing 26 people. After Hurricane Andrew, Miami-Dade County officials commenced an in-depth review of building codes that had been in effect since 1974 as well as code enforcement, resulting in important changes for both within a relatively short period of time. The rest of Florida took four years before changes to the 1974 law were recommended, to include a single statewide code with state oversight, and another two years for the recommendations to be adopted by the state legislature (Florida Association of Insurance Agents 2009). Note that of the four risk management methods discussed here, mitigation is the most comprehensive and costly strategy for reducing risk from natural hazards. However, as the Hurricane Andrew example shows, even in countries with a well-developed infrastructure, robust institutions, strong economy, and established political systems, mitigation is not always an easy process.

3.2.5.2. Preparedness

One of the most important differences between mitigation and preparedness is the time scale involved. As we saw in the Hurricane Andrew example, mitigation can literally take years to accomplish. By contrast, prepared-

---

2. According to businessdictionary.com, hedging is "a risk management strategy used in limiting or offsetting probability of loss from fluctuations in the prices of commodities, currencies, or securities. In effect, hedging is a transfer of risk without buying insurance policies" (www.businessdictionary.com/definition/hedging.html).

ness involves short-term measures and actions necessary for a community's readiness to respond when the event takes place. Examples include developing emergency action plans and aid agreements with neighboring communities, conducting personnel training and public education, procuring and maintaining emergency supplies, and building the necessary physical facilities (to include robust communications) for response and recovery actions (https://training.fema.gov/hiedu/aemrc/booksdownload/fem/).

3.2.5.3. Response

This is another phase with a very short time scale. In fact, the effectiveness of a disaster response can be defined partially by the speed with which casualties are identified and processed, secondary damage is effectively reduced or prevented, and the immediate impacts of the event have been contained. In this phase, proper coordination with other communities and agencies at the state and federal levels is absolutely critical, especially when the spatial scale of damage is very large (e.g., tropical cyclone, earthquake). This is one of the reasons why it is so important to develop and test appropriate agreements and arrangements for outside assistance in the preparedness phase.

3.2.5.4. Recovery

As with mitigation, recovery is a long-time-scale phase. Depending on the scale and magnitude of the disaster event, the recovery period could be months or even years. Typical actions taken during the recovery phase include debris removal, infrastructure repair, restoration of normal services (e.g., energy, water), and providing temporary housing, medical care, etc. The goal of recovery is to bring the affected community back to the same or better standard of living as in the preevent period (FEMA 2018).

In the United States, an important component of disaster management at multiple phases is the assistance available to communities through state and/or federal means. At the federal level, this is accomplished through the Stafford Act, which provides the federal government with the legal authority to assist states during declared major disasters[3] and emergencies.[4] The Stafford Act, which is an amended version of the Disaster Relief Act of 1974, is codified as U.S. Code, Title 42, Chapter 68 (http://uscode.house.gov/). To most people, the best-known part of this law has to do with federal assistance (usually through FEMA) provided to affected areas after a disaster event has taken place. However, Stafford Act assistance is not just restricted to the response phase of a disaster. One of the aid components available to a community after a major disaster declaration is the Hazard Mitigation Grant Program (HMGP), which provides grants to states "for activities that prevent future disasters or reduce their impact if they cannot be prevented." (Lindsay 2012). In this context, the HMGP can be considered assistance as the recovery phase transitions to the mitigation phase. Under the Stafford Act, an emergency declaration can actually be made *before* an event occurs in order to help the communities conduct evacuations and preposition equipment and supplies in order to lessen the impact when the event takes place. In this context, the assistance is actually received in the preparedness phase immediately preceding the event.

3.2.6. THE CASE STUDIES FOR THIS UNIT

The next three chapters in this unit present studies that illustrate some of the environmental security challenges associated with disaster management. In chapter 3.3, Lanicci discusses the use of the simplified vulnerability model as a means of identifying the susceptibility of the U.S. Gulf Coast region to Hurricane Katrina in August 2005. In chapter 3.4, Fisher and Lanicci provide a study

---

3. A major disaster is defined as "any natural catastrophe (including any hurricane, tornado, storm, high water, wind-driven water, tidal wave, tsunami, earthquake, volcanic eruption, landslide, mudslide, snowstorm, or drought), or, regardless of cause, any fire, flood, or explosion, in any part of the United States, which in the determination of the President causes damage of sufficient severity and magnitude to warrant major disaster assistance under this chapter to supplement the efforts and available resources of states, local governments, and disaster relief organizations in alleviating the damage, loss, hardship, or suffering caused thereby" (42 U.S. Code section 5122).

4. An emergency declaration is defined as "any occasion or instance for which, in the determination of the President, Federal assistance is needed to supplement State and local efforts and capabilities to save lives and to protect property and public health and safety, or to lessen or avert the threat of a catastrophe in any part of the United States" (42 U.S. Code section 5122).

of the roles that traditional and social media play in disaster management and in their possible influence on postdisaster public policy. Chapter 3.5 by Mujkic et al. describes how Bosnia and Herzegovina and Serbia were ill prepared for historic flooding and landslides in May 2014 and how the population's vulnerability was influenced by the wars of the 1990s, weak institutions, and widespread government corruption.

In these cases, either the simplified vulnerability model or the PAR model can provide a basis for examining the environmental security issues associated with disaster preparedness and management, whether in more-developed countries such as the United States or in a less-developed region such as the Balkans.

REFERENCES

AMS, 2014: Strengthening social sciences in the weather–climate enterprise. American Meteorological Society, accessed 10 March 2017, www.ametsoc. org/ams/index.cfm/about-ams/ams-statements/ statements-of-the-ams-in-force/strengthening-social-sciences-in-the-weather-climate-enterprise/.

Baird, M. E., 2010: The "phases" of emergency management. Intermodal Freight Transportation Institute Paper, University of Memphis, 50 pp., www.memphis. edu/ifti/pdfs/cait_phases_of_emergency_mngt.pdf.

Burton, C., and S. L. Cutter, 2008: Levee failures and social vulnerability in the Sacramento-San Joaquin delta area, California. *Nat. Hazards Rev.*, **9**, 136–149, https:// doi.org/10.1061/(ASCE)1527-6988(2008)9:3(136).

CRED, 1988: EM-DAT: The international disaster database. Université Catholique de Louvain, accessed 08 Mar 2017, www.emdat.be.

FEMA, 2004: Using HAZUS-MH for risk assessment: How-to guide. FEMA Rep., 226 pp., www.fema.gov/ pdf/plan/prevent/hazus/fema433.pdf.

——, 2008: Glossary and acronyms. FEMA Rep., 20 pp., www.fema.gov/pdf/emergency/nrf/nrf-glossary.pdf.

——, 2018: Emergency program manager: Knowledges, skills, and abilities. FEMA Emergency Management Institute Rep., 26 pp., https://training.fema.gov/ hiedu/downloads/emergprogmgr.doc.

Florida Association of Insurance Agents, 2009: Mitigation: A report card on Florida's quest to harden homes. Florida Association of Insurance Agents Rep., 43 pp., www.sbafla.com/method/portals/methodology/ WindstormMitigationCommittee/2009/20090917_ MitigationWhitePaper9-3-09.pdf.

Gleick, P. H., 2014: Water, drought, climate change, and conflict in Syria. *Wea. Climate. Soc.*, **6**, 331–340, https://doi.org/10.1175/WCAS-D-13-00059.1.

IRDR, 2014: Peril classification and hazard glossary. IRDR DATA Publ. 1, 28 pp., www.irdrinternational. org/wp-content/uploads/2014/04/IRDR_DATA-Project-Report-No.-1.pdf.

Lanicci, J. M., J. D. Ramsay, and E. H. Murray, 2017: Re-conceptualizing environmental security as resilience: Strategic planning for human and national security. *J. Human Secur. Resilience*, **1**, 1–32, www. thinkhumansecurity.org/v1-lanicci-ramsay-murray. html.

Lindsay, B., 2012: Federal emergency management: A brief introduction. Congressional Research Service Rep. R42845, 32 pp., https://fas.org/sgp/crs/homesec/ R42845.pdf.

NGA, 1979: Comprehensive emergency management: A governor's guide. NGA Center for Policy Research Rep., 64 pp., https://training.fema.gov/hiedu/docs/ comprehensive%20em%20-%20nga.doc.

Wisner, B., P. Blaikie, T. Cannon, and I. Davis, 2004: At Risk: *Natural Hazards, People's Vulnerability and Disasters*. 2nd ed. Psychology Press, 471 pp.

3.3

NATURAL HAZARDS VULNERABILITY ALONG THE U.S. GULF COAST: THE CASE OF HURRICANE KATRINA

John M. Lanicci

3.3.1. INTRODUCTION

In this chapter, we apply the simplified vulnerability analysis model introduced in chapter 3.2 to Hurricane Katrina, the costliest natural disaster (to date) in U.S. history [National Centers for Environmental Information 2017]. The chapter begins with a short geographic description of the U.S. Gulf Coast region, with particular emphasis on Louisiana and Mississippi, the states hardest hit by Hurricane Katrina. This description is followed by a summary of the region's important industries (which includes some critical infrastructure) and selected demographic data derived from the 2000 U.S. Census, which can be considered representative of the region's population in the time frame preceding Hurricane Katrina's landfall in August 2005. The natural hazards overview and the industrial and demographic information are intended to help you evaluate the region's vulnerability by applying several of the vulnerability model components illustrated in Figure 3.2.1.

3.3.2. NATURAL HAZARDS IN THE GULF COAST REGION

In section 3.2.2, we suggested that a hazards vulnerability analysis using the simplified model should begin with

a defined geographic region and population for study. Quite often, this will be an arbitrary decision based on data availability and the particular case being studied. Since we are focusing on Hurricane Katrina, we narrow the geographic study to Louisiana and Mississippi, the states most affected. For the natural hazards portion of the analysis, we begin by describing the physical geography and the climatological aspects of the natural hazards.

3.3.2.1. Physical Geography

The physical geography of the southeastern and Gulf Coast regions of the United States is shown in Figure 3.3.1. The three primary physiographic features are the inner coastal plain, the Mississippi alluvial valley, and the outer coastal plain. The inner coastal plain (yellow region in Figure 3.3.1) contains the piedmont regions of Virginia, the Carolinas, and Georgia and extends as far south as the Florida Panhandle, as far west as eastern Texas, and as far north as Arkansas, western Tennessee, southwestern Kentucky, and the "boot heel" of Missouri. The Mississippi alluvial valley (pink region in Figure 3.3.1) contains the floodplain of the Mississippi River, which cuts across the inner coastal plain to the Gulf of Mexico and extends north to the confluence of the Mississippi and Ohio Rivers. The outer Gulf Coast plain (light green

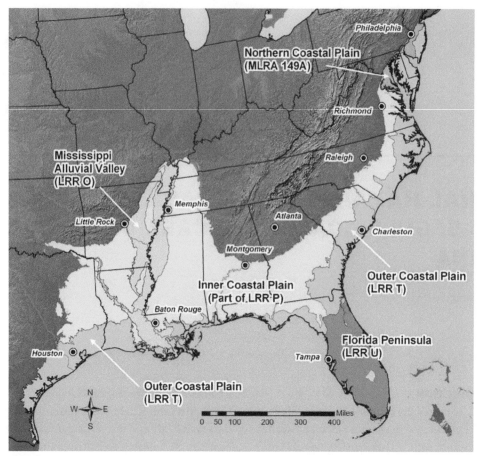

Figure 3.3.1. Major physiographic features discussed in text (see Figure 1 in U.S. Army Corps of Engineers 2010).

region in Figure 3.3.1) includes the areas west of the Mississippi alluvial valley and north of the inner coastal plain. This region includes the barrier beaches along the Gulf of Mexico, the marshes to the north of the beaches that extend into interior Louisiana and southeastern Texas, and the rolling terrain north of the marshlands (www. ereferencedesk.com/resources/state/louisiana.html).

An important component of the outer coastal plain and Mississippi River alluvial valley is the Louisiana coastal wetlands. Louisiana has 40% of the nation's wetlands, and these marshes and swamps contribute approximately $1 billion annually to Louisiana's seafood industry (Williams 2003). However, these wetlands have been rapidly disappearing because of a combination of natural processes involving the Mississippi River itself and the diversion of the river's sediment deposits well south of the delta region by an extensive system of levees constructed along the river channel. The levees prevent

flooding in this region and have allowed Louisiana's shipping industry to flourish over many years. Unfortunately, the loss of these wetlands also means that a natural buffer to landfalling tropical cyclones is being eliminated, and the loss is not without its consequences.

As illustrated by the highlighted topographic map in Figure 3.3.2, a considerable geographic area along the Gulf Coast is within 30 feet of sea level. While much attention has been devoted to the levee system in New Orleans, Louisiana, because of its elevation below sea level, we note that the highlighted area in Figure 3.3.2 is approximately the size of the state of Maryland (about 32,000 km²).

3.3.2.2. Natural Hazards Climatology

While there are a number of natural hazards endemic to the Gulf Coast region, for the purposes of this chapter, we will focus only on the meteorological ones. Table 3.3.1 shows the occurrence frequencies of six types

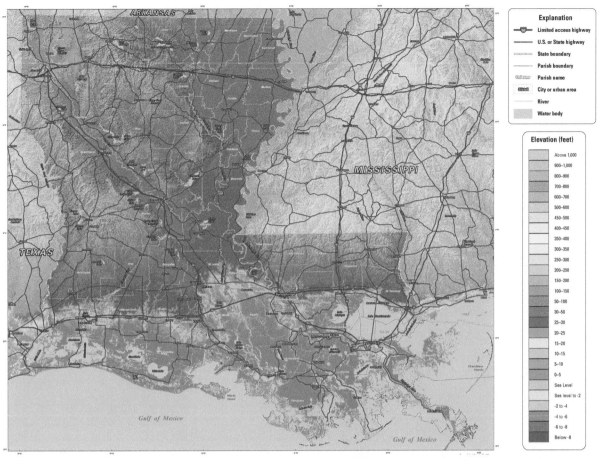

Figure 3.3.2. Topographic map of lower half of Louisiana, Mississippi, and coastal portions of the surrounding states with the lowest 30 feet of elevation above mean sea level, displayed as brightly colored 5-foot elevation bands (courtesy of Kosovich 2008).

Table 3.3.1. Occurrence frequency (number of events) over Louisiana and Mississippi for six types of natural hazards in the U.S. billion-dollar weather disasters compilation.

Hazard/number of events in each state	Louisiana	Mississippi
Severe local storms	14	24
Tropical cyclones	13	12
Droughts	10	12
Winter storms	6	7
Floods	6	4
Freezes	1	2
Total	**50**	**61**

of meteorological hazards [severe local storms (i.e., severe and tornadic thunderstorms), tropical cyclones, droughts, winter storms, floods, and freezes] during the

1980–2016 period that caused significant economic impacts. In order to be considered in the event compilation, the total economic losses across all affected U.S. states had to be equal to or greater than $1 billion; such events are known as *billion-dollar weather disasters* (Smith and Katz 2013; National Centers for Environmental Information 2017). The table shows that the three most frequent types of high-damage hazards over Louisiana and Mississippi were severe local storms, tropical cyclones, and droughts. Keep in mind that although floods were not in the top three in terms of damage, the floods category considered non-tropical-cyclone-related flood events.

Since this chapter is about Hurricane Katrina (a tropical cyclone), we can employ the climatological data archived at the National Oceanic and Atmospheric Administration (NOAA) Coastal Research Center (CRC) to determine hurricane event and intensity frequencies and geographic coverage. Figure 3.3.3 shows a clima-

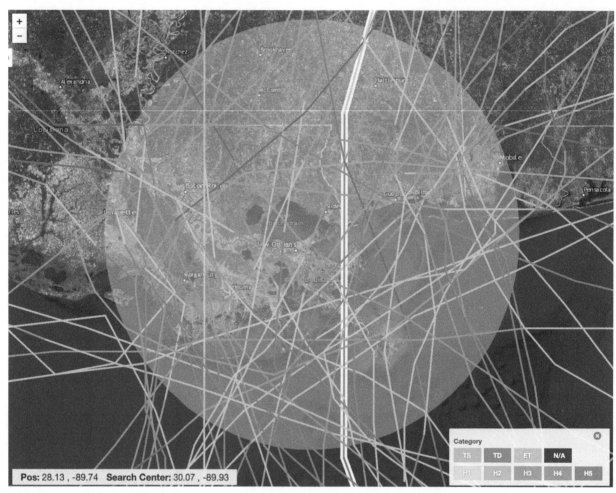

Map labels visible: Natchez, Brookhaven, Alexandria, McComb, Louisiana, Mobile, Baton Rouge, Pensacola, Slidell, Lafayette, Pontchartrain, New Orleans, Morgan City, Houma

Pos: 28.13 , -89.74   Search Center: 30.07 , -89.93

Category
TS TD ET N/A
H1 H2 H3 H4 H5

Figure 3.3.3. Historical hurricane storm tracks within a 200-km radius of New Orleans as derived from NOAA CRC database. Storm categories are indicated by color using legend in lower right. Hurricane Katrina's track is highlighted in white.

tological frequency/intensity analysis for hurricanes of category 1–5 passing within 200 km of New Orleans using the CRC's historical database (https://coast.noaa. gov/hurricanes/?redirect=301ocm). There were a total of 53 storms that tracked through this region using data extending back to 1852. Based on this historical data, we can expect a hurricane to pass within 200 km of New Orleans once every 3.1 years, so during any given year, there is a 32% probability of such a storm transiting this region. Figure 3.3.3 also shows that the majority of hurricanes weakened to either tropical storm or depression strength after making landfall, as indicated by the number of green and blue tracks over the land areas. However, a number of hurricanes maintained category 1–2 intensities well inland from the coast. This information, combined with the geographic features from Figures 3.3.1 and 3.3.2, suggests

that while the vulnerability to tropical cyclones decreases as one proceeds inland from the immediate coastline, the threat is still quite potent over the inland areas.

The remainder of the hazards analysis portion of Figure 3.2.1 involves investigating previous events and current hazards monitoring. We will combine this portion of the analysis with the vulnerability analysis presented in the next section.

3.3.3. A BASIC VULNERABILITY ANALYSIS

In order to facilitate analysis of the occurrences of property, infrastructure, and environmental damage, agricultural loss, and interruption of business from past events, it is helpful to examine the economics, infrastructure, and demographics of the study region.

3.3.3.1. Economics

Louisiana is a major agricultural producer. Its primary crops include cotton, sugar cane, rice, sweet potatoes, pecans, soybeans, and corn, and it is also a major poultry producer. Forestry and tourism are the state's largest industries. Louisiana's major mineral products are petroleum, natural gas, salt, sulfur, carbon black, and gravel. The state ranks second in the nation in oil production, produces over 25% of U.S. natural gas, and has slightly under 10% of all known U.S. oil reserves. Louisiana is the nation's largest producer of shrimp and oysters, and its commercial fishing industry is responsible for about one quarter of all seafood caught in the United States (www. ereferencedesk.com/resources/state/louisiana.html).

Mississippi's economy is not as diversified as Louisiana's. In 2000, Mississippi was the third leading producer of cotton in the nation and is an important producer of rice and soybeans. The state's important industries are apparel, furniture, lumber and wood products, food processing, electrical machinery, and transportation equipment (www.ereferencedesk.com/resources/state/mississippi.html). Although not mentioned in the reference, offshore casinos were an important contributor to the local economy, responsible for some $500,000 a day in state and local tax revenues prior to Katrina's landfall (Solis 2005).

3.3.3.2. Infrastructure

In terms of infrastructure, Louisiana has one of the busiest port complexes in the United States. Each year, more than 11,000 vessels, 500 million tons of cargo, 60% of the nation's grain, and 20% of the nation's coal and petro-chemicals travel through the lower Mississippi River system. Baton Rouge, Louisiana, is the farthest inland port in the United States for seagoing ships, while the port of New Orleans is served by six class one railroads and is connected to 14,500 miles of inland waterways throughout the Mississippi River system, as well as the Gulf Intracoastal Waterway (www.portnola.com/). Mississippi also has important port infrastructure that is vital to its economy. The state is ranked 12th nationally in terms of total inland waterway miles (870). The state has three major ports and was ranked 16th nationally in cargo movement, with 48.6 million short tons in 2012 [American Society of Civil Engineers (ASCE) 2013].

Mississippi is served by 27 freight railroads covering 2,454 miles, ranking the state 29th nationally in terms of rail mileage (ASCE 2013).

3.3.3.3. Demographics

The information presented above suggests that Louisiana has a healthy and diversified economy and infrastructure, while Mississippi's is perhaps not quite as diverse. However, when we examine selected population demographics for both states, a different picture emerges, especially for Louisiana. Figure 3.3.4 illustrates educational levels and poverty rates for Louisiana, Mississippi, and parts of the surrounding states, taken from the 2000 U.S. Census. These figures, created through the MapUSA website (www.s4.brown.edu/mapusa/), show that significant portions of both states are above the national medians for lowest level of education attained (48.2% according to Bauman and Graf 2003) and for poverty rate (12.2% according to Bishaw 2013). Note in particular the higher-than-U.S.-median rates of poverty in both states. These demographic figures suggest that significant portions of the population could be vulnerable to natural disasters; such information is critically important for a pre-Katrina hazard vulnerability analysis of the region. In particular, notice the corridor of parishes[1] that runs south-southwest to north-northeast west of the Mississippi River with the lowest education levels (75%–85%, shown in lavender in Figure 3.3.4a); several of these parishes also have high poverty levels (25%–30%, shown in lavender in Figure 3.3.4b). While Mississippi does not have any counties in the 75%–85% education-level bracket, a number of Mississippi counties in the immediate vicinity of the Mississippi River have poverty levels that are well in excess of 30%; these are bordered by parishes in Louisiana with the same high poverty levels (shown by pink and fuchsia in Figure 3.3.4b).

3.3.3.4. Vulnerability Analysis Results

The geographic analysis suggests that the lowest-elevation areas (including those below sea level) along the coastal areas of both states would be most vulnerable to a tropical cyclone, especially considering the storm-track/intensity climatology from Figure 3.3.3. While the economic analysis shows that Louisiana has a

---

1. In Louisiana, parishes are the same as counties.

Figure 3.3.4. Selected population demographics for Louisiana, Mississippi, and portions of surrounding states from the 2000 Census through the MapUSA project (https://s4.ad.brown.edu/projects/mapusa/index.html): (a) percentage of counties/parishes with the lowest educational level attained (high school or less); (b) percentage of counties/parishes in poverty.

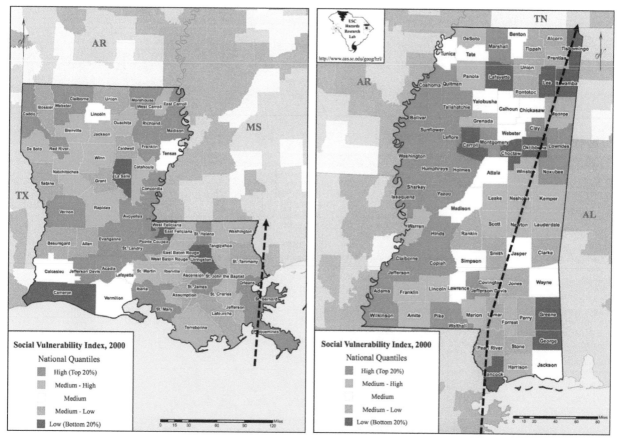

Figure 3.3.5. SoVI-2000 analysis for (left) Louisiana and (right) Mississippi, with Hurricane Katrina path shown by black dashed line with arrow (analyses courtesy of http://artsandsciences.sc.edu/geog/hvri/sovi®-2000-42-variable-state-and-regional-maps).

diversified and robust economy, the large fraction of the economy dependent on lumber production, fishing, and petroleum production and transportation could be greatly disrupted from a large tropical cyclone transiting through this region. Mississippi's agriculture and lumber industries would also be vulnerable, as would their growing offshore casinos. The infrastructure of both states, especially maritime transportation, is particularly vulnerable given the economic interdependencies (e.g., petroleum, fishing). The demographics shown in Figure 3.3.4 would cause us to focus on the interior regions that have higher-than-median poverty rates and lower-than-national-median education. However, when all of the data are considered, we would argue that *the entire territory* of both states should be of concern because of the many types of vulnerabilities uncovered in our cursory examination of geography, natural hazards, economics, infrastructure, and population demographics.

How does this basic analysis compare to that from the social vulnerability index (SoVI)? Figure 3.3.5 shows the SoVI-2000 analysis for Louisiana and Mississippi. Not surprisingly, there are similarities between the SoVI-2000 analysis and the education/poverty demographic analyses in Figure 3.3.4. The areas with highest vulnerability in Figure 3.3.5 are mostly located in the interiors of both states, in close proximity to the Mississippi River, similar to the areas in Figure 3.3.4. The likely reasons for the similarities are that both analyses used the same source data (2000 U.S. Census), and the SoVI-2000 used some of the same socioeconomic factors displayed in Figure 3.3.4. We note that Orleans Parish (where New Orleans is located) is in the top 20% SoVI-2000 vulnerability category in Figure 3.3.5, whereas in Figure 3.3.4, its education and poverty levels are close to the national median. This suggests that other factors influenced its placement in the highest vulnerability category in the SoVI-2000 analysis.

Table 3.3.2. Major disaster declarations in Louisiana and Mississippi resulting from hurricane damage and destruction, 1956–2004 (source: www.fema.gov/disasters).

Hurricane disaster declaration: Louisiana	Hurricane disaster declaration: Mississippi
Hurricane (DR-64) Incident period: 4 October 1956 Major disaster declaration: 4 October 1956	
Floods, hurricane (DR-73) Incident period: 16 May 1957 Major disaster declaration: 16 May 1957	
Hurricane Hilda (DR-178) Incident period: 3 October 1964 Major disaster declaration: 3 October 1964	
Hurricane Betsy (DR-208) Incident period: 10 September 1965 Major disaster declaration: 10 September 1965	Hurricane Betsy (DR-210) Incident period: 25 September 1965 Major disaster declaration: 25 September 1965
Hurricane Camille (DR-272) Incident period: 19 August 1969 Major disaster declaration: 19 August 1969	Hurricane Camille (DR-271) Incident period: 18 August 1969 Major disaster declaration: 18 August 1969
Hurricane Edith (DR-315) Incident period: 13 October 1971 Major disaster declaration: 13 October 1971	
Hurricane Carmen (DR-448) Incident period: 23 September 1974 Major disaster declaration: 23 September 1974	
	Hurricane Frederic (DR-599) Incident period: 13 September 1979
	Hurricane Elena (DR-741) Incident period: 29 August–4 September 1985 Major disaster declaration: 4 September 1985
Hurricane Juan (DR-752) Incident period: 26 October–8 November 1985 Major disaster declaration: 1 November 1985	
Hurricane Andrew (DR-956) Incident period: 25–30 August 1992 Major disaster declaration: 26 August 1992	
Tropical Storm Frances and Hurricane Georges (DR-1246) Incident period: 9 September–10 October 1998 Major disaster declaration: 23 September 1998	Hurricane Georges (DR-1251) Incident period: 25 September–5 October 1998 Major disaster declaration: 1 October 1998
Tropical Storm Isidore (DR-1435) Incident period: 21 September–1 October 2002 Major disaster declaration: 27 September 2002	Tropical Storm Isidore (DR-1436) Incident period: 23 September 23–6 October 2002 Major disaster declaration: 1 October 2002
Hurricane Lili (DR-1437) Incident period: 1–16 October 2002 Major disaster declaration: 3 October 2002	
Hurricane Ivan (DR-1548) Incident period: 13–26 September 2004 Major disaster declaration: 15 September 2004	Hurricane Ivan (DR-1550) Incident period: 13–20 September 2004 Major disaster declaration: 15 September 2004

3.3.4. DISASTER PREPAREDNESS IN THE GULF COAST REGION

The simplified vulnerability model from section 3.2.2 suggests that analysis of past events plays an important role in evaluating a region's vulnerability to future disasters. Table 3.3.2 is a list of hurricane-related major disaster declarations in Louisiana and Mississippi prior to Katrina, taken from the Federal Emergency Management Agency (FEMA) database. Recall from section 3.2.5 the criteria for a major disaster declaration ("any natural catastrophe . . . or, regardless of cause, any fire, flood, or explosion . . . which in the determination of the President causes damage of sufficient severity and magnitude to warrant major disaster assistance"), so these can be considered significant historical events. The database, which extends back to 1953, shows that 20 total declarations were made for the two states, 13 for Louisiana and 7 for Mississippi. There were 10 hurricanes where declarations were made for both states. Two of these, Hurricanes Betsy

and Camille, were historically significant for a number of reasons. Betsy, the first billion-dollar damage hurricane, is noteworthy for the rapidity with which federal aid was provided to Louisiana in an era when relations between the southern states and the federal government were rocky (Horowitz 2012). If we count each of the 15 individual storms that affected either or both states during this 49-year period, we can deduce that a declaration occurred an average once every 3.3 years (similar to the hurricane frequency shown in Figure 3.3.3), suggesting that these states should have had ample opportunities over the years to improve their resiliency to tropical cyclones as a result of their cumulative experiences.

While a number of the cases in Table 3.3.2 merit study, the two most significant of these are Hurricane Camille, which made landfall in Louisiana in 1969 as a category 5 storm (the only hurricane to do so in the continental United States in the twentieth century), and Hurricane Betsy in 1965, which flooded many of the same sections of New Orleans as Katrina would 40 years later.

Pielke et al. (1999) prepared a retrospective on the 30th anniversary of Hurricane Camille that included a summary of the economic and physical damages to the region. A map showing the physical damage is shown in Figure 3.3.6, while Table 3.3.3 shows the economic damage (in

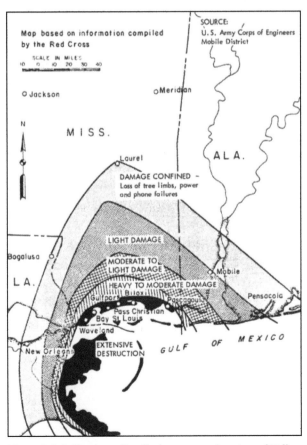

Figure 3.3.6. Hurricane Camille damage map (courtesy of Pielke et al. 1999).

Table 3.3.3. Estimated damage along the Gulf Coast from Hurricane Camille (using data gathered by Pielke et al. 1999).

Sector	Estimated damage (1969 $)
Residential	172,481,000
Commercial and industrial	113,357,000
Schools, churches, and hospitals	31,471,000
Transportation	25,029,000
Government (federal and nonfederal)	28,252,000
Marine	15,623,000
Agriculture	97,059,000
Utilities	29,433,000
Debris removal	21,139,000
Federal assistance	197,358,000
Total	**731,202,000***

*Does not include $250,000,000 estimated damages in Louisiana, which would bring the total to $981,202,000.

1969 dollars). In addition to the physical and economic damages, 143 people along the Gulf Coast lost their lives as a result of Camille. The majority of the physical and economic damages from Camille were in Mississippi. One of the results of this storm was the implementation of the Saffir–Simpson scale in 1973. The scale was developed in the late 1960s and early 1970s as a means to improve the communication of tropical cyclone impacts to first responders and emergency management personnel but became widely used after Dr. Neil Frank became director the National Hurricane Center in 1974 (Iacovelli 1999).

Hurricane Betsy made landfall near Grand Isle, Louisiana, on 10 September 1965 as a high-end category 3 storm. The hurricane caused extensive damage (in excess of $1 billion in 1965 dollars) and 81 fatalities, and the storm surge in Lake Pontchartrain resulted in a breach of levees in New Orleans, which inundated portions of the city. Prior to this event, the New Orleans levees had been designed for river flooding but not a major hurricane (Colten 2006). There were two major policy changes as a result of Hurricane Betsy. The first of these was the installation of a new set of levees around the New Orleans area to mitigate the effects of hurricane-induced flooding—this same set of levees failed during Hurricane Katrina. The second was the National Flood Insurance Act of 1968 (part of Public Law 90-448; www.gpo.gov/fdsys/pkg/STATUTE-82/pdf/STATUTE-82-Pg476.pdf), whose passage was hastened by this storm and concerns about similar flooding that could result from future hurricanes.

3.3.5. WHAT WENT WRONG WITH KATRINA?

Figure 3.3.7 shows a summary of the flooding in Louisiana and Mississippi from Hurricane Katrina. The National Aeronautics and Space Administration (NASA)'s Multiangle Imaging SpectroRadiometer (MISR) took the satellite imagery in Figure 3.3.7a on 14 August 2005 (15 days before landfall; left-hand image) and 30 August 2005 (24 h after landfall; right-hand image). The processing of the MISR data results in false-color composites that show water bodies and saturated soil as blue and purple, while highly vegetated areas appear bright green. The images show the extent of the impact of the flooding from this large storm. In the poststorm image, there are numerous rivers along the Mississippi coast that have swollen as a result of the hurricane's rainfall (estimated between 6 and

9 inches by NASA's Multisatellite Precipitation Analysis; http://earthobservatory.nasa.gov/NaturalHazards/view.php?id=15407). Comparing the two images also reveals the flooding in the Lake Pontchartrain and New Orleans areas and the nearly saturated soils in the Mississippi River floodplain along the Louisiana–Mississippi border. Figures 3.3.7b and 3.3.7c show the areas where the storm surge/tide and wind damage were the greatest, which understandably were closest to the coast. These figures show that while the storm's greatest physical impact was along the Gulf Coast, the vulnerable inland populations with relatively low education and high poverty were also impacted.

Here is a summary of the major impacts from Hurricane Katrina. As you read these, consider how many of these impacts would fit onto the second and third tiers of the environment-to-security cascade model for more-developed countries presented in Figure 3.1b. There were 1,883 deaths directly or indirectly caused by the hurricane with more than 1 million people displaced. After the levees failed, 80% of New Orleans flooded; 70% of the city's occupied housing was damaged, with direct property damage of $30 billion. Overall damages were estimated at $125 billion and over $60 billion in insured losses (Allianz Global Corporate and Specialty 2015). Prior to landfall, 79% of Gulf oil platforms were evacuated, translating to 1.4 million barrels per day of oil and 8.8 billion cubic feet per day of gas being shut in [i.e., available oil or gas that is not being produced from an existing well (www.merriam-webster.com/dictionary/shut-in)]. Katrina destroyed 44 platforms as it passed over the outer continental shelf oil/gas-producing region [U.S. Energy Information Administration (EIA) 2006]. Because of the production shutdown, oil prices jumped to nearly $70 a barrel following Hurricanes Katrina and Rita (which affected western Louisiana and Texas three and a half weeks after Katrina), with gas shortages and pump prices rising to $4 and $5 a gallon in some southeastern U.S. locations. To mitigate the price rise, President George W. Bush authorized the release of 30 million gallons from the U.S. Strategic Petroleum Reserve.

Recall from section 3.2.5 that mitigation is considered one of the most effective but expensive of the four risk management strategies. As we have already seen, there were a number of storms in addition to Betsy and Camille that served as "wake-up calls" for additional mitigation and preparedness actions at multiple levels

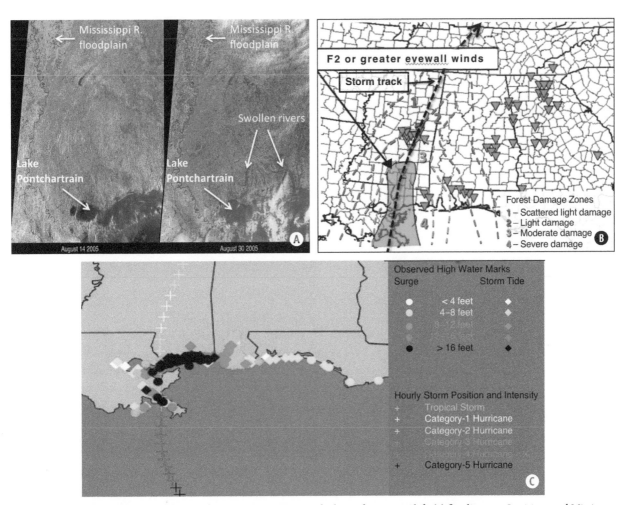

Figure 3.3.7. Physical impacts and damage from Hurricane Katrina, clockwise from upper left: (a) flooding over Louisiana and Mississippi as detected by comparison of NASA MISR satellite imagery taken (left) before and (right) after landfall (www.nasa.gov/vision/earth/lookingatearth/h2005_katrina.html); (b) tornado reports [red triangles; from National Weather Service (NWS) 2006], forest damage zones [separated by dashed lines; from U.S. Department of Agriculture (USDA) Forest Service 2005], with storm track (black dashed line) and area of F2 or greater tornado-equivalent winds from Hurricane Katrina's eyewall (light red shading); (c) hurricane track and intensity (legend in lower right) and storm surge/tide high-water marks over Louisiana, Mississippi, Alabama, and Florida coasts (legend in upper right; adapted from http://surge.srcc.lsu.edu/historical_maps.html).

of government. In fact, previous hurricanes (Georges in 1998 and Ivan in 2004) exposed flaws in Louisiana's evacuation procedures, which were subsequently addressed prior to Katrina. However, there were other actions such as upgrades to and strengthening of the existing levee system around New Orleans as a result of soil subsidence and sea level rise that were never undertaken. What happened to make Hurricane Katrina the worst natural disaster in U.S. history to date? Besides the points we have already made regarding the Gulf Coast region's vulnerability, here are some additional facts related to unintended consequences from legislation meant to

improve mitigation, plans that were never implemented, demographics that were not thoroughly examined, and critical weaknesses in the emergency management organizations that would play a leading role in the initial response to and recovery from Hurricane Katrina:

- *Unintended consequences of mitigation legislation.* The National Flood Insurance Act of 1968 did not discourage development along vulnerable coastline areas. Flynn (2007) points out that Mississippi's three coastal counties grew by almost 90,000 residents between 1995 and 2000.

- *Disappearance of Louisiana wetlands.* Discussed earlier, this natural barrier to tropical cyclones decreased by nearly a million acres between 1935 and 2005 (Flynn 2007).
- *Plans never implemented.* Hurricane Pam, a hypothetical disaster preparedness and response exercise held in 2004 using a scenario of a major hurricane hitting New Orleans, resulted in a number of recommendations for local, state, and federal officials to prepare for a major hurricane strike on New Orleans. However, only a few of these recommendations were acted upon before Katrina hit a year later (Select Bipartisan Committee to Investigate the Preparation for and Response to Hurricane Katrina 2006).
- *Special needs population.* Hurricane Katrina exposed vulnerabilities of residents within the New Orleans city limits beyond poverty and lack of education, such as age, disability, lack of mobility, no means of transportation, and number of children living in nontraditional home arrangements.
- *Organizational flaws exposed.* The FEMA reorganization after the 11 September 2001 terrorist attacks placed the agency under the newly formed Department of Homeland Security (DHS), whose main mission was counterterrorism. From 2001 into 2005, FEMA faced decreased funding, a "brain drain" of experienced personnel who left the agency, and a senior leadership cadre with a lack of emergency management experience (Moynihan 2009). Additional deficiencies at the state level in Louisiana existed because of chronic budget shortfalls and staff shortages (Select Bipartisan Committee to Investigate the Preparation for and Response to Hurricane Katrina 2006).

There were a number of corrective actions that took place as a result of Hurricane Katrina's impact on the Gulf Coast region. One of these, a much-needed reorganization of FEMA, was hastened perhaps by intense media scrutiny during the days and weeks following the hurricane's landfall. This story is told in the next chapter, which examines the role that traditional and social media play in the immediate aftermath of a natural disaster and during the long recovery phase when lessons are learned and remedial actions are recommended, debated, and implemented.

In-Depth Analysis Exercise 3.3.1: Using the PAR model in chapter 3.2 and the data provided in chapter 3.3, examine the *progression of vulnerability* in Louisiana and Mississippi. We suggest "working backwards" from the *unsafe conditions*, through the *dynamic pressures*, to determine if you can identify one or more *root causes* of the population's vulnerability in this region. (Note: while the data provided in this chapter is meant to give you a useful starting point for such an analysis, you will need to collect additional data.) Based on your findings, what can be done to improve the situation in each of these three portions of the PAR model?

In-Depth Analysis Exercise 3.3.2: Given your findings in Exercise 3.3.1, estimate how effective the *risk mitigation* and *hazard preparedness* actions can be in this type of operating environment. What can be done to improve the situation?

REFERENCES

Allianz Global Corporate and Specialty, 2015: Hurricane Katrina 10: Catastrophe management and global windstorm peril review. Allianz Global Corporate and Specialty Rep., 15 pp., www.agcs.allianz.com/assets/PDFs/risk%20bulletins/HurricaneKatrina10.pdf.

ASCE, 2013: 2012 report card for Mississippi's infrastructure. ASCE, http://2013.infrastructurereportcard.org/mississippi/mississippi-overview/.

Bauman, K. J., and N. L. Graf, 2003: Educational attainment: 2000. U.S. Census Bureau Rep. C2KBR-24, 12 pp.

Bishaw, A., 2013: Poverty: 2000 to 2012. U.S. Census Bureau Rep. ACSBR/12-01, 16 pp.

Colten, C. E., 2006: From Betsy to Katrina: Shifting policies, lingering vulnerabilities. *Third Annual Magrann Research Conf.*, New Brunswick, NJ, Rutgers University, http://magrann-conference.rutgers.edu/2006/_papers/colten.pdf.

EIA, 2006: The impact of tropical cyclones on Gulf of Mexico crude oil and natural gas production. U.S. Energy Information Administration Rep., 24 pp., www.eia.gov/outlooks/steo/special/pdf/2006_hurricanes.pdf.

Flynn, S., 2007: *The Edge of Disaster*. Random House, 272 pp.

Horowitz, A., 2012: Seeing the federal light. Slate, www.slate.com/articles/news_and_politics/history/2012/11/sandy_and_chris_christie_lessons_from_hurricane_betsy_in_1965.html.

Iacovelli, D., 1999: The Saffir/Simpson hurricane scale: An interview with Dr. Robert Simpson. *Mar. Wea. Log*, **43**, 10–12, www.vos.noaa.gov/MWL/apr1999.pdf.

Kosovich, J. J., 2008: State of Louisiana—Highlighting low-lying areas derived from USGS digital elevation data: U.S. Geological Survey Scientific Investigations Map 3049, version 1.0, http://biotech.law.lsu.edu/climate/ocean-rise/SIM3049.pdf.

Moynihan, D. P., 2009: The response to Hurricane Katrina. International Risk Governance Council Rep., 11 pp., https://irgc.org/wp-content/uploads/2012/04/Hurricane_Katrina_full_case_study_web.pdf.

National Centers for Environmental Information, 2017: U.S. billion-dollar weather and climate disasters: Overview. NOAA, www.ncdc.noaa.gov/billions/.

NWS, 2006: Service assessment: Hurricane Katrina—August 23-31, 2005. NWS Rep., 50 pp.

Pielke, R. A., Jr., C. Simonpietri, and J. Oxelson, 1999: Thirty years after Hurricane Camille: Lessons learned, lessons lost. University of Colorado Boulder Center for Science and Technology Policy Research, http://sciencepolicy.colorado.edu/about_us/meet_us/roger_pielke/camille/report.html.

Select Bipartisan Committee to Investigate the Preparation for and Response to Hurricane Katrina, 2006: A Failure of initiative: The final report of the Select Bipartisan Committee to investigate the preparation for and response to Hurricane Katrina. U.S. House of Representatives Rep. 109-377, 582 pp., http://katrina.house.gov.

Smith, A., and R. Katz, 2013: U.S. billion-dollar weather and climate disasters: Data sources, trends, accuracy and biases. *Nat. Hazards*, **67**, 387–410, https://doi.org/10.1007/s11069-013-0566-5.

Solis, R., 2005: Mississippi casino boats are moving onto dry land. USA Today, 18 October, https://usatoday30.usatoday.com/news/nation/2005-10-18-casinos-miss_x.htm.

U.S. Army Corps of Engineers, 2010: Regional Supplement to the Corps of Engineers Wetland Delineation Manual: Atlantic and Gulf Coastal Plain Region (Version 2.0), ed. J. S. Wakeley, R. W. Lichver, and C. V. Noble. ERDC/EL TR-10-20. Vicksburg, MS: U.S. Army Engineer Research and Development Center.

USDA Forest Service, 2005: Potential timber damage due to Hurricane Katrina in Mississippi, Alabama and Louisiana—September 22, 2005. USDA Forest Service Rep., 2 pp., www.srs.fs.usda.gov/katrina/katrina_brief_2005-09-22.pdf.

Williams, S. J., 2003: Louisiana coastal wetlands: A resource at risk. U.S. Geological Survey, https://pubs.usgs.gov/fs/la-wetlands/.

MEDIA IMPACTS ON DISASTER MANAGEMENT AND POLICY

John R. Fisher
John M. Lanicci

3.4.1. INTRODUCTION

This chapter focuses on 1) the changing roles of traditional and social media as they relate to disaster management immediately before, during, and in the aftermath of an event; and 2) the potential influence of traditional and social media on maintaining public and policy-maker focus in the aftermath of a natural disaster. It begins with a short case study analysis of the media's coverage of the problems related to disaster management in the postlandfall period of Hurricane Katrina in August–September 2005. The case study shows that in the immediate aftermath of the event, traditional media[1] coverage played an important role in drawing attention to the magnitude of the disaster despite some initial challenges with obtaining accurate information. The case study then provides a short summary of U.S. disaster management policy changes in the aftermath of the event. The chapter concludes with a brief summary of the ways in which social media (in particular,

Twitter) has changed the ways in which the U.S. Federal Emergency Management Agency (FEMA) manages a disaster in real time. This summary, which includes examples from Superstorm Sandy and other recent events, can be compared and contrasted with the ways in which accurate information was difficult to come by in New Orleans, Louisiana, in the hours and days following Hurricane Katrina's landfall.

The case study approach to this chapter was chosen because quantitative research approaches have been unsuccessful in measuring mass media influence on public policy making. Case studies can be defined as "a story of a problem," dealing with actual events, organizations, and decision-makers (Hoag et al. 2001, p. 50). Problem solving "can be measurably improved by the case study method" (Hoag et al. 2001, p. 49). The case study approach may have greater success in establishing a situation-by-situation analysis of how the mass media impacts the policy-making process by examining

---

1. For the purposes of this chapter, traditional media is defined as "any form of mass communication available before the advent of digital media. This includes television, radio, newspapers, books, and magazines" (https://www.igi-global.com/dictionary/mobile-phones-news-consumption-news-creation-and-news-organization-accommodations/47688), while we use Kaplan and Haenlein's (2010) definition of social media as "a group of Internet-based applications that build on the ideological and technological foundations of Web 2.0, and that allow the creation and exchange of User Generated Content."

high-profile natural disaster events such as this one. As valuable as this approach is, one must exercise caution in generalizing the results of a case study to other disaster events, as each takes place within its own unique set of circumstances, albeit (hopefully) with the benefits of lessons learned from previous events.

Before proceeding with this chapter, it is necessary to state some caveats. We believe it is important to understand the increasingly important roles that traditional and social media play in disaster coverage. As this book goes to press (summer 2019), the United States continues to recover from the two most recent natural disasters, Hurricane Florence in the Carolinas and Hurricane Michael along the Gulf Coast and southeast United States. There is much debate within the scientific community about proper messaging for the affected populations in advance of these extreme events. While we could provide examples where social media helps disseminate the message to influence proper decision-making (e.g., evacuations, preparedness for sheltering in place), there are also examples where social media has diluted the message (e.g., accusations of overhyping an event, fake news). One cannot necessarily draw a straight line from preexisting conditions (vulnerability), to the event and associated media coverage, to public policy actions taken in the event's aftermath. And we can only speculate about the media's role in influencing the security implications of the event. However, we believe that the presence (and possible influences) of traditional and social media must be accounted for in management of and recovery from such events (to include public policy actions) and, as such, should be included in a unit on natural disasters and environmental security.

3.4.2. TRADITIONAL MEDIA COVERAGE OF HURRICANE KATRINA AND CHANGES TO U.S. DISASTER MANAGEMENT POLICY IN ITS AFTERMATH

In the days immediately following Hurricane Katrina's landfall in Louisiana and Mississippi, a multitude of reporters besieged New Orleans and reported a city overwhelmed by the devastation of nature, human misery, and crime. Each media report reemphasized a city suffering from a catastrophe. These reports first demonstrated government incompetence and then later showed government response to the problems.

The reports of atrocities in New Orleans shocked the nation and the world. Audiences heard and read about a city in anarchy and subhuman living conditions at the Louisiana Superdome and New Orleans Convention Center. However, many of the reports of violence were false and could not be verified. Reports were based on rumors several times removed from the source. For example, on 5 September 2005, the *Financial Times of London* attributed the following report to unnamed "refugees": "Girls and boys were raped in the dark and had their throats cut and bodies were stuffed in the kitchens while looters and madmen exchanged fire with weapons they had looted." The report claimed that "several hundred corpses are reported to have been gathered by locals in one school alone" in St. Bernard Parish, the badly flooded community just east of the city. A similar report indicated that up to 300 bodies were piled in Marion Abramson High School in east New Orleans. Reporters from the *New Orleans Times-Picayune* canoed to the school, went inside, and found no bodies.

"Stone-age storytelling got amplified by space-age technology," according to Thevenot (2005). Rumors of bodies in the Superdome were retold several times and finally reached the media. When "the media arrived, with satellite phones and modems, BlackBerrys, television trucks with the ability to broadcast worldwide and the technology to post on the Internet in an instant," most of them did not realize that the "normal rules of sourcing no longer ensured accuracy" (Thevenot 2005). The stories went global as officials, hurricane victims, and rescue and security personnel confirmed nightmarish scenarios, sincerely believing what they were saying and wanting desperately to get the word out so that help would come. The media also believed the stories they were telling, repeating without verification the stories being told by the officials. When it was discovered that the stories were false, the media were criticized. However, it was the media who revealed the falsehood of the stories. The only way that the public knew about the bad reporting was that the journalists told them.

Despite these early missteps, the traditional media's coverage of the government response to Katrina had an impact on public opinion almost immediately. Not long after this came the reactions in Washington, D.C. One of these was the firing of Michael Brown, the FEMA director, in the midst of the federal government's response to the hurricane's aftermath. Following Katrina, congressional hearings applauded the unselfish service of over 60,000 volunteers, while at the same time, they were highly critical of the federal government's response (Select Bipartisan Committee to Investigate the Preparation for and Response to Hurricane Katrina 2006). Next came a major reorganization of FEMA itself as a result of the Post-Katrina Emergency Management Reform Act in 2006 (U.S. Congress 2006), which directed FEMA to take the following actions (https://emilms.fema.gov/is230c/fem0101summary.htm):

- "Establishes a Disability Coordinator and develop guidelines to accommodate individuals with disabilities.
- "Establishes the National Emergency Family Registry and Locator System to reunify separated family members.
- "Coordinates and supports precautionary evacuations and recovery efforts.
- "Provides transportation assistance for relocating and returning individuals displaced from their residences in a major disaster.
- "Provides case management assistance to identify and address unmet needs of survivors of major disasters."

As a result of the congressional hearings in the aftermath of Hurricane Katrina, the Department of Homeland Security (DHS; FEMA's parent organization since 2002) changed its focus to consider other forms of disasters in addition to terrorist attacks (Homeland Security Council 2007).

Previous studies (Fisher 1991; Fisher and Soemarsono 2008) have suggested that the media generally has little impact on public policy. While the traditional media bring public attention and the attention of politicians to an issue, they are unable to sustain the kind of coverage that is required to see public policy through. Thus, the media usually play a minor role in the *adoption* of public policy. Over time, the interest of the traditional media in an issue wanes. Haiti's tragic earthquake and the aftermath is an example. The international community reacted quickly to support the victims, in large part due to traditional media coverage. However, little has changed for the victims in Haiti. Many remain homeless. Traditional media attention has faded (Toronto Star 2011). By contrast, in the case of Katrina, the traditional media's coverage of the hurricane's aftermath may have

kept the focus on the disaster long enough to influence the immediate change in FEMA leadership and ignite congressional investigations that eventually led to the FEMA and DHS organizational changes.

To be clear, the media did not act alone in bringing about these changes but rather in concert with pressure from the public and local and state politicians (Fisher 2014). Why was Katrina different from other natural disasters? One possibility is the "issue-attention cycle" proposed by Downs (1972), suggesting that a traumatic event is required to "catapult" an issue to the attention of the public and policy makers. In this case, the horrendous impacts from Katrina kept natural disasters in the forefront of American consciousness. In the policy research community, Hurricane Katrina provided what is known as a "focusing event" (Kingdon 2011) that "shocked" the U.S. policy system and acted as a catalyst for organizational changes at the U.S. federal level. Birkland (2016) provides an overview of focusing events and their influence on U.S. disaster policy using legislation covering the period 1950–2015. Among these were several hurricanes and subsequent legislation described in the previous chapter.

To truly have an impact on public policy, the media must provide consistent and continual coverage to follow up on issues. The press must go beyond simply bringing issues to the public's attention and thoroughly examine the problems and suggest solutions. However, this will only happen if the public also shares an interest in finding solutions to the public policy problems. How might this happen? The advent of social media in the late 2000s and early 2010s may be a way of keeping the attention on these issues, as we will see in the next section.

3.4.3. THE EVOLVING ROLE OF SOCIAL MEDIA IN THE WAKE OF RECENT NATURAL DISASTERS

If Downs' (1972) issue-attention cycle suggests that a traumatic event is required to catapult an issue to the attention of the public and policy makers, then Superstorm Sandy in 2012 appears to have had a sustaining effect on both the public and politicians. In addition to traditional media coverage documenting some of the estimated $19 billion in damage in the New York City, New York, area from this event, the event led to numerous studies on the impact of climate change on disasters (e.g., Thompson and Kahn 2014). From Sandy, there was a wealth of data available to scientists and decision-makers pointing to failures in responding to the storm and to the opportunities that followed the storm (Thompson and Kahn 2014). The data came from "traditional" sources such as weather observation platforms and "nontraditional" sources such as cell phones, security cameras, population surveys, and social media. Additionally, in the aftermath of Sandy, more people used social media to keep informed and to protect themselves.

As was the case with Hurricane Katrina, Sandy could be viewed as a focusing event for the policy-making community, since it did influence legislation in Washington (Birkland 2016, their Table 1). Three months after the disaster, the bipartisan Disaster Relief Appropriations Act of 2013, also known as the "Sandy Supplemental Appropriations Bill" (U.S. Congress 2013), was passed into law. The Sandy Supplemental Appropriations Bill provided supplemental funding to over a dozen federal departments and agencies for poststorm aid and restoration. A small fraction of the bill's $61 billion allocation provided funds to the National Oceanic and Atmospheric Administration (NOAA) for "Procurement, Acquisition and Construction" activities, which included supercomputer acquisition to enable improved numerical weather model forecasts. This portion of the bill was likely influenced by traditional and social media reports of a "superior" medium-range forecast of the event from the European Centre for Medium-Range Weather Forecasts' (ECMWF) global model compared to the U.S. National Centers for Environmental Prediction's Global Forecast System (GFS) model. Rood (2013) provides a short list of online sources that carried this story.

If we contrast the social media environments of Katrina and Sandy, which were seven years apart, we find some interesting differences. When Hurricane Katrina hit the shores of Louisiana and Mississippi in 2005, Facebook® was just getting started, and Twitter did not yet exist. Now, FEMA has a Twitter account that had nearly 400,000 followers in 2015, and former FEMA director Craig Fugate had his own page, @CraigatFEMA, with over 50,000 followers. In FEMA's 2013 national preparedness report, the department indicated that during and immediately following Hurricane Sandy, "users sent more than 20 million Sandy-related Twitter posts, or 'tweets,' despite the loss of cell phone service during the peak of the storm" (Department of Homeland Security 2013).

New Jersey's largest utility company, the Public Service Enterprise Group (PSEG), reported that during Sandy they used Twitter to notify the public of the daily locations of their giant tents and generators (Maron 2013).

While these are hopeful signs, inherent risks exist in using social media. One is misinformation. Sutton (as cited in Maron 2013) claims that "all the fast-paced information available via social media does pose inherent risks when navigating emergency situations." Although false information eventually gets corrected by the "Wikipedia effect," by which other users correct the information, Sutton notes that inaccuracies can also "go viral." Rumor Control, run by FEMA, relies on local emergency personnel to correct misinformation (Department of Homeland Security 2013). Another risk is fraud. The American Red Cross used cell phone technology to raise more than $5 million in the 48 hours following the Haiti earthquake in 2010, but at the same time, cell phone texting and web pages were used by criminals who appealed to emotion to steal cash (Maron 2013).

Since 2010, FEMA has used Twitter during all stages of a disaster, from before the event strikes, during the actual event, and after (Fisher et al. 2015). Prior to a disaster, FEMA monitors local weather reports (and tweets) and advises the public. As an example, in the case of floods, FEMA's posts on Twitter outline the parts of the United States experiencing flooding, share information about flood preparedness, and give advice to people about what they can do. The agency relies on official information, including forecasts from the National Weather Service and links from official emergency management agencies. FEMA typically retweets information from other government agencies. They use a tool to shorten ".gov" web addresses and can track how many hits each individual link draws (Fisher et al. 2015).

The agency also uses social media to try to predict what a state might need to do to prepare for a potential disaster. For example, in one of its first attempts to use social media in September 2010 as Hurricane Earl moved up the U.S. East Coast, FEMA monitored Twitter and was able to see that tourists on the Outer Banks in North Carolina were evacuating, but many residents were not. That information gave FEMA and state agencies the information they needed to develop search-and-rescue plans for those residents (Fisher et al. 2015).

Emergency agencies determine what people are saying by tracking hashtags (#). During the 2011

Groundhog Day Blizzard that affected the central and northeastern U.S. and Canada (NOAA National Centers for Environmental Information 2017), the most commonly used hashtag was #snomg. During those storms, FEMA monitored what was happening by using HootSuite, a Twitter-adaptable program that displays all tweets using a given hashtag. During that storm, FEMA could tell Oklahoma was getting hit by ice and Chicago residents thought the storm had missed them—until they started tweeting as the storm got worse (Fisher et al. 2015).

Twitter also serves as a news service, not only a social network. This is particularly true when tweeters are victims of the disaster. As eyewitnesses of the harm from the disaster, they become first-line reporters of what is happening. A study of the 2009 flooding of the Red River in North Dakota by Starbird et al. (2010) showed that 10% of tweets were new information. However, much of the valuable information resulted from copying or adapting information from others (derivative information) and combining information (synthesis). The researchers found that fully 80% of the information was generated by people living in the location of the disaster, with the remainder being generated by the local and national media (Starbird et al. 2010). The majority of information that was retweeted was news because it did not exist elsewhere or on the Internet.

Another factor that made Twitter unique was that Twitter did not only serve as a means of broadcasting news but also as a platform for informational interaction. This provided a way for people to navigate through the enormous amounts of information, placing "virtual signposts" that they could follow. People retweeted information they felt was important, adding to the amount of information out there, but also signaling to their followers that this was information that needed their attention. Tweeters use retweeting, copying, or adapting information and combining information as a way of organizing information and making sense of the many messages (Fisher et al. 2015).

Twitter may also be a valuable source of information for policy-maker decision-making, although there is some doubt as to whether policy makers can synthesize the enormous amount of information in time to arrive at a consensus about what the information is really saying. Nevertheless, public officials and policy makers can get feedback from their followers on Twitter.

While the "big players" such as Facebook and Twitter still dominate social media, social media do more to equalize the playing field so that the average person has a greater opportunity to receive and relay information. For example, a farmer in India can check social media for weather reports and also report on his crop yields. The use of social media has changed the way the public is informed about disasters and how to recover from them. While the traditional media continue to play a key role, social media has given citizens a means to inform and protect each other as well as to attempt to alter public policy and the official approach to dealing with emergencies. While social media was independently evolving in the years leading up to 2010, the use of social media since that time has made public officials aware of its potential in disaster response. Since then, social media has played an important part in informing and keeping the public safe at both the local and national levels.

3.4.4. CONCLUSIONS

The analysis of the problems faced by the traditional media in the immediate aftermath of Hurricane Katrina in August–September 2005 shows that they were largely due to a lack of reliable communications in the New Orleans area, resulting in the reporting of multiple false narratives that took days to correct. While the inaccurate depictions of murders, rapes, and other atrocities were later recanted, the media appeared to play a role in raising and keeping the public's and politicians' attention on the evacuees' situation and the subpar government response to the disaster. The case study showed that despite the limited informational access and technological challenges, traditional media coverage eventually had an important impact on public opinion, likely contributing to a "focusing event" from a policy-making perspective that subsequently led to changes in U.S. disaster management policy and federal organizational structures.

We also described how the advent of social media over the last 10 years played an important role in altering the ways in which disasters are reported and managed. In particular, Twitter has changed the means by which FEMA manages disasters in real time. While it is unclear what role social media plays in the influence of policy making in the aftermath of a disaster, it appeared to keep a continued awareness of the issues associated with the recovery from Superstorm Sandy long after the traditional media moved on to new stories. While Sandy provided another focusing event for the U.S. policy-making community, it is difficult to ascertain the influence that traditional and social media had on maintaining this awareness and its influence on the passage of the Sandy Supplemental Appropriations Bill. Suffice it to say that this and other aspects of the issue certainly deserve further study.

In-Depth Analysis Exercise 3.4.1: Choose a pair of U.S. natural disasters, one occurring before the advent of social media and smartphone technologies and the other occurring after use of these technologies became widespread among the general population. Compare and contrast the disaster management process before, during, and after each event, and evaluate whether the preparations and responses were better or worse. Can social media be used as a proactive tool in the *risk mitigation* and *hazard preparedness* phases of disaster management as shown in Figure 3.2.6? What are the advantages? What are the disadvantages?

REFERENCES

Birkland, T. A., 2016: Policy process theory and natural hazards. *Oxford Research Encyclopedia of Natural Hazard Science*, Oxford University Press, https://doi.org/10.1093/acrefore/9780199389407.013.75.

Department of Homeland Security, 2010: Quadrennial homeland security review report: A strategic framework for a secure homeland. Department of Homeland Security Rep., 108 pp.

——, 2013: National preparedness report. Department of Homeland Security Rep., 72 pp.

Downs, A., 1972: Up and down with ecology—The "issue-attention cycle." *Pub. Interest*, **28**, 38–51.

Fisher, J. R., 1991: News media functions in policymaking. *Can. J. Commun.*, **16**, 139–145.

——, 2014: Media impact on disaster public policy. *Digital Nation: New Media, Old Teachers, Learning and Citizenship*, R. H. Kuddus, J. O. Jasperson, and A. M. Carter, Eds., Utah Valley University, 119–132.

——, and A. Soemarsono, 2008: Mass media impact on post-secondary policy making: A case study of a failed merger attempt. *Competition Forum*, **6**, 96–102.

——, J. Pitcher, and G. Noll, 2015: Using student case study research to verify Twitter usage in disasters. *Int. J. Interdiscip. Res.*, **4**, 15–26.

Hoag, A., D. J. Brickley, and J. M. Cawley, 2001: Media management education and the case method. *Journalism Mass Commun. Educ.*, **55** (4), 49–59, https://doi.org/10.1177/107769580105500405.

Homeland Security Council, 2007: National strategy for homeland security. Homeland Security Council Rep., 62 pp.

Kaplan, A. M., and M. Haenlein, 2010: Users of the world, unite! The challenges and opportunities of social media. *Bus. Horiz.*, **53**, 59–68, https://doi.org/10.1016/j.bushor.2009.09.003.

Kingdon, J. W., 2011: *Agendas, Alternatives, and Public Policies.* 2nd ed. Longman, 273 pp.

Maron, D. F., 2013: How social media is changing disaster response. Scientific American, www.scientificamerican.com/article/how-social-media-is-changing-disaster-response/.

Office of Homeland Security, 2002: Organizing for a secure homeland. National strategy for homeland security. Office of Homeland Security Rep., 11–14.

Rood, R. B., 2013: To be the best in weather forecasting: Why Europe is beating the U.S. Washington Post, accessed 12 October 2018, www.washingtonpost.com/blogs/capital-weather-gang/post/to-be-the-best-in-weather-forecasting-why-europe-is-beating-the-us/2013/03/08/429bfcd0-8806-11e2-9d71-f0feafdd1394_blog.html?utm_term=.256c1413d012.

Select Bipartisan Committee to Investigate the Preparation for and Response to Hurricane Katrina, 2006: A Failure of initiative: The final report of the Select Bipartisan Committee to investigate the preparation for and response to Hurricane Katrina. U.S. House of Representatives Rep. 109-377, 582 pp., http://katrina.house.gov.

Starbird, K., L. Palen, A. L. Hughes, and S. Vieweg, 2010: Chatter on the Red: What hazards threat reveals about the social life of microblogged information. *Proc. 2010 Conf. on Computer Supported Cooperative Work*, Savannah, GA, Association for Computing Machinery, 241–250, https://doi.org/10.1145/1718918.1718965.

Thevenot, B., 2005: Myth-making in New Orleans. *Amer. Journalism Rev.*, **27** (6), 30–37.

Thompson, A., and B. Kahn, 2014: Two years on: Sandy inspires storm of climate research. Climate Central, www.climatecentral.org/news/two-years-later-sandy-inspires-storm-of-climate-research-18248.

Toronto Star, 2011: Haiti's neglected cholera
crisis. Toronto Star, www.thestar.com/opinion/
editorials/2011/05/14/haitis_neglected_cholera_
crisis.html.

U.S. Congress, 2006: Department of Homeland Security
Appropriations Act of 2007. Public Law 109-295,
www.doi.gov/sites/doi.gov/files/uploads/Post_
Katrina_Emergency_Management_Reform_Act_pdf.
pdf.

——, 2013: Disaster Relief Appropriations Act of 2013.
Public Law 113-2, www.gpo.gov/fdsys/pkg/PLAW-
113publ2/pdf/PLAW-113publ2.pdf.

3.5

WAR AND WEAK INSTITUTIONS AS CONTRIBUTORS TO NATURAL DISASTERS

Edin Mujkic
Lauren Bacon Brengarth
John M. Lanicci

3.5.1. INTRODUCTION

In May 2014, the Balkans[1] faced unprecedented floods. Three countries were particularly affected: Bosnia and Herzegovina, Croatia, and Serbia. A three-week period of above-normal rainfall in the latter part of April and in early May was followed by three days of record-setting rains. The result was flooding and landslides, especially in Bosnia, where the rugged Southern Alps are home to many villages and farms. The floods and landslides were responsible for over 1 million temporarily displaced people and several billion euros in damages and losses. This study shows how the wars of the 1990s, weak institutions, and widespread corruption combined to create a lack of preparedness and ability to respond, especially in Bosnia. This case provides us with another opportunity to apply the Pressure and Release (PAR) model introduced in chapter 3.2 as well as the environment-to-security cascade model in Figure 3.1.

While human civilization has had to deal with natural disasters since the beginning of organized settlement, in the twentieth century and especially in the twenty-first century, the world became more resilient to natural disasters because of better-organized institutions, especially in the more-developed world (Kahn 2005). At the same time, however, because of an expanding human habitat, the population also became more exposed to various natural hazards. Although more-developed countries have great assets at their disposal for disaster preparation and response, we saw in chapter 3.3 with Hurricane Katrina that even these can be overwhelmed if the disaster is severe enough.

While the aftermath of Hurricane Katrina was a shock for Americans and others around the world, lessons from the preparation and response have been exhaustively studied (e.g., Gabe et al. 2005; White House 2006; Senate Committee on Homeland Security and Governmental Affairs 2006; Select Bipartisan Committee to Investigate the Preparation for and Response to Hurricane Katrina 2006). This level of analysis and research is not available in poorer countries, especially those ravaged by wars. In such countries, it is important to study the degree to which disasters can be anticipated and managed. However, as we will see shortly, even the level of anticipation and management often does not

---

1. According to dictionary.com, the Balkans consist of the following countries and territories: Croatia, Bosnia and Herzegovina, Slovenia, Serbia, Montenegro, Kosovo, Macedonia, Romania, Bulgaria, Albania, Greece, and the European part of Turkey.

depend solely on whether a country is rich or poor but on the strength of its institutions (Kahn 2005).

3.5.2. THE BALKAN WARS OF THE 1990S

The former Yugoslavia broke apart officially in 1991 when Slovenia and Croatia declared their independence. Although political institutions in the former Yugoslavia were on a destabilization path since the death of life-long President of Yugoslavia Josip Broz Tito in 1980, the collapse of the Berlin Wall in 1989 accelerated that process (Woodward 1995). Old issues characteristic of the Balkans surfaced together with corruption and fighting for power, which was a recipe for disaster. While war in Slovenia lasted only 10 days [until the Yugoslav People's Army (YPA) pulled out of that country], in Croatia it took a more serious, prolonged path. As the European community and the United States were trying to solve issues in Croatia, Bosnia and Herzegovina was going through its own turmoil, which sounded alarms all across Europe and the United States, considering the very complex religious composition of that country.

In 1992, Bosnia and Herzegovina declared independence from Yugoslavia, which triggered a secessionist movement in Bosnia by the radical Serbs who were supported by Serbia, which controlled the YPA and its resources. The war in Bosnia lasted from 1992 until the end of 1995 and took more than 100,000 lives. The world witnessed the first concentration camps and cases of genocide on European soil since World War II (Vulliamy 1998).

During the war, many areas in Bosnia that were controlled by the legitimate Bosnian government were surrounded and under siege by the Army of the Serb Republic in Bosnia, as well as for some period of time by Croatian forces who tried to use the war in Bosnia to further their own objectives. Some areas were faced with serious shortages of food, electricity, and gas for several years until the Dayton Peace Agreement was signed (Curtis 1995). These shortages led the populace to take extreme measures for gathering heating materials during the harsh Bosnian winters, such as cutting down trees in parks, streets, and hillsides and even using construction materials from houses destroyed by artillery (Curtis 1995).

Once the war was over, Bosnia faced a tremendous number of issues. Prior to 1991, Yugoslavia was an industrialized country, and Bosnia was the heart of Yugoslavian heavy industry, with an emphasis on the military.

Much of that capacity, as well as infrastructure that was on par with western Europe, was now destroyed. That led to a massive effort by the international community to rebuild Bosnia's infrastructure and economy (McMahon 2004). The infrastructure was back to its prewar level by 2002–2004 and even developed further after that time. However, the economy lagged behind because Bosnia was no longer part of Yugoslavia and therefore lost access to a market of 24 million consumers. Also, the YPA in 1991 was one of the largest military forces in Europe, and since most of the former Yugoslavian military industry was located in Bosnia (because of inhospitable mountains that provide good protection) and the YPA ceased to exist, the Bosnian economy was on a slow path to recovery.

The intention of the Dayton Peace Agreement (also known as the Dayton Accords) was first and foremost to stop the war. The idea was that after hostilities ended, the Bosnian people would take matters into their own hands and create a more functional constitution, similar to the American experience. However, most of the political elite who were present before and during the war in Bosnia also continued to be involved in running that country *after* the war. That situation led to further separation of religious groups and emphasis on issues of "rights" for each of the three major religious groups (Muslims, Catholics, and Christian Orthodox), while other groups of people were marginalized (Borger 2015). The continuation of warlike rhetoric, without actual war, in order to preserve the status quo and political positions, led to institutionalized corruption (Nardelli et al. 2014). The consequence of this situation was a lack of funding for any types of agencies where political cronies could not be appointed because of the nature of the job. These agencies included institutions responsible for protecting the environment and population, such as the forest service, civil protection agency, and the military. The military, which became united in the mid-2000s, was particularly underfunded and considered more of a "necessary evil" by nationalists whose goal was always to keep Bosnia from meaningful reforms that might lead to establishment of functional institutions (Hulsey and Mujkić 2010).

At the same time, Croatia and Serbia went different ways. In 1995, Croatia succeeded with Operation "Storm" to establish sovereignty over all its territory, and in 1999, Serbia was bombed by the North Atlantic Treaty Organization (NATO) in Operation Allied Force, after which citizens toppled dictator Slobodan Milosevic in

2000, and the country returned towards a democratic path (McFaul 2005). Unlike Bosnia, Croatia and Serbia suffered limited damage to their infrastructure, and with more streamlined governments (unlike the Bosnian governmental system that has 14 governments and three presidents), had more resources at their disposal to fund agencies responsible for protecting the environment and population.

3.5.3. PROBLEMS WITH POSTWAR DISASTER MANAGEMENT IN BOSNIA AND SERBIA

In order to understand the operating environment with regard to disaster management in present-day Bosnia and Serbia, it is first necessary to get a historical perspective. The former Yugoslavia had a very robust emergency management system dating back to 1932 [Državna Uprava za Zaštitu i Spašavanje (DUZS) 2015a]. In fact, the awareness of and preparation for flooding in this region can be traced back to the Austro-Hungary period, when the government built huge levees in downtown Sarajevo after it annexed Bosnia in 1878. After World War II, the Yugoslav government, together with its six republics (Bosnia and Herzegovina, Croatia, Macedonia, Montenegro, Serbia, and Slovenia) actively worked on forestation of the country for various reasons, one of them being the prevention of landslides. Additionally, the government built large levees in Zenica similar to those in Sarajevo. Besides organized forestation, after the 1960s floods that ravaged Yugoslavia, where the YPA played the largest role in stabilization operations, the country also heavily invested in the Civil Protection Agency (CPA) (Mišković and Mandić 1987). The agency was available to the country's workforce and was also actively engaged with major businesses in utilizing their resources in case of a large disaster. They conducted complex drills at least once a year with their corporate partners in order to prepare for large natural disasters (Mišković and Mandić 1987).

While the Dayton Accords were successful in stopping the war in Bosnia, they also introduced a complicated bureaucratic system that encouraged corruption and nepotism. At the same time, Croatia attempted to befriend NATO and the European Union (EU), which eventually was successful. That had meaningful impact on Croatia's institutions responsible for protecting the population. Considering that Croatia is an important

tourist destination in Europe, the country invested heavily in air force and police search-and-rescue capabilities (DUZS 2015b). On the other hand, Serbia, both during and after the wars, relied on an abundance of military equipment that it took possession of once the YPA disintegrated. However, because of the prevailing corruption and neglect in Serbia, most of the equipment had to be scrapped over time and was not replaced (Femić 2014).

Natural disasters in the Balkans prior to the 2014 flood were a good indicator for what to expect from each newly independent country in a large or unprecedented disaster. For example, Croatia had several major floods and forest fires prior to 2014, and the emergency agencies did their job on par with EU countries. In fact, the Croatian Air Force now has a highly respectable aerial firefighting capability. The Croatian firefighting capabilities and mobilization process are particularly remarkable for such a small country; these include 6 Canadair CL-415 fire suppression planes and 10 smaller Air Tractors (AT-802 and AT-802 Fire Boss) (Croatian Firefighting Association 2015).

By contrast, Bosnia relies solely on the helicopter fire suppression capabilities of their MI-8, MI-17, and UH-1 helicopters, in a country with a similar climate to Croatia (Mediterranean) that is prone to wildfires. In case of larger fires, Bosnia has an agreement with Croatia to call their air force for help using their CL-415 aircraft (Krnić 2013). Although Bosnia faced huge forest fires for several years, disagreements within the government arose over who would have aerial firefighting equipment, which led the country to not invest any meaningful resources to increase such firefighting capabilities (Huseinović 2013). The situation in Serbia is even more alarming, considering the resources that the country took away from the YPA. However, Serbia has an agreement with Russia to station some of its aerial firefighting capabilities during the summer at one of the Serbian Air Force bases (Banković 2015a).

The lack of investment in the necessary emergency management agencies and related institutional capabilities is a known issue for countries in transition, but in Bosnia and Serbia, it took a dramatic path. These countries completely scrapped the emergency management system they inherited from the former Yugoslavia. Unlike Croatia, which heavily invested in their vertical transport capabilities as well as in professional and volunteer firefighting brigades, Bosnia and Serbia mostly

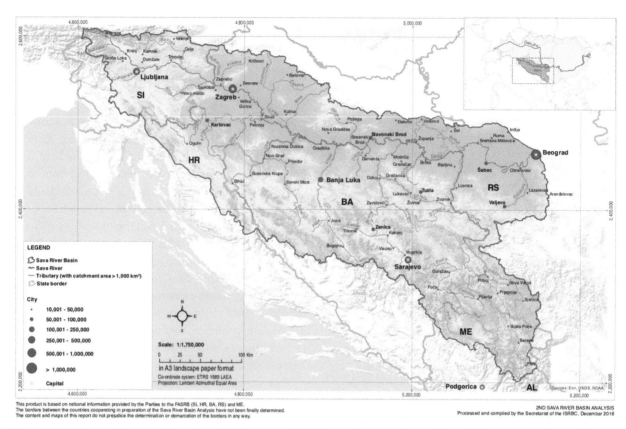

Figure 3.5.1. Topographic map of the regions with the greatest flood damage [source: Wikiwand (www.wikiwand.com/en/Socialist_Federal_Republic_of_Yugoslavia)].

relied on old equipment and donations. In Bosnia, the money that was supposed to be appropriated for the CPA was used instead for "patching budget holes." Every time taxes were paid in the country, part of it should have gone to fund the CPA, which on an annual basis, is around $15 million (U.S. dollars) just for the Federation of Bosnia and Herzegovina. That is a substantial amount of money for a territory that has approximately 2.2 million people (Degrimendžić 2015). As we will show, this corrupt relationship between the government, CPA, and other emergency management agencies resulted in a tragedy that was largely avoidable.

3.5.4. THE BALKAN FLOODS OF MAY 2014

The Bosnia (or Bosna) River (the river after which the country is named) flows for 168 miles (270 km) from suburban areas of Sarajevo in central Bosnia to the Sava River that constitutes the northern border between Bosnia and Croatia. Although the Bosnia River is con-

sidered a mountain river, it flows through flatlands in the northern region of Bosnia, which makes it prone to flooding. Since the majority of its path is through rugged mountains, it collects water generated by extensive fall and spring rains and melting snow. The Sava River starts in Slovenia, goes through the capitol of Croatia, Zagreb, and joins the Danube River in the capitol of Serbia, Belgrade. The Sava is a large river that is an important economic generator for all three countries, as barges travel from the Sava to the Danube River and on to the Black Sea on its waters. Figure 3.5.1 shows a map of the region and its rivers.

From mid-April through early May 2014, rainfall over the Balkans was well above normal on 18 of 21 days (Stadtherr et al. 2016). Then from 13 through 16 May, the region faced unprecedented rainfall, with most areas exceeding 90 mm (3.5 inches) (Stadtherr et al. 2016). The highest three-day rainfall amounts were measured at Tuzla [264 mm (10.4 inches)], Loznica [213 mm (8.4 inches)], Valjevo [190 mm (7.5 inches)], and

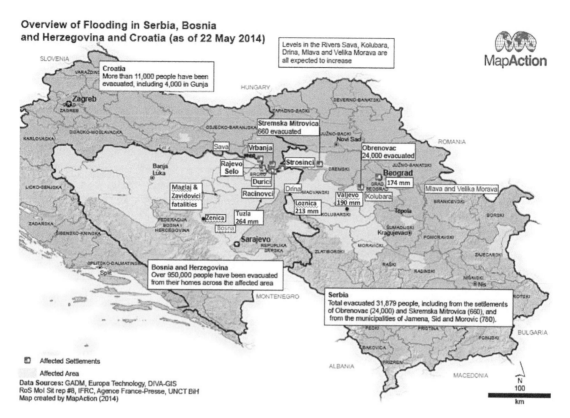

Figure 3.5.2. Regional flood overview map produced by the Assessment Capabilities Project (2014) as part of its 23 May 2014 Briefing Note. Key event locations are shown by white inset boxes with black lettering (including information added by the authors on 72-hour rainfall amounts and locations of fatalities), while rivers are labeled by white inset boxes with blue lettering.

Belgrade [174 mm (6.9 inches)] (Magnusson et al. 2014). To put these amounts in a climatological perspective, Van Oldenborgh (2014) estimated this rain event to have a return period[2] of greater than 60 years, while Magnusson et al. (2014) showed that a European Flood Awareness System river-flow forecast for the Sava River near Belgrade had an event return period of greater than 20 years. Stadtherr et al. (2016) estimated that the daily rainfall amounts during this event exceeded the 99th percentile[3] for the region, based on 65 years of data. Because this rain fell in a region where the soil was already saturated from April and early May rains, extensive flooding occurred throughout the region. A detailed flood map is shown in Figure 3.5.2.

Major cities in Bosnia such as Sarajevo and Zenica were better protected since they are located between rugged mountains (see Figure 3.5.1) and have fairly strong levees that date back to the Austro-Hungarian period (as was pointed out earlier). Cities located downstream in flatlands, however, faced dramatic water spillover. In several cities, such as Maglaj and Zavidovići (locations shown in Figure 3.5.2), dozens were killed and several bridges were destroyed (Mehić 2014). All told, over 3 million people in all three countries were affected, with nearly 1 million evacuated (the majority in Bosnia) (Assessment Capabilities Project 2014). Total death figures vary by source but are generally reported between 53 and 80 (Assessment Capabilities Project 2014; Zurich Insurance Company 2015). Total economic losses were estimated to be 3.3 billion euros (Zurich Insurance Company 2015).

Several issues became obvious during the flooding. Houses that were built after the war in Bosnia were

2. The American Meteorological Society (2018) defines a *return period* as the average time (usually expressed in years) until the next occurrence of a specific event. This is also known as a recurrence interval.

3. This means less than 1% of all the days in the record had daily rainfall amounts greater than 13–16 May.

mostly built in the areas most heavily hit by flooding or landslides, whereas in the time of the former Yugoslavia and even during the Austro-Hungary period, areas that were designated as flooding or landslide prone had a ban on any building there (Karić 2014).

Although the floods did tremendous damage, the real problem was landslides. Besides building houses in the landslide-prone areas, the war in Bosnia left many villages, towns, and cities deforested to a certain extent because of the sieges and need for heating materials (Curtis 1995). While all cities worked on the forestation of parks in the populated areas, the forest service generally neglected the foothills because of lack of funding. To make matters worse, the struggling Bosnian economy moved toward the timber industry as an answer for its economic challenges. While the timber industry in Bosnia prior to the war was extremely strong, there were strict rules on how the forest could be utilized for economic purposes. Also, most of the timber was turned into furniture and other final products in Bosnia, not elsewhere (Marić et al. 2012). After the war, the laws were changed in order to benefit timber exporters, not manufacturers. This led to massive deforestation in Bosnia. Although experts warned for years that deforestation could create problems in the event of extensive rain, the government did not attempt to pass any meaningful laws that would prevent such a practice (Musli 2015).

The economic situation in Bosnia contributed to deforestation in another way. Many villages and small cities were experiencing prolonged economic depression after the 1990s war, which, as mentioned earlier, led to forest theft, where people would steal timber or bribe forest rangers in order get possession of heating materials. Although it has been more than 20 years since the end of the war, one part of Bosnia, the Federation of Bosnia and Herzegovina, still does not have any laws that regulate forestry (Al Jazeera 2015).

The situation described above led to occasional landslides every year. Just like many parts of Europe, Bosnia was also experiencing droughts that had a serious economic impact on the country (Maksimović 2014), and forest fires became a major problem. In 2013, the climate started to return to normal rain and snow amounts, the latter of which helped struggling ski resorts in the country. However, experts warned that in case of historic rains, landslides would be the biggest issue (Maglajlija 2015).

Once the rains started, and it was obvious that the floods were going to be unprecedented, most of the emergency response was focused on the major cities. These cities were better equipped and had infrastructure to deal with the problem compared to the small towns and villages that were getting cut off from the rest of the country because of the river overflows and huge landslides. The military actually proved to be the most organized and most effective during the disaster response, although it was severely underfunded. The Bosnian Air Force managed to dispatch approximately 10 helicopters, rotating them based on servicing needs during periods of high operations tempo. Most were equipped with search-and-rescue equipment for extraction. Before the floods, the biggest achievements of the Bosnian military were deployments to Afghanistan and Iraq. The response of the Bosnian military to the floods was a much more complex undertaking, considering logistical capabilities, and the fact that soldiers of different religions were involved in rescuing people of all religions and nationalities who live in Bosnia. Considering the recent history, that had a huge impact when it came to trust in the central government. Despite their efforts, the Bosnian Air Force was not enough, and the Austrian, Croatian, and Slovenian Air Forces sent their helicopters in order to help extract people who were cut off from the rest of the world. This was the first time after the war that the governments of countries that constituted the former Yugoslavia coordinated in such an efficient way [Obrana i Sigurnost (OBRIS) 2014]. Altogether, over 30 countries provided some type of aid to either Bosnia, Serbia, or both countries during this event. Additional help was provided by the European Union and the United Nations.

The CPA and law enforcement had a hard time coordinating their efforts, even deciding where the staging point should be. Floods and landslides started in central Bosnia, mostly in small towns and villages around the city of Zenica (see Figure 3.5.2). It took the CPA and law enforcement three days to establish a staging point in Zenica where people would be evacuated and, if necessary, treated in a local hospital. Complicating the situation was the political elite deciding to use resources, mainly helicopters, to tour affected areas. This decision actually deprived citizens of necessary resources to aid evacuations (Klix 2014). At the same time, the CPA leadership could not respond to questions about why part of the tax revenue that should have been allocated toward the CPA was used for other purposes, mainly patching budget holes.

As days passed, the European Union and European Union Force (EUFOR; assigned to monitor implementation of the Dayton Accords) could not stand by and watch any longer. They decided to take matters into their own hands and coordinate evacuations with the military of Bosnia and Herzegovina (Slanjankić 2014).

3.5.5. DISCUSSION

The unprecedented floods in Bosnia, Croatia, and Serbia in 2014 will happen again. It is projected that extreme events such as this one will occur more frequently as a result of global climate change (Thompson 2014). The lessons learned from the response to the floods in this region could be, and should be, applied all over the world—regardless of whether the lessons are applied in the countries that were affected. As stated earlier, neither Bosnia nor Serbia invested in the additional vertical transport resources needed since the floods (although Serbia is buying two new helicopters; one is replacing a helicopter lost in 2015) (Banković 2015b). In contrast, Croatia, a member of NATO, is openly discussing the purchase of UH-60 Black Hawk helicopters for their vertical transport fleet. This will increase evacuation capabilities and decrease its dependence on Russia (Jutarnji List 2014).

The failure of institutions and extreme corruption was something that was avoidable. The international community's focus on free elections as a sign of developing democracy was at the expense of monitoring the development of strong governmental institutions, especially those responsible for the protection of the population. This neglect played a very important role in the failed flood response, especially in Bosnia. The international community, which still has a tremendous presence in Bosnia and is sometimes involved in decision-making, also failed to simplify the investment process so that the country could attract more foreign investments. The result was that most lucrative jobs were found in the public administration sector, leading to widespread corruption (Divjak 2005).

While the Dayton Peace Accords focused primarily on stopping the carnage, the agreement did not focus at all on functioning institutions (World Bank 2015).

Richard Holbrook, the late U.S. diplomat who was responsible for bringing all sides in the war to the negotiating table, thought that Bosnians would take the issue seriously and, through legislative bodies in the country, come up with a more streamlined government [Public Broadcasting Service (PBS) 2005]. What Holbrook failed to see is that corruption had already taken root among nationalistic parties. Also, because of the disagreements among parties, who were split among nationalistic and religious lines (and still are), they actually embraced the agreement since it guaranteed their survival as ruling parties. Since this agreement envisioned two entities (the Federation of Bosnia and Herzegovina, where Muslims and Croats are the majority, and the Republika Srpska, where Serbs are the majority), that meant two large governments. Complicating matters further is a central government and the presidency with three presidents, one from each major religious group. In the Federation of Bosnia and Herzegovina, there are 10 cantons (similar to those in Switzerland) with 10 governors and 10 governments (U.S. Department of State 1995). This kind of government structure is consuming 68% of the Bosnian federal budget, while the rest is appropriated for all other needs, including military, first responders, health care, and education (Divjak 2005).

As much as it was a failure of Bosnian parties to streamline government and make resources available for agencies such as the CPA and other first responders, it was also a failure of the international community, considering the role it has in Bosnia. So while deforestation played a significant role in this tragedy, it was not the key to the devastation. The key was the weak institutions that did not address the issue of reforestation or building levees after the war. Probably a more complex problem is corruption that is spreading in the country rapidly, with no effective measures by the government to stop it. Deforestation was a symptom of the bigger problem, which ultimately was the failure to restore the natural environment after the war. As a result, the present Bosnian emergency management system was simply inadequate for such challenges.

Despite the loss, this tragedy also provides opportunity. The governments of Bosnia, Croatia, Serbia, and Slovenia showed unprecedented levels of cooperation. Slovenia, which was not affected by the 2014 floods as the other countries were, sent helicopters to Bosnia and special CPA units to Serbia. Croatia sent two helicopters to Bosnia, and since it had fewer issues with landslides and areas that were cut off, it had enough equipment to help Bosnia during that time. While encouraging, no meaningful protocol has been set up between these governments to help each other in case of another natural disaster.

In-Depth Analysis Exercise 3.5.1: Based on this chapter and additional resources, please answer the following questions:

1. Why does corruption have such dramatic impact on people's security?
2. Why are strong government institutions important for the average citizen?
3. How does multigovernment cooperation impact disaster relief and recovery?
4. What are some other examples of when government action (or inaction) has led to greater devastation during a natural disaster?

In-Depth Analysis Exercise 3.5.2: Based on chapters 3.3, 3.4, and 3.5, compare the disaster preparedness of the United States for Hurricane Katrina to that of Bosnia and Herzegovina for the May 2014 floods in the following disaster management stages:

1. Mitigation
2. Preparedness
3. Response
4. Recovery

For each stage, in addition to the differences, discuss whether there are any similarities between the two governments' approaches.

REFERENCES

Al Jazeera, 2015: Ilegalna sječa uništava BH. šume. Al Jazeera, accessed 13 December 2015, http://balkans.aljazeera.net/vijesti/ilegalna-sjeca-unistava-bh-sume.

AMS, 2018: Return period. Glossary of Meteorology, http://glossary.ametsoc.org/wiki/Return_period.

Assessment Capabilities Project, 2014: Floods in Serbia, Bosnia and Herzegovina, and Croatia. ACAPS Briefing Note, 6 pp., www.acaps.org/sites/acaps/files/products/files/bn_bosnia_serbia_floods.pdf.

Banković, Ž., 2015a: Analiza: Čime će sve Srbija i region gasiti požare iz vazduha ove sezone. Tango Six, accessed 13 December 2015, http://tangosix.rs/2015/24/07/analiza-sa-cime-ce-sve-srbija-i-region-gasiti-pozare-iz-vazduha-ove-sezone/.

——, 2015b: Posle 24 godine: Novi vojni helikopter Vojske Srbije—Ruski Mi-17V-5. Tango Six, accessed 14 December 2015, http://tangosix.rs/2015/19/08/posle-24-godine-novi-vojni-helikopter-vojske-srbije-ruski-mi-17v-5/.

Borger, J., 2015: Bosnia's bitter, flawed peace deal, 20 years on. Guardian, accessed 14 December 2015, www.theguardian.com/global/2015/nov/10/bosnia-bitter-flawed-peace-deal-dayton-agreement-20-years-on.

Croatian Firefighting Association, 2015: The firefighting service in Croatia. Hrvatska Vatrogasna Zajednica, accessed 24 February 2017, www.hvz.hr/en/.

Curtis, P., 1995: Urban household coping strategies during war: Bosnia-Hercegovina. *Disasters*, **19**, 68–73, https://doi.org/10.1111/j.1467-7717.1995.tb00335.x.

Degrimendžić, S., 2015: Vlast protiv zakona uzela novac od Civilne zaštite! Dnevni Avaz, accessed 13 December 2015, www.avaz.ba/clanak/180968/vlast-protiv-zakona-uzela-novac-od-civilne-zastite?url=clanak/180968/vlast-protiv-zakona-uzela-novac-od-civilne-zastite.

Divjak, B., 2005: Corruption in post-conflict reconstruction Bosnia and Herzegovina case study. Transparency International Rep., 4 pp., https://ti-bih.org/wp-content/uploads/Documents/05-12-2007/Post-conflict_reconstruction_and_corruption_in_BiH.pdf.

DUZS, 2015a: Povijest Civilne zaštite. DUZS, accessed 14 December 2015, http://stari.duzs.hr/page.aspx?PageID=156.

——, 2015b: O nama. DUZS, accessed 15 December 2015, https://duzs.hr/o-nama/.

Femić, R., 2014: Obrenovac: Tragedija za čiji razmjer je kriv ljudski faktor. Al Jazeera, accessed 14 December 2015, http://balkans.aljazeera.net/vijesti/obrenovac-tragedija-za-ciji-razmjer-je-kriv-ljudski-faktor.

Gabe, T., G. Falk, M. McCarty, and V. W. Mason, 2005: Hurricane Katrina: Social-demographic characteristics of impacted areas. Congressional Research Service Rep. RL33141, 35 pp.

Hulsey, J., and Mujkić, A., 2010: Explaining the success of nationalist parties in Bosnia and Herzegovina. *Croat. Polit. Sci. Rev.*, **47**, 143–158.

Huseinović, S., 2013: BiH: Neka gori, samo nek' je daytonska. Deutsche Welle, accessed 13 December 2015, www.dw.com/bs/bih-neka-gori-samo-nek-je-daytonska/a-17002782.

Jutarnji List, 2014: Amerika potvrdila 'Pregovaramo s Vladom RH o nabavci helikoptera Blackhawk, ali još je rano.' Jutarnji List, accessed 14 December 2015, www.jutarnji.hr/amerika-potvrdila--pregovaramo-s-hrvatskom-vladom-o-nabavci-mocnih-helikoptera-blackhawk-za-hv-/1231351/.

Kahn, M. E., 2005: The death toll from natural disasters: The role of income, geography, and institutions. *Rev. Econ. Stat.*, **87**, 271–284, https://doi.org/10.1162/0034653053970339.

Karić, S., 2014: Srušene kuće u Tuzlanskom kantonu većinom građene bez dozvola. Olsobođenje, accessed 13 December 2015, https://www.akta.ba/vijesti/srusene-kuce-u-tuzlanskom-kantonu-vecinom-gradene-bez-dozvola/39888 .

Klix, 2014: Izetbegović nakon obilaska poplavljenih područja: Uradit ćemo sve da pomognemo građanima. Klix, accessed 14 December 2015, www.klix.ba/vijesti/bih/izetbegovic-nakon-obilaska-poplavljenih-podrucja-uradit-cemo-sve-da-pomognemo-gradjanima/140515078.

Krnić, D., 2013: Srbi su nam u ratu oteli kanadere, a sad ćemo im mukte gasiti požare. Slobodna Dalmacija, accessed 14 December 2015, www.slobodnadalmacija.hr/Hrvatska/tabid/66/articleType/ArticleView/articleId/218115/Default.aspx.

Maglajlija, V., 2015: Klizišta: Odraz stanja BH. društva na terenu. Al Jazeera, accessed 13 December 2015, http://balkans.aljazeera.net/vijesti/klizista-odraz-stanja-bh-drustva-na-terenu.

Magnusson, L., F. Wetterhall, F. Pappenberger, and I. Tsonevsky, 2014: Forecasting the severe flooding in the Balkans. *ECMWF Newsletter*, No. 140, ECMWF, Reading, United Kingdom, 7–8, www.ecmwf.int/sites/default/files/elibrary/2014/14583-newsletter-no140-summer-2014.pdf.

Maksimović, D., 2014: Deset godina je potrebno za povratak na stanje prije poplava. Deutsche Welle, accessed 13 December 2015, www.dw.com/bs/deset-godina-je-potrebno-za-povratak-na-stanje-prije-poplava/a-17665517.

Marić, B., M. Avdibegović, D. Blagojević, D. Bećirović, A. Brajić, S. Mutabdžija, S. Delić, and Š. P. Malovrh, 2012: Conflicts between forestry and wood-processing industry in Bosnia-Herzegovina: Reasons, actors and possible solutions. *South-East Eur. For.*, **3**, 41–48, https://doi.org/10.15177/seefor.12-05.

McFaul, M., 2005: Transitions from postcommunism. *J. Democracy*, **16** (3), 5–19.

McMahon, P. C., 2004: Rebuilding Bosnia: A model to emulate or to avoid? *Polit. Sci. Quart.*, **119**, 569–593, https://doi.org/10.1002/j.1538-165X.2004.tb00530.x.

Mehić, E., 2014: Poplave u ZDK: Maglaj bez struje i telefonije, kritično u Zenici i drugim općinama. Klix, accessed 13 December 2015, Klix, www.klix.ba/vijesti/bih/poplave-u-zdk-maglaj-bez-struje-i-telefonije-kriticno-u-zenici-i-drugim-opcinama/140515018.

Mišković, I., and M. Mandić, 1987: *Civilna Zaštita u SFRJ.* Poslovna Politika, 202 pp.

Musli, E., 2015: Zašto uništavamo ono što nas štiti? Deutsche Welle, accessed 13 December 2015, www.dw.com/bs/zašto-uništavamo-ono-što-nas-štiti/a-18497759.

Nardelli, A., D. Dzidic, and E. Jukic, 2014: Bosnia and Herzegovina: The world's most complicated system of government? Guardian, accessed 14 December 2015, www.theguardian.com/news/datablog/2014/oct/08/bosnia-herzegovina-elections-the-worlds-most-complicated-system-of-government.

OBRIS, 2014: Poplave u regiji—Solidarnost na djelu. Obrana i Sigurnost, accessed 14 December 2015, http://obris.org/regija/poplave-u-regiji-solidarnost-na-djelu/.

PBS, 2005: A new constitution for Bosnia. PBS, accessed 14 December 2015, www.pbs.org/newshour/bb/europe-july-dec05-holbrooke_11-22/.

Select Bipartisan Committee to Investigate the Preparation for and Response to Hurricane Katrina, 2006: A Failure of initiative: The final report of the Select Bipartisan Committee to investigate the preparation for and response to Hurricane Katrina. U.S. House of Representatives Rep. 109-377, 582 pp., http://katrina.house.gov.

Senate Committee on Homeland Security and Governmental Affairs, 2006: Hurricane Katrina: A nation still unprepared. Senate Rep. 109-322, 737 pp.

Slanjankić, A., 2014: Katastrofalan sistem za zaštitu od katastrofa. Deutsche Welle, 15 December 2015, www.dw.com/bs/katastrofalan-sistem-za-zaštitu-od-katastrofa/a-17670230.

Stadtherr, C., D. Coumou, V. Petoukhov, S. Petri, and S. Rahmstorf, 2016: Record Balkan floods of 2014 linked to planetary wave resonance. *Sci. Adv.*, **2**, e1501428, https://doi.org/10.1126/sciadv.1501428.

Thompson, A., 2014: The climate context for 'unprecedented' Balkans flooding. Climate Central, accessed 14 December 2015, www.climatecentral.org/news/climate-context-balkans-flooding-17468.

Transparency International, 2014: Corruption perceptions index 2014: Results. Transparency International, accessed 14 December 2015,www.transparency.org/cpi2014/results.

U.S. Department of State, 1995: Dayton Accords. U.S. Department of State, accessed 14 December 2015, www.state.gov/p/eur/rls/or/dayton/.

Van Oldenborgh, G. J., 2014: Climate aspects of the floods in Bosnia and Serbia May 2014. Royal Netherlands Meteorological Institute, accessed 23 February 2017, www.knmi.nl/cms/content/119609/climate_aspects_of_the_floods_in_bosnia_and_serbia_may_2014.

Vulliamy, E., 1998: Bosnia: The crime of appeasement. *Int. Aff.*, **74**, 73–91, https://doi.org/10.1111/1468-2346.00005.

White House, 2006: The federal response to Hurricane Katrina: Lessons learned. White House Rep., 228 pp.

World Bank, 2015: Rebalancing Bosnia and Herzegovina: A systematic country diagnostic. World Bank Group Rep., 204 pp.

4

CONFLICT AND ENVIRONMENTAL SECURITY

INTRODUCTION TO UNIT 4

This unit introduces the relationship between environmental security and conflict. It begins by discussing the difference between correlation, when conflict happens in an area that is environmentally insecure, and causation, when conflict causes an environment to become insecure or when environmental insecurity causes conflict. Links between these events, historical, current, and future, are discussed in light of climate change. The chapter then goes on to discuss different types of conflict, political, nonviolent, and violent, and details the roles these different types of conflict have on more-developed countries (MDCs) and less-developed countries (LDCs). It then details conflict within and between MDCs and LDCs to give a greater understanding of the global impact of environmental insecurity in light of climate change.

Two key case studies are presented to evaluate these relationships and the varying types of conflict present in theaters of environmental insecurity—Kenya and the Arctic. The Kenyan case study serves to underscore the relationship between violent conflict, drought, famine, and climate change; it identifies the causal links between environmental insecurity, poverty, and violence. Further, this case also discusses the links between local-level practices and global events. The Arctic case study provides insight into the domain of political conflict. Detailing the contestation of both resources and rights of passage through this increasingly changeable region, this unit underscores the vital role diplomacy plays in the era of climate change in maintaining U.S. national and human security.

STUDENT LEARNING OBJECTIVES

1. Understand the difference between causality and correlation.
2. Identify the different types of conflict usually present in and between MDCs and LDCs and recognize why these differences exist.
3. Discuss the impact climate change will have on conflict generally and violence specifically.
4. Describe how a lack of resources or a perceived lack of resources can impact security.
5. Recognize how climate change can impact U.S. homeland and national security by changing resources, threats, and access to borders.
6. Recognize how conflict can directly and indirectly impact within and between states.

KEY TERMS AND CONCEPTS

Violence The intentional use or threatened use of physical force, usually with some sort of weapon, to cause death or injury; the intentional encroachment upon the physical integrity of the body (Krause 2009)

Conflict An expressed struggle, either physical, psychological, or political, over incompatible interests in the distribution of limited resources (based on Mortensen 1974)

Violent conflict An interaction between at least two individuals, groups, states, or institutions that use violence to pursue their struggle over access to and distribution of resources (see unit 4.2)

Radicalization The process of evolution a society undertakes as it moves away from peace and toward increased conflict, violence, terrorism, and atrocity (Murray 2015)

Terrorism Criminal acts intended or calculated to provoke a state of terror for political purposes in the general public; these acts are in any circumstance unjustifiable, whatever the considerations used to justify them, be they of a political, philosophical, ideological, racial, ethnic, religious, or any other nature (UN General Assembly 1994)

Genocide Any of the following acts committed with intent to destroy, in whole or in part, a national, ethnical, racial, or religious group as such: killing members of the group, causing serious bodily or mental harm to members of the group, deliberately inflicting on the group conditions of life calculated to bring about its physical destruction in whole or in part, imposing measures intended to prevent births within the group, or forcibly transferring children of the group to another group (UN High Commissioner for Human Rights 1948)

Cultural genocide Any deliberate act committed with the intent to destroy the language, religion, or culture of a national, racial, or religious group on grounds of the national or racial origin or religious belief of its members, such as prohibiting the use of the language of the group in daily intercourse or schools or the printing and circulation of publications in the language of the group or destroying or preventing the use of libraries, museums, schools, historical monuments, places of worship, or other cultural institutions and objects of the group (UN Economic and Social Council 1948)

LDC A country-based category established by the UN Committee for Development Policy (CDP). The CDP reviews the list of LDCs every three years and makes recommendations to the UN General Assembly as to the inclusion and graduation of eligible countries based on criteria of income (gross national income per capita), human assets (including the mortality rate of children five years old or under, literacy rate, maternal mortality rate, gross secondary school enrollment ratio, and percentage of population undernourished), and economic vulnerability [including population, remoteness, merchandise export concentration, share of agriculture, hunting, forestry, and fishing in gross domestic product (GDP), share of population in low-elevation costal zones, instability of exports, victims of environmental disasters, and the instability of agricultural production]

MDC Countries that have never been or have graduated from the LDC category upon review of the CDP and acceptance from both the Economic and Social Council and the UN General Assembly

Acute food insecurity phase classifications [Famine Early Warning Systems Network (FEWS NET) 2018b]

Phase 1: Minimal More than four in five households (HHs) are able to meet essential food and nonfood needs without engaging in atypical, unsustainable strategies to access food and income.

Phase 2: Stressed Even with any humanitarian assistance, at least one in five HHs in the area have the following or worse: minimally adequate food consumption but are unable to afford some essential nonfood expenditures without engaging in irreversible coping strategies.

Phase 3: Crisis Even with any humanitarian assistance, at least one in five HHs in the area have one of the following or worse: food consumption gaps with high or above usual acute malnutrition; marginal ability to meet minimum food needs only with accelerated depletion of livelihood assets that will lead to food consumption gaps.

Phase 4: Emergency Even with any humanitarian assistance, at least one in five HHs in the area have one of the following or worse: large food consumption gaps resulting in very high acute malnutrition and excess mortality; extreme loss of livelihood assets that will lead to food consumption gaps in the short term.

Phase 5: Famine Even with any humanitarian assistance, at least one in five HHs in the area have an extreme lack of food and other basic needs where starvation, death, and destitution are evident. Evidence for all three criteria (food consumption, acute malnutrition, and mortality) is required for a region to classify as "famine" (FEWS NET 2018b).

4.1

ENVIRONMENTAL SECURITY AND CONFLICT

Elisabeth Hope Murray

4.1.1. INTRODUCTION

As referenced throughout this book, the relationships between the environment and the various categories of society are complex. Equally, they are hard to disassociate from one another; discussions about food security lead inevitably into questions regarding population flux, which lead to challenges in the economic and energy sectors, leading further into questions of how to strengthen critical infrastructure in light of an environmental emergency. It should be no surprise then that when these complex relationships become tangled, when they refuse to work properly, and when human error, politicking, and the desire for power are prioritized, conflict over environmental issues is an inevitable actor in the thickening plot of human security.

4.1.2. LINKS, CORRELATION, AND CAUSALITY

Before going on to discuss this relationship further, let us take a moment and consider how we can best understand conflict in the context of environmental security (ES). We see conflict emerge in three macrocategories: conflict between more-developed countries (MDCs) and less-developed countries (LDCs), conflict in and between MDCs, and conflict in and between LDCs.

Though these categories may at first seem obvious, how conflict is made manifest does tend to broadly differ between them in sometimes vastly different ways. As mentioned throughout earlier chapters in this book, we must keep in mind that ES threats tend to supersede state boundaries; this is then a challenge in a global system where states tend to be the primary power brokers and state sovereignty is of principal concern in international governance. This means states are highly impractical actors when it comes to managing transnational challenges such as cybercrime, human trafficking, and—most pertinent to our discussion—climate change. Nonetheless, individuals, institutions, and even international organizations look to states to provide answers for these global questions. Because of this tension, many scholars have attempted to persuade states to sacrifice this perception of sovereignty as absolute in favor of supporting the human security mainframe—in short, to address individual and societal security needs, regardless of country or citizenship, in order to provide a stronger state in the long term; however, these suggestions have largely, if not entirely, been overlooked (Harris 2013; Smeulers 2010; Sutch 2009).

In fact, though the scientific consequences of climate change will be very problematic, the political consequences are possibly more impactful and are likely to become more so over the course of the next 50 years. As mentioned in *What's Wrong with Climate Politics and How to Fix It*, Paul Harris details the political impact of climate insecurity, saying "Climate change is a *political* problem every bit as much as it is a scientific one. . . . Governments and other actors, even while expressing increasing interest and concern about climate change, very rarely act in ways that match the scale of the growing environmental and human tragedy" (Harris 2013, p. 2). Indeed, one of the countries with the most convoluted political approach to climate change is one of the countries with the highest number of scientists and social scientists warning it of the probably catastrophic ramifications of climate change and pointing to the fact that human action is responsible for this increased insecurity: the United States.

As we will see in this and upcoming chapters, it is the political ramifications of climate change and the resultant environmental insecurity, whether real or ideologically imagined, that have the greatest capacity to lead to conflict and finally to violence. As mentioned earlier, how and where that conflict is manifested is broadly determined by MDC or LDC status. LDCs constitute states that tend to rank low on human security factors generally, including equal access to education for females, suffrage, and health care; they also to have high percentages of the population that are unemployed or employed in at-risk livelihoods. Finally, they include states with some of the world's lowest gross domestic product (GDP) rankings and highest levels of economic degradation; nonetheless, these low levels of industrialization have led to comparatively extremely low levels of greenhouse gas (GHG) emissions compared to levels produced in MDCs, as we will see below.

The remainder of this chapter focuses on the relationships between and within MDCs and LDCs. Addressing conflict through this lens allows us to focus on the varying environmental security threats and challenges facing these different types of states. This chapter proceeds as follows: First, we will begin by looking at conflict between MDCs and LDCs, specifically addressing how climate change plays a historical role in this relationship. Secondly, we will move on to the relationship between MDCs, highlighting the political nature of the conflict and the institutions in which this conflict takes place. We will also discuss the role climate change denial plays in

American politics and the impact that has on ES more generally in the international sphere. Finally, we will examine LDCs and how environmental insecurity has impacted and affected conflict, both political and violent, in these states. Critically, this section also addresses the role of resource scarcity in conflicts, both modern and historical.

4.1.3. CONFLICT BETWEEN MDCS AND LDCS

To understand the tension between these MDCs and LDCs, perhaps a very brief history of modern anthropogenic climate change is helpful.

The Industrial Revolution resulted in new technologies resident primarily in the global North. Many of these new technologies were both largely manufactured from resources produced in LDCs and resulted in the faster manufacturing of further products for those living in MDCs; colonialism was built on just this premise (Brown 2012; Byrd 2011; Das 2015; Ezrow et al. 2015; Josiah 2011; Maldonado et al. 2014; Perry 2016; Satya 2004). Take, for instance, the British decision to transition from coal to oil in the fueling of its naval vessels after World War I. Prior to this decision, made by Admiral John Fisher with the support of the then–First Lord of the Admiralty Winston Churchill, British ships had run on British coal, a fuel source prevalent in the United Kingdom; oil, on the other hand, was completely nonexistent in Britain and would have to be provided from British colonies overseas.

The British government then purchased a majority stakeholder share (51%) of the Anglo-Persian Oil Company with assurances to receive 20 years of oil under attractive terms (Churchill 1931). The Anglo-Persian Oil Company, now known as British Petroleum (BP), acquired oil from Iran and across the Arabian Peninsula. Investment resulted in a massive improvement in technology for the British Navy (and other industries), offering greater security to British life—particularly in light of the looming Second World War—but did little to improve the economics, education, infrastructure, or technological advancement for those living in the area where the resource was initially withdrawn from the earth (Bamberg 1994). Thus, we see the prioritizing British military security over environmental security in the colonies in the short term limited British and colonial security overall. This example hints that, as suggested in

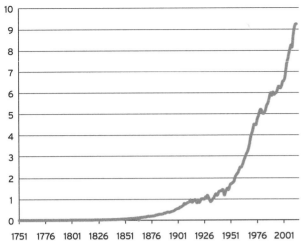

Figure 4.1.1. Average global CO₂ emissions from fossil fuel combustion and cement production, 1751–2014, in billion metric tons per year (Boden et al. 2013).

Figure 4.1.2. Average LDC CO₂ emissions from fossil fuels combustion and cement production, in thousand metric tons per year (Boden et al. 2013).

unit 1, military might in the short term is, for better or worse, frequently prioritized over environmental stability in the long term, leading to a reduction in national security overall. But we will return to this point later.

The environmental aspect is one frequently overlooked in colonialism studies, but the rape of resources from these states forms the basis of many of the challenges facing the global commons today. Indeed, colonialism begins the true divide between MDCs and LDCs, a divide from which we have yet to recover economically, politically, or socially. The technological advances of the Industrial Revolution seated primarily in the global north resulted in vast changes in the global carbon output; indeed, most LDCs participated in the Industrial Revolution primarily as a mine for resources with little concern for the human security of those individuals at risk because of these policies (Davis 2000). Figure 4.1.1 serves as an example of information reflected in many datasets, that between 1850 and 1870, fossil fuel emissions began to increase, with a sharp increase occurring after World War II.

The states responsible for these environmental increases are overwhelmingly MDCs, though this does start to change moderately with the end of colonialism.

The end of colonialism, which time period is considered generally to be between 1949 and 1980, saw the increase in carbon output in LDCs as they took on the mantle of production in an attempt to industrialize and fully participate in a globalizing economy (Berger 2000; Ezrow et al. 2015; Shamir 2005). This increase in indus-

trialization resulted in an unsurprising upswing in carbon outputs, which continues throughout the twentieth and twenty-first centuries, as shown here in Figure 4.1.2.

Though this rise in carbon output does mirror the similar rise in global outputs as shown in Figure 4.1.1, the clear difference in Figure 4.1.2 is the measurement of metric tons of CO₂ emissions from fossil fuels and cement production per year. Figure 4.1.2, tracking LDC emissions output, is tracked in *thousands*; Figure 4.1.1, tracking global emissions output, is tracked in *billions*. For example, of the LDCs being tracked at the time, Myanmar (then Burma) was the worst offender, producing a total of 28,000 metric tons of emissions per year. That same year, Norway produced 2,841,000 metric tons of CO₂ emissions, the Netherlands produced 13,783,000 metric tons of CO₂ emissions, and the United States produced 589,517,000 metric tons of CO₂ emissions from fossil fuels and cement production. Even by 2013, Myanmar was only producing 3,437,000 metric tons of CO₂ emissions, a fragment of the emissions produced by the United States in 1949, much less the CO₂ emissions output in the same year, an overwhelming 1,414,281,000 metric tons (Boden et al. 2013).

Regardless of the staggering differences in carbon and GHG outputs, it is the LDC states that show a much stronger dedication to making changes to livelihoods, education, and technological implementation to mitigate the effects of climate change resultant from the outpouring of GHGs into the environment (Chaudhury et al.

2016; Regmi et al. 2016; Sovacool et al. 2017). This is primarily due to the recognition of the high financial cost of environmental insecurity in many of these countries. In Mali, for example, climate change costs approximately 21% of the overall GDP (Diallo 2015); between 2009 and 2015, Bangladesh spent nearly $385 million (U.S. dollars) of their annual combined budget to cover the cost of climate damage, mitigation, and adaptation, though Bangladesh's annual carbon emissions during that time were a mere 0.012% of those in the United States (UN Environment Programme 2016).

So what does this mean in terms of conflict? We see conflict occurring between LDCs and MDCs in two main ways: 1) nonviolent political conflict, usually voiced in diplomatic arenas, and 2) through military involvement, either directly through "peacekeeping" missions or indirectly through proxy wars.

Let's address option 2 first, conflict through direct violence and military force. This type of conflict is what most people think of when they think of "conflict"; military patrols and Great War–style offenses. Indeed, many, if not all, wars have their basis in the need for resources because resources are one of the key pathways to power. Without resources, political leaders have no access to support themselves or their governments. Even governments with easy access to resources, such as the United States, China, Canada, and Germany, have histories of starting or participating in international wars waged over resources. Perhaps the most famous in recent history is the Holocaust and specifically Nazi incursions into the Eastern Front into countries such as Poland and Czechoslovakia. Indeed, this incursion is considered by many scholars to be an act of colonization (Bloxham 2001, 2009; Bloxham and Kushner 2005; Carmichael 2010; Moses 1998; Zimmerer 2011; Perraudin and Zimmerer 2010). We must remember that the Jews were consistently portrayed as leeches on the German economy, robbing the German citizenry of food and other key resources (Avalon Project 2008a,b; Rubenstein and Roth 1987). The process of ghettoization and of man-made famine within both the ghettos and the camps was at least partially justified as saving the key resources of food—limited via rations in many states at the time—for the "true" citizens, those of Aryan lineage (Adelson et al. 1989; Roland 1992; Smolar 1989).

We see resources surface as a rationale for military action in more modern wars between MDCs and LDCs as well. Take, for example, U.S. intervention in Kuwait during Operation Desert Storm from August 1991 to February 1992. The American government was open in its acknowledgement that the protection of its oil interests in the region was one of the top reasons why the war began. In a speech before Congress on 11 September 1990, President George H. Bush (Bush 1990) maintained that

> Vital issues of principle are at stake. . . . Vital economic interests are at risk as well. Iraq itself controls some 10 percent of the world's proven oil reserves. Iraq plus Kuwait controls twice that. An Iraq permitted to swallow Kuwait would have the economic and military power, as well as the arrogance, to intimidate and coerce its neighbors—neighbors who control the lion's share of the world's remaining oil reserves. We cannot permit a resource so vital to be dominated by one so ruthless. And we won't.

Indeed, the Middle East is well known as a geographic area with a legacy of wars over resources; in fact, the current war in Iraq also has strong ties between resources and the conflict. Though generally understood as being fought for ideological reasons masked by concerns over nuclear stockpiles, continued access to Iraqi oil has been one of the key desired and obtained outcomes of the war. At a cost to the American taxpayer of over $2 trillion (U.S. dollars), the war in Iraq saw changes in the Iraqi oil system from a socialized system largely closed to Western oil companies to a privatized, open system with investments in the industry by major companies such as Halliburton, Chevron, Shell, and BP. Iraq's oil production has increased more than 40% between 2003 and 2013, 80% of which is now exported overseas to MDCs, primarily the United States, India, China, and South Korea (Energy Information Administration 2016; Juhasz 2013; Trotta 2013).

There are, of course, a number of other examples we can point to, many during the colonial period and others in the postcolonial era, where LDCs and MDCs have come to blows over resources. However, particularly since the end of the Cold War—many of whose proxy wars were fought precisely with resources in mind (D'Aveni 2012; Rockoff 2012; Tsygankov 2012)—conflict over resources between LDCs and MDCs have gone the way of option 1 above: nonviolent political conflict, usually voiced in the diplomatic arena.

Note that this move toward diplomacy does not necessarily result in improved compassion, population health, environmental health, or security on many levels. Indeed, one need only look to U.S. relations with the Marshall Islands to see an example of the human security impacts of political conflict, particularly when they intersect—as they so often do—with other aspects of the complex security nexus. During the Cold War, the United States detonated more than 60 nuclear weapons over the Bikini and Enewetak Atolls. They left behind an inadequate nuclear waste storage system that, even when it was newly constructed, would not only fail to pass regulations applicable to similar facilities in the United States (Nuclear Waste Policy Act 1982) but, as Michael Gerrard so aptly puts it, "would not meet today's US standards for the disposal of household waste" (Gerrard 2015, p. 93).

Two massive security breaches arise from this situation: first is the environmental disaster occurring from the poor design, construction, and resultant degradation of the waste site causing nuclear waste to seep into both groundwater in the Marshall Islands and as far afield as the coast of Japan. The effects this nuclear leakage is having and will continue to have in the Pacific are unknown as so few scholars have researched the issue (Gerrard 2015). The second challenge is the resultant crime against humanity; more than 1/6th of the population has left the Marshall Islands because of poor agriculture and health risks associated with nuclear leakage. Some research has determined that the loss of cultural identity associated with the local population qualifies as cultural genocide for which the United States is morally, if not criminally, culpable (Levene 2011; Levene and Conversi 2014; Moses 2004). Equally, as sea level rise and increased typhoon risk occurs as a consequence of climate change, these challenges are expected to continue to increase until the storage site is completely submerged; as the entirety of the Marshall Islands is no more than two meters above sea level, this will mean that the entirety of the islands will be underwater and the entirety of the population will need to relocate (IPCC 2007, 2014). The people of the Marshall Islands have petitioned Congress for funds to help mitigate the response efforts of this disaster, but outside of a pitiful recompense package, these have been repeatedly denied (Gerrard 2015; Pevec 2006). Thus, we see that taking the diplomatic track does not necessarily result in environmental or human security.

Nonetheless, it is largely preferred over direct violence and warfare.

Before going on, we must first remember that conflict is not necessarily violent. In fact, most conflict is nonviolent, revolving around individual disputes (Conrad 1990; Folger et al. 1997; Wall 1985). In the political realm, we see this usually played out in relationships between political institutions such as Democrats versus Republicans or within certain institutions such as the United Nations. Indeed, the numerous international conferences and negotiations held over the past 30 years on climate change prevention and policy provide us with an excellent venue to view the amount of conflict existent between states on this key topic in ES. The various agreements produced by these summits proves the resolution of some of these conflicts, though many of these arise yet again when in-state policy actually needs to be changed.

Perhaps, based on the data and examples above, it is no surprise that the two main "teams" emerging in diplomatic circles are one comprising MDCs and one comprising LDCs. In fact, 48 of the most impoverished states tend to work internationally as a block of actors, attempting to achieve together what is lost to them individually because of limits on economic and political power (Lavender 2016). These LDCs, led at most international forums by the Least Developed Countries Expert Group (LEG), tend to work primarily to achieve environmental stability by putting pressure on MDCs and specifically on India, China, and the United States—the top three GHG emitters (Siddique 2015).

The main point of political conflict is the fact that most economic buoyancy is achieved through the process of industrialization; industrialization takes time, and it has an economic cost. However, a lack of economic success also leads to higher-risk environments with less chance of recovery from environmental disaster and less chance of properly implementing mitigation policies. The goal of most LDCs is to no longer maintain their LDC status; states want to become (and remain) economically secure. The current perception is that in order to do this, further increases in GHGs should be allowed and expected from these states. For example, in a recent interview leading up to the recent 21st Conference of the Parties (COP21) in Paris, France, Bangladesh's LEG representative Qazi Ahmad details the following on the relationship regarding future GHG emissions (Siddique 2015):

We have said that we will not increase our greenhouse gas (GHG) emissions by more than the average of the developing countries. That is our commitment, whatever the average emission are for developing countries. We will not exceed that. We remain below that. We are committed to being a part of the global process to reduce GHG emissions although we emit a very little compared to the developed countries, just 0.3 tons per capita per annum. We are not responsible for climate change yet. Our plan obviously will increase emissions as we need development and we need poverty reduction and for that there will be an increase.

Many LDCs believe all states, though primarily MDCs, should cut GHG emissions low enough to ensure that global temperature warming will rise to only a maximum of 1.5°C; this is in direct comparison to most MDCs, who are generally unwilling to make assurances for GHG emissions reductions much below 2°–2.5°C (Committee on Small Business 2013; Committee on Environment and Public Works 2014). We should also remember that many politicians in certain MDC states such as the United States and China deny that human action has any impact on climate change (Sheppard 2016).

This climate reluctance further exacerbates political conflict between LDCs and MDCs. Lack of critical infrastructure, reliance on at-risk livelihoods, a lack of economic development, low GDPs, interstate conflict, and lack of political will by MDCs mean that LDCs experience the impact of climate change in a way highly detrimental to human security in those states (IPCC 2007). To understand the depth of tension in this area, one need only look to Cameroon, whose major port city and economic capital, Douala, is floundering under the combined attack of heightened levels of flooding, population growth, and climate refugees fleeing desertification, drought, and agroterrorism in the north and flooding in the nearby coastal areas (Tetchiada 2013).

Examples like this one explain why LDCs expect MDCs both to be more politically motivated to make changes within their own states and also to spend the financial capital to take responsibility for climate change and, in doing so, at the least to provide funding for adaptation and mitigation initiatives (Siddique 2015;

Kabi 2015; Sisay 2015; Palden 2015). Exactly what steps LDCs wish to take and exactly what they look to the international community to support are laid out in National Adaptation Programs of Action (NAPAs), strategic plans submitted to the UN Framework Convention on Climate Change (UNFCCC). NAPAs are intended to help offset a key concern of MDCs and a primary rationale for many states to limit climate mitigation funding: government corruption in LDCs.

This lack of faith on both ends has resulted in years of mistrust and political conflict in the international arena. As this continues, the capacity for the shift from political conflict to violent conflict increases. We discussed earlier the history of violence within LDCs perpetrated primarily by MDCs. However, there is a growing body of literature linking environmental insecurity and terrorist activity that will be discussed later in this chapter and in chapter 4.2. It is important to here note that relationships between MDCs and LDCs, though of import, are not the only ones under stress caused by environmental insecurity.

4.1.4. CONFLICT BETWEEN AND WITHIN MDCS

Like most postcolonial relationships between LDCs and MDCs, the overwhelming majority of resource conflict between MDCs is political conflict occurring in the diplomatic theater. However, before moving on to discuss this in depth, let us first address the elephant in the room that exists principally within MDCs: climate change denial.

While there are climate change deniers in most states, the overwhelming majority of those with political power are present in the United States. Indeed, while 74% of Democrats state that human action is responsible for climate change (a number still more than 20 points lower than the average for U.S. climate scientists), only a staggering 24% of Republicans agree, despite overwhelming evidence to the contrary (Funk and Rainie 2015). In fact, a 2016 poll shows that only 47% of political conservatives in the United States believe the climate is changing at all regardless of human activity; what is more staggering is that this is almost double those admitting to the occurrence of climate change in 2014 (Leiserowitz et al. 2016). We know that politicians lie,[1] but why do so many

---

1. For example, President Donald Trump's Politifact Fact Checker scorecard indicates that only 31% of his statements are true (5%), mostly true (11%), or half true (15%), while a whopping 46% were labeled false (32%) or pants on fire (14%) (Politifact 2018).

U.S. politicians lie to their constituents about this one particular issue, causing needless political conflict and hindering action on what can be considered the greatest threat to human and national security the United States has ever faced?[2]

First, many Fortune 500 companies have economic incentives to keep to the status quo—or even to increase investment into environmentally unfriendly policies. Oil companies, fracking companies, energy companies, coal companies, cell phone manufacturers, and the global shipping industry along with many other companies worry they would face production challenges and increased taxation if environmentally friendly policies were put into place. This is further complicated by the fact that many of these companies finance political campaigns through direct campaign contributions and through soft money contributions (Siddique 2015; Dobkowski and Wallimann 2002; Dunlap and McCright 2011; Sisay 2015). The media also has a high-level impact, giving unmerited credence to climate change skeptics who tend to skew scientific evidence to produce unjustified results; pair this with repeated exposure to a single-message media source, and the politicians themselves are likely to disbelieve science in favor of policies that further their own political well-being (Gregoire 2015). Climate change denial in the United States fuels party conflict and furthers radicalization within parties, as well as strengthening the divide between MDCs and LDCs.

Nonetheless, in some areas, the United States continues to make policy based on the reality of climate change; some of these policies bring the U.S. military and other political agencies into direct political conflict with other MDCs, conflict that could, in the future, have the capacity for violence. A key region of such conflict between MDCs is the Arctic.

Encompassing about 6% of Earth's surface, the Arctic is one of the world's regions at high susceptibility to the consequences of climate change because of its polarity;

every year since 2005, we have seen an increase in Arctic temperatures and the melting of sea ice in the area (Casper 2009; Groisman et al. 2011). But why is a region populated almost entirely by scientists and Arctic sea life an area of conflict for MDCs? The Arctic is also considered one of the greatest untapped sinks of natural resources in the world. Both petroleum and natural gas reserves have been found there to a tune of as much as 30% of global natural gas reserves and 13% of global petroleum reserves, ensuring the region as a high-value target to states with high energy demands and dwindling supplies (Bird et al. 2008; Campbell 2005; Dobkowski and Wallimann 2002). As sea ice melts, these limited resources become available to big business; as Ben Stewart of Greenpeace reflects, "there is a bitter irony that the ice melting is being seen as a business opportunity rather than a grave warning" (in Cowling 2011).

Aside from the economic motivation, there are also opportunities to expand military power. Canada, Denmark, Russia, and the United States have all claimed territory in the Arctic under jurisdiction of the UN Convention on the Law of the Sea (UNCLOS) allowing states to extend their sovereignty rights to the edges of their land shelves. Along with the natural resources being politically fought for in the region, military rights of way are also key issues of conflict. Both direct and perceived threats against a state's territorial sovereignty are often used as excuses for military action (Murray, 2015); though direct military conflict in the area has yet to occur on any grand level, most of the four involved states are lobbying for increased military rights and larger military presences in the region directly in response to feared challenges to sovereignty claims (Pugliese 2016). Russia was the first of the four to radicalize its Arctic policy, establishing on 19 May 2011 the 200th Independent Infantry Brigade, an elite fighting force highly trained in cold-climate response based at Pechenga on the Kola Peninsula. In response, Denmark along with

---

2. For example, the former head of the Environmental Protection Agency (EPA), Scott Pruitt, has falsely claimed that carbon dioxide is not a "a primary contributor to the global warming that we see" (in Carroll 2017); in 2017, Pennsylvania's Republican senator falsely tried to explain global warming by claiming "the Earth moves closer to the sun every year—you know the rotation of the Earth. We're moving closer to the sun" (in Oroso 2017); finally, President Donald Trump falsely claimed that there had been an increase in polar ice when he stated in 2018 that if the "ice caps were going to melt, they were going to be gone by now, but now they're setting records, so okay, they're at a record level," despite polar ice being at an all-time low (in Greenberg 2018). These are only a small selection of possible examples. Have any representatives in your state or region made claims about climate change that contradict the science presented in unit 1?

its autonomous region, Greenland, announced plans to establish an Arctic Military Command; the United States and Canada then both followed with demands to increase their own unilateral military presences in the region (Jones 2011; Pegna 2013). Actions such as the recent establishment of U.S. Navy Base Ice Camp Sargo highlight the perception that U.S. sovereignty extends to the Arctic and that the role of the military is to heighten their presence to achieve these ends. As detailed by Vice Admiral and Commander of Submarine Forces at Camp Sargo Joseph Tofalo: "the Arctic environment plays a key role in national defense. With over a thousand miles of Arctic coastline, the U.S. has strong national security and homeland defense interests in the region" (in CNN 2016). Increases in military presence from all major players are set to continue, particularly as tensions over national security between the United States, China, and Russia escalate. This could result in the Arctic being the next theatre of international war between MDCs.

There are other risks to military presence in the Arctic and other areas where sea level rise is directly affecting MDC military policy. We discussed the challenges facing nuclear policy in the Marshall Islands earlier; Arctic ice melt is causing further concern about nuclear material previously buried in Greenland. In 1959, the U.S. Army Corps of Engineers built Camp Century and proceeded, until 1967, to test the feasibility of using the base as a site to launch ballistic weapons, some of which contained nuclear material. When the tests proved largely unsuccessful, the site was decommissioned with little oversight. Both the military and politicians believed that the material would remain frozen in time, buried underneath ever-increasing snowfall (Colgan et al. 2016; Nielsen et al. 2014). However, warming in the region and the resultant ice melt is exposing the nuclear waste; sea level rise threatens to disperse the waste throughout the Arctic Ocean and beyond (IPCC 2014; United Press International 2016); this collision point between climate change, military policy, and human health is once again put to the test—this time not in a far-flung LDC but in a space directly claimed by some of the wealthiest MDCs in the world. The sinking of Camp Century is only one example of challenges felt by military powers who, as we will see below, are on the front lines of climate change, particularly as direct conflict resulting in sometimes extreme violence becomes more visible in society.

4.1.5. CONFLICT BETWEEN AND WITHIN LDCS

Resources have always been at the heart of conflict. As far back as the Peloponnesian Wars and beyond, losing access to food, water, wood, fertile cropland, grazing space, minerals, and ores have been the excuses for engaging in violent conflict. In fact, the fear of resource loss is often just as ideologically powerful as actual resource loss (Murray 2015); we have only to look at the rationalizations states use for denying refugees to see how fear of resource scarcity can be used as an exceedingly motivational factor even in societies with high levels of access to resources. Conservative American media reports that Syrian refugees cost the taxpayer anywhere from $20,000 to $60,000 (U.S. dollars) per year are highly influential in explaining why the majority of Americans are hesitant to support prorefugee legislation despite the fact that the Reception and Placement (R&P) Act only supports the immediate needs of refugees for the first 90 days of their stay in the United States, maximizing a total of a mere $1,800 total per refugee (Brown and Scribner 2014). Though the primary concern is that a refugee will turn out to be a terrorist, the fear of the financial resource loss is nonetheless a great motivator.

We must remember that financial wealth is in itself a resource; it is, at its most base, an outcome of having a resource of value for which individuals and institutions are willing to pay. A lack of financial resources limits individual choice; a large amount of scholarship shows us that to be poor is to increase your chances of being both a victim and a perpetrator of violence because your access to resources is limited (Ajodo-Adebanjoko and Walter 2014; Dodds and Pippard 2005; Ezrow et al. 2015; Graeger and Smith 1996; Kirby 2006; UN High-Level Panel on Threats, Challenges and Change 2005; Rees 2002; Samatar 1993; Smith 1996; Sporton et al. 1999). Thus, the propensity of violent conflict driven by resource scarcity in poorer LDCs is higher than in MDCs.

One example we can look to is genocide in Darfur. Largely understood as the first climate change–driven genocide of the twenty-first century (Brown et al. 2007), aggression in western Sudan between the Janjaweed, government-funded Arab militias, and local Darfur civilians began in 2003 and persist through 2018, resulting in the deaths of more than 480,000 and the displacement of over 2.5 million refugees. These killings are considered by many scholars to be due to increased levels of desertification, threatening livelihoods of herders and

PHASE 1 Minimal	More than four in five households (HHs) are able to meet essential food and nonfood needs without engaging in atypical, unsustainable strategies to access food and income.
PHASE 2 Stressed	Even with any humanitarian assistance at least one in five HHs in the area have the following or worse: Minimally adequate food consumption but are unable to afford some essential nonfood expenditures without engaging in irreversible coping strategies.
PHASE 3 Crisis	Even with any humanitarian assistance at least one in five HHs in the area have the following or worse: • Food consumption gaps with high or above-usual acute malnutrition OR • Are marginally able to meet minimum food needs but only by depletion of livelihood assets that will lead to food consumption gaps.
PHASE 4 Emergency	Even with any humanitarian assistance at least one in five HHs in the area have the following or worse: • large food consumption gaps resulting in very high acute malnutrition and excess mortality OR • Extreme loss of livelihood assets that will lead to food consumption gaps in the short term.
PHASE 5 Famine	Even with any humanitarian assistance at least one in five HHs in the area have an extreme lack of food and other basic needs where starvation, death, and destitution are evident. Evidence for all three criteria (food consumption, acute malnutrition, and mortality) is required to classify Famine.
!	Phase classification would likely be worse without current or programmed humanitarian assistance.

Figure 4.1.3. Acute food insecurity phase descriptions (FEWS NET 2018b). IPC phases (accessed 24 April 2018 from www.fews.net/IPC).

pastoralists (Prunier 2005; de Waal 2005; World Without Genocide 2017; Young et al. 2009); chapter 4.2 details another example of intrastate LDC conflict between these two groups in Kenya where genocide has not occurred but levels of violence are directly linked to climate instability.

Resource insecurity then is both a precursor for and a consequence of violence. Let's look first at some conflicts where resource insecurity is a precursor for violent conflict. World War II is arguably the most researched conflict in history and has its roots in resource insecurity. Hitler and the Nazi party generally made no secret of the fact that they believed their country to be directly threatened by the Jews, who were portrayed as being parasites, sucking the country dry of resources (Hitler 1934). Equally, the Nazis were clear that the current amount of space would not provide enough resources for German citizens, that, in fact, these resources were under threat of being taken away; this fear only increased over the course of the war as the genocide of the Holocaust increased (Hitler 1934; Kamenetsky 1961; Murray 2015). As Hitler expressed, "we must struggle for the existence of our fatherland, for the unity of our nation and the daily bread of our children" (in Hitler 1969, p. 565).

We do not, of course, need to go so far back in history to be able to see these direct links between violent conflict and resources, particularly when we turn our eyes to conflict within and between LDCs. Water, water rights, and access to clean, viable water sources have been and remain key firestarters to violent conflict; LDCs are particularly at risk of violent conflict because of high demographic pressures, high levels of migration and refugees, group grievances exacerbated by lack of access to governance, corruption, unequal education, economic limitations, illegitimate governance actors, challenged security apparatuses, factionalized elites, external intervention, and, in some areas, radicalized ideologies (Fund for Peace 2018). These factors, determined by the fragile states index (FSI), can serve to identify states at risk for violent conflict. Note that not all of the 48 states in the LDC diplomatic partnership discussed above are at risk of violence; nonetheless, all of the states identified as being at "very high alert" in the 2018 fragile states index are in the LDC block with the one exception of Syria, which is currently fighting a war and perpetrating extreme violence against civilians (Katulis et al. 2015; Werrell et al. 2015). As an aside, there is a growing concern among scholars that many violence indication indices, such as the FSI, do not consider or do not weight highly enough environmental instability (IPCC 2014; Werrell et al. 2015). Crucially, of the variables listed above, none are linked to climate or environmental insecurity; however, all states identified by the FSI as being at "very high alert," "high alert," and "alert" levels have also been identified as being among those at highest risk of climate change (IPCC 2014, 2016).

To look at an effect of climate violence in LDCs, let us begin by looking at the recent war in Yemen, largely assessed as a war with environmental insecurity at its roots. Yemen has consistently ranked as one of the states under very high alert under the FSI and, in the 2018 FSI report, is listed as one of the top five "most worsened countries." As of April 2018, only five states are identified by the Famine Early Warning Systems Network (FEWS NET) as being at "emergency" or "famine" levels of food insecurity, as detailed in Figure 4.1.3. As this figure shows, there are considerable levels of food insecurity. Yemen, along with South Sudan, Nigeria, and Ethiopia, continue to be the most food-insecure regions as of autumn 2018; over three quarters of the country is facing "crisis" or higher levels of food insecurity. These levels are expected to rise to emergency levels over the upcoming months—despite a considerable amount of international aid—through at least January 2019, at which point they may worsen depending of sociopolitical factors (FEWS NET 2018a,c,d). Yemen imports nearly 90% of their food stores, and as of autumn 2018, the cost of wheat is 45%–65% higher than in January 2015; retail diesel fuel prices have increased by 100%–125% since January 2015 (FEWS NET 2018d).

Setting the environmental issues aside for the moment, let us turn our attention to the most recent violent conflict in the region. Since President al-Hadi assumed office in February 2012, Yemen has been in a state of on-again, off-again large-scale violence from Houthi rebel groups targeting specific military and policy institutions such as military installations and checkpoints as well as the targeting of government buildings in the capital of Sana'a in the fighting leading to the capture of the city in 2015 (Kerr 2015). Assassinations against military, intelligence, and security personnel have become de rigueur (Sarai 2016), as seen in the December 2017 assassination of former President Ali Abdullah Saleh. Al-Qaeda in the Arabian Peninsula (AQAP) has set themselves against both the government and the Houthi rebels,

further muddying the waters by introducing another radicalized ideological bent into the claims of aggrieved groups. In an attempt to quell further radicalization in the area, Saudi Arabia, backed by the United States and others, began airstrikes in 2013, resulting in the deaths of thousands of civilians and the internal displacement of an estimated 2.5 million people (Fattah 2014; Internal Displacement Monitoring Centre 2018; BBC 2015). Add into this crisis the fear factors considered by the FSI and others as outcomes of the conflict: a sharp rise in overall poverty, an equally sharp rise in inflation, soaring unemployment, a growing budget deficit, less government spending on social systems, a sharp decline in development investments, approximately half of the population relying on international aid, increased reported child labor, a decrease in school attendance, decreased access to sanitation, and approximately 25% of the population no longer receiving basic medical care (Fattah 2014; FEWS NET 2016; Fund for Peace 2016).

This raises the question: Which came first, the violence or the environmental insecurity? The conflict has resulted in limitations to accessing food and water, the destruction of cropland, and the misuse of critically taxed water resources (FEWS NET 2018c). Though the country has one of the world's highest birth rates, child death rates are now at their highest levels: 1 in 10 children will not live to see the age of five, while 60% of the population are now considered "chronically" malnourished (UN Economic and Social Council 2018). With such a large percentage of the total population now dependent on international aid, aid deliveries have become zones of violence, with aid deliveries frequently hampered by the conflict (El Dahan 2014; Fattah 2014; UN World Food Programme 2016). On the other hand, however, we see that these environmental security indicators are not consequences of the conflict, that, indeed, malnourishment, reliance on aid, limited access to food and water, the devastation of land due to climate change, and misuse of development funds by governmental sources were all present before the most recent conflict began (Fund for Peace 2011; Wiebelt et al. 2013). In fact, there is some evidence to suggest that the failure to address these very factors caused Houthi unrest and radicalization among Shia groups (Werrell et al. 2015; BBC 2015).

The moral of this story is that, rather than making things better, things are worse because of the conflict; human security is at greater risk, not less. LDCs are in particular jeopardy of falling foul of the decrease in human security because climate change also reflects this relationship, making society less secure, putting humanity under greater threat. As we have seen, LDCs are at the highest risk of experiencing the negative consequences of climate change with the least capacity to mitigate and respond to those consequences and thus are equally at highest risk of the resultant conflict becoming violent.

There is, however, another lesson to be learned here: environmental insecurity provides an opportunity for radicalization to become manifest in otherwise ideologically malleable societies. Radicalization, or the evolution of a society away from peace and toward increased conflict, violence, and mass atrocity (Murray 2015), occurs for many reasons, but throughout the course of this book and, more specifically, this section, we are beginning to see that governments are failing citizens in action on climate change; in many parts of the world, this failure is resulting in poverty, insecurity, and the destruction of livelihoods. For example, between 2007 and 2012, Syria experienced one of its worst and most extended droughts ever in recorded history. A study from the 2011 Global Assessment Report on Disaster Risk Reduction found nearly 75% of Syrians were dependent on agriculture and thus were at highest risk to the consequences of drought and experienced complete crop failure. The northeastern regions of Syria were hardest hit; these are the regions where the Islamic State in Iraq and Syria (ISIS) has found the strongest foothold and established its seat of governance (Katulis et al. 2015; Marshall 2014; Werrell et al. 2015). We must begin to ask ourselves whether or not our limited action in responding to climate change and environmental insecurity is directly responsible for radicalization and, thus, whether we are—at least in this specific way—responsible for the terrorist attacks that are becoming more frequent, normal mechanisms of public protest.

But why discuss terrorism in this section regarding conflict in and between LDCs? The media would have us believe that MDCs are the primary intended victim of terrorist violence. However, data tell us that the overwhelming majority of terrorist attacks occur in LDCs, frequently by perpetrators originating in the country where the attack is carried out. Equally, we also know that the overwhelming majority of terrorist deaths occur in LDCs; you are considerably less likely to survive a terrorist attack if the attack occurs in an LDC, largely because of poor infrastructure and access to health care—

both problems linked to environmental security and significantly challenged by climate change (Butts 2014; Department of Homeland Security 2012, 2014, 2015).

4.1.6. CONCLUSIONS

This chapter serves as an introduction to the complexities of inter- and intrastate conflict when viewed in the theater of environmental security. We have seen that there is a global history of conflict over resources between LDCs and MDCs. This relationship of conflict and sometimes violence seems prepared to continue as climate change directly challenges a resource base under threat from population growth and industrialization. We are already feeling the consequences of climate change; MDCs are no longer safe from its effects and are haggling over how to staunch the diplomatic loopholes while LDCs are struggling under the dual burden of industrialization and environmental shift. It should be no surprise that environmental insecurity is at the foundation of many of today's conflicts; access to resources is the tangible consequence of power, and power has always been a rationale for violence. The international community has indicated an understanding that transnational challenges require transnational solutions, but few MDCs are willing to sacrifice sovereignty for environmental security, resulting in both violent and nonviolent points of conflict in and between both LDCs and MDCs.

The upcoming case studies on the Arctic and the eastern Horn of Africa give us a deeper perspective on the depth these problems create, both practically through internal policy challenges and diplomatically through external negotiations and tensions challenging both bilateral and multilateral alliances. These cases provide us with the opportunity to address the strengths and weaknesses of our global system and the U.S. response to these challenges. In doing so, we can participate in a larger discussion on how to consider human security in such a way as to better match today's security threats.

This section raises again and again the fact that environmental security crises arise amid a complex grid of social failures. We cannot always know which of these crises will result in violent conflict. What we learn from situations such as those found in the Marshall Islands challenge our belief that violent conflict poses the greatest threat in environmentally insecure areas. In these cases, the environment serves as an interlocutor between the perpetrator of violence and the (often) long-term victim. In a political world suffering from short-sightedness, meeting the needs of our global citizenry continues to challenge us.

REFERENCES

Adelson, A., R. Lapides, and M. Web, 1989: *Lodz Ghetto: Inside a Community under Siege.* Viking, 526 pp.

Ajodo-Adebanjoko, A., and U. O. Walter, 2014: Poverty and the challenges of insecurity to development. *Eur. Sci. J.*, **10** (14), 361–372, https://doi.org/10.19044/esj.2014.v10n14p%25p.

Avalon Project, 2008a: Judgement: Ribbentrop. Yale Law School, http://avalon.law.yale.edu/imt/judribb.asp.

——, 2008b: Judgement: Streicher. Yale Law School, http://avalon.law.yale.edu/imt/judstrei.asp.

Bamberg, J. H., 1994: *The Developing Years, 1901–1932.* Vol. 1, *The History of the British Petroleum Company*, Cambridge University Press, 830 pp.

BBC, 2015:Yemen crisis: Who is fighting whom? BBC, www.bbc.com/news/world-middle-east-29319423.

Berger, S. R., 2000: A foreign policy for the global age. *Foreign Aff.*, **79** (6), 22–39, www.foreignaffairs.com/articles/2000-11-01/foreign-policy-global-age.

Bird, K. J., and Coauthors, 2008: Circum-Arctic resource appraisal: Estimates of undiscovered oil and gas north of the Arctic Circle. U.S. Geological Survey Fact Sheet 2008-3049, 4 pp., https://pubs.usgs.gov/fs/2008/3049/fs2008-3049.pdf.

Bloxham, D., 2001: Jewish slave labour and its relationship to the "Final Solution." *Remembering for the Future: The Holocaust in an Age of Genocide*, J. K. Roth et al., Eds., Vol. 1, Palgrave, 163–186.

——, 2009: *The Final Solution: A Genocide.* Oxford University Press, 416 pp.

——, and T. Kushner: 2005: *The Holocaust: Critical Historical Approaches.* Manchester University Press, 256 pp.

Boden, T., G. Marland, and R. Andres, 2013: Global, Regional, and National Fossil-Fuel CO_2 Emissions (1751–2014), version 2017. Environmental System Science Data Infrastructure for a Virtual Ecosystem, DD MMM YYYY, https://doi.org/10.3334/CDIAC/00001_V2013.

Brown, A., and T. Scribner, 2014: Unfulfilled promises, future possibilities: The refugee resettlement system in the United States. *J. Migr. Hum. Secur.*, **2**, 101–120, https://doi.org/10.14240/jmhs.v2i2.27.

Brown, K. W., 2012: *A History of Mining in Latin America: From the Colonial Era to the Present.* University of New Mexico Press, 280 pp.

Brown, O., A. Hammill, and R. McLeman, 2007: Climate change as the 'new' security threat: Implications for Africa. *Int. Aff.*, **83**, 1141–1154, https://doi.org/10.1111/j.1468-2346.2007.00678.x.

Bush, G. H., 1990: Address before a joint session of Congress. 11 September 1990, University of Virginia Miller Center of Public Affairs, transcript and Adobe Flash audio, 34:12, http://millercenter.org/president/bush/speeches/speech-3425.

Butts, K., 2014: Environmental security and climate change: A link to homeland security. *J. Homeland Secur. Emerg. Manage.*, **11**, 269–279, https://doi.org/10.1515/jhsem-2013-0098.

Byrd, J. A., 2011: *The Transit of Empire: Indigenous Critiques of Colonialism.* First Peoples: New Directions in Indigenous Studies, Vol. 4, University of Minnesota Press, 320 pp.

Campbell, D., 2005: The biopolitics of security: Oil, empire, and the sports utility vehicle. *Amer. Quar.*, **57**, 943–972, https://doi.org/10.1353/aq.2005.0041.

Carmichael, C., 2010: Genocide and population displacement in post-communist eastern Europe. *The Oxford Handbook of Genocide Studies*, D. Bloxham and D. A. Moses, Eds., Oxford University Press, 509–528, https://doi.org/10.1093/oxfordhb/9780199232116.013.0026.

Carroll, L., 2017: EPA head Scott Pruitt says carbon dioxide is not 'primary contributor' to global warming. Politifact, www.politifact.com/truth-o-meter/statements/2017/mar/10/scott-pruitt/epa-head-scott-pruitt-says-carbon-dioxide-not-prim/.

Casper, K., 2009: Oil and gas development in the Arctic: Softening of ice demands hardening of international law. *Nat. Resour. J.*, **49**, 825–881, https://digitalrepository.unm.edu/nrj/vol49/iss3/8.

Chaudhury, A. S., M. J. Ventresca, T. F. Thornton, A. Helfgott, C. Sova, P. Baral, T. Rasheed, and J. Ligthart, 2016: Emerging meta-organisations and adaptation to global climate change: Evidence from implementing adaptation in Nepal, Pakistan and Ghana. *Global Environ. Change*, **38**, 243–257, https://doi.org/10.1016/j.gloenvcha.2016.03.011.

Churchill, W., 1931: *The World Crisis: 1911–1918*. T. Butterworth, 832 pp.

CNN, 2016: U.S. military tests Arctic operations. CNN, 20 March, www.cnn.com/2016/03/20/politics/gallery/u-s-military-arctic-exercise-icex/.

Colgan, W., H. Machguth, M. MacFerrin, J. Colgan, D. van As, and J. MacGregor, 2016: The abandoned ice sheet base at Camp Century, Greenland, in a warming climate. *Geophys. Res. Lett.*, **43**, 8091–8096, https://doi.org/10.1002/2016GL069688.

Committee on Environment and Public Works, 2014: Review of the President's climate action plan. Senate Doc. 113–743, 521 pp.

Committee on Small Business, 2013: The President's climate action plan: What is the impact on small businesses? House of Representatives Doc. 113–031, 67 pp., www.gpo.gov/fdsys/pkg/CHRG-113hhrg81938/pdf/CHRG-113hhrg81938.pdf.

Conrad, C., 1990: *Strategic Organizational Communication: An Integrated Perspective*. 2nd ed. Holt, Rinehart, and Winston, 386 pp.

Cowling, J., 2011: Arctic oil exploration: Potential riches and problems. BBC News, www.bbc.com/news/business-14728856.

Das, P. V., 2015: *Colonialism, Development, and the Environment: Railways and Deforestation in British India, 1860–1884*. 1st ed. Palgrave Macmillan, 189 pp.

D'Aveni, R. A., 2012: *Strategic Capitalism: The New Economic Strategy for Winning the Capitalist Cold War*. McGraw-Hill, 336 pp.

Davis, M., 2000: Late Victorian Holocausts: *El Niño Famines and the Making of the Third World*. Verso, 464 pp.

Department of Homeland Security, 2012: Terrorist attacks 2012: Concentration and intensity. National Consortium for the Study of Terrorism and Responses to Terrorism, www.start.umd.edu/gtd/images/START_GlobalTerrorismDatabase2012dataset_Map.jpg.

——, 2014: Terrorist attacks 2014: Concentration and intensity. National Consortium for the Study of Terrorism and Responses to Terrorism, www.start.umd.edu/gtd/images/START_GlobalTerrorismDatabase_2014TerroristAttacksConcentrationIntensityMap.jpg.

——, 2015: Terrorist attacks 2015: Concentration and intensity. National Consortium for the Study of Terrorism and Responses to Terrorism, www.start.umd.edu/gtd/images/START_GlobalTerrorismDatabase_2015TerroristAttacksConcentrationIntensityMap.jpg.

de Waal, A., 2005: *Famine that Kills: Darfur, Sudan*. Oxford University Press, 288 pp.

Diallo, D. D., 2015: Q&A: Mali is extremely vulnerable and unable to combat climate change impacts. International Institute for Environment and Development, www.iied.org/qa-mali-extremely-vulnerable-unable-combat-climate-change-impacts.

Dobkowski, M. N., and I. Wallimann, 2002: *On the Edge of Scarcity: Environment, Resources, Population, Sustainability, and Conflict*. 2nd ed. Syracuse University Press, 204 pp.

Dodds, F., and T. Pippard, 2005: *Human and Environmental Security: An Agenda for Change*. Earthscan, 270 pp.

Dunlap, R., and A. McCright, 2011: Organized climate change denial. *The Oxford Handbook of Climate Change and Society*, Oxford University Press, 144–160.

El Dahan, M., 2014: Political conflicts worsening Yemen food security: U.N. agency. Reuters, www.reuters.com/article/us-yemen-crisis-food-idUSKCN0HO1FU20140929.

Energy Information Administration, 2016: Country analysis brief: Iraq. Energy Information Administration Rep., 17 pp., www.eia.gov/beta/international/analysis.cfm?iso=IRQ.

Ezrow, N. M., E. Frantz, and A. Kendall-Taylor, 2015: *Development and the State in the 21st Century: Tackling the Challenges Facing the Developing World*. Palgrave Macmillan, 368 pp.

Fattah, K., 2014: Yemen's insecurity dilemma. *Washington Report on Middle East Affairs*, Vol. 33, No. 2, 32–33, www.wrmea.org/014-march-april/yemens-insecurity-dilemma.html.

FEWS NET, 2016: Intensification of conflict limits humanitarian access and activities. FEWS NET Rep., 3 pp., www.fews.net/east-africa/yemen/food-security-outlook-update/august-2016.

——, 2018a: Acute food insecurity: Near term (January 2018). FEWS NET, www.fews.net/.

——, 2018b: Integrated phase classification—IPC 2.0: A common starting point for decision making. FEWS NET, www.fews.net/IPC.

——, 2018c: Staple food prices increase sharply following in further currency depreciation and increased conflict. FEWS NET, http://fews.net/east-africa/yemen/key-message-update/september-2018.

——, 2018d: Staple food prices remain high following the recent blockade. FEWS NET, http://fews.net/east-africa/yemen/key-message-update/march-2018.

Folger, J. P., M. S. Poole, and R. K. Stutman, 1997: *Working through Conflict: Strategies for Relationships, Groups, and Organizations*. 3rd ed. Longman, 318 pp.

Fund for Peace, 2011: The failed states index 2011. Fund for Peace, https://www.pucsp.br/ecopolitica/downloads/failed_states_index_2011.pdf .

——, 2016: The fragile states index 2016. Fund for Peace, http://fundforpeace.org/fsi/2016/06/27/fragile-states-index-2016-annual-report/.

——, 2018: The fragile states index 2018. Fund for Peace, http://fundforpeace.org/fsi/2018/04/24/fragile-states-index-2018-annual-report/.

Funk, C., and L. Rainie, 2015: Americans, politics and science issues. Pew Research Center, www.pewinternet.org/2015/07/01/americans-politics-and-science-issues/.

Gerrard, M., 2015: America's forgotten nuclear waste dump in the Pacific. *SAIS Rev.*, **35** (1), 87–98, https://doi.org/10.1353/sais.2015.0013.

Graeger, N., and D. Smith, Eds., 1996: Environment, poverty, conflict. Peace Research Institute, Oslo (PRIO) Rep. 2.

Greenberg, J., 2018: Donald Trump gets polar ice trend backwards. Politifact, www.politifact.com/truth-o-meter/statements/2018/jan/29/donald-trump/trump-gets-polar-ice-trend-backwards/.

Gregoire, C., 2015: Why some conservatives can't accept that climate change is real. Huffington Post, www.huffingtonpost.com/entry/climate-change-denial-psychology_us_56438664e4b045bf3ded5ca5.

Groisman, P., J. Overland, B. Rudolf, and J. Walsh, 2011: Ongoing climate change in the Arctic. *Ambio*, **40** (Suppl.), 6–16, https://doi.org/10.1007/s13280-011-0211-z.

Harris, P. G., 2013: *What's Wrong with Climate Politics and How to Fix It*. Polity Press, 296 pp.

Hitler, A., 1934: *Hitler-Worte: Aussprüche aus "Mein Kampf" und aus den Reden des Führers*. F. Hirt, 31 pp.

——, 1969: *Mein Kampf*. Hutchinson, 629 pp.

Internal Displacement Monitoring Centre, 2018: Yemen IDP figures analysis. Internal Displacement Monitoring Centre Rep., http://www.internal-displacement.org/countries/yemen.

IPCC, 2007: *Climate Change 2007: Impacts, Adaptation and Vulnerability*. Cambridge University Press, 976 pp., www.ipcc.ch/publications_and_data/publications_ipcc_fourth_assessment_report_wg2_report_impacts_adaptation_and_vulnerability.htm.

——, 2014: *Climate Change 2014: Mitigation of Climate Change*. Cambridge University Press, 1465 pp., www.ipcc.ch/pdf/assessment-report/ar5/wg3/ipcc_wg3_ar5_full.pdf.

——, 2016: Fifth assessment report—Synthesis report. YouTube, www.youtube.com/watch?v=fGH0dAwM-QE.

Jones, B., 2011: Denmark and Greenland plan Arctic military force. *Jane's Defence Weekly*, Vol. 48, No. 24, 10.

Josiah, B. P., 2011: *Migration, Mining, and the African Diaspora: Guyana in the Nineteenth and Twentieth Centuries*. Palgrave Macmillan, 274 pp.

Juhasz, A., 2013: Why the war in Iraq was fought for Big Oil. CNN, www.cnn.com/2013/03/19/opinion/iraq-war-oil-juhasz/.

Kabi, P., 2015: Q&A: Legalise Paris Agreement. International Institute for Environment and Development, www.iied.org/qa-legalise-paris-agreement.

Kamenetsky, I., 1961: *Secret Nazi Plans for Eastern Europe*. Bookman Associates, 263 pp.

Katulis, B., S. al-Assad, and W. Morris, 2015: One year later: Assessing the coalition campaign against ISIS. *Middle East Policy*, **22** (4), 1–21, https://doi.org/10.1111/mepo.12154.

Kerr, S., 2015: Houthis take control of Yemeni government. *Financial Times*, 6 February, www.ft.com/content/358bbb34-ae29-11e4-8188-00144feab7de.

Kirby, P., 2006: Theorising globalisation's social impact: Proposing the concept of vulnerability. *Rev. Int. Polit. Econ.*, **13**, 632–655, https://doi.org/10.1080/09692290600839915.

Krause, K., 2009: Beyond definition: Violence in a global perspective. *Global Crime*, **10**, 337–355, https://doi.org/10.1080/17440570903248270.

Lavender, B., 2016: The LEG work programme for 2016-2017. *29th Meeting of the Least Developed Countries Expert Group*, Bonn, Germany, UN Framework Convention on Climate Change, 1-20.

Leiserowitz, A., E. Maibach, C. Roser-Renouf, G. Feinberg, and S. Rosenthal, 2016: Politics and global warming, spring 2016. Yale Program on Climate Change Communication Rep., 75 pp., http://climatecommunication.yale.edu/publications/politics-global-warming-spring-2016/.

Levene, M., 2011: Beyond Gaddafi: Sustainable prevention in the face of environmental injustice: Some words of praise but also caution! *J. Genocide Res.*, **13**, 209–215, https://doi.org/10.1080/14623528.2011.606682.

——, and D. Conversi, 2014: Subsistence societies, globalisation, climate change and genocide: Discourses of vulnerability and resilience. *Int. J. Hum. Rights*, **18**, 281–297, https://doi.org/10.1080/13642987.2014.914 702.

Maldonado, J. K., B. J. Colombi, and R. Pandya, Eds., 2014: *Climate Change and Indigenous Peoples in the United States: Impacts, Experiences and Actions.* Springer, 174 pp.

Marshall, R., 2014: ISIS: A new adversary in an endless war. *Washington Report on Middle East Affairs*, Vol. 33, No. 8, 8–10, www.wrmea.org/014-november-december/isis-a-new-adversary-in-an-endless-war.html.

Mortensen, C. D., 1974: A transactional paradigm of social conflict. *Perspectives on Communication in Social Conflict*, G. R. Miller and H. W. Simons, Eds., Prentice Hall, 90–194.

Moses, A. D., 1998: Structure and agency in the holocaust: Daniel J. Goldhagen and his critics. *Hist. Theory*, **37**, 194–219, https://doi.org/10.1111/ 0018-2656.00049.

——, 2004: *Genocide and Settler Society: Frontier Violence and Stolen Indigenous Children in Australian History.* Berghahn Books, 344 pp.

Murray, E. H., 2015: *Disrupting Pathways to Genocide: The Process of Ideological Radicalisation.* Palgrave Macmillan, 218 pp.

Nielsen, K. H., H. Nielsen, and J. Martin-Nielsen, 2014: City under the ice: The closed world of Camp Century in Cold War culture. *Sci. Cult.*, **23**, 443–464, https://doi.org/10.1080/09505431.2014.884063.

Nuclear Waste Policy Act, 1982: U.S. Code 42, section 10101, http://energy.gov/downloads/nuclear-waste-policy-act.

Oroso, A., 2017: PA GOPer's climate change theory debunked: Nope, not getting closer to the sun. Politifact, www.politifact.com/pennsylvania/statements/2017/mar/31/scott-wagner/pa-gopers-climate-change-theory-debunked-nope-not-/.

Palden, T., 2015: Q&A: A crucial year for our planet, says prime minister of Bhutan. International Institute for Environment and Development, www.iied.org/qa-crucial-year-for-our-planet-says-prime-minister-bhutan.

Pegna, M. R., 2013: U.S. Arctic policy: The need to ratify a modified UNCLOS and secure a military presence in the Arctic. *J. Marit. Law Commer.*, **44**, 169–194.

Perraudin, M., and J. Zimmerer, Eds., 2010: *German Colonialism and National Identity.* Routledge, 340 pp.

Perry, A., 2016: *Aqueduct: Colonialism, Resources, and the Histories We Remember.* ARP Books, 103 pp.

Pevec, D., 2006: The Marshall Islands nuclear claims tribunal: The claims of the Enewetak people. *Denver J. Int. Law Policy*, **35**, 221–239, http://djilp.org/wp-content/uploads/2011/08/The-Marshall-Islands-Nuclear-Claims-Tribunal-Claims-Enewetak-People-Davor-Pevec.pdf.

Politifact, 2018: All statements from Donald Trump. Politifact, www.politifact.com/personalities/donald-trump/statements/?list=speaker.

Prunier, G., 2005: *Darfur: The Ambiguous Genocide.* Cornell University Press, 212 pp.

Pugliese, D., 2016: Canadian military looks to expand Arctic footprint. Defense News, www.defensenews.com/global/2016/05/23/canadian-military-looks-to-expand-arctic-footprint/.

Rees, W. E., 2002: An ecological economics perspective on sustainability and prospects for ending poverty. *Popul. Environ.*, **24**, 15–46, https://doi.org/10.1023/A:1020125725915.

Regmi, B. R., C. Star, and W. L. Filho, 2016: Effectiveness of the local adaptation plan of action to support climate change adaptation in Nepal. *Mitigation Adapt. Strategies Global Change*, **21**, 461–478, https://doi.org/10.1007/s11027-014-9610-3.

Rockoff, H., 2012: *America's Economic Way of War: War and the US Economy from the Spanish-American War to the First Gulf War.* Cambridge University Press, 357 pp.

Roland, C. G., 1992: *Courage under Siege: Starvation, Disease, and Death in the Warsaw Ghetto.* Oxford University Press, 310 pp.

Rubenstein, R. L., and J. K. Roth, 1987: *Approaches to Auschwitz: The Legacy of the Holocaust.* SCM Press, 422 pp.

Samatar, A. I., 1993: Structural adjustment as development strategy? Bananas, boom, and poverty in Somalia. *Econ. Geogr.*, **69**, 25–43, https://doi.org/10.2307/143888.

Sarai, E., 2016: Amid war, Yemenis face dire food insecurity. VOA News, www.voanews.com/a/amid-war-yemenis-face-dire-food-insecurity/3385108.html.

Satya, L. D., 2004: *Ecology, Colonialism, and Cattle: Central India in the Nineteenth Century*. Oxford University Press, 204 pp.

Shamir, R., 2005: Without borders? Notes on globalization as a mobility regime. *Sociol. Theory*, **23**, 197–217, https://doi.org/10.1111/j.0735-2751.2005.00250.x.

Sheppard, K., 2016: Marco Rubio spouts every type of climate change denial. Huffington Post, www.huffingtonpost.com/entry/marco-rubio-climate-change_us_56e239f3e4b0860f99d8882b.

Siddique, A. B., 2015: Q&A: World leaders must abandon their narrow political interests to deliver the best deal at COP21. International Institute for Environment and Development, www.iied.org/qa-world-leaders-must-abandon-their-narrow-political-interests-deliver-best-deal-cop21.

Sisay, A., 2015: Q&A: Building zero carbon emission economy in a decade. International Institute for Environment and Development, www.iied.org/qa-building-zero-carbon-emission-economy-decade.

Smeulers, A., 2010: *Collective Violence and International Criminal Justice: An Interdisciplinary Approach*. Intersentia, 452 pp.

Smith, D., 1996: Dynamics of contemporary conflict: Consequences for development strategies. Environment, poverty, conflict, Peace Research Institute Oslo Rep. 2/94, 47–90.

Smolar, H., 1989: The Minsk Ghetto: *Soviet-Jewish Partisans against the Nazis*. Holocaust Publications, 175 pp.

Sovacool, B. K., B.-O. Linnér, and R. J. T. Klein, 2017: Climate change adaptation and the Least Developed Countries Fund (LDCF): Qualitative insights from policy implementation in the Asia-Pacific. *Climatic Change*, **140**, 209–226, https://doi.org/10.1007/s10584-016-1839-2.

Sporton, D., D. S. G. Thomas, and J. Morrison, 1999: Outcomes of social and environmental change in the Kalahari of Botswana: The role of migration. *J. Southern African Studies*, **25**, 441–459, https://doi.org/10.1080/03057070.1999.11742768.

Sutch, P., 2009: International justice and the reform of global governance: A reconsideration of Michael Walzer's international political theory. *Rev. Int. Stud.*, **35**, 513–530, https://doi.org/10.1017/S0260210509008638.

Tetchiada, S., 2013: COP21: Climate change and conflict meet in Cameroon. Integrated Regional Information Networks, www.irinnews.org/feature/2015/12/09.

Trotta, D., 2013: Iraq war costs U.S. more than $2 trillion: Study. Reuters, www.reuters.com/article/us-iraq-war-anniversary-idUSBRE92D0PG20130314.

Tsygankov, A. P., 2012: *Russia and the West from Alexander to Putin: Honor in International Relations*. Cambridge University Press, 317 pp.

UN Economic and Social Council, 1948: Ad hoc committee on genocide: Draft report. UN Economic and Social Council Rep. E/AC.25/W.1/Add.3, 8 pp., https://digitallibrary.un.org/record/601996?ln=en.

——, 2018: Least developed country category: Yemen profile. UN Economic Analysis and Policy Division, www.un.org/development/desa/dpad/least-developed-country-category-yemen.html.

UN Environment Programme, 2016: Bangaladesh. UN Poverty-Environment Initiative, http://unpei.org/what-we-do/pei-countries/bangladesh.

UN General Assembly, 1994: Measures to eliminate international terrorism. United Nations, www.un.org/documents/ga/res/49/a49r060.htm.

UN High Commissioner for Human Rights, 1948: Convention on the prevention and punishment of the crime of genocide. UN Resolution 260 (III), www.hrweb.org/legal/genocide.html.

UN High-Level Panel on Threats, Challenges and Change, 2005: Poverty, infectious disease, and environmental degradation as threats to collective security: A UN panel report. *Popul. Dev. Rev.*, **31**, 595–600, https://doi.org/10.1111/j.1728-4457.2005.00088.x.

United Press International, 2016: Melting ice sheet could release frozen Cold War-era waste. Space Daily, www.spacedaily.com/reports/Melting_ice_sheet_could_release_frozen_Cold_War_era_waste_999.html.

UN World Food Programme, 2016: Yemen: Country overview. UN World Food Programme, www.wfp.org/countries/yemen/overview.

Wall, J. A., 1985: *Negotiation: Theory and Practice*. Scott Foresman, 182 pp.

Werrell, C., F. Femia, and T. Sternberg, 2015: Did we see it coming? State fragility, climate vulnerability, and the uprisings in Syria and Egypt. *SAIS Rev. Int. Aff.*, **35** (1), 29–46, https://doi.org/10.1353/sais.2015.0002.

Wiebelt, M., C. Breisinger, O. Ecker, P. Al-Riffai, R. Robertson, R., and R. Thiele, 2013: Compounding food and income insecurity in Yemen: Challenges from climate change. *Food Policy*, **43**, 77–89, https://doi.org/10.1016/j.foodpol.2013.08.009.

World Without Genocide, 2017: Darfur genocide. World Without Genocide, http://worldwithoutgenocide.org/genocides-and-conflicts/darfur-genocide.

Young, H., K. Jacobsen, and A. Osman, 2009: Livelihoods, migration and conflict: Discussion of findings from two studies in West and North Darfur, 2006–2007. Feinstein International Center Briefing Paper, 23 pp., http://fic.tufts.edu/assets/Livelihoods-Migration-and-Conflict.pdf.

Zimmerer, J., 2011: *Von Windhuk nach Auschwitz? Beiträge zum Verhältnis von Kolonialismus und Holocaust.* LIT Verlag Münster, 349 pp.

AN ENVIRONMENT OF INSECURITY: THE RELATIONSHIP BETWEEN ENVIRONMENTAL CHANGE AND VIOLENT CONFLICT IN NORTHWEST KENYA

Jan-Peter Schilling

4.2.1. OVERVIEW

In reading, analyzing, and discussing this case study, students will gain an understanding of

- how environmental changes related to global climate change affect conflicts between pastoral communities in northwest Kenya,
- how conflict impacts human security in pastoral communities, and
- how local conflict dynamics are connected to national and global processes.

4.2.2. INTRODUCTION

We live in a time where we as humans constantly and drastically change our planet. We cut trees in one place and plant new trees elsewhere; we dump our waste into the oceans and the atmosphere and clean up rivers. We blast rocks to build tunnels through mountains and set up national parks to protect nature. Our impact on Earth is so dramatic that some authors suggest calling this period of Earth history the Anthropocene (Steffen et al. 2011). Regardless of what we call our current age, the fact is that there are about 7.4 billion of us, and soon there will be many more [Population Reference Bureau (PRB) 2015]. As we have seen discussed in earlier units, all of us need food, water, shelter, and energy. All of these in turn depend almost exclusively on fossil fuels. Modern society relies on fossil fuels to sustain a modern Western lifestyle (Suranovic 2013). Fossil fuels such as oil and coal are fairly easy to mine and produce; equally, global coal supplies are sustainable for at least the next 100 years (World Energy Council 2015). Sadly, coal is causing health risks locally, and globally, it has another major side effect: climate change. When you burn coal or oil, greenhouse gases such as carbon dioxide (CO_2) are released into the atmosphere; this in turn leads to an increase of the global air surface temperature. For instance, in parts of North Africa, the temperature has increased by 2.5°C since the beginning of mass industrialization (IPCC 2013). Thus, animals, plants, and everything else on Earth must adapt quite quickly to higher temperatures and changes in rainfall. Some studies for instance suggest that climate change is likely to reduce agricultural output (Cline 2007). That would mean we have less food to offer and (many) more people to feed.

In addition, concern is increasing not only that climate change may make it harder to produce enough food but also that climate change through environmental change may contribute to violent conflicts (Scheffran

177

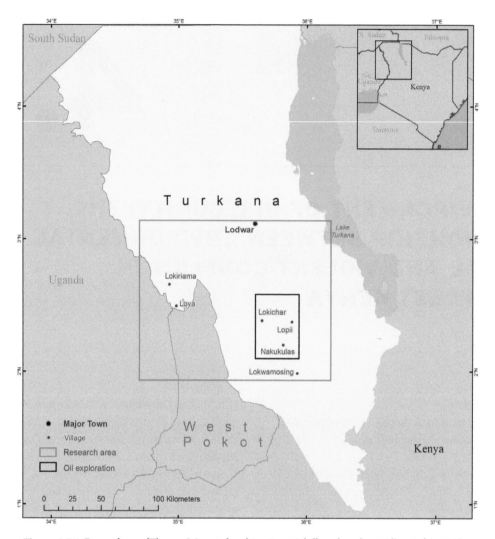

Figure 4.2.1. Research area [Thomas Weinzierl and Jan-Peter Schilling, based on Tullow Oil (2014)].

et al. 2012a). Some examples include when droughts destroy harvests and people then compete for scarce resources (von Uexkull 2014) and when sea level rise floods coastal zones or entire islands. These island populations then have to move somewhere else where they might get into conflict with the host community (Saha 2012).

So far, studies on such potential links between climate and environmental change and violent conflict show mixed results. Some suggest a link, while others do not (Scheffran et al. 2012a,b). The reason for this is that each phenomenon is complex in and of itself. Hence, the relationship and interactions between climate/environmental change and conflict are even more complex. But this does not mean that we should not attempt to understand what is going on.

This chapter will shed some light on the relationship and interactions between climate change and conflict using an example from northwest Kenya. The region is experiencing significant challenges because of both climate change and violent conflicts, phenomena we are equally interested in at present. The challenge here is to determine how they relate to each other.

We start the main body of the chapter with an introductory section on northwest Kenya and will continue along the following three lines: 1) How do environmental changes related to global climate change affect violent conflicts between pastoral communities in northwest Kenya? 2) How do the conflicts impact the human security of pastoral communities? 3) What are the connections between local conflict dynamics and national and global processes?

Figure 4.2.2. Turkana pastoralist with camel (Schilling 2012).

4.2.3. NORTHWEST KENYA

Kenya is divided into 47 counties. The one this chapter is mostly concerned with is called Turkana, located in the northwest (Figure 4.2.1). According to the latest publicly available numbers, Turkana had a population of about 855,400 people in 2009 [Kenya National Bureau of Statistics (KNBS) 2010]. A recent report citing the unpublished county integrated development plan for Turkana gives a population size of almost 1.3 million people for 2015 (Human Rights Watch 2015). Almost all people in Turkana practice nomadic pastoralism, meaning they move around with their livestock in search of water and pasture (Figure 4.2.2). Around Lake Turkana, some fish to sustain their livelihoods. Traditional agrarian farming is rare simply because the climate is too dry to grow most crops. The temperatures do not vary much throughout the year and tend to be quite warm; for example, in the largest city, Lodwar, the annual average temperature is usually above 30°C (Tutiempo 2011). In regular years, Turkana receives most of its rainfall during the "long rains" between March and May and the "short rains" between October and December (McSweeney et al. 2012). The occurrence of these two distinct periods of rainfall is generally known as a bimodal rainfall pattern.

Global climate change is projected to lead to an even warmer climate with less predictable, and hence less reliable, rainfall (Schilling et al. 2014). Pastoralists in this area are well adapted to the harsh climate, but less reliable rainfall makes it harder for them to find water and pasture for their animals (Opiyo et al. 2015). During drought periods, the government of Kenya and international organizations regularly distribute food aid in Turkana to prevent people from starving [UN Office for the Coordination of Humanitarian Affairs (UNOCHA) 2011]. In a formal sense, Turkana is the poorest and least developed county in Kenya, at least when measured in income per capita or school attendance (Kenya Open Data 2011a,b, 2012). The health and road infrastructure in Turkana is also among the worst in the country. For years, the central Kenyan government has largely neglected Turkana (Government of Kenya 2007).

The Turkana are in violent conflict with other pastoral groups and especially with the Pokot of Kenya and neighbouring Uganda (Ide et al. 2014; Schilling et al. 2012). Access to land, water, and livestock are at the heart of these conflicts, as explained in more detail in the next section.

4.2.4. ENVIRONMENTAL CHANGE AND VIOLENT CONFLICT IN THE REGION

To begin, note that though global climate change is one key influential driver of environmental change, it is not the only one. Higher temperatures and less rainfall associated with global climate change can lead to local environmental changes such as drought. However, drought can also be caused by local action, such as deforestation, which contributes directly to the warming of the local climate and the environment (Salih et al. 2013). This section will highlight some results of this research (Schilling 2012), focusing on how environmental changes relating to global climate change affect the conflicts between various pastoral communities in northwest Kenya. Violent conflict, as noted in earlier chapters, can be understood as an interaction of at least two groups who use violence to pursue their aims. Each group sees its aims incompatible with the aims of the other group (see Scheffran et al. 2012c). Simply speaking, the Turkana and Pokot both want the same land, pasture, water, and livestock resources. The conflict between the two groups is mostly visible in violent livestock acquisitions, or raids. In these raids, young men of one group attack the other group with automatic guns to steal their livestock (Schilling et al. 2012).

Before undertaking research in southern Turkana and northern West Pokot (see red square in Figure 4.2.1), it was important to delineate two different explanations of the relationship between environmental conditions and raids. The first line of argument, the scarcity argument, suggests that more raids can be expected during dry periods because key resources such as water and pasture are scarce and hence people are more likely to fight over them (Campbell et al. 2009; Eriksen and Lind 2009; Meier et al. 2007). The scarcity argument draws on earlier work by Thomas Robert Malthus who, in the eighteenth century, stressed that population growth is limited by the availability of resources (Malthus 1798). Other scholars who base their arguments on this assumption are therefore sometimes called Malthusians or neo-Malthusians. One of the most debated scholars who, at least in part, draws on Malthusian ideas is Thomas Homer-Dixon, who claims that resource scarcity coupled with strong population growth and unequal resource distribution leads to or at least contributes to violent conflict (Homer-Dixon 1994, 1999; Homer-Dixon and Deligiannis 2009). All three factors are present in Turkana, and hence, one would expect more conflicts during dry periods.

The second line of argument, known as the "rains and raids" argument, suggests the opposite. Witsenburg and Adano have analyzed raiding and climate data for Marsabit, located in northern Kenya, on the eastern side of Lake Turkana. The authors find that raids are more likely to occur during wet years due to the high grass, strength of the animals, dense brush, and availability of surface water necessary during a long trek (Witsenburg and Adano 2009). In other words, animals are too weak to travel long distances from the location of the raid back to the home camp. For these practical reasons, more raids can be expected during wet climatic conditions when the availability of water and pasture is higher.

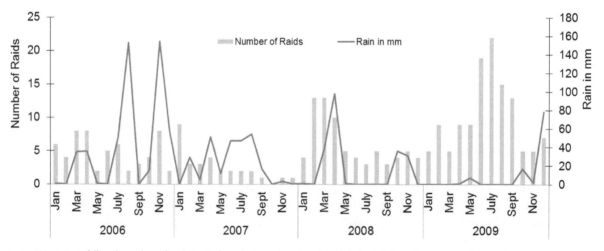

Figure 4.2.3. Rainfall and number of raids in Turkana between 2006 and 2009 [adopted from Schilling et al. (2014)].

Keeping these varying perspectives in mind, the Turkana Pastoralist Development Organization's (TUPADO) data on raids were accessed and analyzed together with data on temperature and rainfall from a weather station in Lodwar. Data were limited to 2006–09; research analysis focuses more on relations between climatic conditions and violence. From this research, we can extrapolate to more informed statements about the future and climate change in general.

Figure 4.2.3 shows the results of the analysis. The bars represent the number of raids in each month between 2006 and 2009, while the curve shows the rainfall. The years 2006 and 2008 throw support to the rains and raids argument as the peaks in rainfall coincide (roughly) with increases in the number of raids. However, 2009 was a drought year, while the number of raids was by far the highest. This supports the scarcity argument. Data from the year 2007 cannot be explained by either of the two arguments.

So how can these opposing findings be explained? Here, the many interviews and focus group discussions with raiders, pastoralists, and community chiefs were very useful. The interviewees explained that in regular years with sufficient rain, raiding is mostly conducted around the long and short rains to make use of the abundance of resources and the fortunate raiding conditions. These conditions include healthier animals, a limited need to care for one's own herds, and substantial vegetation to provide cover when conducting raids and hiding from members of the other tribe. But when rains partly or completely fail in a year such as 2009 and a certain threshold of resource scarcity is reached, raids are conducted despite the less fortunate raiding conditions. These "dry raids" differ from "wet raids" as the purpose of the former is not to steal livestock but to protect or gain control over scarce pasture and water resources.

We can therefore conclude that the relationship between environmental conditions and violent conflict in northwest Kenya is not as simple as one where dry periods result in more raids or wet periods result in more raids. However, in years with regular long and short rains, most of the raiding can be expected in and around the wetter periods, while drought years tend to be more violent overall. Against this background, it is likely that higher temperatures and less reliable rainfalls aggravate insecurity for pastoralists and hence also aggravate violent conflicts.

4.2.5. VIOLENT CONFLICT AND HUMAN SECURITY

Keeping this relationship in mind, let us now take a look at how these violent conflicts impact human security within the communities in Turkana and Pokot. Human security, as noted in earlier chapters, is best understood here as the "freedom from the risk of loss or damage to a thing that is important to survival and well-being" (Barnett and O'Brian 2010, p. 4). We can further break down human security into four key elements (Figure 4.2.4).

These elements of human security are represented in both the direct and indirect effects of raiding and conflict in Kenya. The direct effects of raids include the

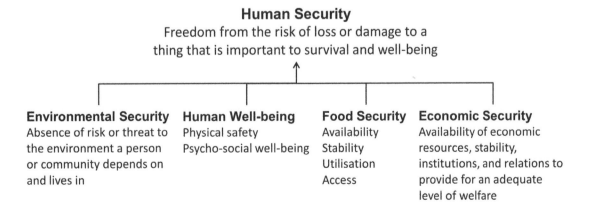

Figure 4.2.4. Elements of human security (based on Barnett and O'Brian 2010; Dalby 2009; Khagram and Ali 2006; Khagram et al. 2003; King and Murray 2001; Schmidhuber and Tubiello 2007; Vivekananda et al. 2014).

loss of life and property, in particular the loss of homes and livestock, and finally, the loss of access to resources, specifically, the loss of pasture, land, and water. These, as we will see further below, signpost many if not all of the four key elements of human security highlighted in Figure 4.2.4. However, these direct losses are further impacted by the increasingly devastating indirect losses raiding and conflict incur: specifically, ineffective resource use, the closing of both schools and markets, and finally, increased obstacles for future investments (based on Schilling et al. 2012). Given the hardships caused by these effects, a deeper look into each indicator gains us further insight into human security.

4.2.5.1. Loss of Human Life

The most detrimental and most direct effect of the conflicts to human well-being is, of course, the loss of human life. Between 2006 and 2009, almost 600 people died in or because of raids in Turkana (TUPADO 2011). Another source reports 640 deaths for Turkana and Pokot in the year 2009 alone [Conflict Early Warning and Response Mechanism (CEWARN) 2010]. Compared to the number of deaths, the number of injuries is fairly low (181 for Turkana between 2006 and 2009) (TUPADO 2011). Possible explanations could include the wide availability of automatic guns and the long distances to medical facilities that can turn even small graze shots into deadly wounds. As mentioned above, the raiders are almost exclusively young men. Thus, the gendered nature of communities within the region lead to further communal devastation when raiders get killed or injured in that these men can no longer serve as communal protection, nor can they continue to look after their herds, activities traditionally held by males in these regions. In the mid- to long term, this undermines the economic security of both Turkana and Pokot communities. This is further entrenched by negative psychological effects and trauma as consequences of the raids (Pike et al. 2010).

4.2.5.2. Loss of Livestock

For the raided community, the raid results in a direct loss of livestock. One might think that there is a balance when two or more groups raid each other as the total number of livestock should fairly stay the same. However, the commercialization of raiding prevents this balance from occurring. The purpose of these commercial raids is not to restock a communities' own herds but to sell the stolen livestock on the market for profit (Eaton 2010). These commercial raids caused a net loss of livestock in Turkana and Pokot of more than 90,000 animals between 2006 and 2009 (CEWARN 2010). Livestock is highly mobile and therefore hard to count; nonetheless, this number was echoed in interviews where 75% of pastoralists and raiders reported to have lost livestock because of raids and drought (Schilling et al. 2012). This is particularly critical as pastoralism revolves around livestock. Livestock means food, income, and prestige. Thus, a loss of livestock negatively affects each element of human security (Figure 4.2.4). As noted by a Pokot raider, "without cattle, you are useless" (Schilling et al. 2012).

4.2.5.3. Loss of Resources and Homes

Raids are also used as an instrument to secure or gain access over key resources, such as pasture, land, and water. Without access to these resources, livestock cannot be kept alive. As we have seen in unit 2, water in particular is a key resource for environmental security. Over the course of this research, the author stayed in a Turkana village called Lokiriama (see Figure 4.2.1). At night, he could often hear nearby exchanges of gunfire. In the morning, community members explained that the Turkana were fighting the Pokot, who were trying to access the nearby borehole at night after having travelled long distances without access to drinking water.

The border region between the Turkana and the Pokot is particularly affected by violent conflict, going beyond raids to direct physical attack of particular villages. Twenty smaller settlements, called homesteads, were looted and destroyed between 2008 and 2011 in the conflict corridor between the Turkana and Pokot (Schilling et al. 2012). Sometimes, entire villages such as Nauyapong are abandoned because of insecurity. A loss of home means loss of shelter, but it also means the loss of an organizational unit for a community. These direct effects are dire, but as noted above, the indirect effects can have equally lasting consequences for communities, further undermining human security in affected regions.

4.2.6. ENVIRONMENTS OF INSECURITY

Almost 90% of the interviewed Turkana and Pokot community members reported that they feel either insecure or highly insecure (Figure 4.2.5). Interviewees on both sides repeatedly stressed that they fear "the enemy," meaning either the Pokot or Turkana, respectively.

This strong perception of insecurity contributes to the three indirect consequences of human insecurity: ineffective resource use, the closing of both schools and markets, and finally, increased obstacles for future investments. The first, ineffective resource use, is best illustrated in Figure 4.2.6. This picture was taken in Loya, a homestead in the border region between Turkana and West Pokot (see also Figure 4.2.1).

Despite overall resource scarcity in the greater region, neither the Turkana nor the Pokot were grazing their animals in this green lowland plain because both parties were afraid of the violence that would result from such action. Similarly, a market in the area remained unused because of the environment of insecurity (Figure 4.2.7). Insecurity further limits pastoral mobility, which is a key strategy to adapt to changing climatic conditions (Opiyo et al. 2015).

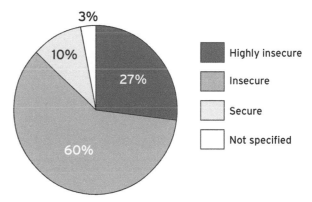

Figure 4.2.5. Perception of insecurity in southern Turkana and northern West Pokot (based on author's interview data).

Women in several Turkana villages noted that they have reduced picking of wild berries and that they fear to go off alone to bathe or use the restroom because of the danger of being attacked, raped, or killed. Teachers

Figure 4.2.6. Underutilized pasture near Loya, Turkana.

Figure 4.2.7. Unused livestock market near Loya, Turkana.

report that schools in Lokiriama and Lobei had to be closed temporarily as conflicts intensified; bullet hole marks in several of the schools in the conflict area further testify to this point. In addition to these effects on the community, insecurity means that any attempts to formally develop the region with roads and other infrastructure face obstacles. For example, the road between Lokiriama and Lorengipi has not been completed because of the high level of insecurity in the area caused both by the conflicts and road banditry.

4.2.7. LOCAL CONFLICTS AND NATIONAL AND GLOBAL PROCESSES

Conflicts between the Turkana and the Pokot are mostly limited to local communities as they revolve around local resources, including water, land, pasture, and livestock. However, these local conflicts do not take place

in isolation from national or even global processes. At the national level, Kenya is currently going through a process of *devolution* that began in 2010. Devolution is a political process during which responsibilities and financial resources are handed down from the national level to lower levels of government. It can also be expressed, as James Lomenen, member of parliament for Turkana South noted in a 2014 interview, as "bring[ing] services to the people." Indeed, one of the key aims of devolution is to reduce the development deficits from which regions like Turkana are suffering (Vasquez 2013). As a consequence, Turkana was among the counties in Kenya that received the highest financial support from the devolution pool. In the 2015–16 financial year alone, Turkana received KES 10.2 billion (about 97.3 million U.S. dollars) (Nairobi News 2015). If this money trickles down to the communities and they see the changes in terms of improved transport, education, and health infrastructure, devolution will definitely be beneficial for Turkana. However, visible improvements in the area are, as yet, limited.

However, in 2014, a new development began to dominate the political and economic scenery: the discovery of oil (see Schilling et al. 2015). Most importantly, the discovery of oil created great expectations among community members in Lokichar, Lopii, and Nakukulas for employment at oil plants as well as improved water supply and economic development in general. Sadly, while oil companies have shared some of the newly drilled water with the communities, these expectations have been largely disappointed both by oil companies and by the government. In fact, the unmet expectations in combination with a lack of transparency, communication, and compensation for land taken from the communities have resulted in company–community conflict. These become visible when the communities block roads, protest, or even storm oil exploration sites (Daily Nation 2013). The communities feel poorly informed by oil companies and by the government about what is going on. Additionally, issues of soil, water, and air pollution are likely to aggravate the relationship between the communities and oil investors (Schilling et al. 2015).

Oil exploration can also have effects on the conflicts between the Turkana and the Pokot. The Turkana expressed fears that the Pokot are now increasing their claims on the land where oil has been found. This shows that not only global climate change but also the global demand for oil can interact with local conflicts.

4.2.8. CONCLUSIONS

The pastoral communities in northwest Kenya remain in an environment of insecurity. Rising temperatures and less reliable rainfall patterns, likely to be aggravated by global climate change, make it increasingly difficult for communities to feed themselves and their livestock. Environmental conditions also affect the intercommunal conflicts, but research suggests that the relationship between environmental and conflict variables is more complex than one might expect. In regular years with sufficient rain, raiding is mostly conducted around the rainy seasons because animals are healthier and can travel longer distances and raiders find cover for their attacks. But when rains partly or completely fail and a certain threshold of resource scarcity is reached, raids are conducted to gain or secure control over scarce pasture and water resources.

The raids and violent conflicts severely undermine the human security of pastoral communities. This happens directly through loss of human life, livestock, resources, and homes. Indirectly, the high level of perceived insecurity results in ineffective resource use, closing of livestock markets and schools, and increased obstacles for investment. Oil has now been added as a third influential factor, contributing to the environment of insecurity. Largely unmet community expectations for employment, water, and development have resulted in conflict between communities and the oil company.

Just as the drivers of the environment of insecurity are not exclusively local, solutions have to be found at different levels. The national government of Kenya needs to ensure that laws are developed and enforced to protect communities from losing their land without proper compensation and to mitigate oil pollution. All levels of government should make sure that local communities benefit from both oil revenues and the financial and infrastructural benefits associated with the devolution process. On the local level, oil companies should be transparent with plans and actions; these should be communicated in a timely manner to the communities in order to help manage local expectations. If these points are taken seriously by the involved actors, there is a chance the region might enjoy an environment of security in a hopefully not too distant future.

4.2.9. ACKNOWLEDGMENTS

The authors appreciate the helpful comments of the reviewers. The field research was made possible by International Alert and Universität Hamburg. The overall work is supported through the Cluster of Excellence Integrated Climate System Analysis and Prediction (CliSAP), Universität Hamburg, funded by the German Science Foundation (DFG).

4.2.10. DISCUSSION QUESTIONS

1) Does resource scarcity lead to violent conflict? Why or why not?

Answer guide. No, resource scarcity does not necessarily lead to violent conflict. When trying to understand interactions between resources and conflict, one must always consider the specific context. In northwestern Kenya, for instance, some theories suggest that, in regular years, most raids happen during and around the rainy seasons, or in times of relative resource abundance. However, between 2006 and 2009, the drought year, 2009, was the one in which the most violence occurred. This suggests that extreme scarcity contributes to conflict, while the purpose of these "dry raids" (control over land and pasture) differs from "wet rains" (restocking of herds). The relationships between resources and conflict are hence more complex than one might expect.

2) What should the government of Kenya do to strengthen the environmental security of the pastoral communities in northwestern Kenya?

Answer guide. The chapter mentions that Turkana has been strongly neglected by the central government. This trend needs to be reversed. Based on the acknowledgement of pastoralism as a productive and suitable livelihood for the dry northwest of Kenya, the government should strengthen the capacity of the pastoral communities to adapt to the changing climatic conditions. As mobility is a key adaptation strategy, ensuring free and safe mobility for the pastoralists would be a promising entry point. Intercommunal peace meetings between the conflicting pastoral groups are likely to improve intercommunal trust and mitigate conflicts.

3) Is the discovery of oil a blessing or a curse for the pastoral communities in Turkana?

Answer guide. Arguments for a blessing are improved (road) infrastructure, some water provided by the oil company, and perhaps more attention paid to the region in general. However, the chapter gives the impression that the oil is more likely to be a curse for the pastoral communities, whose expectations for employment, water, and economic development have largely been disappointed so far. Loss of land and environmental pollution further increase the chances of oil being perceived as a curse, particularly in the long term.

4) What are the main drivers of the conflict between the pastoral communities and the operating oil company? Are developed countries responsible as well?

Answer guide. The main drivers are the disappointed community expectations for employment, water, and economic development. Developed countries consume huge amounts of oil. Without the global demand for oil, the oil reserves in Turkana would not be explored. We also know that the international community can strongly impact the workings of oil companies and national policies regarding oil investments. When we compare Turkana with Sudan, we can see how Russia and China have been instrumental in blocking UN legislation that would help stop genocide in Darfur in order to maintain their strong oil trade agreements with the Sudanese government. Thus, developed countries, and the citizens who live in these countries, are responsible both for educating themselves about the ramifications of international trade on local-level violent conflict and for influencing their political leaders to institute policies of trade that ensure human security in other areas.

REFERENCES

Barnett, J., R. Matthew, and K. O'Brian, 2010: Global environmental change and human security: An introduction. *Global Environmental Change and Human Security*, R. Matthew et al., Eds., MIT Press, 3–32.

Campbell, I., S. Dalrymple, R. Craig, and A. Crawford, 2009: Climate change and conflict: Lessons from community conservancies in northern Kenya. International Institute for Sustainable Development and Saferworld Rep., 62 pp., www.iisd.org/sites/default/files/publications/climate_change_conflict_kenya.pdf.

CEWARN, 2010: CEWARN country updates: September–December 2009. CEWARN Rep., 19 pp., www.cewarn.org/index.php/reports/archived-early-warning-reports/alerts/uga-1/2009-4/42-uga-sept-dec09/file.

Cline, W., 2007: *Global Warming and Agriculture: Impact Estimates by Country*. Center for Global Development, 250 pp.

Daily Nation, 2013: Turkana MP under probe over riots against Tullow Oil firm. Daily Nation, www.nation.co.ke/news/MP-under-probe-over-Turkana-riots/1056-2053848-1o796jz/index.html.

Dalby, S., 2009: *Security and Environmental Change*. Polity Press, 197 pp.

Eaton, D., 2010: The rise of the 'traider': The commercialization of raiding in Karamoja. *Nomadic Peoples*, **14**, 106–122, https://doi.org/10.3167/np.2010.140207.

Eriksen, S., and J. Lind, 2009: Adaptation as a political

process: Adjusting to drought and conflict in Kenya's drylands. *Environ. Manage.*, **43**, 817–835, https://doi.org/10.1007/s00267-008-9189-0.

Government of Kenya, 2007: National policy for the sustainable development of arid and semi-arid lands. Government of Kenya Rep., 73 pp.

Homer-Dixon, T., 1994: Environmental scarcities and violent conflict: Evidence from cases. *Int. Secur.*, **19** (1), 5–40.

——, 1999: *Environmental Scarcity and Violence*. Princeton University Press, 253 pp.

——, and T. Deligiannis, 2009: Environmental scarcities and civil violence. *Facing Global Environmental Change*, H. G. Brauch et al., Eds., Springer, 309–323.

Human Rights Watch, 2015: "There is No Time Left": Climate change, environmental threats, and human rights in Turkana County, Kenya. Human Rights Watch Rep., 15 pp., www.hrw.org/sites/default/files/report_pdf/kenya1015_brochure_web.pdf.

Ide, T., J. Schilling, J. S. A. Link, J. Scheffran, G. Ngaruiya, and T. Weinzierl, 2014: On exposure, vulnerability and violence: Spatial distribution of risk factors for climate change and violent conflict across Kenya and Uganda. *Polit. Geogr.*, **43** (1), 68–81, https://doi.org/10.1016/j.polgeo.2014.10.007.

IPCC, 2013: *Climate Change 2013: The Physical Science Basis*. Cambridge University Press, 1535 pp., https://doi.org/10.1017/CBO9781107415324.

Kenya Open Data, 2011a: Poverty. ArcGIS Hub, accessed 1 October, www.opendata.go.ke/Poverty/Poverty-Rate-by-District/i5bp-z9aq.

——, 2011b: School attendance. ArcGIS Hub, accessed 24 June 2015, www.opendata.go.ke/Counties/2009-Census-Vol-II-Table-1-Population-3-years-and-/jkkd-epmw.

——, 2012: Employment. ArcGIS Hub, accessed 24 June 2015, www.opendata.go.ke/Employment/2009-Census-Vol-II-Table-4-Activity-Status-by-dist/c3yj-8gpj.

Khagram, S., and S. Ali, 2006: Environment and security. *Annu. Rev. Environ. Resour.*, **31**, 395–411, https://doi.org/10.1146/annurev.energy.31.042605.134901.

——, W. Clark, and D. F. Raad, 2003: From the environment and human security to sustainable security and development. *J. Hum. Dev.*, **4**, 289–313, https://doi.org/10.1080/1464988032000087604.

King, G., and C. J. L. Murray, 2001: Rethinking human security. *Polit. Sci. Quart.*, **116**, 585–610, https://doi.org/10.2307/798222.

KNBS, 2010: 2009 Kenya population and housing census. KNBS, 74 pp.

Malthus, T. R., 1798: *An Essay on the Principle of Population*. St. Paul's Church-Yard, 134 pp.

McSweeney, C., M. New, and G. Lizcano, 2012: UNDP climate change country profiles: Kenya. UN Development Programme Rep., 26 pp., www.geog.ox.ac.uk/research/climate/projects/undp-cp/UNDP_reports/Kenya/Kenya.lowres.report.pdf.

Meier, P., D. Bond, and J. Bond, 2007: Environmental influences on pastoral conflict in the Horn of Africa. *Polit. Geogr.*, **26**, 716–735, https://doi.org/10.1016/j.polgeo.2007.06.001.

Nairobi News, 2015: Nairobi and Turkana to get biggest share of county cash. Nairobi News, http://nairobinews.nation.co.ke/nairobi-and-turkana-to-get-biggest-share-of-county-cash/.

Opiyo, F., O. Wasonga, M. Nyangito, J. Schilling, and R. Munang, 2015: Drought adaptation and coping strategies among the Turkana pastoralists of northern Kenya. *Int. J. Disaster Risk Sci.*, **6**, 295–309, https://doi.org/10.1007/s13753-015-0063-4.

Pike, I. L., B. Straight, M. Oesterle, C. Hilton, and A. Lanyasunya, 2010: Documenting the health consequences of endemic warfare in three pastoralist communities of northern Kenya: A conceptual framework. *Soc. Sci. Med.*, **70**, 45–52, https://doi.org/10.1016/j.socscimed.2009.10.007.

PRB, 2015: 2015 world population data sheet. PRB Rep., 23 pp., https://assets.prb.org/pdf15/2015-world-population-data-sheet_eng.pdf.

Saha, S., 2012: Security implications of climate refugees in urban slums: A case study from Dhaka, Bangladesh. *Climate Change, Human Security and Violent Conflict: Challenges for Societal Stability*, J. Scheffran et al., Eds., Hexagon Series on Human and Environmental Security and Peace, Vol. 8, Springer, 595–611.

Salih, A. A. M., H. Körnich, and M. Tjernström, 2013: Climate impact of deforestation over South Sudan in a regional climate model. *Int. J. Climatol.*, **33**, 2362–2375, https://doi.org/10.1002/joc.3586.

Scheffran, J., M. Brzoska, J. Kominek, P. M. Link, and J. Schilling, 2012a: Climate change and violent conflict. *Science*, **336**, 869–871, https://doi.org/10.1126/science.1221339.

——, ——, ——, ——, and ——, 2012b: Disentangling the climate-conflict nexus: Empirical and theoretical assessment of vulnerabilities and pathways. *Rev. Eur. Stud.*, **4** (5), 1–13, https://doi.org/10.5539/res.v4n5p1.

——, P. M. Link, and J. Schilling, 2012c: Theories and models of climate-security interaction: Framework and application to a climate hot spot in North Africa. *Climate Change, Human Security and Violent Conflict: Challenges for Societal Stability*, J. Scheffran et al., Eds., Hexagon Series on Human and Environmental Security and Peace, Vol. 8, Springer, 91–131.

Schilling, J., 2012: On rains, raids and relations: A multimethod approach to climate change, vulnerability, adaptation and violent conflict in northern Africa and Kenya. Ph.D. dissertation, University of Hamburg, 241 pp., http://ediss.sub.uni-hamburg.de/volltexte/2012/5748/pdf/Dissertation.pdf.

——, F. Opiyo, and J. Scheffran, 2012: Raiding pastoral livelihoods: Motives and effects of violent conflict in north-western Kenya. *Pastoralism*, **2**, 25, https://doi.org/10.1186/2041-7136-2-25.

——, M. Akuno, J. Scheffran, and T. Weinzierl, 2014: On raids and relations: Climate change, pastoral conflict and adaptation in northwestern Kenya. *Conflict-Sensitive Adaptation to Climate Change in Africa*, U. Bob and S. Bronkhorst, Eds., Berliner Wissenschafts-verlag, 241–268.

——, R. Locham, T. Weinzierl, J. Vivekananda, and J. Scheffran, 2015: The nexus of oil, conflict, and climate change vulnerability of pastoral communities in northwest Kenya. *Earth Syst. Dyn.*, **6**, 703–717, https://doi.org/10.5194/esd-6-703-2015.

Schmidhuber, J., and F. Tubiello, 2007: Global food security under climate change. *Proc. Natl. Acad. Sci. USA*, **104**, 192703–192708, https://doi.org/10.1073/pnas.0701976104.

Steffen, W., and Coauthors, 2011: The Anthropocene: From global change to planetary stewardship. *Ambio*, **40**, 739–761, https://doi.org/10.1007/s13280-011-0185-x.

Suranovic, S., 2013: Fossil fuel addiction and the implications for climate change policy. *Global Environ. Change*, **23**, 598–608, https://doi.org/10.1016/j.gloenvcha.2013.02.006.

Tullow Oil, 2014: East Africa: Kenya. Tullow Oil, www.tullowoil.com/operations/east-africa/kenya.

TUPADO, 2011: Turkana Pastoralist Organization incident register 2000–2010. TUPADO Rep.

Tutiempo, 2011: The weather in cities of Kenya. Tutiempo, www.tutiempo.net/en/Weather/Kenya/KE.html.

UNOCHA, 2011: Humanitarian report eastern Africa: Nairobi. UNOCHA Rep., Vol. 3, 11 pp.

Vasquez, P. I., 2013: Kenya at a crossroads: Hopes and fears concerning the development of oil and gas reserves. *Int. Dev. Policy*, **4** (3), 3–26, https://doi.org/10.4000/poldev.1646.

Vivekananda, J., J. Schilling, S. Mitra, and N. Pandey, 2014: On shrimp, salt and security: Livelihood risks and responses in south Bangladesh and east India. *Environ. Dev. Sustainability*, **16**, 1141–1161, https://doi.org/10.1007/s10668-014-9517-x.

von Uexkull, N., 2014: Sustained drought, vulnerability and civil conflict in sub-Saharan Africa. *Polit. Geogr.*, **43**, 16–26, https://doi.org/10.1016/j.polgeo.2014.10.003.

Witsenburg, K., and W. Adano, 2009: Of rain and raids: Violent livestock raiding in northern Kenya. *Civ. Wars*, **11**, 514–538, https://doi.org/10.1080/13698240903403915.

World Energy Council, 2015: Energy resources: Coal. World Energy Council, www.worldenergy.org/data/resources/resource/coal/.

4.3

U.S. MILITARY STRATEGY AND ARCTIC CLIMATE CHANGE

Tobias T. Gibson

4.3.1. OVERVIEW

Throughout this case study, students will gain an understanding of

- how environmental changes related to global climate change affect conflicts in the Arctic,
- how conflict impacts national and human security in regions making claims over Artic resources,
- how national military engagement is likely to change because of shifts in the Arctic climate, and
- how international law regarding naval operations should receive further consideration by the United States to ensure future human security domestically and internationally.

4.3.2. INTRODUCTION

In recent years, there has been a massive retreat of the Arctic ice, which has led to a scramble—politically, diplomatically, scientifically, economically, and importantly, militarily—between competing nations and interests in the Arctic Circle. In the United States, unlike most of the developed world, there is a political debate about global climate change and its impact on the nation and world. This chapter takes a position similar to former U.S. Northern Command (NORTHCOM) and North American Aerospace Defense Command (NORAD) commander General Charles Jacoby, who in a 2014 speech about Arctic ice said that he "doesn't care why it's melting. It's melting." General Jacoby went further and noted that Russia's military is now more active in the Arctic than it had been in several decades (Gibson 2014).

This chapter proceeds as follows: First, evidence of a massive ice melt will be marshaled to illustrate the importance of the climate change in the Arctic Circle. Second, recent diplomatic developments between the five Arctic littoral states and other interested nations will be discussed in the context of the breadth of global interest in the melting Arctic. Third, the military activities of competing nations will be discussed at some length, with an eye toward Russia, the primary historical antagonist to the United States and her allies. There is then a brief section on the importance of the UN Convention on the Law of the Sea (UNCLOS) and why the United States should become a signatory member. Finally, the chapter concludes with an eye toward the future, and potential complications facing the Arctic, and the United States interests within the area.

4.3.3. RECENT ICE MELT IN THE ARCTIC

In recent years, there has been a massive ice melt in the Arctic (Figure 4.3.1). While there is some debate about the reasons for this melt, the fact that the ice is melting is indisputable (O'Rourke 2015, 16–19). The results of the ice melt have led to increased activity by cooperating and competing nations in the region.

In the United States, the political debate over climate change generally and Arctic ice melt specifically has led to "politicized science." Many U.S. politicians, especially those on the political right, have made a career of publicly questioning climate change and thwarting proposed policies intended to limit the impact of these changes. While these denials occasionally rise to humorous interpretations (Colbert 2014), politicians ignore the preponderance of scientific evidence of global climate change, which may lead to dire consequences of human, homeland, and national security.

The vast majority of scientists and nations have noted not only that climate change is occurring but that it can and will impact security. Scientists fear that climate change will impact, and in fact already has impacted, security in a variety of ways. Retired U.S. Navy Admiral David Titley, who is a leading expert on security and the climate, in a speech at Westminster College in Fulton, Missouri, noted that evidence of global climate change can be seen in the consistent decrease of Arctic ice since at least 1980. He also noted that, in the same period, the number of weather related catastrophes has increased (Titley 2015).

A recent paper (Strauss et al. 2015, p. 132508) notes that "substantial research indicates that contemporary carbon emissions, even if stopped abruptly, will sustain or nearly sustain near-term temperature increases *for millennia* [emphasis added] because of the long residence time of carbon dioxide in the atmosphere and inertia in the climate system." Thus, according to current research, even if in the best-case scenario in which a vast amount of carbon emissions ended immediately, the damage wrought would likely extend and expand for thousands of years. The authors suggest that this will lead to the submersion of several U.S. population centers, including New York City and Boston, over the next century.

The impact of carbon emissions is especially troublesome in the Arctic, because the Arctic ice is younger and thinner than the ice in Antarctica, which makes it more likely to melt. As the ice melts, the region becomes more at risk for continued, increased ice melting because of the diminishment of the cooling white ice and the increased exposure of the dark land and sea—both of which then absorb solar radiation (Titley and St. John 2010).

4.3.4. ECONOMIC IMPACTS OF THE OPENING OF THE ARCTIC

As the Government Accountability Office (GAO) noted, "melting ice could potentially increase the use of three trans-Arctic routes: the Northern Sea Route, Northwest Passage, and Transpolar Route, saving several thousands of miles and several days of sailing between major trading blocs" (GAO 2015, p. 7). The opening of the Northern Sea Route (NSR) would allow goods to be shipped from Europe to Asia much more quickly and efficiently. For example, the current route from Rotterdam, Netherlands, to Yokohama, Japan, through the Suez and the Indian Ocean to Japan is 11,200 nautical miles. The NSR would allow goods between those cities to be shipped along a route of only 6,500 nautical miles (Borgerson 2008).

This boon to the shipping industry comes with accompanying perils, however. One such issue is the likelihood of invasive species taken along for the ride as ships cut through the northern shipping routes. There is concern that as species are introduced to a region where they have never appeared, there will be enormous biological complications. According to Lewis Kizka, of the U.S. Department of Agriculture, invasive species can "use

Figure 4.3.1. Walt Meier, National Aeronautics and Space Administration. Adapted from dataset sea ice index: Shows the total ice reduction from 1979–2000 as nearly 50% of total ice coverage.

up the lion's share of resources, and whatever biodiversity that was there falls apart" [as quoted in Palmer (2013)].

Greenland's climate has become much milder, leading to a farming boom, including seasons allowing for crops such as broccoli and hay (Borgerson 2008). Indeed, as fossil fuel riches are discovered, and Greenland becomes increasingly independent of Denmark, "Greenland might well become the first country born from climate change" (Borgerson 2013, p. 85). And there are several other economic boons likely awaiting the Arctic. Previously remote outposts, such as Anchorage, Alaska, and Reykjavik, Iceland, "could someday become major shipping centers and financial capitals—the high-latitude equivalents of Singapore and Dubai" (Borgerson 2013, p. 78). The region's geography may offer vast opportunities for hydropower development, and an increasingly mild environment may offer highly secure data storage centers (Borgerson 2013, p. 81–82).

The opening of the Arctic may lead to a boon in many sectors. The Arctic is home to about 13% of the world's petroleum reserves. The U.S. exclusive economic zone (EEZ) may hold billions of barrels of oil and massive amounts of natural gas reserves. The world's oil companies have already begun to see the region as a new source of untold revenue (Titley and St. John 2010).

4.3.5. THE ARCTIC AND U.S. SECURITY

In 2007, the "Maritime Strategy" released jointly by the Navy, Marine Corps, and Coast Guard noted that "climate change is gradually opening up the waters of the Arctic, not only to new resource development, but also to new shipping routes that may reshape the global transport system. While these opportunities offer potential for growth, they are potential sources of competition and conflict for access and natural resources" [as quoted in Titley and St. John (2010, p. 42)].

Thus, from a national security perspective, the overwhelming consensus of scientific research suggests that the United States take the Arctic ice melt and all of the threats and opportunities seriously going forward. It is time for the United States to act and plan with an eye toward the impacts of an opening Arctic. Yet even climate change deniers should take lessons from military leaders. As noted above, former NORTHCOM commander General Charles Jacoby suggests that the ice melt has already afforded the Russians opportunity in the Arctic. Retired

U.S. Navy Admiral Titley, too, has concerns over U.S. national security because of global climate change, noting that there are several pieces of evidence that indicate that the world's climate is changing and that there is a particularly disruptive change in the Arctic (Titley 2015).

Retired U.S. General Gordon R. Sullivan, former member of the Joint Chiefs of Staff, has stated that "people are saying they want to be perfectly convinced about climate science projections. . . . But speaking as a soldier, we never have 100 percent certainty. If you wait until you have 100 percent certainty, something bad is going to happen on the battlefield" [as quoted in Femia and Werrell (2014)]. In an April 2015 press briefing, the then–NORTHCOM and NORAD commander Admiral Bill Gortney echoed his predecessor by saying about the Arctic that "there's going to be more activity up there, and it's actually more dangerous today than when we had a stable shelf [prior to the massive reduction of ice]" [Department of Defense (DoD) 2015]. Huebert (2011, p. 205) notes succinctly that "it is clear that the Arctic is about to be a much more significant region in the international system."

It is revealing that the United States seems to be ill prepared on this front. Regional competitors, and some genuine foes, have spent much more time and resources preparing for the security threats of the future than the United States. For example, Russia, which has the most Arctic coastline of any of the Arctic nations, has 41 commissioned ice breakers and plans to build 11 more; Canada has about a dozen. China and South Korea, both non-Arctic states, have new ice breakers. As of late 2015, the U.S. Coast Guard had three icebreakers—two of which were commissioned in 1976—one of which experienced massive engine failure and has not been active since 2011 (Borgerson 2013; Davis 2015). In September 2015, while visiting Alaska, President Barack Obama suggested that new ice breakers be built and put into service by 2020. Republican Senator Dan Sullivan (Alaska) responded that "the highways of the Arctic are paved by icebreakers. Right now, the Russians have superhighways, and we have dirt roads with potholes" (Davis 2015). Russia's massive military presence is intended to further its economic claims over Arctic natural resources and mineral and territory rights (Ramsay and O'Sullivan 2013).

Although the United States thus far has been slow to respond to Arctic threats in some ways, it has not been completely inactive. In 2012, the United States buttressed its Arctic relationship with Canada by signing the Tri-Command Framework for Arctic Cooperation between the militaries of both countries. According to the Department of Defense, the agreement allows "the U.S. and Canadian militaries [to] support other departments and agencies in response to regional threats and hazards" (Miles 2012); however, little more has been done to ensure North American influence in the region. If the United States continues, its lack of action, preparation, and vision in the Arctic "will leave the United States playing a game of strategic catch-up or worse" (Rosenberg et al. 2014, p. 1).

Arctic Zephyr, a joint search-and-rescue (SAR) training exercise with United States, Canada, Denmark, Finland, Iceland, Norway, and Sweden, illustrates the need for continued and increased cooperative actions in the Arctic region. According to the Coast Guard (2015),

> The objectives of Arctic Zephyr were to advance the understanding of Arctic nations' SAR capabilities and the means for coordination, and command and control among mission partners and relevant stakeholders; to identify and recommend improvements for coordination and interoperability; to identify the challenges associated with increased human access and environmental changes and their impact on international Arctic SAR operations; to evaluate the complexities involved in conducting remote mass search and rescue operations; and to develop a core set of implementation recommendations to be presented to the Arctic Council.

While clearly important, Arctic Zephyr was intended as a civilian training exercise, and some pundits and national security professionals have expressed some concern over the lack of joint military training with a similar international community. Russia was not a part of this exercise.

It is worth noting, however, that the United States, Canada, and Denmark, all founding members of NATO, have "come together" in an effort to buttress military capabilities in the north (O'Rourke 2015a, p. 57), including increased spending on naval capacity in the Arctic, placing command centers in the region, and working to improve already standing relationships. The U.S. European Command (EUCOM) helped to establish the Arctic Security Forces Roundtable, which is composed of senior officers from the Arctic Council, France, Germany, the Netherlands, and the United Kingdom (O'Rourke 2015, p. 58). Norway, too, has moved toward considering the Arctic as a "strategic balcony" and has a keen national interest in its resources and playing a role in managing those resources (Flikke 2011, p. 73).

Moreover, Presidents George W. Bush and Barack Obama have issued directives related to Arctic security. National Security Presidential Directive 66, issued by President Bush in 2009, makes the Departments of Defense and Homeland Security jointly responsible for implementing the nation's Arctic security plan, including missile defense, maritime presence, and preserving the free navigation and overflight of the region (GAO 2015).

The number of stakeholders in the Arctic region underscores the complex issues facing the U.S. interests in the Arctic. The following U.S. agencies have a role in protecting the national interests in the Arctic Circle:

- the Navy, as the primary protector of waterways globally;
- NORTHCOM and NORAD, a joint defensive venture of the United States and Canada;
- EUCOM and U.S. Pacific Command (USPACOM), because of the actors in the Arctic, including Norway, Denmark, China, and India;
- the Coast Guard, the primary agency for the Department of Homeland Security (DHS) in the region;
- the Department of State, which intercedes diplomatically with Canada, the four other littoral Arctic nations, and U.S. regional allies and competitors;
- and, finally, diverse groups including the National Science Foundation, which is responsible for scientific research in the region (GAO 2015, 10–12).

Moreover, because of threats posed by Russia and China in the Arctic, the U.S. intelligence community (IC) is becoming increasingly interested and active in the region. The majority of the agencies in the IC have analysts responsible for the region, analyzing data collected from U.S. satellite imagery and Navy sensors and also collected from allied intelligence services, including at least Canadian and Norwegian resources (Bennett and Hennigan 2015).

National security threats stem from global climate change; thus, the subsequent opening of the Arctic will likely pose threats to the United States. As the ice melts, sea lanes that heretofore were not navigable become available to both private sector shipping and military forces; not all of these military forces and private sector businesses implement policies supporting global human security, U.S. national security, or economic security interests. Thus, there results a heightened probability for a diplomatic or even military crisis as states compete for resources, populations shift, and unknown future threats arise. There is no doubt that the ice melt due to climate change will result in the Arctic being a point of increased contention between other states globally. Even now, Arctic states, non-Arctic states, and global industries are laying the foundations to benefit from the opening sea lanes and access to natural resources.

Russia, already the "pre-eminent power in the High North" (Rosenberg et al. 2014, p. 1), has become much more active in the region in past decade. The military threats introduced in the quotes by General Jacoby and Admiral Gortney are illustrative of the threat posed by Russia's increased military interest in the Arctic. But the threats go much deeper. In 2001, Russia attempted to claim a 460,000-square-mile region in the Arctic. Although rebuffed by the United Nations, Russia then staked its claim by planting its flag at the bottom of the Arctic Ocean and flew bombers over the region for the first time since the conclusion of the Cold War. Russia is also actively conducting exercises in the region—including one in 2015 that included nearly 40,000 servicemen, 50 or more surface ships and submarines, and 110 aircraft (BBC 2015). In addition, Russia has reopened at least 10 bases and 14 airfields on the Arctic seaboard and is building more nuclear-powered submarines with the intention to use them in Arctic regions (Bennett and Hennigan 2015). Russia's interest in the Arctic, when coupled with the continued dispute with the United States over areas in the Bering Sea (GAO 2015), and increasingly hostile actions toward the United States and her NATO allies, including Turkey, Syria, Crimea, and Ukraine, suggest the severity of volatile issues facing the United States and Russia globally. This is not merely a hypothetical issue: Canada boycotted an Arctic Council meeting held in Moscow to protest Russian annexation of portions of Ukraine (Rosenberg et al. 2014, p. 4; O'Rourke 2015a, pp. 53 and 60). The cold relationship between Russia and NATO is especially troubling because, in 2009, Russia informed NATO that it would not work with the security organization in the Arctic.

And, in 2010, then-President Medvedev said that Russia "views [possible NATO] activity [in the Arctic] with quite serious tension" [as quoted in O'Rourke (2015, p. 59)]. Other scholars note that the Russian disagreements with the United States and NATO—even prior to incursions into Crimea, Ukraine, and Syria—over NATO enlargement and the reaction of these nations to the Russian war with Georgia, "have had ripple effects on perceptions of the state of security . . . in the Arctic," and helps to explain the massive Russian military interest in the Arctic (Zysk 2011, p. 90).

China, too, has begun to flex its muscle by expanding into the Arctic. China is "challenging American military maritime supremacy" (Cassotta et. al 2015, p. 201), including in the Arctic. This has been done in a myriad of ways, including an increased presence in the region and achieving permanent participant status in the Arctic Council (Cassotta et. al 2015). In addition, China is trumpeting a claim that the Arctic is part of the "global commons" and as such nations cannot have sovereignty claims (O'Rourke 2015a, p. 54). In an effort, perhaps, to hedge its bets on the sovereignty claims, China has been aided, in part, in furthering its interest in the Arctic by Russia. In 2013, the two nations announced that China would be granted exploration rights in the Arctic in exchange for purchasing oil from Russia (O'Rourke 2015, p. 52).

The opening of the Arctic also has future homeland security implications, especially in light of increased shipping and tourism. As with existing border security issues in the U.S. Southwest, for example, the porous borders of Alaska, which are now largely unregulated and open (Rosenberg et al. 2015) will have to be secured. This is an area where little research has been done, and therefore, we can only hypothesize that refugees, traffickers, and other illegal activities will increase as sea ice melts, further challenging both national and international laws.

4.3.6. THE ARCTIC AND UNCLOS

The UNCLOS was negotiated in 1982 and took effect in 1994. Part VI of the convention is the most relevant portion of the agreement regarding disputes in the Arctic. UNCLOS gives resource rights to the coastal state of its coastal shelf. Because of the receding ice, continently shelves are becoming much more accessible. The United

States abides by the Law of the Sea Convention (Titley and St. John 2010, p. 40), but Congress has yet to fully ratify the treaty. Nonetheless, the Obama administration announced the national strategy for the Arctic region in 2013; this piece of policy includes goals of protecting the Arctic environment, enhancing security in the region, and accession to UNCLOS (O'Rourke 2015, p. 55). Perhaps, this is due to the fact that "[t]he convention advances and protects the national security, environmental, and economic interests of all nations . . . codifying the navigational rights and freedoms that are critical to American military and commercial vessels" (Titley and St. John 2010, p. 40).

The accession to joining the Law of the Sea Convention would support the U.S. regional goals. As a UNCLOS nonmember state, the United States is unable to submit sovereignty claims nor act as a member of the Commission on the Limits of the Continental Shelf, the decision-making body of UNCLOS regarding sovereignty issues. Thus, the United States is doubly disadvantaged in the Arctic as sovereignty claims, and therefore resource claims, are made (Titley and St. John 2010, 14–15). This is important to keep in mind as Russia makes broad sovereignty claims (Zysk 2011) and China claims use of Arctic passages based on the Arctic being part of the global commons (Cassotta et al. 2015).

Additionally, the United States has no legal recourse if any UNCLOS member state denies its scientists access to waters in a claimed EEZ (Rosenberg et al. 2014). Recent support for joining the UNCLOS has come from the previous and current presidential administrations, military service chiefs, and many corporations (Borgerson 2008, p. 64), so perhaps the time is nigh in which the Senate will allow the United States to be a signatory to the convention.

4.3.7. CONCLUSIONS

As the Arctic continues to open because of massive ice melt in the region, there are both promises and perils for the United States that are directly and indirectly tied to the region. While the adapted climate in the High North will offer economic benefits, including shortened shipping routes, access to resources, and increased tourism, these benefits come with pitfalls. The Alaskan border as entry into the country, increased conflict over shipping lanes with adversarial nations, additional biological

impact due to increased shipping, the likelihood of oil spills, and heightened security threats such as piracy and shipwrecks are all examples of security considerations in the Arctic Circle as sea lanes open and remain open year-round in the future. While most security experts doubt that there will be war in the Arctic (Kraska 2011), it should be noted that adversarial countries such as China and Russia, countries with which the United States is contending with in the South China Sea, the Middle East, eastern Europe, and in cyberspace, are active in the Arctic and seek to become even more so.

Although the United States recently has begun to take steps to secure its interests in the region, by formalizing the lead stakeholders in the region, by working closely with allies in a variety of contexts, and by providing guiding documents for the region moving forward, the United States lags behind the Arctic states in important ways. The number of operational icebreakers is woeful, and the Obama administration's move to build another and move its commission date forward was a step in the right direction but fails to address the shortcoming between U.S. capability and that of Russia, Canada, and even China.

The United States needs to be cognizant of potential conflict with Canada over the sovereignty of the Northwest Passage and other trappings as the Arctic opens. There are also decades-old issues that remain unresolved, such as Russia's Cold War–era dumping of 18 nuclear reactors in the Arctic Ocean and the need to clean up this travesty, as well as consideration for the rights of the indigenous peoples in the region (Borgerson 2008, 72–75; Kraska 2007, pp. 262, 267).

The unwillingness of the Senate to accept the UNCLOS is another reason why the United States is at a disadvantage as the Arctic region opens to the rest of the world. It is time that the Senate make the United States a party to the convention, or the United States will continue to lack the full resources of the UNCLOS—despite already recognizing its governing provisions.

Finally, it is time that the U.S. government as a whole recognizes that the climate is changing and that humans have agency to mitigate this change. It is not enough that the military is trying to plan for the future. The current and future presidents and members of Congress must recognize that the United States can and should play a role in limiting and preventing future climate change. As noted above, even if the United States and the rest of the world act now, the impact may not be felt for thousands of years.

4.3.8. DISCUSSION QUESTIONS

1) What are the short-term promises and perils in the Artic?

Answer guide. In the short term, the environmental change in the Arctic suggests that natural resources that were previously unavailable are now accessible to the global community. Oil, minerals, diamonds, and farmland in Greenland may benefit the world as energy sources become scarce and as the global population increases and needs new food sources. Shorter shipping routes may lead to economic benefits as goods become less expensive and arrive earlier. On the other hand, there are biological concerns associated with increasing the world's supply of fossil fuels, as use of these fuels contribute to the warming globe. Easier shipping may impact invasive species and lead to security issues such as piracy and conflicts between nations. Perhaps most importantly, the opening Arctic provides another region in which already adversarial relations between Russia, China, the United States, and Canada, among others, may lead to conflict or serve to exacerbate historical rivalries.

2) Describe the relationships of states interested in having an Arctic footprint.

Answer guide. On the one hand, many of the states already have strong relationships. Four of the five Arctic states—the United States, Canada, Norway, and Denmark—are members of NATO and have joint operations in the Arctic. Russia has good ties with China, who has a strong interest in the Arctic region. Russia and Norway also have taken steps to ameliorate their relationship and act cooperatively in the Arctic. On the other hand, both Russia and China have made sovereignty claims in the region that are counter to the U.S. interests in the region, including the extraordinary step of Russia planting a flag on the seabed. Moreover, even traditional allies have some competing claims in the region, including the Canadian claim that the Northwest Passage is Canadian only rather than open for general global use. In short, the Arctic remains a very complex region, in which many states have competing interests that are difficult to resolve because it has historically been nearly inaccessible.

3) What steps can the United States take to remain a key player in the Arctic?

Answer guide. There are at least three issues that the United States must resolve as the Arctic melts. First, while the United States globally has the most powerful navy, U.S. Arctic assets are woefully behind Russia and Canada and at best equal to nations such as China and South Korea—neither of which is actually an Arctic state. Second, the United States needs to accede to the UNCLOS so that it can use the relationship to make claims and, even more importantly, play a role in official decisions when competing nations such as Russia and China make claims that are contrary to U.S. and global interests. Finally, the U.S. citizenry and politicians need to take science seriously and understand that the climate is changing and that the United States must play a major role in mitigating future climate disasters and responding to those that occur.

REFERENCES

BBC, 2015: Russia makes renewed bid for contentious Arctic regions. BBC, accessed 7 August 2015, www.bbc.com/news/world-europe-33777492.

Bennett, B., and W. J. Hennigan, 2015: U.S. builds up Arctic spy network as Russia and China increase presence. *Los Angeles Times*, 7 September, www.latimes.com/world/europe/la-fg-arctic-spy-20150907-story.html.

Borgerson, S. G., 2008: Arctic meltdown: The economic and security implications of global warming. *Foreign Aff.*, **87** (2), 63–77, www.foreignaffairs.com/articles/arctic-antarctic/2008-03-02/arctic-meltdown.

——, 2013: The coming Arctic boom: As the ice melts, the region heats up. *Foreign Aff.*, **92** (4), 76–89, www.foreignaffairs.com/articles/global-commons/2013-06-11/coming-arctic-boom.

Cassotta, S., K. Hossain, J. Ren, and M. E. Goodsite, 2015: Climate change and China as a global emerging regulatory sea power in the Arctic Ocean: Is China a threat for Arctic Ocean security? *Beijing Law Rev.*, **6**, 199–207, https://doi.org/10.4236/blr.2015.63020.

Coast Guard, 2015: U.S. Coast Guard and federal partners lead Arctic search-and-rescue exercise. Coast Guard News, https://coastguardnews.com/coast-guard-and-federal-partners-lead-arctic-search-and-rescue-exercise/2015/10/28/.

Colbert, S., 2014: The Republicans inspiring climate change message. *The Colbert Report*, season 11, episode 20, accessed 30 November 2015, www.cc.com/video-clips/sc6mpp/the-colbert-report-the-republicans--inspiring-climate-change-message.

Davis, J. H., 2015. Obama calls for more Coast Guard icebreakers to gain foothold in Arctic. *New York Times*, 2 September, A17.

DoD, 2015: Department of Defense press briefing by Admiral Gortney in the Pentagon briefing room. Department of Defense, https://dod.defense.gov/News/Transcripts/Transcript-View/Article/607034/department-of-defense-press-briefing-by-admiral-gortney-in-the-pentagon-briefin/.

Femia, F., and C. E. Werrell, 2014: Climate and security 101: Why the U.S. national security establishment takes climate change seriously. Center for Climate and Security Rep. 23, 4 pp.

Flikke, G., 2011: Norway and the Arctic: Between multilateral governance and geopolitics. *Arctic Security in an Age of Climate Change*, J. Kraska, Ed., Cambridge University Press, 64–84.

GAO, 2015: Arctic planning: DOD expects to play a supporting role to other federal agencies and has efforts under way to address capability needs and update plans. GEO Rep. GAO-15-566, 50 pp., www.gao.gov/products/GAO-15-566.

Gibson, T. T., 2014: Threats facing the homeland. The Hill, accessed 28 November 2015, http://thehill.com/blogs/pundits-blog/defense/220482-threats-facing-the-homeland.

Huebert, R., 2011: Canada and the newly emerging international Arctic security regime. *Arctic Security in an Age of Climate Change*, J. Kraska, Ed., Cambridge University Press, 193–217.

Kraska, J., 2007: The Law of the Sea Convention and the Northwest Passage. *Int. J. Mar. Coastal Law*, **22**, 257–281, https://doi.org/10.1163/157180807781361467.

——, 2011. The new Arctic geography and U.S. strategy. *Arctic Security in an Age of Climate Change*, J. Kraska,

Ed., Cambridge University Press, 244–266.

Miles, D., 2012: U.S., Canada expand Arctic cooperation, military training. Department of Defense, accessed 7 August 2015, http://archive.defense.gov/news/newsarticle.aspx?id=118768.

O'Rourke, R., 2015: Changes in the Arctic: Background and issues for Congress. Congressional Research Service Rep. R41153, 105 pp., https://www.hsdl.org/?abstract&did=813513.

Palmer, L., 2013: Melting ice will make way for more ships—And more species invasions. Scientific American, accessed 7 August 2015, www.scientificamerican.com/article/melting-arctic-sea-ice-means-more-shipping-and-more-invasive-species/.

Ramsay, J. D., and T. M. O'Sullivan, 2013: There's a pattern here: The case to integrate environmental security into homeland security. *Homeland Secur. Aff.*, **9**, 6, https://www.hsaj.org/articles/246.

Rosenberg, E., D. Titley, and A. Wiker, 2014: Arctic 2015 and beyond: A strategy for U.S. leadership in the High North. Center for a New American Security Rep., 13 pp., https://www.cnas.org/publications/reports/arctic-2015-and-beyond-a-strategy-for-u-s-leadership-in-the-high-north.

Strauss, B. H., S. Kulp, A. Levermann, 2015: Carbon choices determine US cities committed to futures below sea level. *Proc. Natl. Acad. Sci. USA*, **112**, 132508–132513, https://doi.org/10.1073/pnas.1511186112.

Titley, D., 2015: Climate change and security. C-SPAN, 3 October 2015, www.c-span.org/video/?328003-2/climate-change-security.

——, and C. St. John. 2010. Arctic security considerations and the U.S. Navy's roadmap for the Arctic. *Nav. War Coll. Rev.*, **63** (2), 5, https://digital-commons.usnwc.edu/nwc-review/vol63/iss2/5.

Zysk, K., 2011: Military aspects of Russia's Arctic policy: Hard power and natural resources. *Arctic Security in an Age of Climate Change*, J. Kraska, Ed., Cambridge University Press, 85–106.

5

CONCLUDING POINTS: INTEGRATING ENVIRONMENTAL SECURITY INTO NATIONAL SECURITY PLANNING

James D. Ramsay
John M. Lanicci
Elisabeth Hope Murray

5.1. INTRODUCTION

If you are reading this, it means that you have completed the materials in units 2–4 and are now attempting to "sum up" what you have covered and determine what may come next in your study of environmental security. You are not alone. It should be obvious to you by now that environmental security is an area that is difficult enough to define, much less implement into any type of policy-making apparatus. Yet in order for environmental security to have some relevance, it must find its way into the policy-making arena in a meaningful way, which is not as a "competitor" to traditional nation state–based notions of security but instead as a complement and "force multiplier" to them. Thus, we will spend this concluding unit discussing various ways of mainstreaming environmental security into the policy-making process. You may have your own ideas regarding the best ways to implement what you have learned in this text—if this is the case, then this text has accomplished its goal!

5.2. THE IMPORTANCE OF CLEAR DEFINITIONS FOR HOMELAND, NATIONAL, AND HUMAN SECURITY

The term *national security* does not generally have a universally accepted definition outside of the general understanding that it refers to the security and perpetuation of governmental institutions and can mean different things to different U.S. presidential administrations. Traditionally within U.S. political discourse, national security has largely been the domain of both the Department of Defense and the national intelligence community in concept and execution and has typically involved protecting U.S. interests from foreign threats (specifically military threats and by military means).

In a similar vein, the definition of *homeland security* has been relatively ill defined, as pointed out by Reese (2013). Reese goes on to state the critical importance of having a clearly defined concept in order to produce a viable security strategy and goes further by confirming earlier observations by Bellavita (2008) regarding the many and varied definitions of homeland security. An ill-defined concept such as homeland security presents challenges in describing how environmental security may relate to it. Presumably, since it is the domain of a separate U.S. federal department, homeland security has developed a different primary focus than that of national security. Since September 11th (and arguably before), the concept of homeland security seems to have been primarily concerned with domestic (i.e., civilian) safety and affairs; that is, homeland security seems to be more concerned with threats to public safety and civil security than with the security of the nation state itself.

If we also bring *human security* into the discussion, its core concepts challenge more traditional security norms (e.g., Furtado 2008; Newman 2010). As discussed in units 1 and 4, human security typically prioritizes individual security over the security of the state when individual rights are threatened by external factors. For example, human security would emphasize establishment of food and water, economic, and political security for the general population as critical mechanisms to achieve a more stable level of state security. Thus, human security can contain elements and objectives of both homeland (civil security/public safety) and national (security/stability of the nation state) security.

Regardless of whether the term security means or refers to the same thing when used in national security, homeland security, or human security contexts, any appropriate definition of environmental security should consider characteristics of both foreign and domestic threats articulated at multiple levels of social expression: individual, local, regional, state, and, particularly because of the transnational character of climatic events, international levels. That is, environmental security can help link the theoretical and operational concepts of national, homeland, and human security. Prevention, sustainability, and resilience will play a role in making countries more secure not just from the threats of international and domestic terrorism but also from the disruption to the economy and homeland security from catastrophic natural disasters (e.g., Flynn 2007).

It was not the intent of this book to define these terms in black and white but instead to point out the difficulties associated with arriving at a definition upon which everyone can agree. Even if there is dissent (and there will always be in a diverse political landscape), at least we have an established framework within which we can work and (hopefully) conduct a productive dialogue in the context of determining what belongs in working definitions for "environment" and "security" and what constitutes environmental security for the purposes of developing and implementing a viable national strategy. Having said this, we provide our thoughts on one possible way to incorporate environmental security into strategy development.

5.3. USING ENVIRONMENTAL SECURITY AS A "PROCESSOR" IN STRATEGY DEVELOPMENT

If we agree with the notion that a useful national security policy connects homeland with national security and includes elements of human security in its development, it is necessary to include factors that are common to these security domains. We believe that environmental security can serve as a "nexus" of sorts between these because of the number of different issues that environmental security touches.

In order to integrate environmental security into both homeland and national security strategic planning, we propose three important environmental security "policy principles" [taken from Lanicci et al. (2017)]:

1) Failure to secure the environment has the propensity to act as a threat multiplier, especially in fragile states or regions with pervasive conflict; knowing how to avoid or offset catastrophic environmental changes is in a nation's vital interest.

2) Environmental security may manifest differently across different states and macroregions; that is, failure to secure the environment may destabilize the political economy and more fragile livelihoods of less-developed countries, potentially leading to radicalization of the population, but may also act to create critical infrastructure vulnerabilities in more-developed countries.

3) Environmental security can be incorporated into both broad national security objectives as well as a long-term homeland security strategy that produces enhanced levels of human security.

While these principles may sound noble, there still is the question of how environmental security can provide a viable framework within which to develop security strategies. We present one possible way below.

Figure 5.1 illustrates one approach for integrating environmental security into strategic planning. We wish to acknowledge Bartholomees (2012), whose national strategy planning model used at the U.S. Army War College contributed important components to this diagram. The left side of Figure 5.1 begins with the high-level policy guidance directed by the Office of the President. Each government department has planners whose job is to develop long-range strategies for action consistent with presidential guidance and any legal directives driving the department. We propose to incorporate major compo-

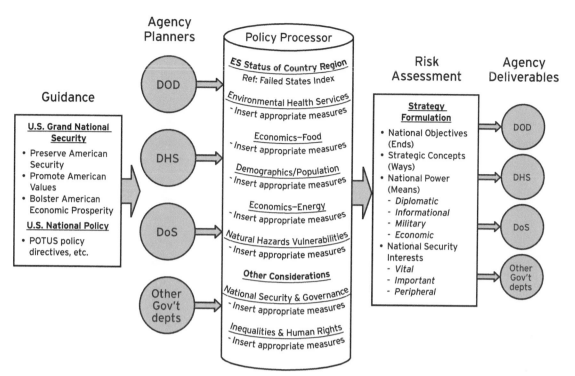

Figure 5.1. Strategic planning model incorporating elements of the Army War College strategy model (rectangular boxes) along with environmental and other factors in the "policy processor" (shown by the cylinder), which could be employed by various agencies (green circles) in their strategy planning processes.

nents of environmental security into a policy analysis "processor" that functions as a "central knowledge bank" of environmental security and other important global monitoring indicators (the cylinder in the middle portion of Figure 5.1), thus providing departmental planners with a "snapshot" of current issues in different parts of the world, and providing an appropriate context for how well or poorly a nation may be postured for dealing with both environmental as well as nonenvironmental problems. There are a number of available comprehensive global databases that characterize all countries' stabilities, using a number of parameters such as vulnerability to effects of climate change and socioeconomic factors such as demography, presence of refugees, and poverty levels. Two examples of such indices are shown here: 1) the fragile states index (Fund for Peace 2017) and 2) the Notre Dame Global Adaptation Initiative (ND-GAIN) index (ND-GAIN 2016).

Using such indices and other data as a starting point, evaluations can be made of a state's or region's environmental health; food, water, and energy security; population dynamics and demographics; and vulnerability

to natural hazards/disasters, along with other considerations important in determining the nation's or region's ability to cope with perturbations to these conditions. For example, consider the environmental security factor of natural hazards vulnerabilities, which provides a means of comparing how developing and developed countries are impacted differently by natural hazards. (You may want to review the discussion of natural hazards vulnerability in unit 3.) Recall that natural hazards factors include meteorological, climatic, and geophysical phenomena capable of producing natural disasters.

Figure 5.2a shows the geographic proportion of environmental disaster events by casualty and economic loss in 2015; Figure 5.2b shows weather-related-loss events in from 1980 to 2014. The trend toward more and more expensive annual loss events seems clear.

Analysis of the detailed disaster data used to construct Figure 5.2 can reveal how such events impact countries differently. For instance, in 2010, the countries that experienced the greatest number of disaster-related fatalities were Haiti (220,000+ from an earthquake—an extreme event), Russia (55,000+ from a heat wave—a

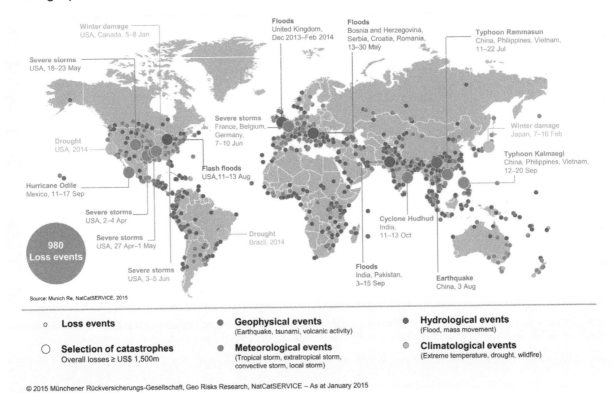

Loss events worldwide 2014
Geographical overview

Munich RE

Winter damage
USA, Canada, 5–8 Jan

Severe storms
USA, 18–23 May

Floods
United Kingdom,
Dec 2013–Feb 2014

Floods
Bosnia and Herzegovina,
Serbia, Croatia, Romania,
13–30 May

Typhoon Rammasun
China, Philippines, Vietnam,
11–22 Jul

Drought
USA, 2014

Severe storms
France, Belgium,
Germany,
7–10 Jun

Winter damage
Japan, 7–16 Feb

Typhoon Kalmaegi
China, Philippines, Vietnam,
12–20 Sep

Hurricane Odile
Mexico, 11–17 Sep

Flash floods
USA,11–13 Aug

Severe storms
USA, 2–4 Apr

Drought
Brazil, 2014

Cyclone Hudhud
India,
11–13 Oct

980
Loss events

Severe storms
USA, 27 Apr–1 May

Severe storms
USA, 3–5 Jun

Floods
India, Pakistan,
3–15 Sep

Earthquake
China, 3 Aug

Source: Munich Re, NatCatSERVICE, 2015

○	**Loss events**	●	**Geophysical events** (Earthquake, tsunami, volcanic activity)	●	**Hydrological events** (Flood, mass movement)
○	**Selection of catastrophes** Overall losses ≥ US$ 1,500m	●	**Meteorological events** (Tropical storm, extratropical storm, convective storm, local storm)	◐	**Climatological events** (Extreme temperature, drought, wildfire)

© 2015 Münchener Rückversicherungs-Gesellschaft, Geo Risks Research, NatCatSERVICE – As at January 2015

Figure 5.2.a. Global economic and human impact of environmental disaster and [courtesy of Hoeppe (2016)].

climatic anomaly), China (nearly 7,000 from three different extreme events), and Pakistan (nearly 2,000 from atypical monsoon flooding—a climatic anomaly) (Guha-Sapir et al. 2011). By contrast, the countries that made it onto the "top five" list of greatest disasters by economic damages were Chile (30 billion U.S. dollars from an earthquake—an extreme event), China (18 billion U.S. dollars from atypical summer flooding—a climatic anomaly), Pakistan (8.5 billion U.S. dollars from atypical monsoon flooding—a climatic anomaly), Haiti (8 billion U.S. dollars from an earthquake—an extreme event), and New Zealand (11 billion U.S. dollars from an earthquake—an extreme event).

In this brief examination of 2016 natural disaster data, we see that one country (China) made it onto all three top-five lists (number of disasters, fatalities, and economic damages), followed by Haiti and Pakistan with two each (fatalities and economic damages). We now want to cross-check each of these three countries' ranks

on the 2016 ND-GAIN, vulnerability, and readiness indices as well as the 2017 fragile states index (Fund for Peace 2017) to examine their geopolitical stabilities based on several factors tied to climate security, writ large. ND-GAIN measures overall vulnerability by considering six life-supporting sectors—food, water, health, ecosystem service, human habitat, and infrastructure (ND-GAIN 2016). Similarly, vulnerability refers to a country's exposure, sensitivity, and capacity to adapt to the negative effects of climate change, while readiness refers to a country's ability to leverage investments and convert them to adaptation actions. ND-GAIN measures overall readiness by considering three components—economic readiness, governance readiness, and social readiness (ND-GAIN 2016). Although China made it onto all three disaster lists for 2016, according to these two stability indices, they are geopolitically more stable than either Pakistan or Haiti, as shown in columns two and four of Table 5.1. It should not come as a surprise

Weather-related loss events worldwide 1980 – 2014
Overall and insured losses

Munich RE ≣

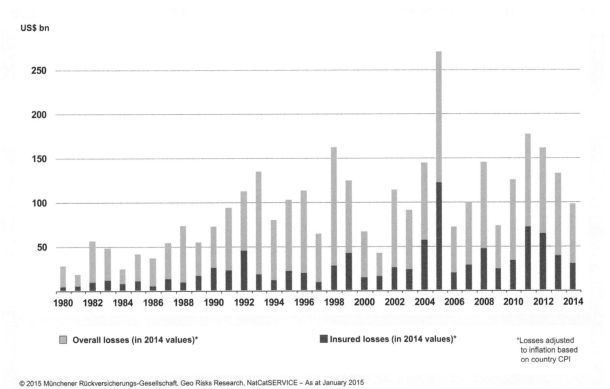

© 2015 Münchener Rückversicherungs-Gesellschaft, Geo Risks Research, NatCatSERVICE – As at January 2015

Figure 5.2.b. Weather-related-loss events worldwide 1980–2014 [courtesy of Hoeppe (2016)].

Table 5.1. The 2016 ND-GAIN index and fragile states index scores and ranks for China, Haiti, and Pakistan (see https://gain. nd.edu/our-work/country-index/rankings/ and http://fundforpeace.org/fsi/data/).

Country	ND-GAIN index[1]	ND-GAIN index rank	ND-GAIN vulnerability[1]	ND-GAIN readiness[2]	Fragile states index[3]	Fragile states index rank[2]
China	53.5	59/181	0.389; 63/181	0.459; 69/191	74.7	85/178
Pakistan	38.8	138/181	0.506; 132/181	0.281; 154/191	98.9	17/178
Haiti	31.4	173/181	0.556; 154/181	0.185; 186/191	105.3	11/178
United States	68.0	15/181	0.339; 21/181	0.699; 11/191	35.6	158/178

1. The higher the score, the worse the country's conditions are.
2. The lower the score, the worse the country's conditions are.
3. The higher the score, the worse the country's conditions are.

that when a natural disaster occurs in Pakistan or Haiti, the human security implications are dramatic and can largely influence neighboring states through aggressive social shifts such as mass migration, which can impact those countries' economies. By contrast, although China has had its share of losses in terms of casualties and economics, they are better postured to cope with and recover from such disasters (relatively speaking), largely because of differences in critical infrastructure and fragile livelihoods.

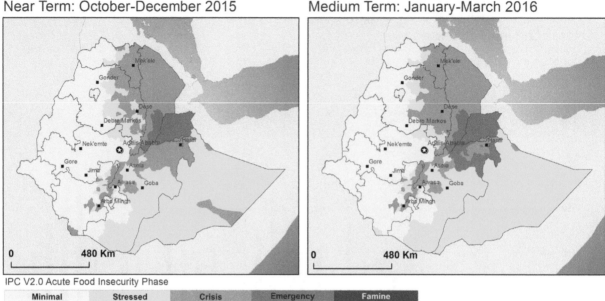

Near Term: October-December 2015   Medium Term: January-March 2016

IPC V2.0 Acute Food Insecurity Phase

| Minimal | Stressed | Crisis | Emergency | Famine |

Figure 5.3. Ethiopian food insecurity changes from October 2015 – March 2016. The highest regions of concern were those in Central-Eastern Ethiopia where the food insecurity phases were heightened from "stressed" to "crisis" and "crisis" to "emergency" is a significantly wide region. Source data for (a) and (b) came from FEWS NET, along with the U.S. Geological Survey and Climate Hazards Group Infrared Precipitation with Station Data (CHIRPS). Images courtesy of FEWS NET ((http://fews.net/east-africa/ethiopia/food-security-outlook-update/december-2015).

The cursory examination above illustrates how one of the factors in the policy processor during a single year can reveal a great deal about three states' abilities to withstand perturbations to their environmental living conditions from the types of extreme environmental events and climatic anomalies described in unit 3. The United States is added to convey a sense of comparison.

Many environmental security problems can occur after a single extreme event or anomalous season and often take humanitarian "first responders" such as nongovernmental organizations by surprise. Continuous environmental surveillance of known vulnerable regions can provide nongovernmental organizations and governments alike with timely warning of potential humanitarian catastrophes. A good example is the Famine Early Warning System Network (FEWS NET) operated by the U.S. Agency for International Development (www.fews.net). FEWS NET combines remotely sensed environmental information with key agricultural and economic data into a set of products designed to assist decision-makers and relief agencies in planning for and responding to humanitarian crises. Such monitoring capabilities can be successful in identifying areas for national and international action. Pulwarty et al. (2018)

provide one such example where FEWS NET identified an emerging food security crisis in Ethiopia in 2015–16, allowing agencies to intervene before food-related conflict could take place. Figure 5.3 shows the FEWS NET assessment of the most vulnerable areas from this event.

5.4. CONCLUDING POINTS: BETTER INTEGRATION OF ENVIRONMENTAL SECURITY INTO NATIONAL SECURITY STRATEGIC PLANNING IS WARRANTED AND NECESSARY

Over the last 10–15 years, environmental security has received renewed interest from the U.S., European, and other countries' policy-making communities because of the concerns about connections between global climate change and national/international security. We suggest here that infusing environmental security principles into the current U.S. national security mindset—if not the overall strategic planning process—is not only warranted but would improve the vision, scope, and nature of the national security strategy. This integration will not only allow the United States to better (i.e., more comprehensively) conceptualize risks to critical infrastructure and vital/important overseas national interests more completely, it will allow a more financially sustainable approach to achieving both homeland and national security objectives. As a result, such integration would provide greater human security on an international scale. When one considers the percentage of people on Earth living in LDCs (nearly 75%), the number of nations suffering water scarcity, the types and frequency of conflict, the issues mass migration presented to the Middle East and Europe following the Arab Spring, etc., the role both environmental and human security policy and initiatives could play in overall national security becomes somewhat obvious. Indeed, a more comprehensive national security strategy could enhance our political leadership's ability to more fully and more effectively use all instruments of national power to predict, interdict, or mitigate factors that influence the development of transnational insurgencies and destabilization of already weak governments or that harm public health.

The interdependencies of energy, water, and food security and the economic impacts from large-scale natural disasters and global climate change combine to impart an important array of security and policy challenges to the United States (Ramsay and O'Sullivan 2013). Such impacts present challenges for the broader civilian domestic security construct (aka homeland security), as well as for practitioners and academic theorists alike. Consequently, environmental security can be employed within an integrated framework for policy and strategic security planning through use of geopolitical stability indices that allow evaluations of human security criteria such as environmental health, food and energy security, population dynamics and demographics, vulnerability to natural hazards/disasters, gender mainstreaming, economic security, etc. Such information can be integrated with other important facts and characteristics to determine a country or region's ability to cope with perturbations to the natural environment from extreme weather events and climatic anomalies, thus better enabling a national security strategy to anticipate either potentially failing governments (such as Syria, Ethiopia, Sudan, or Eritrea) or the rise of asymmetric transnational extremist groups (such as ISIS) (O'Sullivan and Ramsay 2014).

Integrating environmental security into homeland and national security strategic planning would certainly elevate the environmental security discipline and deepen the nation's commitment to its grand national strategic imperatives such as peace, opportunity, democratic governments, and a stable international order. That is, better integration of environmental security into U.S. homeland and national security policy development is not only prudent but provides a unique opportunity to better integrate human security by extension. Indeed, and in stark contrast to the notion of a threat multiplier, a robust integration of environmental, human, and national security strategy could actually become a global peace multiplier. Additionally, such integration could improve the U.S.'s ND-GAIN index, vulnerability, and readiness scores. Last, for a more thorough treatment of how environmental security might be more deeply integrated into homeland and national security strategy, the reader is referred to Ramsay and O'Sullivan (2013) and O'Sullivan and Ramsay (2014).

REFERENCES

Bartholomees, J. B., Jr., 2012: U.S. Army War College guide to national security issues—Volume II: National security policy and strategy. 5th ed. U.S. Army War College Rep., 433 pp., https://ssi.armywarcollege.edu/pubs/display.cfm?pubID=1110.

Bellavita, C., 2008: Changing homeland security: What is homeland security? *Homeland Secur. Aff.*, **4**, 1, www.hsaj.org/articles/118.

Flynn, S., 2007: *The Edge of Disaster*. Random House, 240 pp.

Fund for Peace, 2017: The fragile states index. Accessed 29 March 2018, http://fundforpeace.org/fsi/data/.

Furtado, F. J., 2008: Human security: Did it live? Has it died? Does it matter? *Int. J.*, **63**, 405–421, https://doi.org/10.1177/002070200806300212.

Guha-Sapir, D., F. Vos, R. Below, and S. Ponserre, 2011: Annual disaster statistical review 2010—The numbers and trends. Université Catholique de Louvain Centre for Research on the Epidemiology of Disasters Rep., 50 pp., http://www.cred.be/sites/default/files/ADSR_2010.pdf.

Hoeppe, P., 2016: Trends in weather related disasters—Consequences for insurers and society. *Wea. Climate Extremes*, **11**, 70–79, https://doi.org/10.1016/j.wace.2015.10.002.

Lanicci, J., J. Ramsay, and E. Murray, 2017: Re-conceptualizing environmental security as resilience: Strategic planning for human and national ecurity. *J. Hum. Secur. Resilience*, **1**, www.thinkhumansecurity.org/v1-lanicci-ramsay-murray.html.

ND-GAIN, 2016: Methodology. Accessed 29 March 2018, https://gain.nd.edu/our-work/country-index/methodology/.

Newman, E., 2010: Critical human security issues. *Rev. Int. Stud.*, **36**, 77–94, https://doi.org/10.1017/S0260210509990519.

O'Sullivan, T., and J. Ramsay, 2014: Defining and distinguishing homeland from national security and climate-related environmental security, in theory and practice. *J. Homeland Secur. Emerg. Manage.*, **12**, 43–66, https://doi.org/10.1515/jhsem-2014-0003.

Pulwarty, R. S., S. Goodman, and A. King, 2018: Disruptive weather and water events: Framing the national and international security dimensions. *Sixth Symp. on Building a Weather-Ready Nation: Enhancing Our Nation*, Austin, TX, Amer. Meteor. Soc., 5.7, https://ams.confex.com/ams/98Annual/webprogram/Paper329468.html.

Ramsay, J., and T. O'Sullivan, 2013: There's a pattern here: The case to integrate environmental security into homeland security strategy. *Homeland Secur. Aff.*, **9**, 6, https://www.hsaj.org/articles/246.

Reese, S., 2013: Defining homeland security: Analysis and congressional considerations. Congressional Research Service Rep. R42462, 18 pp.

INDEX

accessible water, 57

accumulation, 92–93

acute food insecurity phase classifications

    phase 1: minimal, 156, 167

    phase 2: stressed, 156, 167

    phase 3: crisis, 156, 167

    phase 4: emergency, 156–157, 167

    phase 5: famine, 157, 167

Afghanistan, 31

agricultural drought, 109–110

agriculture

    climate change effects on, 26–29

    corn production, 25–26

    extreme environmental event effects on, 28

    global warming effects on, 28

    urbanization effects on, 63

    water usage for, 59, 62–63

    world production growth, 28

air pollution, 90

al-Assad, Bashar, 81

American Enterprise Institute, 88

American Legislative Exchange Council, 88

American Meteorological Society (AMS)

    drought as defined by, 109

    environment as defined by, 4

    flood as defined by, 107

    return period as defined by, 149

Anthropocene era, 42, 55

anthropogenic climate change

    definition of, 15–16

    description of, 88

    human rights effects of, 90

anthropomorphic climate change, 4

aquifer, 57–58

Arab–Israeli War, 50

Arab Spring, 50

Arctic, 165, 189–195

Athabasca tar sands, 91–93

Australia, 93–94

avoidance, 120

Azerbaijan, 49

Balkans. *See also specific country*

    floods in, 145, 148–151

    natural disasters in, 147

    wars in, 146–147

Bangalore, 63

Bangladesh, 31

battery, 48

billion-dollar weather disasters, 125

biogeochemical, 21. *See also specific biogeochemical*

biogeochemical cycling

    definition of, 57

    water and, 57–59

biogeochemicals, 57

biological hazards, 103–104

Bolivia, 64
Bosnia, 145–146, 149–150
Bosnia River, 148
bottled water industry, 63
BP *Deepwater Horizon* Gulf oil spill, 10
Brown, Michael, 138
Burkina Faso, 31

Cameroon, 32
Canada, 93
Capetown, South Africa, 55
capitalism, neoliberal, 90–91, 94
carbon, 57
carbon capture and storage (CCS), 47
carbon dioxide (CO_2) emissions
    from fossil fuels, 18, 161
    increases in, 88
    reduction in, 47
carrying capacity, 21, 27
case studies, 137
Centre for Research on the Epidemiology of Disasters (CRED),
        103, 118–119
China, 32, 193
Civil Protection Agency (CPA), 147–148, 150–151
Clean Air Act, 52
Clean Power Plan, 46
Clean Water Act, 51–52
climate
    definition of, 4
    weather versus, 15
Climate Action Plan, 51
climate change
    agriculture affected by, 26–29
    anthropogenic, 15–16
    in Arctic, 189–195
    conflicts and, 29, 33
    crop yields affected by, 27
    definition of, 4
    economic impact of, 33
    education on, 17
    first assessment report (1990) on, 17
    floods associated with, 65
    food scarcity and, 29
    food systems affected by, 27
    fossil fuels and, 12
    greenhouse gases as cause of, 16–17, 161–162
    human rights violations caused by, 90
    humans as cause of, 16
    introduction to, 15–17
    Middle East affected by, 50
    migration caused by, 34–35
    national security and, 7–8, 192–193
    proof of, 16

renewable energy and, 42–43
    second assessment report (1995) on, 17
    strong states and, 33
    threats associated with, 11, 16
    violent conflict and, 177–182
    water cycle affected by, 63
    water-related hazards secondary to, 59, 62, 65
climate security, 9
climatic anomaly, 101
climatological hazards, 103–104
coal
    energy from, 87
    global reserves of, 87
    health risks caused by burning of, 177
    U.S. consumption of, 45
coal-bed methane (CBM), 93
coal seam gas (CSG), 93
"Cochabamba Water War," 64
colonialism, 161
Colorado River basin, 64
common security, threats to, 9
conflict
    climate change and, 29, 32, 33, 178
    definition of, 156
    environmental security and, 75, 159–175
    food scarcity-based, 30–32
    Israeli–Palestinian, 82
    local, 184–185
    between more-developed countries and less-developed
        countries, 160–164
    natural resources as cause of, 70
    political, 162–163
    resource scarcity and, 30–32, 185–186
    violent, 156, 167, 177–182
    water allocation, 81, 83
    water scarcity as cause of, 80–81
ConocoPhillips, 88
corn, 25
*Corporation: The Pathological Pursuit of Profit and Power,
        The*, 89
corruption, 151
Counter-ISIL Finance Group (CIFG), 73
Croatia, 145–147, 151
crop production
    climate-driven changes on, 34, 182–184
    extreme environmental events and, 28
    water usage and, 59
crude oil, 70, 72
cultural genocide, 156
cyclones, tropical, 104–107

Darfur, 166
Dartmouth Flood Observatory, 114

Dayton Peace Agreement, 146–147, 151. *Also referred to as Dayton Peace Accords.*

deforestation, 150–151

Democratic Republic of Congo, 70

demographics, 55, 116, 126–129, 133, 199, 203

Department of Defense (DoD), humanitarian relief by, 7

Department of Homeland Security (DHS), 134

devolution, 184

Diamond, Jared, 44, 52

disaster
    definition of, 4, 101, 118
    natural. *See* natural disasters
    water-related, 59, 62

disaster management
    mitigation phase of, 120, 132
    overview of, 119–120
    preparedness phase of, 120–121
    recovery phase of, 121
    response phase of, 121

Disaster Relief Act of 1974, 121

Disaster Relief Appropriations Act of 2013, 140

distributed solar capacity, 48–49

distributed wind power, 47

drinking water
    global use of, 79
    lack of access to, 59

drought, 25–26, 59, 64–65, 104, 109–111, 169, 178–181

ecological security, 9

economic security, threats to, 9

Egypt, 31

electric power, 45

electric vehicles, 41

emergency declaration, 121

Emergency Events Database (EM-DAT), 119

emergency management (EM), 119

Endangered Species Act, 52

energy
    food security and, 49–50
    human progress and, 42, 52
    nonrenewable, 87–88. *See also* fossil fuel(s)
    renewable. *See* renewable energy
    sources of, 45
    U.S. policy on, 50–52
    wars caused by, 50

"energy cliff," 89, 93

energy conservation pyramid, 47

energy insecurity, 49

energy pyramid, 43

energy return on investment (EROI)
    definition of, 22
    energy sources and, 45
    examples of, 49

extreme energy, 89

energy security, 41–52
    climate change and, 43
    as collective action problem, 43
    components of, 44
    definition of, 22, 44
    diminishing of, 44
    economics of, 49
    environmental security and, 42
    long-term, 44
    in Persian Gulf region, 88
    short-term, 44

energy-use models, 42

environment
    anthropogenic climate change effects on, 90–91
    definition of, 4–5
    instability caused by, 4
    international law for protection of, 75

environmental accidents, 10

environmental change, migration caused by, 34

environmental degradation
    conflicts associated with, 32
    energy security affected by, 44–45
    human security affected by, 10
    sources of, 12

environmental disruption, 29

environmental insecurity, 169, 182–184

environmental migrants, 34

Environmental Protection Agency (EPA), 50, 165

environmental refugees, 34–35

environmental security
    armed conflict and, 75
    conflict and, 75, 159–175
    definition of, 3, 8–10
    disaggregation of, 9–10
    energy security and, 42
    governments in, 9–10
    history of, 6–8
    human security and, 10–12
    ISIS oil looting and smuggling effects on, 71–73
    in national security planning, 197–203
    natural disasters' effect on, 99–100
    nongovernmental organizations in, 10
    in policy making, 7
    policy principles of, 198
    power and, 10
    in U.S. security strategy, 10
    working definition of, 9

environmental stresses, 64

Ethiopia, 31, 202

Euphrates River, 81

evaporation, 109

evapotranspiration, 109

extraterrestrial hazards, 103–104

extreme climate event, 21, 28

extreme energy, 89–90, 92, 94

extreme environmental events

    agricultural output affected by, 28

    crop production affected by, 28

    definition of, 28

extreme weather events

    definition of, 21, 101, 103

    resilience to, 33

Exxon Mobil, 88

Faces of Hunger, 25

Falkenmark water stress index, 79–80

famine, 157, 167

Famine Early Warning Systems Network (FEWS NET), 168, 202

Federal Emergency Management Agency (FEMA)

    description of, 10

    hazard as defined by, 103

    reorganization of, 134, 139

    social media, 140

fifth assessment report (2013, 2014), 18–19

Financial Action Task Force (FATF), 71, 74

first assessment report (1990), 17

flash flood, 108

floods

    in Balkans, 145, 148–151

    causes of, 107–109

    climate change and, 65

    definition of, 107

    hazard classification of, 108

    from Hurricane Katrina, 132

    as natural hazards, 104–105

    precipitation as cause of, 107–108

    social media coverage of, 140

    tropical cyclones as cause of, 105

    tsunamis as cause of, 108–109

focusing event, 139

food availability, 30

food commodity prices, 49

food economics, 50

food prices, 30

food protests, 30

food riots, 30–32

food scarcity

    climate change and, 29

    conflicts caused by, 30–32

    global, 28–29

    introduction to, 25–26

    political instability caused by, 30

    acute food insecurity phase 1: minimal, 156, 167

    acute food insecurity phase 2: stressed, 156, 167

    acute food insecurity phase 3: crisis, 156, 167

    acute food insecurity phase 4: emergency, 156–157, 167

    acute food insecurity phase 5: famine, 157, 167

food security

    definition of, 21, 26

    energy and, 49–50

food systems, 27

forced migration, 35

foreign exchange currencies, 49

Foresight report, 34

fossil fuel(s). *See also* coal; natural gas; oil

    carbon dioxide emissions from, 18, 161

    climate change and, 12

    energy from, 46, 89

    food production and, 49

    pollutants caused by, 90

fossil fuel extraction

    ecosystems affected by, 91–93

    fracking, 45, 62, 89, 93–94

    water usage for, 62–63

fourth assessment report (2007), 17–18

fracking, 45, 62, 89, 93–94

fragile states index (FSI), 167, 199

free trade-oriented globalization, 42

freshwater, 59

Fukushima Daishi nuclear plant, 10, 109

gas fracking, 45, 62

Gaza Strip, 81

General Motors Corporation (GMC), 41

genocide, 156, 166–167

geophysical hazards, 103–104

ghettoization, 162

glaciers

    water bound up in, 79

    freshwater content from, 56, 57, 59

    shrinking, 88

Global Fire Monitoring Center, 114

globalization, free trade-oriented, 42

global warming

    agriculture affected by, 28

    environmental effects of, 88

    greenhouse gases as cause of, 50

global war on terrorism, 7

Global Water Partnership, 65

Golan Heights, 81

governments, in environmental security, 9–10

greenhouse gases (GHGs)

    anthropogenic emission of, 18–19

    climate change caused by, 16–17, 161–162

    definition of, 21

    emission of, 18–19, 164

    global warming and, 50

    types of, 21

Gulf Coast region, 123–124

Haiti, 31
Harmer, Chris, 74
hashtags, 140–141
hazard(s)
    classification of, 103
    definition of, 101, 103
    natural. *See* natural hazards
    technological. *See* technological hazards
Hazard Mitigation Grant Program (HMGP), 121
Hazards U.S. Multi-Hazard (HAZUS-MH), 115–116
hazards vulnerability analysis, 114
heavy rains, 105–106
hedging, 120
Herzegovina, 145
high winds, from tropical cyclones, 106
homeland security, 3, 197, 203
Homer-Dixon, Thomas, 180
human security
    core concepts of, 198
    definition of, 3
    elements of, 181
    environmental degradation effects on, 10
    environmental security and, 10–12
    ISIS oil looting and smuggling effects on, 71–73
    "optical solutions" to, 12
    threats to, 9, 11
    violent conflict and, 181–184
"hunger wages," 26
Hurricane Harvey, 106
hurricane(s), 104, 123–135
Hurricane Andrew, 120
Hurricane Betsy, 131–132
Hurricane Camille, 131–132
Hurricane Earl, 140
Hurricane Florence, 138
Hurricane Katrina
    description of, 6, 100, 105
    as focusing event, 139
    natural hazards vulnerability analysis of, 123–135
    traditional media coverage of, 138–139
Hurricane Michael, 138
Hurricane Pam, 134
Hussein, Saddam, 70
hydraulic fracking, 45, 62, 89, 93
hydrological drought, 109–110
hydrological hazards, 103–104
hydrologic cycle, 57

ice melt, 165–166, 189–194
Indonesia, 32
industrial accidents, 103–104

Industrial Revolution, 42, 50, 160–161
infrastructure failure, 103–104
Integrated Research on Disaster Risk (IRDR), 119
Intergovernmental Panel on Climate Change (IPCC)
    composition of, 4
    crop yield predictions, 27
    definition of, 4
    description of, 16
    fifth assessment report (2013, 2014), 18–19
    first assessment report (1990), 17
    fourth assessment report (2007), 17–18
    members of, 16
    peer-review process, 16
    second assessment report (1995), 17
    third assessment report (2001), 17
International Criminal Court, 75
International Energy Agency (IEA), 22, 44
International Freshwater Treaties, 80
International Law Commission (ILC), 76
international migration, 35
International Organization for Migration (IOM), 34–35
International Risk Management Institute (IRMI), 103
Iraq
    ISIS oil looting in, 70, 72–73
    water allocation conflicts in, 81
Islamic State in Iraq and Syria (ISIS)
    airstrikes against, 72–76
    climate change and, 50
    definition of, 22
    oil looting and smuggling by, 69–76
    oil well burning by, 72
    scorched-earth policy of, 72–73
Israel, 81–82
issue-attention cycle, 139
Ivory Coast, 31

Jordan basin, 81–83
Jordan River, 81–83

Kaplan, Robert, 35
Kenya, 177–186
Koch Industries, 88–89
Kyoto Protocol, 21

land degradation, 32
landslides, 150, 152
land use and development patterns, 63
law of tolerance, 43–44
Least Developed Countries Expert Group (LEG), 163
less-developed countries (LDCs)
    conflict in, 160–164, 166–169
    criteria for classification as, 17
    definition of, 156, 160

less-developed countries (LDCs) (*continued*)
energy insecurity in, 49
in first assessment report, 17
more-developed countries and, conflict between, 160–164
natural disaster effects on, 100
water use in, 62
Limits to Growth, The, 87, 90–691
lithium-ion battery, 48
Lloyd-Davies, Edward, 89
local conflict, 184–185
long-term energy security, 44
Louisiana, 124–125, 127–128

major disaster, 121
Malin, Stephanie, 90
Malthus, Thomas Robert, 29, 80, 180
Marcel, Roxanne, 93
Marshall Islands, 163, 169
Mauritania, 32
McMichael, A.J., 28
mean precipitation, 28
media
social, 101, 137, 139–141
traditional, 101, 137–139
meteorological drought, 109
meteorological hazards, 103–105
methane, 16, 21, 88
Middle East
climate change effects on, 50
wars in, 162
water needs in, 80
migration
climate change as cause of, 34–35
forced, 35
movement patterns, 35
mining, 26
miscellaneous accidents, 103–104
Mississippi, 123, 125, 128
Mississippi River, 124
mitigation phase, of disaster management, 120, 132
Montreal Protocol, 21
more-developed countries (MDCs)
climate change denial in, 164–166
conflict in, 160–166
criteria for classification as, 99
definition of, 156, 160
in first assessment report, 17
less-developed countries and, conflict between, 160–164
natural disaster effects on, 100
water use in, 62
Morocco, 31
Myanmar, 161

National Adaptation Programs of Action (NAPAs), 164
National Flood Insurance Act of 1968, 132–133
National Oceanic and Atmospheric Administration (NOAA)
Coastal Research Center of, 125–126
natural hazards information from, 114
weather as defined by, 15
National Patriotic Front of Liberia, 70
national security
climate change and, 7–8, 192–193
climate-induced migration and, 34–35
definition of, 3
environmental security in planning of, 197–203
threats to, 9
National Weather Service (NWS), 105
natural disasters. *See also* disaster; *specific disaster*
definition of, 118
destabilizing effects of, 99–100
environmental security affected by, 99–100
fatalities caused by, 119
global statistics, 200
Pressure and Release (PAR) model of, 100, 116–118
social media coverage of, 139–141
threshold for declaring of, 118
natural gas
limits to growth and, 87
U.S. consumption of, 45
natural gas liquids (NGLs), 88
natural hazards
classification of, 103
definition of, 101
droughts, 25–26, 59, 64–65, 104, 109–111, 169, 178–181
floods. *See* floods
mitigation of, 120
population vulnerability to, 100
tropical cyclones, 104–107
natural hazards vulnerability
description of, 113–116
Hurricane Katrina case study of, 123–135
natural resources
conflicts associated with, 70
overexploitation of, 44
scarcity of, 30–33
neoliberal capitalism, 90–91, 94
neoliberalism, 22
neo-Malthusians, 180
net energy, 89
nitrogen, 57
nitrous oxide, 88
nongovernmental organizations, in environmental security, 10, 202
nonrenewable energy sources
carbon dioxide emissions from, 88
fossil fuels. *See* fossil fuel(s)
"limit to growth" caused by depletion of, 87

North Africa, 80
northwest Kenya, 177–186
Notre Dame Global Adaptation Initiative (ND-GAIN) index,
    199–201, 203

Obama, Barack, 51, 74
Office of U.S. Foreign Disaster Assistance (OFDA), 33
Ogallala aquifer, 57–58
oil
    and conflict, 41–54, 184–186, 191–194
    Islamic State in Iraq and Syria looting and smuggling of, 69–76
    limits to growth and, 87
    Syrian reserves of, 69–70
    tar sands extraction of, 91–93
    U.S. consumption of, 45
    water usage for extraction of, 62
oil well burning, 72
Operation Allied Force, 146
Operation Tidal Wave II, 74
Organization of Petroleum Exporting Countries (OPEC), 49–50
ozone, 16, 21

Pakistan, 32–33, 65
Palestinian Authority, 82
Palestinians, 81–82
Paris Climate Agreement, 50, 65
peak oil, 22, 92
peer-review process, 16
Philippines, 31
phosphorus, 57
Poitras, George, 93
Pokot, 179–184
political conflict, 162–163
political economy, 22
political instability, food scarcity-driven, 30
population growth
    Malthusian drivers of, 29, 80
    water scarcity and, 80
potable water, 57
poverty, water-related, 55, 65
power, environmental security and, 10
precipitation
    mean, 28
    trends in, 28
preparedness phase, of disaster management, 120–121
Pressure and Release (PAR) disaster model, 100, 116–118
producers, 43
Program on International Law and Armed Conflict (PILAC), 73
Pruitt, Scott, 165

radicalization, 156, 169
rainfall
    floods caused by, 107–108

from tropical cyclones, 105–106
recovery phase, of disaster management, 121
refined oil, 70
reflectors, 48
renewable energy
    cheapness of, 52
    climate change and, 42–43
    definition of, 22, 46
    Energy Information Administration definition of, 46
    energy production from, 45–46
    as security, 47–49
    solar energy/power, 42, 45, 48, 50–51
    sources of, 42
    total U.S. distribution and consumption of, 46
    wind energy, 45, 47–48
resource distribution, Malthusian drivers of, 29
resource scarcity
    conflicts caused by, 30–32, 185–186
    weak state and, 33
response phase, of disaster management, 121
retention, 120
return period, 101, 149
riots, food, 30–32
risk, 4

Saffir–Simpson hurricane intensity scale, 106
Sandy Supplemental Appropriations Bill, 140, 142
Saudi Arabia, 49
scarcity. See food scarcity; resource scarcity; water scarcity
scorched-earth policy, 72–73
sea level rise, 11, 16, 30, 33, 88, 133, 163, 166, 178
seasonal flooding, 108
second assessment report (1995), 17
security
    definition of, 5
    energy. See energy security
    environmental. See environmental security
    features of, 5
    human. See human security
    types of, 9
    water. See water security
security strategy, 3
Senegal, 31
Serbia, 145–147, 151
shale oil extraction, 45
short-term energy security, 44
Slovenia, 145–146
social media
    definition of, 101, 137
    natural disaster coverage on, 139–141
social vulnerability index (SoVI), 115, 129
socioeconomic drought, 111
solar energy/power, 42, 45, 48, 50–51

solar thermal power systems, 48
South Africa, 55
Soviet Union, 6
Stafford Act, 121
standardized precipitation evapotranspiration index (SPEI), 111, 114, 117–118
state capacity, 32
Stone Age, 42
storm surge, 105, 107
storm tide, 105
strong states
    characteristics of, 32
    climate change and, 33
    definition of, 21–22
    resource scarcity and, 32
sulfur, 57
SunShot Initiative, 51
Superstorm Sandy, 137, 139–142
Syria
    drought in, 169
    energy security in, 74
    heavy crude in, 72
    ISIS oil looting and smuggling effects on, 71–72
    oil resources in, 69–70
    water allocation conflicts in, 81
    water scarcity-related conflicts in, 65

Tamir, Avraham, 80
tar sands
    Athabasca, 91–93
    definition of, 92–93
    water usage for extraction of, 62
Taylor, Charles, 70
technological hazards
    classification of, 103–104
    definition of, 101
    floods as cause of, 109
terrorism
    definition of, 156
    global war on, 7
Thailand, 31
third assessment report (2001), 17
"tight oil," 93
Tobago, 31
tornadoes, 106–107
Toronto Project on Environmental Change and Acute Conflict (TPECAC), 29
traditional media
    definition of, 101, 137
    Hurricane Katrina coverage by, 138–139
transfer, 120
transnational corporations (TNCs), 22
transport accidents, 103–104

Trinidad, 31
tropical cyclones, 104–107
tropical depression, 104
tropical storm, 104–105
Trump, President Donald
    climate change and, 12, 164
    statements by, 164
    U.S. energy policy under, 50–51
tsunami, 108–109
Turkana, 179–184
Turkey
    ISIS oil looting in, 70–71, 73
    water allocation conflicts in, 81
21st Conference of the Parties (COP21), 46–47, 163
Twitter, 140–141
typhoon, 104

United Arab Emirates, 31
United Nations (UN)
    Food and Agriculture Organization, 26
    human development report, 10
    Security Council, 73, 75
    sustainable development goals, 10–11
    21st Conference of the Parties, 46–47, 163
    Watercourses Convention of 1997, 83
    water security as defined by, 59
United Nations Environment Programme (UNEP)
    conflicts caused by natural resources, 70
    Convention on the Law of the Sea, 165, 189, 193–194
    fracking warning from, 94
    Intergovernmental Panel on Climate Change, 4, 16
United Nations Framework Convention on Climate Change (UNFCC), 16, 164
United States
    anti-ISIS airstrikes by, 73–76
    Corn Belt of, 25
    Energy Information Administration, 45–46
    energy policy of, 50–52
    energy sources in, 45
    European Command, 192
    National Weather Service, 3
    oil consumption in, 41
    State Department, 7
    Transportation Command, 7–8
    water usage statistics in, 62
UNOSAT, 72
urbanization, 63
utility-scale solar electrical-generation systems, 48, 50
utility-scale wind, 47
Uzbekistan, 32

Venezuela, 49
Vilsack, Tom, 25

violence, 156
violent conflict, 156, 167, 177–182
"virtual water," 80
vulnerability
    definition of, 101, 113
    natural hazards, 113–116
vulnerability analysis
    description of, 113–114
    Hurricane Katrina case study of, 126–130

wars
    Balkan, 146–147
    energy as cause of, 50
Warsaw Pact, 6
water
    access to, 55, 65, 82
    agricultural use of, 59, 62–63
    biogeochemical cycling and, 57–59
    distribution of, 56
    for fossil fuel extraction, 62–63
    freshwater, 59
    global use of, 62, 79
    Israeli access to, 82
    Palestinian access to, 82
    shipping uses of, 64
    transportation uses of, 64
    twenty-first century challenges for, 59
    U.S. consumption of, 62
    usage of, 59
    virtual, 80
    World Bank statistics regarding, 64
water cycle, 55–56, 59, 63
water-population-food-energy nexus, 62–63
water-related hazards, 59
water-related poverty, 55
water scarcity
    conflicts associated with, 80–81
    factors that cause, 59, 61

Falkenmark index, 79–80
    global statistics regarding, 61
    standard of living affected by, 79
    Syrian civil conflicts caused by, 65
water security
    definition of, 22, 59
    description of, 59–62
    importance of, 65
    issues related to, 63–64
    land use and development patterns, 63
    United Nations definition of, 59
water stress, 79–80
water vapor, 16, 21, 55, 62, 109
weak states
    as conflict pathway, 32–33
    definition of, 22
    resource distribution in, 33
weather
    climate versus, 15
    definition of, 3, 15
    National Oceanic and Atmospheric Administration definition
        of, 15
West Bank, 81
wildfires, 118
wind energy, 45, 47–48
wind turbines, 47
World Bank
    water availability statistics, 64
    water security statistics, 59
World Meteorological Organization (WMO), 4
World Trade Organization (WTO)
    definition of, 22
    free trade-oriented globalization, 42

Yemen, 32
Yugoslavia, 146

Zimbabwe, 34